DEBORAH K. VAN DEN HOONAARD
LISA-JO VAN DEN SCOTT

FOURTH EDITION

QUALITATIVE RESEARCH IN ACTION

A CANADIAN PRIMER

OXFORD

OXFORD
UNIVERSITY PRESS

Oxford University Press is a department of the University of Oxford.
It furthers the University's objective of excellence in research, scholarship,
and education by publishing worldwide. Oxford is a registered trade mark of
Oxford University Press in the UK and in certain other countries.

Published in Canada by
Oxford University Press
8 Sampson Mews, Suite 204,
Don Mills, Ontario M3C 0H5 Canada

www.oupcanada.com

Copyright © Oxford University Press Canada 2022

The moral rights of the authors have been asserted

Database right Oxford University Press (maker)

First Edition published in 2012
Second Edition published in 2015
Third Edition published in 2019

Library and Archives Canada Cataloguing in Publication

Title: Qualitative research in action : a Canadian primer / Deborah K. van den Hoonaard, Lisa-Jo
van den Scott.
Names: Van den Hoonaard, Deborah K. (Deborah Kestin), 1951- author. | Van den Scott, Lisa-Jo K.,
1977- author.
Series: Themes in Canadian sociology.
Description: Fourth edition. | Series statement: Themes in Canadian sociology | Includes
bibliographical references and index.
Identifiers: Canadiana (print) 2021018440X | Canadiana (ebook) 20210184426 | ISBN 9780190165970
(softcover) | ISBN 9780190165987 (EPUB)
Subjects: LCSH: Qualitative research—Methodology. | LCSH: Qualitative research—Canada—
Methodology.
Classification: LCC H62 .V33 2021 | DDC 300.72—dc23

Cover image: © iStock/piranka
Cover design: Farzana Razak
Interior design: Sherill Chapman

Oxford University Press is committed to our environment.
This book is printed on Forest Stewardship Council® certified paper
and comes from responsible sources.

Printed and bound in the United States of America

Contents

List of Boxes   vii
Preface   viii
Acknowledgements   ix

1 **Introduction**   1

Learning Objectives   1
Introduction   1
What Is Qualitative Research?   1
About This Book   6
Summary   9
Questions for Critical Thought   10
Exercises   10
  In-Class Exercise   11
Suggested Readings   11
Related Websites   11

2 **Asking Questions and Identifying Goals**   12

Learning Objectives   12
Introduction   12
Underlying Assumptions and the Research Process   14
The Research Process   20
Generic Social Processes   27
Summary   31
Key Terms   32
Questions for Critical Thought   32
Exercises   32
  In-Class Exercise   33
Suggested Readings   33
Related Websites   33
Notes   33

3 **Strategies for Designing Research**   34

Learning Objectives   34
Introduction   34
Origins of Qualitative Studies   35
Where to Find Ideas for Research Topics   40
How to Begin Your Own Study   46
Summary   53

Key Terms   54
Questions for Critical Thought   54
Exercises   54
    In-Class Exercise   55
Suggested Readings   55
Related Websites   55

4   Ethics on the Ground: A Moral Compass   56

Learning Objectives   56
Introduction   56
Ethical Principles of Research in Canada   56
Research Involving Indigenous Peoples in Canada   59
Applying the Principles of Ethics to Qualitative Research   60
Writing Up Research   71
Summary   73
Key Terms   74
Questions for Critical Thought   74
Exercises   74
    In-Class Exercise   74
Suggested Readings   74
Related Websites   75
Notes   76

5   Observing Social Life through Field Research   77

Learning Objectives   77
Introduction   77
Historical Antecedents of Contemporary Fieldwork   78
Conducting a Field Study   84
Innovations in Virtual Ethnography   99
Summary   101
Key Terms   102
Questions for Critical Thought   102
Exercises   102
    In-Class Exercise   103
Suggested Readings   103
Related Website   103
Notes   103

6   In-Depth Interviewing   105

Learning Objectives   105
Introduction   105
Standardized Interviews   105

In-Depth Interviews   109
Conducting an In-Depth Interview Study   113
What You Should Do after the Interview   121
Innovations in Interviewing   123
Summary   126
Key Terms   127
Questions for Critical Thought   127
Exercises   127
  In-Class Exercise   128
Suggested Readings   128
Related Website   128
Notes   128

7   **Focus Groups   129**

Learning Objectives   129
Introduction   129
Planning Focus Groups   132
Conducting Focus Groups   140
Analyzing the Data and Group Interactions   144
Summary   147
Key Terms   147
Questions for Critical Thought   147
Exercises   148
  In-Class Exercise   148
Suggested Readings   148
Related Website   148

8   **Unobtrusive Research   149**

Learning Objectives   149
Introduction   149
Analyzing Pre-existing Documents   151
Analyzing Documents of Social Institutions   156
Analyzing Media Content and Reflections of Reality   157
Analyzing Physical Objects   162
Innovations in Research   164
Summary   169
Key Terms   169
Questions for Critical Thought   170
Exercises   170
  In-Class Exercise   170
Suggested Readings   171
Related Websites   171
Notes   171

9   Trust the Process: Analyzing Qualitative Data   173

Learning Objectives   173
Introduction   173
Beginning with Memos   175
Coding Interview Transcripts and Field Notes   176
Innovations in Analysis of Research   188
Summary   193
Key Terms   194
Questions for Critical Thought   194
Exercises   194
   In-Class Exercise   195
Suggested Readings   195
Related Website   195
Notes   196

10   Writing Up Qualitative Research   197

Learning Objectives   197
Introduction   197
Getting Started   197
Writing Your Report   200
Attending to Matters of Style   210
Cleaning It All Up   212
Presenting Research with Indigenous Communities   214
Innovations in Presenting Research   214
Summary   217
Key Terms   217
Questions for Critical Thought   218
Exercises   218
   In-Class Exercise   218
Suggested Readings   218
Related Websites   219
Notes   219

Appendix A: A Guide to Student Presentations   220

Appendix B: Sample Field Notes   224

Appendix C: Checklist for Writing Research Reports   226

Glossary   227
References   234
Index   253

List of Boxes

1.1 Selected Papers Presented at the Qualitative Analysis Conference 3
2.1 A Twenty-First-Century Breaching Experiment 19
2.2 Generic Social Processes: Accomplishing Activity 29
3.1 The Sociological Imagination 37
3.2 The Characteristics of Participatory Action Research (PAR) 40
4.1 Core Principles of Ethics 57
4.2 Preconceived Ideas That Stood in the Way of Doing Ethical Research 63
5.1 The Hobo 80
5.2 The Chicago School and McGill: Carl Dawson and Everett C. Hughes 82
5.3 Connecting with a Sponsor to Gain Access 91
5.4 Building Trust in the Research Setting 93
5.5 Addressing Gender in Establishing a Research Identity 94
5.6 Advice for Making Jottings 96
6.1 Feminist Critiques of Standardized Interviews 107
6.2 Sample Interview Guide 118
6.3 Photovoice in Indigenous Research 126
7.1 Interactions in Focus Groups: An Example 130
7.2 Using Talking Circles with Indigenous Communities 134
7.3 Sample Topic Guide 138
7.4 Sample Focus-Group Introduction 142
8.1 Discovery in the Library 155
8.2 Interpretive Content Analysis 159
8.3 Meaning in Trash 164
9.1 Sample Memos 176
9.2 Memo: Ideas for Chapter on Widows' Relationships with Men 179
9.3 Narrative Analysis: Stories and Themes 193
10.1 Notes on Widows and Driving 202
10.2 Excerpt and Commentary 205
10.3 Opening Sentences That Draw the Reader In 209

Preface

Qualitative Research in Action is an introduction to qualitative research methods that is geared to undergraduate students who do not have experience doing qualitative research. The book provides both a discussion of the theoretical underpinnings of qualitative research and practical advice to help students get their feet wet by trying out some qualitative methods.

We have described our own experiences carrying out qualitative research to make the book more personal and alive and have used an accessible and conversational style to make the book readable and interesting. Our theoretical approach borrows heavily from symbolic interactionism, and this preference is clear throughout the text. However, the basic skills of interviewing, observation, and analysis are useful regardless of one's theoretical perspective, and students will learn to adapt them to suit their own approaches.

The book is unabashedly Canadian. In fact, one of the most pleasurable aspects of writing it has been discovering and thinking about qualitative work done by Canadian scholars. For years, Deborah used excellent American textbooks in her classes, but she never realized how few Canadian studies they cited until she began working on the first edition of *Qualitative Research in Action*. To correct this omission, we have included many examples from Canadian research not often cited in other methods texts.

In our years of teaching, we have found that many students are full of trepidation when they start a research methods course because they fear the class will be difficult or boring. In reality, a qualitative methods class that gives students an opportunity to get their hands dirty by doing a few in-depth interviews, observing participants in a social setting, and analyzing documents (say, magazine advertisements) is often very exciting. This book does not pretend that qualitative research is not a lot of work. It does, however, include moments of discovery and euphoria, and we try to communicate these high moments throughout the text. When students complete the class, they are often eager to carry out their own studies. By the end of the term, it is not unusual for a student to come to one of our offices to ask, "How do I get to do what you do?" When that happens, we know the student has caught the bug of doing qualitative research. In writing this book, it was our goal to pass on this bug.

Brief Overview of the Book

Qualitative Research in Action begins by introducing the inductive approach that qualitative researchers use. Students will discover how qualitative researchers build concepts and theories based on the data they have collected, and they will see how these methods stand in contrast to the deductive approach of testing theories through research. Further, students will learn how the questions researchers ask determine, to some extent, the answers they find, and they will learn how to develop a research question. The book then provides a consideration of the ethical dimensions of doing research, challenging students to engage with principles of research ethics: respect for persons, concern for human welfare, and justice.

With the foundation in place, the book moves on to discuss various methods of collecting data to address research questions. Throughout these discussions, students will encounter numerous examples of researchers' actual strategies and experiences, including observation, in-depth interviews, and analysis of pre-existing documents. The fourth edition has added discussions and more examples of Indigenous research that, we believe, enrich the book.

Later chapters discuss analyzing data and writing up research reports. These chapters also include lively examples and hints about how to approach these challenging phases of research.

Acknowledgements

Deborah:

It was with real surprise and pleasure that I received the invitation from Susan McDaniel and Lorne Tepperman to write a textbook on qualitative research methods. Writing this book has been an adventure from start to finish, and I am very grateful for the opportunity.

As I gathered material for *Qualitative Research in Action*, I relied on the experiences I have acquired over years of teaching qualitative methods. Over these years, my students have inspired and challenged me to think of new ways to talk about conducting qualitative research and have thereby contributed to this volume in untold ways. In addition, the students who took my class in the winter of 2010 read early drafts of the core chapters and provided comments that surely improved them.

While writing this text, I became very aware of the rich legacy of qualitative research we have in Canada. I enjoyed finding Canadian work to use as examples, and I am thankful for all the qualitative researchers who have long been working "in the vineyard." In particular, the collegiality, friendship, and inspiration over the years from participants at the annual (Canadian) Qualitatives have been invaluable.

I would like to thank the many people who helped me bring everything together for this book. Rick Helmes-Hayes and Emily Milne contributed Box 5.2 on the history of ethnography in Canada. They agreed to write the material, which makes a substantial contribution to the chapter, on very short notice. I would also like to thank Jacqueline Anderson, Jean Carrière, Vera Kohler, Elza Y. Passini, Kira Shingareva, Miriam H. Zaar, and photographer Jesus Reyes for sharing their stories and generously giving us permission to include their photo in Chapter 6.

My research assistant, Kristen Gallant, searched for and found many of the websites that deal with qualitative research. She read each chapter for the first edition as I wrote it and provided helpful comments. Kristen put together the initial list of terms for the glossary. Her enthusiasm for the work has been a real contribution. Gillian Steeves helped with editing the revised manuscript. In particular, she carefully checked the accuracy of each reference.

My assistant, Lehanne Knowlton, helped in too many ways to name. She was always there to proofread and help with formatting issues that I found impossible to remedy. I also knew that I could go into her office at any time to decompress and eat a piece of chocolate from her stash. Who could ask for more than that?

My colleagues at St Thomas University are unfailingly supportive. The members of the Gerontology Department always celebrate each other's accomplishments, a rare state of affairs that makes me feel very fortunate. Dawne A. Clarke of the Criminology Department gave the manuscript a trial run in her methods class. The late Rosemary Clews, former assistant vice-president of research, was a constant source of encouragement and companionship during our long friendship, and Gayle MacDonald, previous assistant vice-president of research at St Thomas University, is an ongoing source of support and friendship. For the second edition, Michelle Lafrance provided helpful comments for the revision of the section on discourse analysis. My research assistant, Angela Priede, found many of the articles that contributed to updating the text, and colleagues at the Qualitative Analysis Conference sent me word of their new publications. Joel Eatmon, my summer student, provided valuable input regarding the tone of my writing from a student's perspective. Dr Sandra Wachholz shared one of her qualitative content analysis assignments with me and gave me permission to adapt it for use as an exercise.

For the third edition, Gary Hansen, director of institutional research at St Thomas University, unearthed a copy of the focus-group study I did on student culture for the university in 2001. Adding material on Indigenous research methods was an exciting but daunting part of the new edition. Dr Lynne Gouliquer of Laurentian University provided references for texts on Indigenous methods. Miima'gan, Elder to the Aboriginal Student Body at St Thomas University, met with me and generously read several of the new sections on Indigenous research. Dr Gul Çalişkan, colleague and friend, told me about several works of Indigenous research of which I was unaware. Her arrival in town has been a true gift. With every edition, I have been fortunate to work with editors who provide timely and encouraging comments. The third edition was no different. Lauren Wing and Colleen Ste Marie joined this generous group. A number of reviewers—including Dawn Currie, Brant Downey, Rick Fehr, Lynne Gouliquer, Stephen Lin, Caroline McDonald-Harker, Michael Mopas, Vivian Stamatopoulos, and Andreas Tomaszewski of Mount Royal University, as well as those who wish to remain anonymous—also provided valuable feedback.

I have been fortunate to receive funding for my studies of widows (Health Canada), widowers (Social Sciences and Humanities Research Council of Canada [SSHRC]), and Iranian Bahá'í refugees to Atlantic Canada (Metropolis, New Brunswick and Atlantic Studies Research and Development Centre). I served as

Canada Research Chair for qualitative research and analysis from 2006 to 2016, which provided me with the resources and the time to complete *Qualitative Research in Action* in a timely manner.

My family is a continuing source of joy and inspiration. My children, Lisa-Jo, Cheryl, and Jordan, take real pleasure in my work and keep me laughing and learning. Lisa-Jo, a sociologist, has read and commented on drafts of most of the chapters in *Qualitative Research in Action* and has come on as co-author for the fourth edition. I do not have a favourite child.

My husband, Will C. van den Hoonaard, is a support and inspiration in everything I do. He readily agreed to write Chapter 4, "Ethics on the Ground," and has read every word of this text at least once. Will has always believed in my work even more than I have and has been a staunch supporter of qualitative research methods in Canada. It is to him that this book is dedicated.

Lisa-Jo:

Let me begin by saying how honoured I am to have been invited onto *Qualitative Research in Action*. I was fortunate to have studied at Northwestern University. There, I benefitted from the mentorship of many excellent qualitative researchers, particularly my supervisor, Gary Alan Fine. I have modelled the current qualitative methods workshop that I facilitate for graduate students on his ethnography workshop.

Many others helped to shape my path, my thinking, and my approach to qualitative research. As my postdoc supervisor, Andrea Doucet launched me into my career. The annual (Canadian) Qualitatives provides a collegial and constructive space for qualitative researchers of every ilk to gather and support each other. I have benefitted from the mentorship of Cheryl and Daniel Albas, Dorothy Pawluch, and Scott Grills, among others, through these meetings. My many colleagues who have encouraged me along the way, read my work, and offered theirs include (alphabetically) Judy Adler, Savina Balasubramanian, Stephen Crocker, Clare Forstie, Stacey Hannem, Steven W. Kleinknecht, Stacy Lom, Staci Newmahr, Stephanie Peña-Alves, Antony Puddephatt, Carrie B. Sanders, Christopher J. Schneider, Deana Simonetto, and Karen Standbridge. Many of these people overlap with the *Society for the Study of Symbolic Interaction*, to which I am indebted for many opportunities and support over the years.

As with many of us, ultimately my verve for qualitative work is maintained by seeing everything anew through the eyes of my students. Thank you to my graduate students for your enthusiasm, dedication, and devotion to sociology.

I would also like to thank the Government of Canada and the Social Sciences and Humanities Research Council for their previous support of my work.

If you have not already figured it out, Deborah is my mother. Both my parents are remarkable scholars and sociologists. I am humbled to be able to learn from them and now to be publishing with them. I know of few mother-daughter teams in sociology, but I can certainly recommend it as a fulfilling and rewarding path. When I was expelled from high school, I hardly think she ever imagined we would end up here! In short, my parents are my heroes, and I aspire to their insight, skill, and talent.

My husband, Jeffrey D. van den Scott, and I have worked together, published together, and supported each other since we met when he was 19 and I was 20. We are coming up on our 20th anniversary now. It is a delight to be members of the qualitative research community together. He has championed me, fortified me, and sacrificed for me to be where I am today.

Deborah and Lisa-Jo:

For the fourth edition, we'd like to thank Peter Weeks for bringing Deborah Tanen's article on how we greet each other during the pandemic to our attention. Lisa-Jo's MA student, Nathan W. DeVenne, helped with bibliographic cross-referencing and formatting.

Thank you, also, to the many members of the annual (Canadian) Qualitatives conference listserv who forwarded their own and others' recent work.

For this edition, Amy Gordon and Kaitlin Thornber have come on as developmental editors. As with all the editors we have worked with at Oxford University Press, they have been unfailingly helpful and encouraging.

Both of us have had the wonderful opportunity to know and be encouraged by the late Kathy Charmaz, whose influence on qualitative methods is beyond measure. It is to her that this fourth edition is dedicated.

1 Introduction

Learning Objectives

- To get a sense of what qualitative research is and what it can accomplish
- To acquire an overview of the coming chapters
- To look forward to learning how to carry out your own qualitative study

Introduction

What do dog-walkers, customers at beauty salons, outlaw bikers, adopted children and their birth mothers, tattoo artists, self-cutters, and widows have in common? They have all inspired qualitative researchers to study their experiences. In fact, almost any type of person or activity you can think of has been or could be the inspiration for an insightful and fascinating qualitative study. *Qualitative Research in Action* will introduce you to many of these studies and provide you with the tools to try out qualitative research on your own.

As you take your first plunge into qualitative research methods, you may fear that the material will be too difficult, or you may worry that it will be boring and you will lose interest. These feelings are normal. Yet we believe you will find that once you begin to think about your own research interests and to practise collecting your own data, you will become very excited about what you are learning. Our hope is that, through reading this text and trying out some of the exercises at the end of each chapter, you will catch the bug of doing qualitative research.

In this introductory chapter, we look at some examples of qualitative research and get an overview of the chapters and how they fit together to provide what we hope is an interesting and useful introduction to doing qualitative research.

What Is Qualitative Research?

Every spring, we attend the Canadian Qualitative Analysis Conference (commonly referred to as the "Qualitatives"). It is the one academic conference we never miss. We go with the anticipation of meeting colleagues we see only once a year and listening to talks about methodological issues and topics directly related to our research interests. We also look forward to listening to fascinating presentations on topics we know little about and that we are quite unlikely to research ourselves. And we are never disappointed. In the 25+ years that we have been attending the conference, speakers have presented papers that explore the social worlds of such diverse groups as veterinarians, divorced people, birdwatchers, dragonfly aficionados, mixed-martial-arts participants, exotic dancers, gun owners, and World Wrestling Entertainment (WWE) performers and enthusiasts. Box 1.1 includes a selection of titles from the Qualitatives that illustrates the breadth of topics covered at these conferences.

Qualitative research encompasses a variety of approaches through which researchers attempt to understand the everyday lives and social settings of those they study. These scholars use many different methods, including in-depth interviewing, focus groups, participant observation, and document analysis, to develop a rich understanding of the social processes involved in everyday life.

Qualitative research methods are powerful because, unlike the quantitative research methods you are probably more familiar with, they allow the studied people to define what is central and important in *their* experience. To illustrate some differences between qualitative and quantitative methods, let's examine how each method might approach a study of widowhood, one of Deborah's major areas of study.

Quantitative surveys about widowhood tend to be rather dry. They often reduce one of the most challenging transitions a woman might endure to a series of correlations that sum up successful adjustment as well-being. For example, a survey designed to determine a widow's well-being might ask her how often she sees her adult children: more than once a week, once a week, several times a month, once a month, or less frequently. To draw meaning from the response, researchers must assume that the respondent experiences a high level of well-being if she sees her children frequently. They also assume that the relationship is a positive one and that the widow receives support from her children. This approach reduces a widow's relationship with her children to a count of how often she sees them. There is no way for the researchers to find out what the frequency of visits means to her or to discover other aspects of the relationship that are important to her.

In contrast, when Deborah employed qualitative methods to explore widows' well-being, she was able to open a discussion through which widows could define their experiences in their own terms. For example, when Deborah asked them if they saw or spoke to their children very often, she discovered that for some women, "often" means more than once a week; for others, it means once a month or less. By encouraging the women to explain how frequent "very often" is and what the particular rate of contact meant to them, Deborah was able to understand that widows' subjective expectations of how often their children *should* be in touch is more meaningful than an objective measurement such as "once a week." In addition, some widows interpreted frequent contact as an aspect of their children's overprotectiveness, while others associated it with close relationships (D.K. van den Hoonaard 2003).

Box 1.1 Selected Papers Presented at the Qualitative Analysis Conference

2019, University of New Brunswick, Fredericton, New Brunswick

"Can Women Be Forgiven?: Competing Media Representations of Karla Homolka's Return to Canada," Deana Simonetto and Mary McCluskey

"Relating Hegemonic Whiteness to Definitions of Right-Wing Extremist Groups," Kayla Preston

"What's the Deal with Small Talk?: A Sociological Analysis of Self-Help Books," Shekara Grant

"Missing and Murdered Indigenous Women and Girls: The Claims-Making Process and Lorelie Williams," Tyra Grant and Rachel Storey

"Constructions of 'Faking Orgasm' in Women's Magazines," Briea Malloy and Monica Stelzl

"Creaky Floors and Doors: A Characterization of Haunted Houses in North American Horror," Shannon Pearson

"Pedestrian Behaviours: Crosswalk Etiquette," Alaina Dostenko

"'That's the Way They Are Made': Canadian Women Firefighters and the Issue of Ill-Fitting Personal Protective Wear," Mackenzie Sharkey et al.

2018, St Thomas University, Fredericton, New Brunswick

"'Truckers Don't Cry': Difficult Data Collection amidst a Culture of Suspicious Masculinity," Michael Fleming

"Container Capitalism: Organizers, Clients, and the Contemporary Obsession with Becoming Organized," Melinda Milligan

"The Scattering of Ashes: Conflict over Risk in the Disposal of Unbounded Cremains of the Deceased," Leonie de Vries and Allision Kirkman

"'Should I Knock?': Door Politics and the Sociology of Access," Stephanie Pena Alves

"'It's the Most Judgemental Place That I've Ever Been': Reconstituting Group Fitness Spaces," Lisa Thomson

"Engineering Design in the Construction of Bionic Hands," David Foord

"Unsettling Education: The Limits and Possibilities for Education as a Key to Reconciliation in Canada," Shannon Mullen

"Performing Danger: Creep Catchers Canada and Vigilante Social Media Performances," Duncan Philpot

"Light on Supreme Court of Nova Scotia Gladue Sentencing Decisions: A Two-Eyed Seeing Approach," Alexandra Jewett

Qualitative methods can also uncover details that allow researchers to gain a deeper understanding of the participants than they could acquire through quantitative methods. For example, Kyriakides and colleagues (2018a, 2018b) developed a more nuanced understanding of the experience of people who came to Canada as part of the Syrian Refugee Resettlement program by asking participants in the refugee sponsorship program to tell them about their experiences. In contrast to the government, which defines successful resettlement "partly as . . . accomplished through securing employment that can sustain a livelihood" (Kyriakides, McLuhan, Anderson, and Bajjali 2018a:295), participants explained that social recognition of their self-worth was an important part of successful resettlement. It was important to participants that their sponsors and others recognized that their identity did not start with being granted refugee status in Canada. Rasha's (a pseudonym) story exemplifies this understanding. Rasha told Kyriakides et al. (2018b) about entering the house her sponsors had furnished and prepared for her in advance of her arrival. She was "mortified by the 'condition of the bedsheets,' and much to the consternation of her sponsors, she immediately stripped the bed." Rasha's sponsors did not expect her to have "high standards of cleanliness" (64). Kyriakides and colleagues use this story to explain that the clean sheets were a symbol of Rasha's status role, in which she took great pride, as housewife and mother in Aleppo. This, and other stories the participants told, allowed the researchers to go beyond the superficial and objective definition of successful resettlement and to understand how the participants saw themselves (as self-rescuers rather than victims) and what successful settlement in Canada meant to them.

Qualitative Research in Daily Life

Qualitative researchers often use experiences from everyday life to develop their research ideas. In addition, they use what they have learned as qualitative researchers to go about their daily lives. As Glassner and Hertz (1999:x) comment, "the job of the scholar is to take the ordinary events and make them extraordinary and to demonstrate how the extraordinary is routine." For this reason, people sometimes think that what qualitative researchers uncover and describe is only common sense.

However, this so-called common sense is usually invisible to us unless we are paying close, sociologically informed attention. To illustrate this principle to our students, we have often asked them to consider the gendered use of space. We begin by reminding them that, generally, men sit in such a way as to take up as much room as they can, while women take up as little space as possible when they sit. Most students believe us, but they often think that they do not fit this pattern. They all know about "manspreading" but think that they are exceptions to the rule. So then we ask them to look around the room. They notice that many of the men sit with their legs extended and their arms outstretched along the backs of their chairs, while many of the women have their legs crossed or pushed back under their chairs and their arms close to their bodies. The students are surprised when they see that they are not exceptions. We have noticed this pattern *because* experience as qualitative researchers has trained us to be very aware of our environment, who is in it, and how they are acting and interacting. Similarly, when Deborah gave a guest lecture to a class in forestry, she noticed that the men were sitting on one side of the classroom and the women on the other. When she asked the class about it, she discovered that no one (including the professor) had noticed it. Are these patterns obvious? Are they just common sense? Sure, but only once you have noticed them.

Candace West, an American researcher, has written an essay in which she describes how her sociological knowledge and qualitative experience contribute to the way she understands and interprets what is going on around her in her daily life (see West 1999). In one example, she talks about the different routines she has for waking up on school days and weekends. She notes that, even though she can take her time on the weekends, she still thinks about articles she is writing and mulls over her students' concerns as she prepares for her day. As a professional, her work commitments do not remain at the office as yours might if you work at Tim Hortons to help pay for your university education. While most non-researchers might accept this distinction and move on, West uses the sociological understanding of what it means to be a professional to explain her experience of feeling "on call" all the time (Zerubavel 1979 as cited in West 1999:3).

Our favourite part of West's article involves a story of her taking her dog to the leash-free area of her local park. West notices a newcomer and tries to start up a conversation with them about their dogs, as one would with any newcomer to the park. She notes that this person does not really act like a dog owner. They do not release their dog to play, and they ask questions about her that seem inappropriate for this social setting. It turns out that the person is an undercover animal control officer looking to catch people whose dogs are not appropriately licensed. To explain how qualitative research contributed to her initial discomfort with the animal control officer, West refers to a classic ethnographic article, "Dogs and Their People" (Robins, Sanders, and Cahill 1991 as cited in West 1999:5), which observes that, among dog owners, it is inappropriate for newcomers to ask for personal information until they have become regulars. Rather, newcomers talk about their dogs and ask about others' dogs as they work their way into the social group. (If you have a dog, you are probably familiar with the practice that strangers often have of talking to and through each other's dogs rather than directly to each other.) When the animal control officer in West's account asked if she "lived around here," West knew something was wrong; they were not who they seemed to be. In the end, West had to pay a fine for failing to register her dog.

Another sociologist, Shulamit Reinharz, has described how she uses her knowledge as a sociologist and her experience as a researcher to notice and interpret the preponderance of warnings in her (and our) everyday life:

> As a qualitative sociologist trained in participant observation, I suffer from the occupational hazard of being extremely attentive to the social and built environment . . . to notice patterns in the mundane experiences of everyday life. . . . Everyday life thus becomes a source of rich data for developing hypotheses about social problems, social structure, and social change. (1999:31)

Reinharz's situation is not unique.

This fascination with everyday routines truly is an occupational hazard of qualitative researchers. We also are unsuccessful at keeping our professional lives as qualitative researchers and our personal lives entirely separate. Lisa-Jo was at a party several years ago, when the topic of reality television came up. She could not resist applying her sociological imagination. Based on this experience, Lisa-Jo convinced a few of her colleagues, Clare Forstie and Savina Balasubramanian, to spend some time watching reality television. She baked hundreds of cookies, and they settled in. For countless episodes, they watched the five minutes, or so, of the segments when participants who were getting kicked off the show and had the chance to say a few words about what Lisa-Jo and her colleagues thought of as "symbolic death." They covered six different reality shows of various genres and ultimately developed the concept of "eulogy work" to describe the social process of framing a loss while in the public eye (van den Scott et al. 2015). Now Lisa-Jo is extending this concept in a study of women who have lost political elections (van den Scott and Martin in press).

In Deborah's life, she also finds that she simply cannot turn off her analytical thinking—especially when she watches TV. In particular, she is often troubled by the portrayal of girls and women as submissive and sexualized. When she watches TV with those closest to her, particularly her children, Deborah can't help sharing her opinions. Ultimately, she believes that such observations enrich the TV-watching experience, and that it is beneficial to be able to identify the patterns behind events. Deborah is certain that her observations affected her children in a positive way, enriching their process of growing up as they came to understand how social norms, beliefs, and atmospheres influenced their development, which Lisa-Jo can attest to. (In fact, as Lisa-Jo, Deborah's oldest child, likes to recount, this type of thinking helped her on her first sociology exam—before answering each question, she asked herself, "What would Mom say about this?" She got an A and today teaches sociology at Memorial University of Newfoundland.) As you can see, we find social life so fascinating that we cannot resist thinking about the social processes involved in our everyday social environments.

As you read this book and try out the various exercises that appear at the end of each chapter, you may discover that you, too, are beginning to see patterns in your everyday life that you did not notice before. This sort of analytical thinking certainly makes life more interesting.

About This Book

This text is designed to help you to think like a qualitative researcher. It introduces you to qualitative methods and provides practical advice on how to use them. As you read through the discussions in each chapter, you will encounter many real-life examples. We have drawn extensively on our own research to write about the actual experience of doing qualitative work, for our experiences are those we know best.

We have also included many examples that demonstrate the range of approaches that other researchers take. In addition to a number of significant examples from international sources, there are many Canadian examples that will give you a sense of the use and importance of qualitative methods in this country. Ultimately, these examples should not only help you understand how qualitative research intersects with the real world but also inspire you to develop your own questions and conduct your own studies in the future.

Content Overview

The chapters in this book describe the process of carrying out research, from generating ideas for topics and research questions and thinking about ethical considerations to designing studies and collecting and analyzing data to writing up the research. This edition also expands the discussion of Indigenous epistemologies and doing research with Indigenous peoples. Several chapters conclude with a discussion of innovations in qualitative research.

Chapter 2, "Asking Questions and Identifying Goals," focuses on the importance of questions in doing research. It explains basic assumptions associated with both quantitative and qualitative approaches to research and identifies the major differences between these two approaches. The chapter includes a brief discussion of symbolic interactionism, the theoretical approach we use in our own research, as well as Indigenous research methods.

Chapter 3, "Strategies for Designing Research," examines the sociological imagination, undermining the hierarchy of credibility, beginning your research from where you are, and turning a topic into a question. The chapter also covers the range of origins of particular qualitative studies—including personal experience, serendipity, and casual observation—and illustrates the ways many researchers combine the theoretical with the personal in their studies.

Will C. van den Hoonaard, one of Canada's foremost writers on research ethics and research ethics review, has contributed Chapter 4, "Ethics on the Ground: A Moral Compass." In this chapter, van den Hoonaard identifies principles of ethical research, particularly as they are outlined in Canada's *Tri-Council Policy Statement: Ethical Conduct for Research Involving Humans*. He also relates ethical concerns to the various stages of the qualitative research process, offering advice on how you can take an ethical approach in your own qualitative studies.

Chapter 5, "Observing Social Life through Field Research," presents the first substantial method of carrying out a qualitative study: field research, or participant observation. The chapter traces the historical antecedents of contemporary field research and describes classic ethnographies of the Chicago School of Sociology. It then provides a brief overview of the history of ethnography in Canada and early uses of ethnography in Canadian anthropology. The heart of the chapter outlines the steps of a field study, from planning and gaining access to a research setting to entering the field and collecting data. The chapter also contains a detailed discussion on how to make jottings to record your observations in the field and then write good field notes based on your jottings. Throughout the chapter are examples that make field research come alive.

Chapter 6 discusses "In-Depth Interviewing," a prominent method of collecting qualitative data. The chapter begins by distinguishing between standardized interviews and in-depth interviews, demonstrating how the latter allow research participants to talk about what is important to them rather than limiting the discussion to topics the researcher chose in advance. The chapter explains that interviews are interactive events in which participants use strategies to locate themselves and the researcher in relation to one another. Researchers can analyze these strategies in addition to what participants talk about as sources of data. In other words, it is not just *what* people say but also *how* they say it that matters. The chapter provides an overview of how to plan and conduct an in-depth interview study, from identifying participants and developing an interview guide to conducting interviews that encourage participants to give rich, expansive answers. Finally, the chapter gives advice on how to transcribe interviews.

Chapter 7 introduces "Focus Groups," which straddle the line between interviews and observation. Researchers convene focus groups comprising individuals who are knowledgeable about or have thought about the topic of research. This chapter identifies the origins of focus-group research during World War II and shows how researchers use what participants say as well as the interaction among focus-group members as data. The chapter includes advice on how to plan and carry out focus-group research and discusses how talking circles may be more appropriate for research with Indigenous communities than traditional focus-group research.

Chapter 8, "Unobtrusive Research," looks at unobtrusive methods, particularly qualitative content analysis. It emphasizes taking an inductive approach. This chapter is different from the previous chapters in that it demonstrates through example. Instead of furnishing an in-depth discussion on how to go about conducting a content analysis, it describes an array of studies in which researchers used unobtrusive methods to analyze diverse items. The chapter shows how researchers have found valuable data in such diverse sources as maps, letters, social media, autobiographies, fictional accounts, professional publications, newspapers, advertisements—and even trash! Ultimately, the imagination of the researcher is the only limit to the types of data that can be analyzed. We had a great deal of fun finding studies to use as exemplars of content analysis for this chapter, and we think that you will enjoy reading about them and coming up with ideas of other types of artifacts you might use as data.

Chapter 9, "Trust the Process: Analyzing Qualitative Data," looks at how researchers go about making sense of the mountains of data that are characteristic of qualitative research. The mantra "Trust the process" will help you to avoid being intimidated by the data or worrying that you will not find anything of importance in the data. Part of doing your analysis is having faith that your data include important themes and that you will find them. The chapter also introduces qualitative coding, which is a process different from the coding you may have done in quantitative research. You will also learn about the importance of using sensitizing concepts to understand your participants' perspectives. Finally, you will discover how generic social processes figure into data analysis. Throughout the chapter are practical examples to demonstrate how researchers have interpreted their own data.

While you are analyzing your own data, it is time to start writing, and Chapter 10 outlines ways to go about "Writing up Qualitative Research." Once again, we ask you to trust the process—this time, the process of writing. Although this chapter is separate from the chapter on data analysis, writing is an integral part of the analysis process. As you write your research report, you will find that you get new ideas about your research and may need to revisit your data. The chapter familiarizes you with the parts of a qualitative research report, encourages you to start writing early, and explains how to include data in your report. The chapter concludes by offering advice on how to improve your writing skills. We hope this chapter will encourage you to make the time to produce a good report, one of which you can be proud.

At the end of each chapter are questions that will ask you to think critically and exercises that will help you to hone your qualitative skills. Each chapter also includes an exercise that is short enough to try in class. As well, there are suggestions for further reading and useful websites. We have tried to identify sources that are both informative and interesting to read. A good qualitative study can be as much of a page-turner as any suspense novel. We have chosen these page-turners whenever possible.

You will also find three appendices at the end of this text. Appendix A is a guide to giving presentations about qualitative research. This appendix provides suggestions about what to include and advice on how to create a focused and clear presentation. Appendix B presents sample field notes from a study of wetlands that Deborah conducted in 2002. The notes present examples of the types of details you should include in your qualitative research. Finally, Appendix C contains a checklist for writing your own research reports. This learning tool will help you to polish your work in order to produce well-written academic papers.

The arena of qualitative research is dynamic and exciting. This textbook provides only a taste of what it is like to do your own study. The best way to learn how to do qualitative work is to be brave and to go out and try it.

Summary

This chapter has provided a brief introduction to qualitative research and a summary of what each chapter of this text covers. Now you should begin to look forward to becoming familiar with some examples of classic qualitative studies and, ultimately, acquiring the tools to implement a qualitative research project of your own.

As you begin your studies, you should note that while Chapters 5 (on field research), 6 (on interviewing), 7 (on focus groups), and 8 (on unobtrusive research) each focus on only one qualitative method, it is quite common for researchers to combine various methods in their work. For example, when Deborah studied a Florida retirement community, she primarily used field methods, but she also interviewed many residents of the community and analyzed 10 years' worth of the community's monthly newsletter. When Lisa-Jo examined symbolic death on reality television competitions, she used unobtrusive methods by watching television episodes and analyzing the exit rituals of these shows.

At this point, we encourage you to turn to the end-of-chapter suggested readings and look for a study that tickles your fancy. Start reading books and articles that pique your interest. Reading qualitative studies will inspire you in your own work, provide ideas about possible topics, and broaden your understanding of social processes.

Questions for Critical Thought

1. Do you have any misgivings about taking a course on qualitative research methods? How has this chapter addressed your concerns?

2. You have probably noticed someone wandering around your campus who did not seem to belong there. What aspects of the person's behaviour, demeanour, or dress gave you the feeling that they just did not fit in?

3. Think about your daily life. What aspects of it might lead you to develop an idea for a research topic?

4. What do you think are important virtues a qualitative researcher must have to conduct ethical research?

5. What might be some good places to people-watch? How might this be done in a systematic way? Would you go at the same time every day or at different times? Would you sit in the same place every day or vary your vantage point? How might this affect what you notice?

Exercises

1. Look through an issue of a qualitative research journal. You can do this online or in person at your university library. Note the range of topics that the articles report on.

2. Find an article in a qualitative research journal that interests you. Read the methods section and skim the rest of it. How does this approach access information and experiences not available through other methods?

3. The next time you enter one of your classes or go to a coffee shop or pub, notice how much space the women take up compared to the men by virtue of the way they sit. If your class is online, notice the way people present themselves online. Look carefully around the room (or "room") for other interesting patterns of behaviour.

4. Watch a few episodes of a family sitcom. Take note of the different ways parents interact with their children based on their gender. Perhaps sexuality also comes into play. Think about the kinds of advice fathers give their sons and how that might shape gender expectations.

In-Class Exercise

Take the next 10 minutes to look closely at the classroom you are in, and write a detailed description of it. Think about the way the chairs or desks are set up and who is sitting or standing where in the room. Or maybe you are in an online forum—how do people orient themselves to the camera? What do these observations tell you about the organization and culture of a university classroom?

Suggested Readings

Barry Glassner and Rosanna Hertz, eds. 1999. *Qualitative Sociology as Everyday Life.* Thousand Oaks, CA: Sage. In this edited text, various seasoned qualitative researchers describe how doing qualitative research has affected their everyday lives and how their everyday lives have influenced the research they do.

Jing Li, Danièle Moore, and Suzanne Smythe. 2017. "Voices from the 'Heart': Understanding a Community-Engaged Festival in Vancouver's Downtown Eastside." *Journal of Contemporary Ethnography.* doi:10.1177/0891241617696808. This moving article reports on a study of the Heart of the City Festival that takes place annually in the Downtown Eastside of Vancouver. The authors used a variety of methods, including interviews, observation, and analysis of visual articles and festival documents, to carry out their ethnography. This readable article demonstrates the potential for community festivals to give voice to members of groups who are usually marginal and silenced in mainstream media.

Stephen W. Klienkecht, Lisa-Jo K. van den Scott, and Carrie B. Sanders, eds. 2018. *The Craft of Qualitative Research: A Handbook.* Toronto: Canadian Scholars Press. This engaging reader includes first-person accounts written by qualitative researchers who use a variety of methods. It makes for fascinating reading that provides insight into the challenges and rewards of qualitative research. Its personal approach includes practical advice for those beginning the journey of becoming qualitative researchers.

Related Websites

International Institute for Qualitative Methodology (IIQM)
www.iiqm.ualberta.ca/
IIQM, operating in association with the University of Alberta, hosts research seminars and educational programs. It also produces the *International Journal of Qualitative Methods*, an online open-access journal.

The Qualitative Report Guide to Qualitative Research Websites
https://tqr.nova.edu/
This site contains a list of websites dealing with every possible approach to qualitative research. *The Qualitative Report* is a weekly newsletter that includes articles as well as notices about publications and conferences related to qualitative research.

National Centre for Truth and Reconciliation
http://nctr.ca/reports.php
This site provides links to the publications of the Truth and Reconciliation Commission of Canada, including its full report and the "94 Calls to Action" from the commission (http://nctr .ca/assets/reports/Calls_to_Action_English2.pdf). The report is an important document and provides a good foundation for anyone considering undertaking Indigenous research.

2 Asking Questions and Identifying Goals

Learning Objectives

- To understand the importance of questions in social research
- To understand the underlying assumptions associated with qualitative research
- To comprehend the differences between qualitative and quantitative research
- To learn about generic social processes and how scholars use them in their research
- To examine how researchers' assumptions affect their research questions

Introduction

"Any questions?"

It is the first day of class, and the professor has just walked into the room. They have not handed out the course outline or given any introduction. "Any questions?" After a few minutes of awkward silence, a student asks whether there will be a final exam. Another asks what the assignments for the course will be like. Other questions follow, and the professor responds to each one in turn. By starting the class in this way, the professor has effectively communicated the importance of questions and of having a question in mind at the start of any project. Without questions, there are no answers.

The questions a person asks indicate what is most important to that person. When we ask our students on the first day of class if they have any questions, they typically ask about course requirements and evaluation. We infer two things from their questions. First, many are still shopping around for the classes they want to take. Some will withdraw from the class if we include oral presentations as a requirement, while others might stay because they like the fact that our classes do not have a final exam. Second, most of the students plan to do only the work that we will evaluate. Some will not do anything that does not receive points. To be fair, however, our assumptions about our students are not necessarily correct; they simply reflect our beliefs. To find out if we are right, we would need to ask the students themselves how they came up with their questions. We would have to do research.

Deciding what questions to ask is not always a simple matter. The way we ask questions determines what kinds of answers we get. For example, if we say, "What is your favourite food: (a) steak, (b) pasta, or (c) fish?" you cannot answer, "ice cream."

The answers to some questions might, moreover, be hard to interpret. Imagine that we ask, "How often do you go drinking with your friends?: (a) more than once a week, (b) once a week, (c) less than once a week but at least once a month, or (d) less frequently?" Those options provide an exhaustive list, but they will not tell us if you consider going out drinking with your friends once a week enough or too much, very often or not often. We would not find out what the answer means to you.

We also know that if we, as researchers, do not ask people why they have particular opinions or act in certain ways, we will guess—we will, in effect, invent their motives. Often, we will be wrong. Herbert Blumer, one of the founders of symbolic interactionism, noted that if we do not ask people why they do things and what those things mean to them, we will nevertheless still talk about their meanings and, "of necessity, invent them" (Becker 1996:58). According to Howard S. Becker, one of the most important qualitative researchers of the 20th century, the problem is that we are just as likely to guess wrong as to guess right. Because our experience and understanding likely differ from those of the people we study, "what looks reasonable to us will not be what looked reasonable to them" (Becker 1996:58).

A number of years ago, Deborah's university took a poll among students and professors to find out whether they preferred classes that met three times a week for 50 minutes or two times a week for 80 minutes. The students preferred the shorter classes and the professors the longer. Then it got interesting. Some professors guessed at the students' motivations for preferring shorter classes. They suggested that the students had short attention spans or were too lazy to pay attention for a whole 80 minutes. No one actually asked the students why they liked the shorter classes; perhaps it was easier for them to juggle work and school schedules if the classes were shorter. Deborah does not know why the students preferred the shorter classes, and neither did the professors who provided their own explanations. They were, in fact, guessing and then assuming they were right. It is likely that the students also made guesses that assumed particular motives on the part of the faculty.

To illustrate this principle, Becker (1996) tells a story about a student of his who was studying the culture of mail carriers. This student wanted to know what kinds of delivery routes the mail carriers preferred. They guessed that mail carriers would prefer routes they perceived to be most safe, such as those in middle-class neighbourhoods or where there were few dogs. Perhaps they preferred to deliver mail in areas where people got fewer heavy packages or catalogues. All of these possibilities made sense, but none was correct. When the student actually asked the mail carriers what kinds of routes they preferred, they answered that they preferred routes in flat areas where they would not have to walk up and down hills. Becker's student would never have come up with that answer on their own because they did not share the experiences of their **research participants**. By asking for their preferences and the reasons for those preferences, the student did not have to "invent" the viewpoint of the mail carriers. Rather, they discovered the mail carriers' actual motives. If the professors at Deborah's university had asked the students why they liked shorter classes, they might have found that the students, like the mail carriers, had good reasons for their preference.

In this chapter, we look at the assumptions associated with quantitative and qualitative approaches in social research and the primary differences between these approaches. Each approach has its own distinctive ways of asking questions, and the approach researchers choose reflects the way in which they understand the social world. This chapter will present more information about the underlying philosophy of qualitative research and give examples of how researchers use sociological concepts in their work. It will also introduce Indigenous research methods and discuss how they differ from Western approaches.

Underlying Assumptions and the Research Process

At this point, you may already be familiar with some of the ways in which qualitative research differs from quantitative research. In general, a researcher's choice between engaging in quantitative research and engaging in qualitative research often comes down to the researcher's theoretical perspective and, by extension, the types of information that they want to find. This section introduces some of the theories and assumptions commonly associated with each approach. To prepare you for the more in-depth discussions to come, Table 2.1 provides a brief overview of the basic assumptions that commonly lead researchers to prefer one approach over the other.

Quantitative Approaches

If you have some background experience with quantitative research methods, you may already know that these methods were first developed for the social sciences by Auguste Comte (1798–1857). Impressed by the advances he observed in the natural sciences, Comte argued that researchers could adapt the quantitative methods of

Table 2.1 Comparing Qualitative and Quantitative Approaches: Differences in Basic Assumptions

Qualitative Research	Quantitative Research
• Research should focus on human lived reality.	• Research should focus on theory development and testing.
• Inductive reasoning (from the specific to the general) leads to understanding.	• Deductive reasoning (from general to specific) leads to truth.
• Participants' meanings are key.	• Researchers' meanings are key.
• Researchers must identify the definition of the situation.	• Researchers must find "objective" definitions.
• Social settings are highly complex and can affect the outcome of an experiment.	• A valid experiment should arrive at the same conclusion no matter where it is performed.
• Understanding exists in our agreed-upon experiences.	• Truth is an objective reality.

science for use in the social sciences. He developed these methods in accordance with his theoretical perspective, which he called **positivism**. Positivism has three principal attributes: (1) adherence to a *realist perspective*, (2) trust in *causal knowledge*, and (3) reliance on *deductive reasoning*. Today, many quantitative researchers still support these principles and the assumptions that they entail. Let us take a look at each of these elements.

A **realist perspective** assumes that reality is out there, waiting to be discovered, or, in the case of psychology, that reality is in there waiting to be discovered. For positivists, therefore, the objective of social science is to uncover the "laws" of human behaviour—what Émile Durkheim (1858–1917) called "social facts" (1897/1951). Because reality is out there like a planet waiting to be discovered, truth is the criterion that social scientists attempt to meet. This approach implies predictability. If we discover the "truth" about social life, we ought to be able to predict how people will act in particular situations, just as we can predict, based on the "truth" of gravity, that an object will fall if we drop it. And, just as we can stop an object from falling because we understand why it will fall, we will have the potential to control social situations once we understand why they occur. Therefore, the emphasis in positivism is on both prediction and control (Prus 2005:9).

Trust in **causal knowledge** involves a belief that the world is made up of causes and effects that are external to individuals, observable, and measurable. This perspective borrows from the natural sciences and, indeed, has the goal of making social science worthy of the term *science*. Because positivists believe that all interactions involve objective causes and effects, they hold that objectivity is achievable in social science research. They have, therefore, emphasized operationalism, the development of research techniques that emphasize quantification and precision. This type of research relies on statistical significance and often uses sophisticated techniques, such as multiple regression, to interpret data.

Deductive reasoning is a form of reasoning that uses a process of inference to derive conclusions from general laws or premises. When researchers use a deductive approach, they develop a theory, **operationalize** the theory (that is, put it into a testable form by developing hypotheses based on the theory), collect data, and then perform an analysis. If the results confirm the hypotheses, the theory is considered plausible, and the researcher writes up the results.

Qualitative Approaches

For nearly 100 years, positivism ruled social science. In the early 1960s, however, experimenters began to realize how heavily an individual's behaviour is influenced by their social situation and past experiences. This revelation led to an interest in the dynamics of interpersonal exchange. For example, researchers began to question how an interviewer's gender identity or cultural background might affect a research subject's responses and, in turn, how a subject's gender identity or cultural background might influence how they respond to an interviewer.

In addition, the social unrest of the 1960s led to the questioning of the status quo. In 1962, Thomas Kuhn published *The Structure of Scientific Revolution* (1962/1970), which showed how traditional methods of observation are "theory laden" and emphasized that data do not "speak for themselves." Soon others began to understand that even very careful researchers are likely to see what they expect to see and to interpret data in line with their own theoretical assumptions. Later research into the social-psychological aspects of psychological experiments (for example, a 1968 study conducted by Cannell, Fisher, and Marquis) confirmed that an experiment involving human participants is an interpersonal event and that the experimenter's perspective can influence the results.

In response to these and similar developments, sociologists began to express a renewed interest in qualitative approaches to research. Since the 1960s, this interest has continued to grow, and qualitative methods are frequently used in sociological research today, even though positivism is still dominant. Anthropologists, health researchers, and even some psychologists also use qualitative methods. Modern researchers adopt qualitative research methods for a variety of reasons, but many do so because they believe in the importance of two concepts developed in the first half of the 20th century—*sympathetic understanding* and *definition of the situation*.

The first of these concepts, sympathetic understanding, was introduced by the social theorist Max Weber (1864–1920). Although he believed in such quantitative ideals as value-free research, Weber (1949) exhorted researchers to seek a level of **verstehen** (a German word that translates as "sympathetic understanding"). He suggested that researchers should strive to put themselves in their research subjects' shoes, to try to see their world through their eyes. For example, in Deborah's research, she has worked with many older widows and, through interviews, she has developed a sympathetic understanding of the enormity of their loss. This understanding, in turn, has helped Deborah to interpret the information that she gathers from the interviews in a way that is appropriate to the widows' experiences. This understanding has also helped Deborah on a personal level. When her father passed away, her sympathetic understanding of widows' situations helped her to understand how devastated her mother was. As a result, Deborah arranged to stay with her for a longer period of time than she would have if she had not done her study of women's experiences as widows.

The second of these concepts, **definition of the situation**, was introduced by the American sociologist W.I. Thomas (1863–1947). As Thomas (1937) described it, this concept means that if we define a situation as true, it is true in its consequences. For example, when Deborah started a job as a waitress when she was in university, the person who was training her told her that women were poor tippers and that she should, therefore, not worry too much about how well she served them. That was her definition of the situation, and many servers in restaurants shared this definition. The consequence? Women often receive poorer service than men do. In response to poor treatment by servers, some women will, indeed, give a small tip, thus reinforcing the servers' definition of the situation.

Many contemporary qualitative researchers are also influenced by the principles of **symbolic interactionism**. This perspective, first formulated by Herbert Blumer (1900–87), based on the theoretical approaches of George Herbert Mead (1863–1931), suggests that the meaning of an object evolves through individuals' shared understandings of and interactions with that object. The object, or "thing," has no intrinsic meaning except for the ones we give it. For example, in the West we take for granted that black is the colour of mourning. However, the colour black, in itself, has no inherent meaning. Hence, in some Asian cultures, black signifies experience or respect while white is the colour of mourning. Such "things" also include people. Generally, in Indigenous cultures, elders represent wisdom, and people seek their advice before making important decisions. In contemporary Western societies, on the other hand, we often see older people through the lens of ageism, and, as a result, they occupy marginalized social positions.

Questions of meaning have led researchers to investigate what events and social roles mean to people. As Howard S. Becker has written, "all terms that describe people are relational." Hence, a trait, such as being tall, is not simply a "fact but rather an interpretation of that fact" (1998:122, 134). In Canada, at five feet two inches, Lisa-Jo is considered pretty short. In Vietnam, she would be considered tall. Even though the objective fact of her height remains the same, it is interpreted differently when the average height of the population changes.

Researchers who adopt qualitative methods are often interested in the ways in which the meanings that things have for us emerge out of our interactions with other individuals, within groups, and within social institutions. Consequently, many qualitative researchers design studies to achieve the goal of understanding those interactions and the emerging meanings that grow out of such interactions. They are also interested in the ways in which we see ourselves as "things" and define ourselves through our interactions with others. Charles Horton Cooley (1902) referred to the self we define through this process as the "**looking-glass self**." Many later researchers have shared his belief that our sense of self is a result of our perceptions of how others see us.

Similarly, many researchers use qualitative methods to investigate how we rely on social meanings to define ourselves as members of certain groups. Consider the concept of an ethnic group. As Everett C. Hughes (1971/1984) pointed out, many people who use the term *ethnic group* would say that one ethnic group is distinguishable from another by some objective criteria: language, physical characteristics, religion, customs, and so forth. He argued that when we take that approach, we have it backwards. An ethnic group is not an ethnic group because of objective, observable differences. Rather, it is an ethnic group because people—both inside and outside the group—recognize it as one. As such, the identification of an ethnic group depends on an established relationship with that group. For example, when Deborah went to China, she, as a foreigner, could not tell that there were any discernible ethnic groups. But Deborah's Chinese guides could immediately identify the members of ethnic groups within their society because they had learned, through social interactions, the meaningful attributes of local ethnic groups. At the same time, we rarely consider mainstream "white" society as an ethnicity because it has become the dominant model, the group that sets the norms. Peggy McIntosh (1988) writes about white privilege and reminds us that whiteness is often invisible except in how we define other groups against whiteness. She argues that we need to learn to see whiteness to strive for social justice. This understanding of identity as a social construct has led many sociologists to replace the term *race*, which implies that "races" are objectively real, with *racialized*, which demonstrates that the concept of "race" is socially constructed rather than real, even though its impact is profound.

Hughes's solution to the problem of deciding who is a member of a particular ethnic group was simply to ask people. They know whether or not they are members of a particular group regardless of any criteria social scientists might come up with. Think of the Québécois in our own country: we know that they are Québécois not because they speak French but because they see themselves as Québécois and because they and non-Québécois Canadians see each other as belonging to different groups.

Other researchers take a slightly different approach. For example, Harold Garfinkel (1967) took the question of a socially constructed reality even further and introduced his own approach, **ethnomethodology**. He questioned how people go about everyday life in the absence of visible or formal rules, and he sought to discover the unwritten rules by which we communicate. For example, if your friend texts you and asks, "Do you want to go to the movies?" you do not reply "Yes," put the phone in your pocket, and set off to see a movie by yourself. You know that the person is really asking you to go to the movies with them and that they expect you to understand this intention and to continue the conversation to discuss which movie you will see, when you will go, and where you will meet.

To make these tacit understandings visible, Garfinkel designed **breaching experiments**, qualitative experiments in which the researcher intentionally breaks one of the unspoken laws of interaction. For example, if you were to meet a friend on the street and ask, "How are you?" you would likely expect the person to say "Fine" and continue walking. If your friend were doing a breaching experiment, they might answer, "How am I in regard to what? Finances? School work? Love life?" When Garfinkel's students tried this out, people sometimes lost their temper and shouted that they were not really interested, they were just being polite (Garfinkel 1967). Ultimately, these experiments reveal the tacit understandings that underlie social life. Our trust that both parties know the unspoken rules—for example, that "How are you?" is usually a pleasantry rather than a serious question—is what makes everyday interactions possible. In extraordinary times, such as during the COVID-19 pandemic, these tacit understandings may no longer apply. In a way, they provide a natural breaching experiment. While we were in the throes of the pandemic, asking "How are you?" became a meaningful question (Tannen 2020). Our noticing this phenomenon has suddenly made obvious our previously tacit understandings. Box 2.1 describes a breaching experiment carried out by a criminology class. It not only demonstrates a contemporary way to break an unstated law of being in a public place but also shows how the challenging step of breaking such a norm in public created a sense of community for the students.

There are a number of assumptions that can lead researchers to adopt qualitative methods. Most qualitative researchers share an understanding that they must pay attention to how participants perceive and interpret their situation within their social context. To accomplish this task, researchers have developed a variety of methods with which to collect and analyze data: field methods, interviews, focus groups, document analysis, and photo elicitation, among others. Later chapters of this book introduce some of these methods and provide opportunities to try them out.

Box 2.1 A Twenty-First-Century Breaching Experiment

Deborah Landry carried out a breaching experiment with her students. When discussing flash mobs in class, a student exclaimed, "We should do that," and another suggested that it could "be our final exam." Although the suggestion seemed "absurd" at first, within 20 minutes it was all arranged, and the majority of the students chose to participate.

The plan was for the students to meet in Confederation Square, a few blocks from Parliament Hill. A car would "blare out 'Are We Human' by The Killers." Landry told the students she would pay any fines but "could not prevent their images being captured on the CCTV system." The students were interested in how people would react to the flash mob, and, indeed, they hoped to "make people uncomfortable for the purpose of later analysis." Landry reports that, "Some pedestrians pretended we were not there but many others chose to play with us," including one man who danced as he walked through the mob of dancing students.

The "transgression" of norms also had unexpected effects on the students themselves as they braved being out of the ordinary and contravening the accepted way of being in a public place. Some were at first very nervous, but participating in the flash mob also created an unanticipated sense of camaraderie among the students.

When we read about Deborah Landry's students, we were very impressed with their courage. A number of years ago, Deborah asked her students to contravene a script when ordering a hamburger at a fast-food restaurant. Not one out of 100 tried because, as one told Deborah, they were afraid. When Lisa-Jo, as a teenager, ordered a hamburger at a fast-food restaurant in a way that was slightly subversive to the expected script, her friend was mortified. To this day, he still remembers, with horror, that breaching of tacit rules. The courage needed to participate in even the gentlest of breaching experiments lets us know how fundamental the tacit rules of interaction and behaviour are.

Source: Deborah Landry, 2013, "Are We Human? Edgework in Defiance of the Mundane and the Measurable," *Critical Criminology* 21(1):1–14.

The Research Process

Qualitative Versus Quantitative Methods

As you might expect, the research process in qualitative research is different from the process in quantitative research. In qualitative research, which generally follows an inductive approach, researchers usually start with the social world and then develop a theory that is consistent with what they see. In quantitative research, which generally follows a deductive approach, researchers tend to begin with a theory and then test that theory in the empirical world. Because qualitative researchers often begin the process of collecting data before they define their specific research question, qualitative research tends to be more open to the unexpected.

To illustrate some of the fundamental differences between qualitative and quantitative methods, let us use the analogy of planning a vacation.[1] If you were to take a vacation using an inductive method of planning, you would know what guidebooks to take—say, one from Lonely Planet and one from Fodor's—but you would not be sure what parts of each guidebook would prove to be most useful. You would have some idea of what you wanted to see and do. However, you would not be locked into a fixed itinerary, so you would have flexibility to explore what you wanted to see along the way. You would be free to change plans as new adventures enticed you. Quantitative research, in contrast, is more like taking a package tour. You do the research of possible tours up front and choose the one that looks most interesting. But once you have begun, you pretty well have to go where the tour guide leads you, even if things are not quite as interesting as you expected or if something else catches your attention. Qualitative strategies often lead to unplanned yet highly worthwhile experiences. So how does qualitative research encourage us to find the unexpected? At its most fundamental level, such research is flexible and open to change.

Indeed, qualitative research allows you to adjust the design of the research as you go. Thus, the design itself is **emergent**. Often, adjustments are necessary to correct for preliminary assumptions that turn out to be incorrect. For example, while doing research in a hamlet in Nunavut, Lisa-Jo decided to ask participants to draw a mental map of their hamlet. She was hoping to learn about important or frequently visited areas of town. However, in her first interview, when she asked her interviewee to "draw a map," her participant looked at her in shock. The task seemed enormous to them. In the end, Lisa-Jo learned that her participants viewed the spatial organization of their hamlet through a lens of interconnectedness. Her participant would have had to draw every single house and all the relationships between and among those houses. Even after living in this hamlet for five years, this experience enabled Lisa-Jo to come to a better sympathetic understanding of Inuit perspectives on space and social structure. Because of the flexibility of qualitative research, Lisa-Jo was able to amend her interview guide to more reasonable requests of her participants, as well as to learn something new and unexpected. Also, because data collection and analysis go on simultaneously in qualitative research, you can adjust the breadth of your study as you progress. You can start with broad questions and then narrow down your questions as you discover what

Table 2.2 Comparing Qualitative and Quantitative Approaches: Differences in Typical Methods

Qualitative Research	Quantitative Research
• Involves little or no advance knowledge of the type(s) of data to be collected	• Involves advance knowledge of the type(s) of data to be collected
• Allows participants to define how the study progresses and what the data mean	• Minimizes participants' input into types of data collected
• Strives for accuracy: researchers do not invent the actor's viewpoint	• Strives for reliability: researchers make sure the findings can be replicated
• Often involves in-depth interviews	• Often involves questionnaires or surveys
• Relies on subjective observation	• Relies on objective experiments
• Includes a literature review at the end of the study	• Includes a literature review at the outset of the study

is important. You can stop when you are no longer learning anything new, a stage called **theoretical saturation**. You can also expand your selection of participants as new questions arise. For example, when Deborah noticed that snowbirds, individuals who spend only the winter in Florida, did not seem to be well integrated into the retirement community, she made sure that she interviewed a few snowbirds to get their points of view (see D.K. van den Hoonaard 2002). (Chapter 6 discusses how the interviewing process works.)

In addition, in a qualitative research project you can adjust your questions throughout the life of the study. This flexibility allows you to examine new ideas and themes that emerge as you go along. Another example from Deborah's retirement-community research illustrates this aspect of qualitative work. One day she was interviewing a widow about how becoming widowed had changed her experience of living in the community. The widow's housecleaner walked into the room and remarked that the biggest problem for widows was negotiating who pays for dinner when they go out with couples. The woman Deborah was interviewing agreed and commented that deciding who pays is a contentious issue. Deborah had not known about this topic when she walked into the house for the interview, but it became a standard and important point of discussion during the rest of the study (see D.K. van den Hoonaard 1994). Had she been carrying out survey research, Deborah would not have been able to add new questions once she had begun collecting data.

Before we move on to discuss how qualitative and quantitative methods can work together, take a moment to review the key aspects of each method. Table 2.2 presents an overview of the major differences.

Mixed-Methods Research

In recent years, **mixed-methods research** has been propounded, whereby researchers use both quantitative and qualitative methods and integrate the findings in a single study. Those who promote mixed methods argue that it is a "third approach alongside quantitative and qualitative approaches" (Creswell and Plano Clark 2007:16). They suggest that a combination of qualitative and quantitative approaches provides more complete understandings of a phenomenon than either one alone. To get a better idea of how researchers have used mixed methods, let us take a look at a few studies that use this approach.

John H. Parmelee, Stephynie C. Perkins, and Judith J. Sayre (2007) decided to use a mixed-methods approach to investigate why a high proportion of young people abstain from voting in national elections in the United States—a phenomenon that is not uncommon in Canada. In particular, they wanted to find out why so few young people voted in the 2004 US presidential election. These researchers therefore decided to examine why the political ads for the election did not engage university students. They designed a mixed-methods study that involved holding focus groups made up of students and conducting a quantitative content analysis of more than 100 ads to see why the members of the focus groups felt alienated. The researchers used a deductive approach, in that they chose the theory they would use (framing theory) in advance of collecting quantitative and qualitative data. Focus-group participants believed that the political ads neglected their age group in both style and substance and that the ads showed every demographic except young adults. The way the advertisements framed the issues resulted in a perception that the issues did not matter to young adults. The researchers' content analysis confirmed that the ads ignored the students' concerns. In this case, the quantitative content analysis played a secondary role because it was the qualitative interviews that revealed a reason for young people's not voting. Even if the students had been mistaken about the *actual* content of the ads, it would not change the fact that they *believed* that the advertisements neglected them and the issues they cared about.

Travis L. Jones and colleagues (2019) combined a survey (quantitative) with qualitative interviews to learn about how individuals think about the future. They explain, not surprisingly, that their interviews provided "richer data" while the surveys allowed them to "collect empirical material from a wider variety of people." They argue that surveys "are particularly useful for quick, automatic responses that capture deep-seated or unconscious beliefs" while interviews provide "more time for self-reflective, intentional elaboration." Hence, their mixed methods (although they did not use that term) "balanced depth . . . with breadth" (157). These researchers used a qualitative approach to interpret their data. They "wanted to let the respondents speak for themselves," and they used "inductive theory construction" (158) in their analysis. Jones and colleagues found remarkable consistency in their data. They explain that their participants most often thought of the intermediate future (5–10 years out), which was "characterized by detailed and optimistic enthusiasm . . . with extraordinary specificity in these imagined scenes" (162–3). In contrast, participants did not think very much about the distant future and focused on the routine and the mundane when they thought of the immediate future (tomorrow or next week). The authors almost poetically observe, "The immediate future is a schedule of certainties; the intermediate future is a dreamscape of possibilities" (169). This is one of the rare mixed-methods studies that prioritizes a qualitative approach in the analysis.

These two studies demonstrate the diversity of mixed-methods research. National committees that adjudicate research-grant applications have seen a growth in the number, particularly in the area of health services, that involve mixed methods. Many of these studies begin with what Thomas W. Christ has described as an "exploratory qualitative component" followed by "confirmatory survey research" with a goal of "generalization" (2007:226). Mixed-methods studies may also use a complementary approach, whereby the qualitative component is used "not merely for illustration" but also to provide "depth of interpretation" one cannot get from quantitative data (Small 2011:65).

One of the biggest challenges for such research is to find ways to truly integrate the findings so that the qualitative components do not disappear in the analysis (D.K. van den Hoonaard 2019). In locating and reviewing mixed-methods studies, Creswell and Plano Clark (2007) report that three out of four studies have a quantitative emphasis while only one out of four has a qualitative emphasis. Similarly, Walker and Baxter (2019) report that in their study looking at mixed-methods studies of the social acceptance of wind energy, they found quantitative dominance in nearly half (47 per cent) of the articles they analyzed while only 29 per cent of the publications showed qualitative dominance. Lynne S. Giddings, a proponent of mixed-methods research, cautions that "the positivist scientific tradition continues to be privileged as a way to know; its dominance is strengthened, rather than challenged, by mixed-method research" (2006:202).

Perhaps the best way to ensure that the richness of qualitative research is not marginalized in mixed-methods research is for investigators who have skill and experience in qualitative research to be responsible for the qualitative component. Hence, before attempting a mixed-methods study, it is important to understand and know how to use qualitative research methods.

Indigenous Methodologies

In the 1990s, recognition of Indigenous knowledge systems and methodologies began to emerge (Kovach 2015:48) around the world. Unlike Western approaches that identify the individual as "the basic building block of society" (Smith 2012:51), Indigenous cultures do not conceive of what it means to be a person in this individualistic way. Rather, they see one's self as connected to other human beings, to "the land, ancestors and animals" (Bull 2016:172). This more collective outlook requires a different approach to carrying out research that involves including the community and elders at all stages of one's research (Bull 2019).

In addition, the history of Canadian research "on" Indigenous peoples has created a situation that calls for reflection and sensitivity, as noted in the *Report of the Royal Commission on Aboriginal Populations* (Erasmus and Dussault 1996) and the more recent *Report of the Truth and Reconciliation Commission*, which states that "[b]y establishing a new and respectful relationship between Aboriginal and non-Aboriginal Canadians, we will restore what must be restored, repair what must be repaired, and return what must be returned" (Truth and Reconciliation Commission of Canada 2015:1).

In recognition of this history, Linda Tuhiwai Smith explains that "storytelling, oral histories, the perspectives of elders and of women have become an integral part of all indigenous research" (2012:145). **Indigenous methodologies** reject work *on* Indigenous communities that is "exclusively positivist, reductionist, and objectivist" as being "colonialist" and, often, "pernicious" (Evans et al. 2009:894).

Taiaiake Alfred (2015) goes beyond the concept of reconciliation and promotes using research in a process of **Indigenous resurgence**. Alfred sees resurgence as a paradigm that includes rootedness in the land, accountability to the community, and transformation accomplished through awakening to the impact of colonization and through knowledge that is transformational and involves connectedness to the land.

Much research with Indigenous peoples in recent years has subscribed to the practice of "**two-eyed seeing**." Mi'kmaw elders Albert and Murdena Marshall introduced this practice in 2004 to facilitate and to make more effective research carried out by Indigenous and non-Indigenous researchers who are working together. This approach requires that researchers treat both Indigenous and Western ways of knowing equally. They explain:

> Two-eyed seeing refers to learning to see from one eye with the *strengths* of Indigenous knowledges and ways of knowing, and from the other eye with the *strengths* of Western knowledges and ways of knowing and using both eyes together, for the benefit of all. . . . [it] further enables recognition of Indigenous Knowing as a distinct and whole knowledge system side by side with the same for mainstream (Western) science (Bartlett, Marshall, and Marshall 2012: 335).

When research teams use two-eyed seeing, all involved should learn "to use both eyes together for the benefit of all" (Bartlett, Marshall and Marshall 2012: 337). This practice should result in researchers' considering Indigenous Knowledges and Western approaches as equally legitimate. In order to do this, Indigenous research methods require a focus on true, genuine relationships with the communities involved. As Kovach (2017) suggests, trust is critical in these research relationships. The building of trust and the establishment of relationships are time-consuming and require our commitment to the individuals and communities with whom we conduct research.

As we look at different qualitative methods in the following chapters, we will include discussions on how they have been adapted and used in Indigenous research.

Identifying Researcher Perspectives and General Assumptions

We create theories all the time, even when we do not realize it. We have ideas about why certain people get paid more than others, why the Atlantic Provinces have traditionally been "have-not" provinces, or why professors act the way they do. Our theories help us to explain what our senses tell us about the empirical world. When our theories are reinforced by enough empirical data, they often become assumptions—theories we hold without question.

Our assumptions about social life and society influence how we approach topics and interpret data when we do research. When beginning any research project, we need to ask ourselves what we think we know and how we know it. As well, we need to examine our biases and investments in particular issues. Although many social scientists believe that research *ought* to be unbiased, most of us who do qualitative research agree that this goal is unrealistic. Everyone has preconceptions. And while our research will be better if we can identify our biases and take them into account, it is impossible for us to recognize all of them or to completely eradicate those we do recognize.

In addition, some bias is inherent in any research process. Recall the underlying assumptions associated with quantitative and qualitative research that we discussed earlier. In adopting a research perspective, a researcher will necessarily be influenced by the assumptions associated with that perspective. In turn, those assumptions will influence the types of questions the researcher asks and the ways in which they ask those questions. To get a better idea of the kinds of basic assumptions that researchers make, let us take a closer look at the assumptions involved in symbolic interactionism, one of the major research perspectives that qualitative researchers can adopt.

In Symbolic Interactionism

The primary assumption of symbolic interactionism is that we, as social actors, create, or construct, social reality. In fact, symbolic interactionists believe that it is only as members of a community or society that we come to understand and believe "what is" and "what is not" (Prus 2005:10–13). Contained within this assumption is the belief that humans are social—as opposed to individualistic—beings. Therefore, as a research perspective, symbolic interactionism assumes that we cannot examine the actions of an individual person without also considering the social context in which that person exists.

Symbolic interactionists also assume that language is the essential mechanism for meaningful knowing and acting. Those who object to using a specific word to describe a particular group of people understand the importance of language as a signifier of meaning. They see that naming a group using a particular word affects both the way people see and act towards members of that group and the way members think about and act towards themselves. For example, members of various social movements have long advocated a move away from the term *handicapped* to refer to individuals who are physically disabled. They believe that the handicaps people experience, rather than residing in the individual, result from the barriers society has constructed. For example, by not universally building ramps to go into buildings, we "disable" people who cannot climb steps. When we install ramps, therefore, we make it easier for all kinds of people to enter buildings, including, for example, those pushing a baby stroller or those in wheelchairs. By choosing terms that avoid labelling an individual based on their physical "ability," we not only give that individual an identity as an *individual*, but we change the connotation—from seeing the individual as the problem to seeing the social context, which can be changed, as the problem.[2]

Symbolic interactionists also believe that we give meaning to things by the ways we act towards them and, in turn, that we act towards things based on the meanings we have for them. Further, symbolic interactionists believe that we create and adapt those meanings by watching how other people act towards and react to those things. Many qualitative researchers identify *sensitizing concepts* (sociological concepts researchers develop based on expressions their participants use) to get at those meanings. (Chapter 9 discusses how researchers identify and use such concepts in their research.) In a classic study by Howard S. Becker et al. (1961/2009), researchers used a sensitizing concept to understand how medical students define certain patients and then adjust their behaviour towards those patients based on their definitions and on their challenges as medical students. Becker (1993) tells the story of how he found out what medical students meant when they referred to a patient as a "crock." As a sociologist, he anticipated that the students would hold a shared definition of the concept of a "crock" and that their definition would reflect their own interests. With this knowledge in mind, Becker asked the students, "What's a crock?" They responded that a crock was someone who was a hypochondriac, a person with complaints but no pathology. For the students, this concept was implicitly negative because the crocks wasted what little time the students had to get practical experience in the field. Of course, such patients would not hold the same meaning for others—a doctor whose aim is to make money by seeing as many patients as possible might enjoy treating hypochondriacs. In the end, by attending to the meaning those patients had *for the students*, Becker learned much about the social context of being a student in a medical school.

Another commonly accepted symbolic-interactionist principle holds that social meaning is negotiable. Individuals do not blindly accept norms, values, and behaviours. In fact, many people engage in influencing understandings of normative behaviours. Howard S. Becker, in his pioneering work *Outsiders* (1963), gave the example of **moral entrepreneurs**, who engage in campaigning to establish certain social behaviours as deviant and illegal (such as using marijuana). The persisting debates around abortion also provide examples of the strategies that groups with different understandings use to persuade the community of their particular moral position. Similarly, we can see the strategies gay–straight alliances use to challenge outmoded ideas about sexual orientation and gender identity.

In relation to self-identity, symbolic interactionists believe that we can only know ourselves through our relationships with other people. These relationships allow us to understand how society works and what our place is in that society. In addition, a shift in these relationships reflects a changing understanding of the social order. Consider the changing role of students in universities. In the past, most students saw themselves as apprentices who were learning from masters in the academic community. Today, students are more likely to see themselves as consumers rather than as apprentices. As such, they expect universities to see them as customers and to serve their needs and wants in that light. By extension, students as consumers see knowledge as a product and judge whether their professors are capable of delivering that product.

Finally, symbolic interactionists understand group life in terms of social processes. They see our lived experience as active and emergent because we are always engaged in negotiating relationships: we negotiate with others, with ourselves, and with broader social structures.

From these examples, you can see the many ways in which theoretical assumptions can influence a researcher's work. When you conduct your own research, remember that all researchers make assumptions, but the *best* researchers avoid making unfounded or careless assumptions.

Generic Social Processes

Unlike quantitative research, qualitative research is not in the business of seeking generalizable findings. At the same time, qualitative researchers do recognize that certain social processes are often consistent across different social settings. Thus, as Canadian sociologist Robert Prus (2005) has noted, researchers can identify several social processes of a "general or transcendent nature." These **generic social processes** include (1) acquiring perspectives, (2) achieving identity, (3) doing activity, (4) developing relationships, (5) experiencing emotionality, and (6) achieving linguistic fluency (Prus 2005:19). These categories reflect researchers' interest in the emergent nature of human life. Researchers do not simply look at perspectives but also at the process of *acquiring* perspectives and not just at identity but also at how people go about *achieving* their identities.

Generally, researchers look for generic social processes within a specific group of individuals. By observing the behaviour of members within this population, researchers can identify common elements of a process that are shared across that population. A good example of a study that examined the social process of acquiring identity comes from the work of Jack Haas and William Shaffir (1994, 1987/2009). In their study, the researchers examined identity formation within a group of medical students. They wanted to find out how medical students transform their identities from those of lay people to those of professional doctors. They noticed that the students observed doctors' ways of working and the neutral demeanour characteristic of doctors in hospitals. In turn, the students began to imitate the behaviours of those doctors. Using the concept of **impression management**, Haas and Shaffir demonstrated that each student participated in a process of adopting a "cloak of competence" through which they communicated to themselves and others a confident, professional self.

In a more recent study, Ashley Austin (2016) explored the process through which young people negotiated a transgender or gender-nonconforming (TGNC) identity. Through interviews, she identified the process of "navigating a TGNC identity in the dark." This concept recognizes that the process is "often silent and invisible," and, because the individuals' gender identity is outside accepted gender norms, they must navigate their experiences "in the dark." Austin found that the process of acquiring and negotiating this identity involved six components: "moving from uncertainty to knowing, finding me, recognizing self in others, explaining work, struggling for authenticity, and evolving self-acceptance" (221).

Identifying a generic social process can also help a researcher expand the scope of the research project to uncover hidden aspects of the participants' collective experience. For example, when Deborah interviewed widows, her overarching research question was "What is the social meaning of being a widow?" As Deborah discussed this topic with her participants, it became clear that the process of identity formation was central to their experiences. This realization led Deborah to explore how becoming a widow had forced the women to form new identities and how this process of identity formation affected their lived experiences. They revealed that, in losing their husbands, their identities as wives disappeared (D.K. van den Hoonaard 2001, 1997). They seemed like different people to themselves and to others. As a result, they had to negotiate new relationships with their children and with their closest friends. They also had to integrate the fact of their being widows into their own identity and self-perceptions.

Identity foreclosure, the concept Deborah developed, was then very useful to Lisa-Jo when the necessity of reforming Inuit identity in a context of colonization and relocation emerged. Inuit have experienced a dramatic form of identity foreclosure and found reshaping their identities under new social contexts to be central to their contemporary experience (van den Scott 2016). Lisa-Jo was even able to see this same social process in play when examining how reality television show contestants frame their symbolic death when they are voted out of the competition and their identities as contestants is suddenly foreclosed upon (van den Scott, Forstie, and Balasubramanian 2015).

Another example, from the work of Daniel and Cheryl Albas, demonstrates how researchers can use a generic social process to categorize subsections within a population. In a classic study, Albas and Albas (1988) studied the process of acquiring an identity within a population of university students. First, they noticed that students acquire an identity related to how well they do in their classes. Through observation, the researchers identified three subgroups within the student population: (1) aces, who saw themselves as overachievers and tended to do very well in their classes; (2) bombers, who tended to fail or just scrape by; and (3) moderates, who got decent grades but did not stand out as high achievers. The process of identity formation drew students within each subgroup closer together because the students were attracted to other students who participated in identity-formation processes similar to their own and therefore had similar identities and perspectives, particularly in relation to study habits.

With these categories in place, the researchers could then expand their analysis to cover the ways in which the students negotiated their relationships with others based on their identities as aces or bombers. Most interesting were the strategies students used when their professors returned exams or assignments. Aces would not want to give the impression that they were showing off, but they would want others to know that they had gotten a good grade. Some reported that they might "accidentally" leave their papers on their desk with the grade showing or "drop" their paper so that the mark would be visible when someone picked it up. Alternatively, they might underplay their grade by a remark, such as "I did okay," if they wanted to avoid bragging. Conversely, bombers would hide their grade or say something like, "Not too bad" when asked how they did. In the end, the categories of students that researchers were able to develop based on the observed generic social process of identity formation allowed the researchers to gather a great amount of information on the social study habits of students. Box 2.2 includes a discussion from the Albases' work on how aces and bombers accomplish study activity.

Box 2.2 Generic Social Processes: Accomplishing Activity

The accomplishment of the study activity typically comes to a climax in a period of about two weeks before the examination period. A new atmosphere seems to emerge on campus . . . [T]he nearer to exam time, the more sensitive students become to exam-related stimuli and the more intensely they concentrate on study . . . [S]tudents are entirely on their own and must rely on their own self-discipline to apply themselves or experience drift—according to their category (Ace or Bomber).

Aces: Keeping "Noses to the Grindstone"

These diligent students are characterized by an awareness of the necessity to keep their "noses to the grindstone." . . . They studiously avoid the distraction of itinerant Bombers who ask irrelevant questions and "waste their time."

> As exams approach, those who have not yet begun their preparations always seem to want to start up conversations. Though it might sound impolite, I try to discourage them by answering in monosyllables. I hardly look up from my work. It eventually gets through to them that studying is the most important thing to me at that time.

continued

Aces tend to view any frivolity or present pleasure as resulting inevitably in future pain . . .

> At the beginning of the year I felt guilty if I refused to go out with my friends and instead stayed home to study. . . . At exam time I would feel even more guilty if I did go out with them.

Bombers are students who procrastinate about studying . . . Perhaps the most typical characteristic of this category of students is their propensity to use fritters [i.e., time wasters] as a rationalization for avoiding study . . . For example:

> The last day of lectures is when the professor ties everything together and says the most important things. It's a waste of time to start studying before then.

> [or]

> When I start to study, I'm particularly sensitive to the smallest speck of dust on my desk. When I dust that off, it seems necessary to get the whole room in order before I can settle down to study.

[*Moderates*] have multiple roles to enact and consequently are the group most likely to experience problems of role competition . . . Moderates are characterized by a non-calculated effort to achieve sense of balance in their lives.

> If you can have fun and get half decent grades, you're in the best position to have a good university life.

Source: Daniel Albas and Cheryl Albas, 1984.

How Researchers' Assumptions Affect Their Research Questions

So far, we've discussed a number of assumptions that researchers can and do make. Now we consider how our most basic assumptions shape the ways in which we formulate and ask research questions. At the most fundamental level, the questions behind qualitative research are motivated by a researcher's assumption that research should shed light on people's real lived experiences. We want to know what people do and what people say they do in real life. How do people go about their daily lives? What sort of meanings do they attach to what they do and say? We are not interested in what they should or should not do. So, rather than ask *why* people do things, we ask *how* they participate in a particular process or *how* they start, maintain, or break their relationships with other people. If we asked you *why* you are taking a class in research methods, you might tell us that the course is required, or that it falls at the right time of day, or even that your friend is taking it. If we ask you *how* you ended up taking the class, you might talk about how you got interested in sociology or anthropology or whatever discipline you are studying. You might talk about how you came to attend your university or about how a professor encouraged you to consider taking courses that would prepare you for graduate school. When we ask you "how," we usually discover "why," but we also have the potential to learn much more about your experiences, your relationships, and the process of being in university.

Because we do not know what we will find when we enter a research situation, we must be very detailed in our observations (Prus 2005:16). Our early observations will then help us to define our central research question. (Chapter 5 will explain and give you an opportunity to try taking initial field notes.)

When Deborah was a graduate student, she learned the importance of taking detailed field notes before developing a research question for a qualitative study. In a field methods class, the professor, Howard S. Becker, began by asking everyone to choose a research setting. Then he instructed them to go to their settings and take detailed field notes. It was only after about a month of note-taking, and thinking about those notes, that they each developed their own actual research question. With a research question in mind, they were ready to do more observation and to carry out interviews with research participants that would help them to understand their observations. This method is characteristic of the Chicago School of Sociology, in which researchers are told "to go out among the people whose cultures" they want to learn about (Shaffir, Dietz, and Stebbins 1994:30).

In Becker's class, one student was interested in the panhandlers who approached people in a particular park. After a few weeks, the student noticed that the panhandlers approached some people but not others. The student could not figure out why they chose certain people. After much discussion, the class came up with a more fruitful research question about the process involved: *How* do the panhandlers know whom to ask for money? *How* do they decide who is more likely to respond positively rather than just walk away? At this point, it became necessary for the student to initiate direct contact with the panhandlers to ask them what kinds of people they approached, how they had learned to identify the most approachable people, and how they decided who would be most likely to respond to them positively.

Canadian anthropologist Jean Briggs (2000) did fieldwork among Inuit in the 1960s and 1970s. She has written about how being ostracized by an Inuit family led her to explore culturally appropriate emotions and how they motivate behaviour. This work led to her ground-breaking book, *Never in Anger* (1970). When she began her research, she did not know that emotions would figure in her work.

Summary

And so we have come full circle. We looked at the way questions affect research, and we examined some common underlying assumptions that researchers make. As well, we discussed basic differences in the ways that qualitative and quantitative researchers design and carry out research. We saw examples of how researchers go about discovering generic social processes. Along the way, we noticed that both social life and qualitative research are emergent. Finally, we returned to talking about the importance of questions in the research process. In the next chapter, we will continue to explore this topic as we go through the step-by-step process of developing a research question.

Key Terms

breaching experiment	impression management	positivism
causal knowledge	Indigenous methodologies	realist perspective
deductive reasoning	Indigenous resurgence	research participants
definition of the situation	looking-glass self	symbolic interactionism
emergent design	mixed-methods research	theoretical saturation
ethnomethodology	moral entrepreneurs	two-eyed seeing
generic social processes	operationalize	*verstehen*

Questions for Critical Thought

1. Think of an example of how a particular definition of the situation had consequences in your life. How might a different definition have led to different results?

2. What are the fundamental differences between qualitative and quantitative research?

3. How well do the identities of "aces," "bombers," and "moderates" fit your experience? If you do not recognize students who fit these descriptions, what identities have you noticed?

4. Think of a time that someone inadvertently broke a tacit norm. What tacit norms were broken? How did the situation resolve itself? List five tacit norms you encounter throughout a normal day.

5. Thank about how people react when they trip or make a mistake. How is this an example of a generic social process?

Exercises

1. With a partner, go to a public place on campus where people are gathered. Observe for about 20 minutes, and take careful notes of everything you think is important. Then meet with another pair from your class, and compare your notes. Alternatively, with a partner, you can do this exercise by watching a home-improvement show.

2. To practise becoming sensitive to your environment, count and record how many security cameras you see during one full day. Are there more than you expected? Were there any in places that surprised you?

3. Make a list of differences between being a consumer and being an apprentice. Focus on the assumptions you associate with each role. Which of these roles more closely relates to how you see yourself as a student? How has your perception affected how you think about and what you expect from your university?

In-Class Exercise

With a partner, discuss the process through which you acquired the identity of a university student. Perhaps it involved wearing university-labelled clothes rather than clothes with your high school logo. What other changes did you make that expressed your identity as a university student?

Suggested Readings

Ginna Husting. 2015. "The Flayed and Exquisite Self of Travelers: Managing Face and Emotions in Strange Places." *Symbolic Interaction* 38(2):213–34. This very interesting article looks at how travellers deal with the discomfort they feel when in a place where they do not know the tacit rules of interaction. If you have done any travelling, you might find some of the feelings very familiar.

Pat Armstrong and Susan Day. 2017. *Wash, Wear, and Care: Clothing and Laundry in Long-Term Residential Care.* Kingston, ON: McGill-Queen's University Press. This fascinating book demonstrates the connection between what seems like meaningless patterns around laundry and clothing and their far-reaching implications for residents' quality of life.

J. Haas and W. Shaffir. 1987. *Becoming Doctors: The Adoption of a Cloak of Competence.* Greenwich, CT: JAI Press. This book, based on a participant-observation study, documents how medical students acquire the identity of professional doctors.

Lisa-Jo K. van den Scott. 2019. "Symbolic Interactionism." In *SAGE Research Methods Foundations*, edited by Paul A. Atkinson, Sara Delamont, J.W. Sakshaug, and Richard Williams. Sage. doi: 10.4135/9781526421036807692.

Related Websites

Web Center for Social Research Methods: Qualitative Measures
www.socialresearchmethods.net/kb/qual.php
This website includes a nice discussion of the differences between qualitative and quantitative research and an overview of the methods that qualitative researchers use.

Society for the Study of Symbolic Interaction
https://symbolicinteraction.org/
This is the website for the academic association of those who use symbolic interactionism in their work. It includes links to interactionist resources as well as to its journal, *Symbolic Interaction*.

Institute for Integrative Science & Health
www.integrativescience.ca/
This website explains how the process of two-eyed seeing developed. It includes the principles on which two-eyed seeing is based, how they were developed, and examples of how it has been used in research.

Notes

1. Although Deborah has developed this analogy further, she first came across it in Rubin and Rubin (1995), in which the authors compare designing a qualitative interview study to planning a vacation.
2. One indication that a term has a negative connotation is the use of changing terminology or euphemisms to escape a connotation that results from prejudice. Until the connotation changes, the new term will also eventually attract negative associations, a new term will appear, and the cycle will continue.

3 Strategies for Designing Research

Learning Objectives

- To understand the origins of qualitative studies, including the role of the sociological imagination
- To discover common sources of inspiration for research topics
- To learn to develop researchable questions based on a topic

Introduction

Because social life is pervasive, almost any aspect of experience can be the basis of qualitative research.

The COVID-19 crisis illustrates the principle that one can look at anything and come up with important sociological questions. Think, for example, about how hand-sanitizing stations proliferated during the crisis. By thinking about *how* they suddenly came to be everywhere, we can learn about our cultural practices and beliefs around cleanliness, the relationship between health fields and private industry, or how we experience policy and health measures in our day-to-day lives. In other words, any aspect of collective life can tell us something interesting and theoretically important, but the research questions we choose to explore will depend on our perspective.

Deborah was passing by a bulletin board at her university a few years ago, and she noticed a poster that was advertising for someone to donate her eggs to a couple who were unable to have a baby. At the bottom of the poster there were tear-off tabs with an email address. As soon as Deborah saw that poster, her mind began to swirl with potential research questions. As a sociologist, her first questions surrounded the social meaning of being an egg donor. If she were a social worker, Deborah might have wondered about what kinds of programs might be available to assist both the donor and the recipient throughout the process. If Deborah were an anthropologist, she might ask about the function of surrogate mothers in a particular culture or compare functions between two different cultures. As you can see, the perspective we bring to our work partially dictates the kinds of questions we will ask.

In this chapter, we will look at how you can move from the kernel of an idea or from a basic question—a question about something you have noticed going on among your friends or family or even in the media—to a *researchable* question. At this point, you may be wondering exactly where to begin looking for an idea for a study. Researchers are often interested in a topic because of a personal experience or because they feel strongly about an issue. Sometimes, a researcher's professional experience may lead to a study. In other cases, a topic may be the result of serendip-ity—researchers may, through chance, find themselves in a situation that inspires a study. A researcher may also develop an interest in a topic by hanging around in a certain setting or because it is convenient. Finally, the idea for a topic might come from a researcher's interest in a theoretical challenge. But before we look at exam-ples of where researchers find inspiration, let us consider what drives researchers to conduct studies in the first place.

Origins of Qualitative Studies

The Sociological Imagination

In identifying potential topics for a sociological study, researchers manifest what C. Wright Mills (1959/1976) famously called "the **sociological imagination**"—the capac-ity to recognize the connection between individuals and their social context. Mills referred to the sociological imagination as "the promise of sociology" because it allows us to identify social issues and determine the questions that need to be asked to under-stand those issues. So how can you use the sociological imagination to develop your own research questions? Let's consider a few examples that stem from Mills's work.

Mills believed that the sociological imagination could lead us to understand the connections between biography and history. In other words, he thought that we could use the sociological imagination to explain why particular types of people are tied to particular periods in history. For example, "the greatest generation," the gen-eration of young adults who were willing to sacrifice and remain steadfast during World War II, was defined by the experiences through which those young adults lived. Thus, we can identify social influences that contributed to shaping that gen-eration. We can apply this concept to contemporary society as well. In recent years, we have seen the growth of celebrity culture. Everywhere we look, we see celebri-ties' faces. Many people look at celebrities and their fans solely as individuals and associate them with "unflattering personality traits" (Ferris 2004:375). However, if we see the ubiquitous obsession with celebrity as a characteristic of this period in history (Furedi 2010), we can use a sociological lens to explore this situation. We can then ask questions that will help us to explain the sociological factors behind the situation: What is it about today's society that encourages a focus on celebrities? How does celebrity culture encourage all of us to become self-promoters (Furedi 2010)? How does the growth of social media and the entrance of "influencers" affect celebrity culture and the "attention economy" (Drenton, Gurrieri, and Tyler 2018:42)? We might also look forward and wonder what future scholars will ask about the COVID-19 generation.

Mills also believed that the sociological imagination could help us to differentiate between private problems, which exist "within the character of the individual," and public issues, which have to do "with matters that transcend [the] local environment of the individual and . . . his inner life" (1959/1976:8–10; see Box 3.1). The classic example Mills used to illustrate the distinction between private problems and public issues has to do with unemployment. If one person is unemployed in a large city, it is likely a result of their private problems. In such a case, the solution is individual: perhaps that person needs to take some job-training courses or learn how to identify job opportunities. However, if a significant segment of the population is unemployed, then this is a public issue, and it is the sociologist's task to investigate the situation: Why are there not enough jobs? How did we arrive at a situation in which so many people are jobless? How has the situation affected the morale of unemployed adults and their families?

The sociological imagination allows us to develop an understanding of how the social context shapes many phenomena that we often treat as individual problems. This approach has the potential to avoid blaming the victims of structural challenges for difficulties that are beyond their control. Framing a question in terms of a public issue has the potential to lead to very rich qualitative research as well as to transcend an individualistic, psychologistic approach.

Patti and Peter Adler have used the sociological imagination in *The Tender Cut: Inside the Hidden World of Self-Injury* (2011). Their analysis moves our understanding from the arena of private problem, in which the practice of self-harm is a symptom of a psychological disorder, to the level of public issue that takes the social context into account. Their study not only explores how individuals begin, practise, and act within online communities of self-harmers but also chronicles the phenomenon's evolution from "ancient, ritualistic and hidden" periods to a "trendy fad" (Adler and Adler 2011:199).

Undermining the Hierarchy of Credibility

In any group, people tend to take it for granted that those with the highest social status have the right to define the situation. We often believe that they have the full story or are less biased and, therefore, have the right to explain the way things are. In contrast, we generally assume that those at the bottom of the social hierarchy function with incomplete information or without the skills or background to interpret things correctly. These usually tacit assumptions lead us to take more seriously, or consider more legitimate, the definition of reality advanced by the superordinate group. Sociologists refer to this tendency as the **hierarchy of credibility** (Becker 1967:241).

In conducting qualitative research, sociologists often seek to give a voice to members of groups whose opinions are frequently ignored or unknown—those

Box 3.1 The Sociological Imagination

Perhaps the most fruitful distinction with which the sociological imagination works is between "the personal troubles of milieu" and "the public issues of social structure." This distinction is an essential tool of the sociological imagination and a feature of all classic work in social science.

Troubles occur within the character of the individual and within the range of his immediate relations with others; they have to do with his self and with those limited areas of social life of which he is directly and personally aware. Accordingly, the statement and resolution of troubles properly lie within the individual as a biographical entity and within the scope of his immediate milieu—the social setting that is directly open to his personal experience and to some extent his willful activity. A trouble is a private matter: values cherished by an individual are felt by him to be threatened.

Issues have to do with matters that transcend these local environments of the individual and range of his inner life. They have to do with the organization of many such milieux into the institutions of an historical society as a whole, with the ways in which various milieux overlap and interpenetrate to form the large structure of historical and social life. An issue is a public matter: some value cherished by publics is felt to be threatened. Often there is debate about what that value really is and about what it is that really threatens it . . . An issue, in fact, often involves a crisis in institutional arrangements. . . .

Source: C. Wright Mills. 1959. *The Sociological Imagination*. New York: Grove Press, 8–9. By permission of Oxford University Press, Inc.

Note: This is a direct excerpt from the work. While we prefer the use of the gender-neutral singular pronoun "they," this was not a common practice in the 1950s.

at the bottom of the traditional hierarchy of credibility. Thus, researchers seek to undermine the hierarchy of credibility by giving individuals in less influential positions the opportunity to explain, in their own terms, how they experience and understand their everyday lives.

When designing a qualitative study, you must never assume that you can get the "best" information from the experts. For example, if you wanted to study new mothers and their experiences with childbirth, you wouldn't rely on delivery-room doctors to describe the experiences of their patients. Yes, these doctors are well educated and understand the technical side of childbirth, but they would not fully understand the *situation* of giving birth unless they have done so themselves. In Deborah's own research on older women's experiences of everyday life, she has had to navigate through many levels of the hierarchy of credibility. Think about how we know what we know about older women, in general. The information usually comes from "the experts." Who are these people? Well, at the top are the doctors, followed by other health-care and social-care professionals. Then come family members: often a daughter, followed by a spouse who may be considered too emotionally involved (and, in many cases, too old!) to see things "objectively." Finally, when there is no one else, we are left with the woman herself. She is at the bottom of the hierarchy, even though she is the only person who truly knows what she feels and thinks about her own situation. In designing her studies, Deborah has rejected this commonly accepted hierarchy by choosing to interview the women themselves, thus giving a voice to a marginalized segment of the population. Similarly, Adler and Adler (2011) did not interview psychologists to gain an understanding of self-injury. Rather, they interviewed people who had participated in self-harming activities about their perceptions and experiences.

Claudia Malacrida (2015) took a similar approach. In Alberta, she studied the experiences, in the first half of the 20th century, of the inmates of the Michener Centre, an institution that housed children considered "mentally defective":

> In [the] dominant model, patients (or in this case, inmates) are conceived of as little more than their diseases or conditions and patients' subjective knowledge is regarded as irrelevant . . . The power of [their] narratives [is that they] reclaim knowledge by making memories public . . . to affirm personal perspectives . . . as real and legitimate and to challenge dominant health care ideologies. (p. 242)

The shortcomings of relying on the hierarchy of credibility have been particularly damaging in the legacy of research involving Indigenous peoples. In the past, Indigenous people or groups have been looked at by researchers as "subjects" (Assembly of First Nations 2009) and have had their stories told by outsider researchers (Kovach 2015), who often used a deficit model that marginalized rather than honoured Indigenous perspectives and knowledge (Strega and Brown 2015).

Lisa-Jo navigated these challenges with hierarchies of credibility when she decided to bypass government organizations, policy-makers, social workers, and other professionals to interview the Inuit residents of Arviat themselves about what it is truly like to live in the Western-style houses as Inuit, how it impacts their daily lives, and how they work agentically to overcome the difficulties they face. This approach privileged their voices rather than those of the "experts."

Similarly, postcolonial researchers, such as Lori A. Chambers (2018), undermined the Eurocentric hierarchy of credibility to avoid recreating colonial power relations by questioning Euro-Western world views as "THE ways in which *we should know*" (p. 55). In her study of African women living with HIV, Chambers recognized and acknowledged the women of African descent whom she interviewed as knowledge generators who have made sense of their social worlds. Chambers adapted her research methods to "feature the varied communicative qualities of oral narrative that made sense in the cultures" of the women she spoke to (p. 84). Chambers was able to upend the hierarchy of credibility to prioritize not only the knowledge and experiences of her participants but also their *ways* of knowing and telling.

Because qualitative researchers often seek to discover the point of view of people at the bottom of the hierarchy of credibility, they "provoke the suspicion that [they] are biased in favour of the subordinate parties" (Becker 1967:241). Yet, as we discussed in Chapter 2, it is impossible to do research that is "objective"; we always have a point of view. So, we must ask ourselves, as Howard S. Becker (1967) asked in a classic article, "Whose side are we on?" Many sociologists would answer that they intentionally take the side of the subordinate members of society, those who are at the bottom of the hierarchy of credibility, those whose voices or points of view are generally absent from any discussion. Hence, sociologists interviewed activists involved in the Occupy Wall Street movement rather than politicians or the police (see, for example, Milkman, Lewis, and Luce 2013). And, as we discuss next, some researchers take a further step of involving participants in the design of the research in an attempt to more fully address issues of social justice and oppression.

Participatory Action Research (PAR)

One way to involve participants is through **participatory action research** (PAR), a form of **community-based research** that attempts to democratize the research process by taking a critical approach and working "with (as opposed to on) . . . marginalized and oppressed groups to improve and empower their position within society" (Jordan 2008:603). This approach includes participants in all stages of the research, from planning to data collection to action, to create a situation that involves "genuinely equal participation" (Esterberg 2002:138). In this way, the researcher and community members collaborate equally in all phases of the research (Benjamin-Thomas, Corrado, McGrath, Laliberte Rudman, and Hand 2018). Often, these collaborations are highly effective in identifying the needs and priorities of the group, and a common goal of PAR is to use research findings to influence social policy or to develop interventions that improve the group's situation. Box 3.2 lists the characteristics of PAR.

As an example of what PAR can accomplish, let us consider Geraldine Dickson's (2000) project involving older Indigenous women—"grandmothers"—in a mid-size Canadian city. Dickson describes her approach to PAR as "inquiry by ordinary people acting as researchers to explore questions in their daily lives, recognize their own resources, and produce knowledge and take action to overcome inequities" (2000:189). Because the "grandmothers" were partners in the research and did not want it to focus on their problems (as more traditional research might), the interviews were designed to elucidate their strengths. Dickson documents a number of actions the women took as a result of their participation in the project. She comments that these "demonstrations of assertiveness and advocacy" reflect the grandmothers' "growing self-confidence and improved self-esteem" (2000:201).

PAR can also offer diverse ways of reporting data that works towards achieving two goals. First, because PAR focusses on social change, PAR researchers may produce reports, "white papers" that advocate specific solutions, policy documents, and documents prepared for hearings, trials, or lawsuits. Second, because PAR emphasizes co-ownership of data and results, and therefore a broader dissemination

Box 3.2 The Characteristics of Participatory Action Research (PAR)

- Involves collaboration between researchers and participants in all phases of research
- Progresses through active involvement
- Reflects and mobilizes participants' desires and needs
- Emphasizes co-construction of knowledge
- Promotes self- and critical awareness leading to individual, collective, and/or social change
- Addresses issues of oppression

Sources: Adapted from A. McIntyre. 2008. *Participatory Action Research*. Los Angeles: Sage, p. 5; and O. Fals-Borda. 1987. "The Application of Participatory Action Research in Latin America." *International Sociology* 2(4):329–47.

of findings in ways that a lay public can consume, researchers may also produce documentaries, poetry, plays, blogs, or other creative endeavours. PAR, then, works to both inform and inspire change across society and reports data in ways that encourage action from the bottom up, as well as top-level policy action informed by the grassroots level.

Where to Find Ideas for Research Topics

Now that we have considered several of the motivations behind conducting a qualitative study, let us examine some of the more practical considerations involved in designing a research project.

Through Personal Experience

The topics of many studies come from a researcher's personal experience. This experience may originate in childhood or be something that happened when the researcher was an adult; it may be tied to the researcher's personal life or to their occupation.

Norman K. Denzin, who spent 30 years studying alcoholism and its treatment, traces his interest in the topic to his early life experiences. At the time that he was beginning his study, most researchers who studied alcoholism focused on trying to identify a specific personality type associated with presumed character flaws of alcoholics. The common perception was that the problems of alcoholics rested on some objective, innate weakness (Denzin 2009:154). As a sociologist, Denzin was more interested in identifying treatments that might help alcoholics than in developing a so-called objective definition. As he notes, his interest in this topic was highly personal:

> The topic of alcoholism is biographically meaningful to me since I have alcoholics in my family. I wanted to make sense out of what it means to live in an alcoholic family. I wanted to know how alcoholics experienced treatment and how they came to terms with their own problems with alcohol. (2009:158)

While there are many significant sociological reasons for studying alcoholism, Denzin's decision to study the topic was rooted in his personal connections with alcoholics.

Difficult or unexpected personal experiences can also provide the source for qualitative research. Claudia Malacrida did the research for her book *Mourning the Dreams: How Parents Create Meaning from Miscarriage, Stillbirth and Early Infant Death* partly to understand her own experience of losing a baby: "My experience was not abnormal. In undertaking this project, I felt a compelling need to find something outside myself that might account for the devastation I experienced" (1998:1). In an equally personal example, researcher Jennifer Dunn, who had been a victim of stalking, developed a study to reveal the "workings of patriarchal culture" that dismissed the impact of stalking or even condoned such practices (2009:277). As well, Stacey Wilson-Forsberg (2012) traces her interest in the kind of welcome young immigrants receive to her own experience as a high school exchange student in a small town in Mexico. She received such a warm welcome that she still considers the town her second home. This experience led her to wonder how people in small cities and towns in Canada, specifically in New Brunswick, respond to young immigrants. This deep interest led Wilson-Forsberg to do a study of immigrant adolescents' experiences in two towns in New Brunswick.

Other researchers have developed an interest in an area on the basis of their professional experiences. Donileen R. Loseke found aspects of the women's shelter in which she worked in the 1970s difficult. As she puts it, she wore "many hats" and had "divided loyalties" as a PhD student, evaluator, and volunteer at the shelter (2009:265). Like many researchers who work with abused or marginalized individuals, Loseke ran into beliefs that victims, in this case battered women, were at least partly to blame for their situation. When Loseke was working in the shelter, several situations puzzled her. First was the distinction workers made between "battered" and "not-battered" women. Second was the unequal treatment the women received from the workers. Loseke's research grew out of her desire to understand these two phenomena.

Sociologists have even found their experiences as professors to be good sources of research ideas. Daniel and Cheryl Albas, whose research we discussed in Chapter 2, found that their encounters with students led to a research topic that has spanned their careers. They observed that their students' obsession with their marks manifested itself in questions about exams starting in the very first class. As young academics, the Albases wanted to learn as much as they could about their students' ways of life. They hoped to use this knowledge to draw out the students' "own best academic efforts" as well as to do their jobs as educators effectively (Albas and Albas 2009:105).

Lesley D. Harman, who carried out the first Canadian ethnography of homeless women, also drew inspiration from her experiences as a professor. She writes:

> I was giving a lecture in the sociology of deviance at York University, and one student asked, "What's all this about 'bag ladies'? I've never seen one and I don't think we have any in Toronto." (Harman 1989:9)

Harman's student's offhand comment led her to identify a topic that interested her and that had not been adequately explored from a sociological perspective at the time. Ginna Husting (2015) also got an idea for research from her students' reactions when she was teaching a semester abroad. When Husting asked her students how things were going, she noticed that they became unusually quiet. One student eventually "burst out, 'Why do they hate us?'" This comment led to further conversation and, eventually, to Husting's conducting a study using interviews and travel blogs to discover how the dislocation of being a traveller can challenge people's sense of themselves as competent persons.

Often, a research topic develops out of a combination of personal and professional experiences. Kathy Charmaz, for example, author of *Good Days, Bad Days: The Self in Chronic Illness and Time* (1991), a wonderful study about individuals' experiences of chronic illness, locates the origin of her study in a combination of the personal—both in childhood and as an adult—and the professional. In looking back, she has written, "I grew up in the shadow of disability and illness" (Charmaz 2009:48). Before becoming a sociologist, Charmaz practised as an occupational therapist. In that role, she noticed things that troubled her:

> I observed instances of staff blaming patients for their lack of progress, inadequate motivation, denial of their disabilities, and I attended several patient–staff conferences that dissolved into degradation ceremonies. . . . I saw first-hand the powerful consequences of professionals' derogatory definitions of patients whose view of their situations clashed with staff's. And I realized that staff and patients lived in separate worlds. (2009:49)

The final inspiration for her study came from an experience she had with a friend who had spent much of her life in a wheelchair. She was with her friend when a branch from a nearby tree fell and knocked into the arm of the woman's wheelchair. The woman exclaimed in surprise, "It *hit* me!" At this moment, Charmaz realized that the wheelchair "had become part of the woman's self-concept" (2009:49). All these observations came together in the form of a research question focusing on how chronic illness affects an individual's sense of self and of time. Charmaz's example suggests an element of serendipity in the chance occurrence of witnessing a branch strike her friend's wheelchair.

Through Serendipity

Among the most fascinating and theoretically rich studies are those that originate with **serendipity**. In relation to qualitative research, *serendipity* refers to accidental discovery and spontaneous invention (Stebbins 2008). When we talk about serendipity in the development of a research question, we are referring to situations in which the scholar accidentally discovers a social setting or research area when not specifically looking for one.

Clinton Sanders, author of *Customizing the Body: The Art and Culture of Tattooing* (1989; Sanders and Vail 2008), states that his interest in tattooing was the result of "simple chance." He was in San Francisco for several days without any commitments. He decided to browse through the Yellow Pages to find an interesting museum to visit, and he happened upon a listing for the Tattoo Art Museum. He decided to visit the museum, even though he knew nothing about tattooing and had never even been in a tattoo shop. By the time he left the museum, he had visited the "adjacent tattoo shop [and] impulsively chose[n] a small tattoo" (Sanders and Vail 2008:63)—thus was born his research interest.

Another example of a serendipitous meeting that led to a study comes from Timothy Diamond's *Making Gray Gold: Narratives of Nursing Home Care* (1992). In the introduction, Diamond reveals that he first became interested in nursing-home culture when he happened to encounter two nursing assistants in his local coffee shop. Over the course of several months, Diamond developed a friendship with the women and enjoyed hearing about their work. Then, suddenly, the two women stopped coming to the café. This second unexpected event left Diamond with many unanswered questions and increased his curiosity, leading him to develop his important research project on life inside a nursing home (Diamond 1992:1–3). Thus, in Diamond's case, two instances of serendipity—his initial meeting with the nursing assistants and the sudden interruption of their friendship—led him to develop his study.

A final example comes from Deborah's experience. Deborah had studied with Helena Z. Lopata, who carried out the first major studies of women's experiences as widows, but she had never thought about doing a full-fledged study herself. Then a student lent Deborah a short book by M.T. Dohaney, *When Things Get Back to Normal* (1989), in which the author records her experiences during her first year as a widow. By the end of the book, Deborah was so deeply moved that she cried along with the author and felt that, for the first time, she was beginning to understand the huge emotional impact that becoming a widow has on a woman's life. The book made such a strong impression on her that Deborah found herself collecting and analyzing all the published first-hand accounts of widowhood she could find. That initial study eventually led to Deborah's larger interview study of widows and her first book, *The Widowed Self: The Older Woman's Journey through Widowhood* (2001), and then to her study of older men's experiences as widowers and her second book, *By Himself: The Older Man's Experience of Widowhood* (2010). She has spent the past 20 years studying widowhood all because a student unexpectedly lent her that first short book.

By "Hanging Around"

Related to serendipity is what we sometimes call "hanging around" or "mucking around." In this approach, the potential researcher spends time in a setting that looks as though it might be a fruitful site of research. Frida Furman describes such a situation as the genesis of her study of beauty-shop culture:

> The very first time I went to Julie's International Salon to get my hair cut, some eight years ago, I could sense that there was something compelling about it, though I could not quite put my finger on what exactly was going on there. But it had to do with older women congregated together in an all-female salon, manifestly for the purpose of hair and nail care, who seemed to be part of a lively and affirming community. For the next three years, I toyed with the idea of doing a study of this beauty salon. . . . Finally, in 1991, I could resist the place no longer. (1997:1)

The simple act of going to a salon to get her hair cut inspired Furman to develop a research project. The setting was so engaging that it simply pulled her in and wouldn't let go.

In other cases, a researcher might be inspired to design new research while hanging around a setting for professional reasons. Jaber F. Gubrium (2009) narrates a situation in which he visited a nursing home, Murray Manor, with the intention of gathering preliminary information to help him design a survey on the impact of environmental living designs on quality of life in nursing homes. While he was "mucking about," he spoke with the residents and staff informally, to "get a feel of nursing-home life" (2009:123). In the end, these conversations led him to carry out an ethnographic study of Murray Manor.

Because It Is Convenient

Some sociologists end up picking topics because they are convenient. This was the case for Patricia and Peter Adler, whose studies have involved their own children. They write:

> Our children's social worlds enticed us as an object of study, not only because they were fresh, challenging, important, and unbelievably complex, but because studying them offered us the ancillary benefit of spending more time with our children during their important and formative years. (2009:226)

In the end, they conducted research on children's experiences and wrote their book *Peer Power: Preadolescent Culture and Identity* (1998) not only because they found their own children's daily experiences fascinating but also because it was convenient for them to involve their children in their study.

Deborah had a similar beginning to her research on retirement communities, *The Aging of a Florida Retirement Community* (1992, 1994). Deborah's parents had moved to a condominium-type retirement community in Florida, where she found the social world intriguing. By doing her master's and doctoral research on their community, Deborah was able to study something fascinating while giving herself and her children more time with their grandparents.

By Combining Personal with Theoretical Questions in Research

Although the above studies were inspired by the researchers' experiences, they succeeded because the authors had good theoretical reasons to conduct them. In some cases, though, researchers work the other way around, starting with a theoretical challenge and then locating their particular study in personal experience.

A good example of this approach comes from Leslie Bella's *The Christmas Imperative: Leisure, Family and Women's Work* (1992). In designing her feminist study, Bella began with a desire to critique what she calls "the androcentric bias in leisure theory." She believed that men had developed the concept of leisure to explain the part of their lives when they were not at work. Women, she felt, did not experience leisure because they were always working around the home. As Bella notes, after establishing the theoretical foundation of her work, she turned to observations from her family life to support her perspective:

> I narrowed my empirical study to family celebrations of Christmas for reasons that initially had more to do with my personal pain around the season than with the theoretical justification. . . . I coined the phrase "the Christmas imperative" to capture this compulsion to reproduce Christmas and began the research needed to explain its origins, describe its impact, and promote its transformation. (1992:11–12)

In other cases, a researcher may arrive at a topic through an equal combination of personal and theoretical interests. This was the case for Andrea Doucet in her study *Do Men Mother?*

> Three particular instances sparked my interest in the "do men mother?" question. One was an observation at home, the second was a decade of academic inquiry, and the third was an inquisitiveness about embodied gender differences and parenting. (2007:10–11)

Jaqueline Low (2020) has an ongoing interest in fashion media. When she noticed the presence of models with disabilities in New York Fashion Week of 2016, the idea for a study was born. She searched to find the first instance of a model with disabilities and analyzed images that appeared between 2012 and 2018. The concept of "celebration of diversity" as a "mode of stigma management" (p. 2) emerged through Low's process of analyzing the images. (Chapter 8 has a discussion of analyzing visual data in qualitative research.)

Many researchers also find themselves returning to a single theoretical interest, even if their studies address seemingly disparate topics. Deborah has studied widows, widowers, older women, and Iranian Bahá'í refugees who have settled in the Atlantic provinces of Canada. These topics are united by her overriding interest in the experience and social meaning of being a member of a marginalized social group.

How to Begin Your Own Study

What can we learn from the experiences of the researchers we have talked about? First, the topic you decide to study should be one that "grabs you" (Pawluch 2009), one about which you have "a powerful compelling curiosity" (Heilman 2009:198). Qualitative research takes a lot of work, but that work will be very exciting if you are really interested in your topic. Second, you can find your research ideas anywhere. As Bruce Berg (2009:21) has written, "the world is a research laboratory. . . . [Y]ou merely need to open your eyes and ears to find numerous ideas."

By Starting Where You Are and Acknowledging Your Limitations

To begin, you should choose a topic or setting with which you have some familiarity—something you are interested in or care about. Lofland and Lofland (1995) call this "starting where you are" and suggest that you find something you care about independent of your interest in social science.

You must also recognize that not all topics are appropriate for all researchers. For example, if you are too emotionally involved in a topic, you may be unable to "meet the standards of good, scientific work," and, therefore, "[your] unavoidable sympathies [might] render [your] work invalid" (Becker 1967:246). In addition, if you find a topic too difficult to discuss, you should acknowledge that you might not be in the best position to study that topic. Deborah recognizes, for example, that she would not be comfortable interviewing women who had lost a child because she would find it too emotionally overwhelming. Similarly, Lisa-Jo knows that she would find herself in an emotional quagmire if she were to study bullying. As such, Deborah has never conducted a study on the topic of losing a child, nor has Lisa-Jo researched the topic of bullying, yet researchers (see, for example, Malacrida 1998; Mishna et al. 2020) who feel more comfortable with these topics have conducted in-depth studies on them. A student in Deborah's qualitative research methods classes interviewed a widow to complete an assignment. Whenever the woman became emotional, the student steered the interview onto another topic because she found it uncomfortable and embarrassing when the widow began to cry. Obviously, this student could not do a thorough study on women's experiences of widowhood.

Although you will not always be able to identify how you will react to interpersonal discussions in a research setting before you begin, you should try to be honest with yourself about whether you can tackle a particular topic. Joseph Alex Maxwell (2005:27) suggests that someone considering a particular topic write a "researcher identity memo" that includes their "goals, experiences, assumptions, feelings, and values." This memo will allow you to see if there are any concerns about the viability of your taking on a particular topic and enable you to identify your own particular strengths and resources. Kalyani Thurairajah (2018) recommends writing down everything that makes you who you are, including gender identity, religion, nationality, age, and even whether you prefer the Maple Leafs or the Canadiens. She suggests that such a list helps us to see the pieces of who we are and our own narrative. By recognizing these "social locations" (p. 10), we can reflect on our own situations and the impact they may have on our choice of research questions and how we understand our findings.

Starting where you are will also help you to avoid topics that are not feasible for you to address. For example, you may be unable to gain access to some settings. In many cases, you will be limited by personal factors, such as your age, experience, background, and even gender. Social settings that involve social elites—politicians, corporate executives, "A-list" celebrities, and so on—are notoriously difficult for "outsiders" to penetrate.

At the same time, your personal characteristics or experience may give you a way of approaching a group that other researchers would find impossible to access. This was the case for anthropologist Daniel Wolf, author of *The Rebels*, a study of an outlaw motorcycle gang. Wolf grew up in a lower-class neighbourhood and witnessed his friends being sent to prison for crimes such as grand theft auto. He managed to get work in a factory to pay for his university education, but he also participated in the motorcycle culture and shared some of the bikers' views. It was this background that gave him the wherewithal to carry out his study:

> I bought myself a ... motorcycle [and] ... rode with lean women. ... But it was more than that. I rode my motorcycle in anger; for me it became a show of contempt and a way of defying the middle class that had put me down. ... In retrospect, I believe that it was this aspect of my non-academic background—the fact that I had learned to ride and beat the streets—that made it possible for me to contemplate such a study, and eventually to ride with the Rebels. (1991:10)

In other words, it was Wolf's class background and experience that allowed him to find a way into this challenging social setting. At the same time, Lisa-Jo, coming from a middle-class background, to say nothing of her gender, could never dream of studying a group like the Rebels.

In another example, Aamir Jamal (2015) studied possible means to overcome barriers to girls' education among the Pashtun tribes of Pakistan. He notes that because he is Pashtun himself and, therefore, did not encounter challenges of "language, access, and cultural legitimacy" (2015:276), the barriers to his doing the study were "significantly reduced." On the other hand, he was aware that having been educated at Western universities and being Canadian could have "created the impression that I am a Pashtun man who has been heavily influenced by Western culture" (p. 276).

If you are considering doing research with Indigenous people, it is necessary to consider how open you are to an attitude of learning and to appreciating Indigenous world views. As discussed in Chapter 2, because of Canada's and other Western countries' colonial legacy, the decision to conduct research with Indigenous people and communities requires careful consideration. Margaret Kovach points out that Indigenous knowledge systems are the "heartbeat" of Indigenous methodologies. Hence, we cannot carry out Indigenous research without a "foundational understanding" of these knowledge systems (2015:57). Western philosophies and research traditions see the individual as the "basic building block of society" and tend to assume that Western ideas are the only way we can make sense of the world (Smith 2012:51, 58). Indeed, the history of research *on* Indigenous peoples mirrored the colonial paradigm. Therefore, if we are considering carrying out research *with* Indigenous communities, we must avoid assuming that problems originate in Indigenous individuals or their communities. Rather, we need to understand that they, like anyone, are embedded in social or structural contexts and that colonialism presents complications to those contexts (Smith 2012:95). Elders, who "carry the traditional teachings, the ceremonies, and stories," must be included at all stages of the research (Lavallé 2009:27).

Understanding this situation will help us to avoid falling into the trap of conducting "parachute research," a common practice in the past, which involved the participants' feeling that their only purpose was to advance the career of the researcher (Bastida et al. 2010:16) who dropped into the community, collected some data, and left. The legacy of parachute research requires us to be very sure to work *with* rather than *on* Indigenous communities. Far from the "objective" distanced research model of positivism, research with Indigenous peoples requires the researcher to build real relationships with the communities they are working with. "Ideally," it is the Indigenous communities, themselves, that identify both the "research priorities" and the "research question" (Bull 2019:242). Lisa-Jo faced these challenges in her work with Inuit. Even though she had lived in Arviat for five years and was well integrated into the community, she still had to take the time and consideration to be reflexive about her trust-based relationships with the participants (van den Scott 2018). The transition from friend to researcher involved careful consultation with participants and for Lisa-Jo to privilege Inuit ways of knowing and being.

Another potentially limiting factor to take into account is the amount of time and money you might need to study a topic. Particularly as a student, you might have very tight time constraints. Thus, whenever you are designing a study, always consider whether the project is doable in the time allotted.

Finally, remember that while you want to start where you are when you choose a topic, you do not want to end in the same place where you began. Your topic should take you beyond the point of view you had when you started. Lynn Davidman, for example, studied the topic of secular Jewish women turning to the very conservative, traditional denomination of Orthodox Judaism for *Tradition in a Rootless World* (1991). This topic arose partly from Davidman's background. She was following the dictum, start where you are. Her initial research question was "Why in the world would anyone do this?" (Notice the strong bias implicit in the question.) But Davidman did not end where she started. She was open enough to develop more "suitable questions," such as "What is the meaning of this experience for the people who choose it?" and "How can I better understand . . . their attraction to Orthodox Judaism?" (1999:82).

In recent years, it has become very common for students to want to study the same topic, related to a strong experience they have had, in every class they take. For example, if a student's parents are divorced, they may want to write papers only on the topic of what it means to be the child of divorced parents. Such a narrow focus, however, can lead to "me-search" rather than research. If you find yourself in this situation, try to branch out and explore other topics. This approach will help you to develop as a researcher and to end up in a place that is different from where you started.

By Developing Research Questions

Once you have chosen a research topic, you need to develop research questions that will allow you to create a plan for collecting and analyzing data. In developing questions for a qualitative study, remember that your aim is to produce results that are descriptive and analytical rather than **prescriptive**. You might decide to collect data about what people believe about climate change, how they learned about climate change, or how they have altered their behaviour in response to learning about climate change. You cannot, however, answer questions about whether it is right or wrong for people to change their behaviour in light of what they know about climate change.

A first step in choosing research questions for your study is to brainstorm a list of questions. As you develop this list, keep in mind that these questions are preliminary: you will likely need to adjust your questions as time goes on in response to what you learn. (Chapter 9 elaborates on how the research question can change during the process of analysis.) Also, you should focus on developing questions that you find interesting and that will hold your attention for the duration of the study.

A good way to begin brainstorming is to think about how generic social processes, which we discussed in Chapter 2, relate to your topic. As an example, let us look at how we might use these processes to develop research questions to address the topic of first-year students' transition to university.

First, consider the process of "acquiring perspectives." This process refers to how we learn to define objects in certain ways or to have particular attitudes towards objects or individuals. When we think about students who are entering university for the first time, we might develop a number of questions related to this generic social process: How do first-year students learn the attributes of a "good prof" compared to a "bad prof"? How do they learn to believe that the only things that count are grades and, as a consequence, worry more about how they will be graded than what they actually learn in class?

Next, consider the process of "achieving identity." This process relates to how one becomes an object to oneself. It includes the "associations and negotiations" that people have with others (Prus 1987:275). As you might expect, this process is particularly salient when one is undergoing a transition. In the case of transitioning from high school to university, most individuals look forward to leaving behind their old identity; they associate being a university student with social prestige, and they often make efforts to display their new status. Knowing this, we might ask questions about how students display their new status: How do they convey to themselves and to others that they are now *university* students? Do they trade in their high school jacket for a sweatshirt with their university's name emblazoned on it? If so, how does changing the paraphernalia—that is, jackets, bags, notebooks, and so on—from that of their high school to that of their university contribute to students' acquiring the identity of a university student? Figure 3.1 shows three high school students who are wearing T-shirts with the logos of the universities they are planning to attend emblazoned across the front. They are anticipating, with obvious pleasure, their forthcoming identity as university students.

Once you have settled on several questions that will guide your research, you will ascertain whether your questions are suitable to be addressed using qualitative research methods. If you ask questions related to generic social processes and you are looking for results that are *descriptive* and *analytical*, then qualitative methods are for you. If you want to address a puzzling issue or one that we know little about and you want

Photo courtesy of Sarabeth Kawugule

Figure 3.1 Looking forward to adopting new identities as university students

to allow participants to explain their points of view, then qualitative methods are for you.

By Determining a Theoretical Stance

As we noted in Chapter 2, one of the strengths of qualitative research is its flexibility: you do not need to be wedded to a particular theoretical perspective throughout the life of your study. Often, you will adapt your perspective based on your findings. But you do have to have an initial standpoint when you are developing your research questions. Hence, someone with a feminist stance would likely develop questions related to issues of gender. Someone whose standpoint tends towards a Marxist approach might develop questions that focus on the accomplishments of labour. In many cases, a researcher will combine elements from multiple perspectives to establish his or her own approach. For example, Meg Luxton, in her seminal book *More Than a Labour of Love* (1980), combined feminist and Marxist approaches to conceptualize the work women do in the home as labour. She did this to emphasize her idea that this type of work is not valued as highly as work in the paid labour force.

Michael Atkinson (2003) had an interest in the sociology of the body, and this influenced his approach to and interpretation of the phenomenon of tattooing. As a result, he approached his topic as one particular "body project" in an era when being "fit" and staying "young" have created multi-billion-dollar industries. In contrast, Clinton Sanders, who was interested in the sociology of deviance (1989), focused more on acquiring the identity of a tattooed person and how that person managed his or her impression as a "normal" person. When we compare Atkinson's and Sanders's research questions, we can see that tattooing became more legitimate between the times of the two studies.

Think of your theoretical stance as a jumping-off point for your research. Your findings may lead you to query unexpected theoretical issues. Your ability to remain open to this possibility will add richness to your work. As an example, although Deborah approaches much of her work through a gender lens, she had not expected to focus on masculinity when she began her study of widowers. Because she was open to new approaches as the data demanded them, Deborah incorporated issues around masculinity into her analysis.

By Choosing a Method

Once you have chosen your topic and identified your research interests, you will need to start thinking about what method or methods you will use. We will discuss several options in greater depth in future chapters, but for now you should consider how your choice of a method relates to the questions you want to explore.

If you are interested in an activity that is connected with a specific geographical location, you will likely want to conduct an observational study. For example, if you want to learn about the culture of your favourite pub, you will need to spend time in that location. You will have to "muck around." (In Chapter 5, we will talk in more depth about how to conduct an observational study.)

In contrast, if you are interested in "amorphous social experiences—those facets of everyday life that are unique to individuals and not to specific kinds of settings" (Kotarba 1980 as cited in Lofland and Lofland 1995:20), then you will be more likely to use qualitative interviews to collect your data. You will have to consider what kinds of people are likely to have the answers to the questions you want to address. As you are deciding whom to interview, avoid relying on the hierarchy of credibility—whenever possible, interview the individuals closest to the lived experience you want to study. (Chapter 6 discusses the processes involved in conducting in-depth interviews.)

Focus-group research combines attributes of qualitative interviews and observational research (Morgan 1997). It brings together small groups of participants who share a similar experience and asks them to discuss their views and experiences on a particular topic. It allows you to see not only what people think and say about the particular topic but also how they interact when discussing it. During a focus group, the participants share ideas and insights and often come up with new understandings based on the discussion (Litosseliti 2003). (Chapter 7 addresses how to go about planning, conducting, and analyzing focus groups.)

In some cases, you may not need to interact directly with research participants at all. For example, if you are interested in how the media contribute to our social definitions, you could gather your data through unobtrusive methods, such as reading newspaper articles, following blogs or Twitter, or watching television programs. (We shall examine various methods of unobtrusive research in Chapter 8.)

Of course, many studies use a combination of methods to collect data. For example, when Deborah was interviewing Bahá'í refugees from Iran about their experiences in Atlantic Canada, she found it useful to attend Bahá'í meetings to observe how these immigrants fit into the wider Bahá'í community. Observing these individuals in this setting helped her to understand the definition of the situation in that culture. In their study of women who have lost elections, Lisa-Jo and her co-author, Emma Martin, began the research by doing an unobtrusive study of online videos of concessions speeches. At some point they might interview some of those women themselves to find out what those speeches meant to them and how they framed their social death in different ways when in private circles versus in the public eye.

In thinking about carrying out your study, you will also need to take into account ethical issues related to doing research. These issues include your participants' voluntary participation in your research as well as confidentiality and settings that might make your participants vulnerable. Chapter 4 provides an in-depth discussion of these issues.

By Consulting the Literature

Most qualitative researchers do at least some reading about their research topic and setting before they begin their research. Literature reviews in qualitative research, however, serve a different purpose from literature reviews in most quantitative studies.

In quantitative studies, the researcher reads literature related to his or her topic to develop hypotheses to test in the process of research. The researcher then collects data to see if they confirm the hypotheses. So, for example, you might read literature that suggests that people who have more education display lower levels of prejudice. You would then design a study by developing **indicators** of prejudice—for example, being unwilling to live on the same street as a person from this or that group and not wanting one's daughter to marry a person who is a member of a particular group. You would then design a questionnaire that collects information about the level of education your respondents have and where they would fall on your scale of prejudice. Finally, you would analyze your data to see if there were, indeed, a correlation between education and prejudice.

In a qualitative study, the literature serves quite a different purpose. Qualitative researchers read broadly in the area they are interested in, and about similar social settings, to help sensitize themselves to the issue they plan to study. Qualitative researchers read very broadly because diverse social settings may involve similar social processes. Thus, if you were studying how divorced people acquire an identity, you might read Helen R. Ebaugh's book *Becoming an Ex: The Process of Role Exit* (1988), which looks at people who have left the clergy, ceased practising as medical doctors, or gone through other types of identity transitions.

As is the case in quantitative studies, having a good idea of what has been published on your topic will help you to situate your study within the greater body of research. It will also give you an idea of what has already been done, and it may even inspire you to create a new study to fill a gap in the existing literature.

Summary

In this chapter, we have looked at how researchers come up with topics for their studies. We talked about how the sociological imagination drives researchers to study the social factors that shape individuals' daily lives. We also discussed the qualitative researcher's goal of undermining the hierarchy of credibility. In addition, we looked at where you can find ideas for research topics. We observed that many studies originate in the personal experiences of the investigators, but we also noted that researchers must have strong theoretical reasons to carry out a study. Most important, we learned that it is often a good idea to start where you are, but you do not want to end up where you began.

The questions you want to answer will determine the research methods you will use to collect and analyze your data. The next chapter discusses how to think about and conduct research in an ethical fashion. The four chapters after that deal with how to implement specific data-collection techniques. The fun is just beginning!

Key Terms

community-based research   participatory action research   sociological imagination
hierarchy of credibility   prescriptive
indicators   serendipity

Questions for Critical Thought

1. What is the difference between a private problem and a public issue? Is there a problem on your campus that might be solvable if people understood that it was a public issue?

2. Have you observed any social issues that you would like to address in a qualitative study? How might you approach this topic to give voice to those at the bottom of the traditional hierarchy of credibility?

3. Is there an aspect of your life that you would like to conduct research on? If you were to design a study based on your experience, do you think that you could be open enough to "start where you are" without ending where you started?

4. How does the "sociological imagination" provide a unique vantage point on a research topic? Think back to a time when you were surprised by someone's behaviour. How might a sociological imagination allow you to think about this behaviour differently?

5. How do the different assumptions underlying qualitative and quantitative research affect the ways in which researchers use literature reviews in each of these approaches?

Exercises

1. Often, when we read about the so-called crisis of obesity, the suggested source of the problem involves private problems: individuals "eat too much" and "don't exercise enough." Design one or two research questions that would result in understanding widespread obesity as a public issue rather than as a series of individual, private problems.

2. Think about doing a study on the topic of student life. Identify any social processes involved in this topic, and then write down all the questions you can think of that might lead to a qualitative research project.

3. Imagine that you had to conduct a study about what life is like for prisoners in a jail. Make a list of the participants in prison life, indicating which ones would be at the top of the hierarchy of credibility and which ones would be at the bottom. Decide how you would go about undermining the hierarchy of credibility in your study. Can you think of any ethical issues that might affect studying this population?

In-Class Exercise

Spend 15 minutes studying the posters on a bulletin board in a popular location or the ads posted on a social media marketplace site. What do these posters or ads tell you about the social setting? Develop several researchable questions based on one of the posters.

Suggested Readings

Howard S. Becker. 1998. *Tricks of the Trade: How to Think about Your Research While You're Doing It.* Chicago: University of Chicago Press. In this practical book, Howard S. Becker shares techniques he has learned that help us to think about our research projects. You will find this book useful at all stages of your research process, from the inception of an idea through collecting data to finally writing up the results.

Jacques M. Chevalier and Daniel Buckles. 2019. *Participatory Action Research: Theory and Methods for Engaged Inquiry.* London: Routledge. This practical book explains the foundations of PAR and takes the reader through its various aspects and strategies for carrying out PAR studies.

Joseph A. Maxwell. 2012. *Qualitative Research Design: An Interactive Approach.* 3rd ed. Thousand Oaks, CA: Sage. This practical book, part of Sage's research methods series, provides a good step-by-step guide to designing qualitative research.

Antony J. Puddephatt, William Shaffir, and Steven W. Kleinknecht. 2009. *Ethnographies Revisited: Constructing Theory in the Field.* New York: Routledge. In this eminently readable book, authors of classic qualitative studies write about their experiences carrying out research. Topics include the genesis of a researcher's interest in a particular topic and how to transform general interests into studies.

Related Websites

Howie's Home Page
http://howardsbecker.com/
This is the website of Howard S. Becker. Here, you will find information on Becker, copies of his articles, and links to many interesting and useful sites.

The Qualitatives
www.qualitative.ca
This is the website for the annual Qualitative Analysis Conference held in Canada. The website includes past programs and a section on featured students and their work.

4

Ethics on the Ground: A Moral Compass

Will C. van den Hoonaard

Learning Objectives

- To understand the importance of promoting respect for persons, concern for human welfare, and justice in qualitative research
- To be aware of creating ethical spaces in research involving Indigenous peoples in Canada
- To develop a moral compass to guide you through the qualitative research process
- To remember to reflect ethically when writing up research

Introduction

In this chapter, we discuss the ethical dimensions of qualitative research. First, we encounter the three ethical principles that form the basis of many official research ethics codes: (1) respect for persons, (2) concern for human welfare, and (3) justice. We discuss these principles as they are set out in Canada's official guide to conducting ethical research, the *Tri-Council Policy Statement: Ethical Conduct for Research Involving Humans* (CIHR, NSERC, and SSHRC 2010). This chapter also incorporates some key ideas related to ethics in Indigenous research. Then, we move on to explore how you can take an ethical approach in your own research and how ethical considerations relate to what you are hoping to learn in this book. We also delve into the real-life experiences of researchers as they grapple with ethical issues in planning, conducting, analyzing, and writing up their research. As you will discover, the purpose of this chapter is not only to underscore the general principles of ethical research but also to help you develop a moral compass that will allow you to steer your way through qualitative research.

Ethical Principles of Research in Canada

The *Tri-Council Policy Statement* (TCPS) in Canada lays out ethical considerations for researchers working with human participants. Canada's three federal research bodies (the Canadian Institutes of Health Research [CIHR], the Natural Sciences and Engineering Research Council of Canada [NSERC], and the Social Sciences and Humanities Research Council of Canada [SSHRC]) jointly created the TCPS. These

ethics codes are teaching researchers to sharpen the ethical dimensions of their research. Today, all Canadian researchers—including student researchers—who conduct studies involving humans must submit their research plans to their university's **research ethics board (REB)** for approval. The *TCPS* specifies how REBs must review research plans. Initially, the government was inspired to create these codes to protect the public against medical research of questionable ethics. Thus, the first version of the *TCPS* (CIHR, NSERC, and SSHRC 1998) was directed more towards biomedical research, and it did not explicitly discuss ethical concerns in qualitative studies. But in 2010, the agencies released a heavily revised version of the publication with an aim to better reflect the issues faced by qualitative researchers. The new *TCPS* (CIHR et al. 2010), therefore, has a separate chapter devoted to qualitative research that, read as a whole, serves as a guide to conducting social research in general and qualitative studies in particular. Still, the biomedical model of ethics in research remains the dominant model of conducting ethical research.

The *TCPS* states that it is the researcher's duty to preserve the dignity of their participants. To help researchers meet this goal, as mentioned, the document identifies three ethical principles that stand at the core of all research projects involving human participants: (1) respect for persons, (2) concern for human welfare, and (3) justice. Box 4.1 provides brief definitions of these principles.

Box 4.1 Core Principles of Ethics

Respect for Persons

Respect for persons recognizes the intrinsic value of human beings and the respect and consideration that they are due. It encompasses the treatment of persons involved in research directly as participants and those who are participants because their data . . . are used in research. Respect for persons incorporates the dual moral obligations to respect autonomy and to protect those with developing, impaired, or diminished autonomy.

Autonomy includes the ability to deliberate about a decision and to act based on that deliberation. Respecting autonomy means giving due deference to a person's judgment and ensuring that the person is free to choose without interference. Autonomy is not exercised in isolation but is influenced by a person's various connections to family, to community, and to cultural, social, linguistic, religious, and other groups.

Concern for Human Welfare

The welfare of a person is the quality of that person's experience of life in all its aspects. Welfare consists of the impact on individuals of factors such as their physical, mental, and spiritual health, as well as their physical, economic, and social circumstances.

continued

Thus, determinants of welfare can include housing, employment, security, family life, community membership, and social participation, among other aspects of life.

Justice

Justice refers to the obligation to treat people fairly and equitably. Fairness entails treating all people with equal respect and concern. Equity requires distributing the benefits and burdens of research participation in such a way that no segment of the population is unduly burdened by the harms of research or denied the benefits of the knowledge generated from it.

Source: CIHR, NSERC, and SSHRC. 2010. *Tri-Council Policy Statement: Ethical Conduct for Research Involving Humans*. Ottawa: CIHR, NSERC, and SSHRC, 8–10. https://ethics.gc.ca/eng/tcps2-eptc2_2018_chapter1-chapitre1.html.

Given the stature of the *TCPS* in Canada, it is understandable that national academic societies, such as the Canadian Sociological Association (CSA) and the Canadian Anthropology Society/la Société Canadienne d'Anthropologie (CASCA), try to align their professional ethics with those of the *TCPS*. The CSA's Statement of Professional Ethics covers six areas related to research: namely, organizing and initiating research, protecting people, informed consent, covert research and deception, security and storage of data and personal information, and dissemination of findings. Table 4.1 offers an extract related to the dissemination of findings; readers

Table 4.1 Extracts from the Canadian Sociological Association Statement of Professional Ethics (approved June 2012)

Dissemination of findings

30.	Researchers have an obligation to disseminate results openly except those likely to endanger research participants or to violate their anonymity or confidentiality.
31.	If they do so desire, research participants have a right to be given feedback on the results and, where practicable, to be consulted over publications.
32.	Researchers should consider carefully the social and political implications of the information they disseminate . . .
33.	The researcher should not falsify or distort his or her findings or omit data which might significantly alter the conclusions. He or she should attempt to make explicit the methodological and theoretical bases of the study, including stating the limitations of the data.
34.	Researchers are obliged to try to clarify any significant distortion made by a sponsor or client of the findings of a research project in which they have participated.
35.	Research reports should disclose all sources of financial support for the research and any other sponsorship or special relationship with investigators.
36.	Sociologists have a responsibility to speak out publicly, both individually and collectively, on issues about which they possess professional expertise . . . and refrain from offering expert commentaries on material which as researchers they would regard as comprising inadequate or tendentious evidence.

(Permission is granted by the CSA to copy and distribute this document, from which this section is extracted, for research, teaching, and other professional and/or administrative purposes. Please note, pronouns have been left as quoted in the original material. The authors prefer to use singular *they*.)

Source: www.csa-scs.ca/files/www/csa/documents/codeofethics/2012Ethics.pdf. Used with the permission of the Canadian Sociological Association.

can consult the URL at the bottom of the table if they wish to read other pertinent sections of the Statement of Professional Ethics.

The CASCA (Canadian Anthropology Society) has decided not to develop formal ethics guidelines. Ethnographic research is both complex and varied, making it impossible to develop one standard set of guidelines (many of which are already captured in *TCPS 2*, especially Chapters 9, "Research Involving the First Nations, Inuit, and Métis People of Canada," and 10, "Qualitative Research"). The guidelines linked to the American Anthropological Association (AAA) are cumbersome and reflect an American orientation. Anthropologists are keen on relating the ethics of their research to the exigencies of culture and communities.

Research Involving Indigenous Peoples in Canada[1]

Creating ethical spaces for research involving First Nations, Inuit, and Métis peoples of Canada derives from the histories, cultures, and traditions that are strikingly different from the conventional ethical practices attached to research in general. The core value of Indigenous life is reciprocity, and that forms the basis of the relationship between researchers and the Indigenous community. Because in the past, non-Indigenous researchers carried out so much research *on* Indigenous peoples, Indigenous peoples are now understandably apprehensive or mistrustful of such research. The newly created ethical spaces call for respectful relationships that leave plenty of room for collaboration and engagement between researchers and Indigenous participants. Trust is the essence of these relationships, and its development takes time. The art of attaining trust requires the involvement of Indigenous peoples from the earliest conception of the research, through the design and analysis, and finally to the dissemination of the findings. The Cree scholar Willie Ermine (2007:193) discusses the role of "ethical space" when two societies "with disparate worldviews . . . are poised to engage each other." This space between them allows the formation of a new framework to examine "the diversity and positioning of Indigenous peoples and Western society."

No doubt the researcher will encounter pitfalls along the way; the most in-grained one involves the researcher's own assumptions and taken-for-granted ways of conducting research. The other issues that both the researcher and the Indigenous partner(s) must agree upon include acknowledging the proper balance between individual and collective interests. In this connection, the role of Elders and Knowledge Keepers (and Indigenous governance structures) is key to the foundational shift from individualistic to collective interests. The nature of the collaborative relationship is not always easy to delineate: on one hand, the research partners must fathom each other's strengths in conducting the research; on the other hand, the research engagement requires the partners to reflect on their role in reviewing and approving the research or even the extent to which the Indigenous partner wants to be engaged in the research. Some of these concerns speak directly to the notions of "cultural safety" and "cultural humility" (Baba 2013).

While Chapter 9 of the *TCPS* is devoted to research with Indigenous peoples, researchers are increasingly relying on OCAP (Ownership, Control, Access, and Possession) and other Indigenous-based principles to gain relevant insights about such research (www.fnigc.ca/ocap.html). These principles outline a new template of research ethics, requiring the researcher and the Indigenous research partner(s) to reflect on academic freedom, the engagement of the next generation with respect to the research, the meaning of welfare or harm engendered by research, and the incorporation of spiritual values deeply attached to nature, to the individual, and to collective life.

Cultural misappropriation and the existence of plural and divergent perspectives are fair notions that any partners in the research must address, especially in light of exploitative practices and essentialist views on "race" and ethnicity that see group characteristics as fixed traits, discounting variation among group members. Finally, researchers need to give special consideration to the use of language (and interpretation).

Those interested in pursuing research ethics from Indigenous perspectives will find works by the following authors very instructive: Julie R. Bull (2010, 2016); Fern Brunger, Julie R. Bull, and Darlene Wall (2014); Fern Brunger, Rebecca Schiff, Julie R. Bull, and Melody Morton-Ninomiya (2014); and Fern Brunger and Julie R. Bull (2011).

Applying the Principles of Ethics to Qualitative Research

At this point, you may be wondering exactly how you can ensure that you respect the dignity of the participants in your own qualitative research studies. Here is some proven advice to help you build your moral compass.

First, enter the research situation with an open mind. As a qualitative researcher, you should never expect your participants to confirm your own assumptions, and you should never invent or rush in to explain your participants' motives. Remember that you are not the expert on the situation. You have no way of knowing what a particular experience is like for your participants, why they do the things they do, or why they *think* they do the things they do. You must allow participants to explain their situation and their motives in their own words.

Second, it will be helpful to ask "how" questions rather than "why" questions. As you will learn in Chapter 6, "why" questions can make participants feel defensive, as if their motives are being questioned. Asking someone *how* something happened rather than *why* they did something also encourages that person to discuss their motives in context—to create a **vocabulary of motives**. Such a discussion will provide you with more useful qualitative data than would the short, direct answer that a "why" question might elicit.

Third, acknowledge the various constraints that can intrude in a social setting that might also affect respect for the person. The *TCPS* notes several such constraints:

> Certain factors may diminish a person's ability to exercise their autonomy, such as inadequate information or understanding for deliberation, or a lack of freedom to act due to controlling influences or coercion. Such constraints may include the fear of alienating those in positions of authority, such as professional or personal caregivers, researchers, leaders, larger groups, or a community to which one belongs. (CIHR et al. 2010:9)

In short, you should be mindful of the fears that a research participant has by virtue of their precarious personal and social position.

Fourth, use an approach that fits the circumstances of the individual participant, group, community, and/or culture. If you are doing field research, ensure that your level of participation is appropriate to the setting. Also, ensure that your approach shows your respect for your participants' values. Remember that you are a guest in the setting and that you must adapt your behaviour to fit with the community's social norms.

Fifth, forgo a "remedial" attitude. Your job is not to find a remedy for a problem or to "fix" things. Recall that qualitative research is descriptive and analytical rather than prescriptive. Thus, you should focus on observing what you see and assessing it in its own terms. You should also remember this approach when you write up your research. (We will look at *ethical writing*—writing that strives towards accuracy, precision, and clarity and offers a balanced perspective—in more depth later in this chapter.)

Finally, try to form authentic relationships with your participants. You should treat your participants as valued partners in the research process, not as subjects to be studied from a distance. Getting to know your participants as individuals will also help you to dispel your own biases. This goal is essential to conducting ethical research—you must be able to step out of your own immediate cultural and social worlds in order to understand the world of your research participants.

To illustrate the importance of this final point, let's look at the example Timothy Diamond set in his study of nursing homes, which you encountered in Chapter 3. In his study, Diamond demonstrated high ethical resolve and established authentic relationships with the staff and the residents of nursing homes. As he notes, these genuine relationships permitted him to identify and overcome his own prejudices and stereotypical views of nursing homes. Box 4.2 presents some of Diamond's self-identified assumptions and his reactions to becoming aware of his faulty views. In addition, by abandoning his preconceived ideas and by having an open and observant attitude—in other words, by bursting out of his own bubble—Diamond was able to transform his original question—"What can we do for them?"—into a more productive qualitative research question: "What is their life like?"

Developing a Research Question

As you have already learned, the birth of a research question often begins with a fascination with a topic or a social setting. For example, Herbert J. Gans's classic 1967 study of the "Levittowners" started when he and his wife mortgaged a home in Levittown, New Jersey, and he began taking notes on the social interactions among neighbours, newcomers, and local rural residents.[2] Although it is easy to get caught up in the excitement of developing your own ideas in the early stages of your research project, to do ethical research, you must remain open-minded as you take notes and investigate your research questions. Almost invariably, you will make these necessary early notes long before you have the opportunity or enough detailed knowledge to submit your research ideas to a research ethics board.

One barrier to such an approach is trying too hard to support your early ideas. The advice in Chapter 3, that you should not end the research where you start, is meaningful when it comes to doing ethical research. When we start a research project, we tend to imagine what the answers to our research question(s) might be. Yet, given our limited experience and unfamiliarity with the life-world of the groups and peoples we wish to study, it is unlikely that our imagined answers will reflect the reality of the situation. After all, if you do not belong to a group, how can you know what it is like to be a member? All too often, such imaginings can lead us to start "defining and inventing" the motives of others (Conn 1971:78; Becker 1996). The predispositions, stereotypes, and prejudices we bring to the research environment render a disservice to the people we aim to study: these pre-established notions, in effect, pre-empt participants' explanations, experiences, and points of view.

A second barrier to open-mindedness arises when there is a conflict of interest. When the public insists that social research be "relevant" or "applied," as is increasingly the case today, researchers may feel pressure to secure funding from organizations that aim to develop social policy. Often, these agencies purport to be interested in "solving" social problems. At first glance, these might seem like praiseworthy objectives, but there is a downside to associating your research process with outside interests. To begin with, the kinds of questions you might ask under these conditions of funding are likely to represent the interests of funders or administrators rather than those of research participants. Merlinda Weinberg (2002), for example, learned that the administrators of the maternity home she was studying wanted to see her reports and field notes about how the residents were being cared for; the administrators planned to use these forms to comply with an external funder's requirement. External influences also present you with a more tenacious problem: Should you leave it to those who fund the research to define the social problem to be studied? Such a definition could force you to take an approach that is too narrow. For example, if you were asked by a school board to study the "problem" of high school dropouts, the organization might insist that you look for

Box 4.2 Preconceived Ideas That Stood in the Way of Doing Ethical Research

- Assumption: Minimum wage is a liveable wage:

  Eventually, the very concepts of job and wage versus unemployment and poverty that I had brought with me began to break down. . . . Full-time work meant earning less than the cost of subsistence; it did not alleviate poverty.

- Assumption: Under-paid workers should simply find new jobs:

  Among the many insults that nursing assistants absorb. . . . I came to think of none more naive than to enquire why they don't just get another job.

- Assumption: Patients in nursing homes are bedridden:

  I had been under the impression that nearly all people in nursing homes were bedridden. In fact, many were up and dressed, walking around, and free to leave the building during certain hours.

- Assumption: Public aid provides a safety net:

  [P]ossessions were continually being lost and not replaced, having fallen through the large holes in the net. . . . What sometimes initially appeared as crazy behaviour emerged over time as rational, desperate attempts to guard what was slipping away.

- Assumption: Life in nursing homes is better than life on the streets:

  I clung for a while to the notion that residence in a nursing home must at least be better than living on the streets. [Yet an encounter with a homeless woman who said she would rather live in an abandoned building than in a nursing home] had opened even this assumption up for debate.

- Assumption: People who live in nursing homes have been abandoned by their families:

  It is an easy explanation, but. . . . it rests on oversimplification. Listening to the residents' everyday conversations about their families did not lead to the inference that they were abandoned.

- Assumption: People who live in nursing homes lead lives of passivity:

  I had thought of residents as on the receiving end of human activity, acted upon rather than acting. . . . Getting to know the residents, however, dissolved that notion.

- Assumption: Nursing homes are silent, lonely places:

  Not only did people in the day room have a lot to say to the nursing staff, but quiet friendships bloomed throughout the room.

Source: Quotations from Timothy Diamond. 1992. *Making Gray Gold: Narratives of Nursing Home Care.* Chicago: University of Chicago Press, pp. 44–5, 46, 63, 68, 69–70, 70, 84–5, 100.

factors outside the school environment to explain the phenomenon. Yet, to focus on finding "answers" that will satisfy the constituents of the supporting organization, you would have to ignore the many school-based factors that could lead students to leave school before they graduate. In the end, your study would not accurately reflect the situations of your participants.

Doing Ethical Fieldwork

Doing fieldwork has a surprising number of unexpected—and unpredictable—ethical dimensions. In general, fieldwork entails a long period of study. As you can see from the list of studies presented in Table 4.2, a qualitative researcher might spend several months or more than eight years making observations in the field.[3] In addition, it can take another two or three years (or even longer) to publish the study. The intensity of time and energy required to complete a field study presents researchers with an ever-shifting environment in which they must consider the ethical dimensions of the study. Still, whether long or short, the time spent doing fieldwork entails gaining access to the research setting, spending time in the community, and finally leaving the field. Each of these aspects demands ethical reflection on the part of the researcher. In addition to the time it takes to be out in the field, researchers devote considerable time preparing research-grant applications (which sometimes involves collecting preliminary data) and following through

Table 4.2 Length of Time in the Field

Topic of Study	Time Spent in the Field	Researcher and Publication Date
Freemasons	9 years	J.S. Kenney, 2016
School in military town	8 years	D. Harrison and P. Albanese, 2016
Household work	8 years	A.R. Hochschild, 1989
Shoplifting	8 years	M.O. Cameron, 1973
Tattoo shops	7 years	C. Sanders, 1989
Provincial training school	7 years	C. Malacrida, 2015
Hotel staff	5 years	R. Prus and S. Irini, 1980
Doomsday cult	4 years	J. Lofland, 1977
Drug dealers	4 years	P.A. Adler, 1985
Homeless women	4 years	E. Liebow, 1993
Unwed mothers	4 years	P. Rains, 1971
Biker gangs	3 years	D. Wolf, 1991
TV news studio	3 years	D.L. Altheide, 1976
Urban youth	3 years	E. Anderson, 1976
Medical school	2 years	H.S. Becker et al., 1961
Hobos	1 year	N. Anderson, 1923
Magicians	5 months	R.A. Stebbins, 1984

with more data even when their work is about to be published. Some, like Scott Kenney (2016), who has devoted some nine years to his research although he confessed that he has been "living his research" since 1999 (or some eight years before he formally began), spend many years carrying out their research.

Gaining Access to the Field

In most field research, unless you are conducting covert research (discussed later in this chapter), you will need to explain your presence to those whose lives you are planning to study. Generally, you will contact a community leader—a gatekeeper— to get permission to study in a particular setting. While you might find it intimidating to approach a community leader, your efforts will always pay off in the end. When I was beginning my first field research project in a remote Icelandic village of 500 inhabitants, I had to approach the highly respected *oddviti*, the chairman of the village, to ask for entry into his community. To make the situation more nerve-racking, I was in an unfamiliar country, I had just ridden on a regional bus for two hours, and I'd had no hand in choosing the village. (An Icelandic agricultural economist whom I had befriended and who learned of my wish to study a fishing village had put me on the bus and suggested I get off at the end of the ride!) As I stepped off the bus, into rain that swept horizontally across the landscape, the environment seemed utterly forlorn to me. Yet, when the *oddviti* greeted me as I stepped out of the bus, I respectfully expressed my desire to study "his" village. Fortunately, he agreed, and my time in the village was productive. Being honest about my intentions foreclosed any future problems.

The ethics involved in studying a private organization or a corporation are often more complex. Gaining formal approval from a company's CEO or president might involve the company's legal department. In general, very few corporations grant researchers access to their internal workings. Libels, lawsuits, the inevitable fall of "whistle-blowers," and the power of multinationals can be disincentives to any kind of research in a corporate setting. When a corporation does grant access, it often wants to direct the research, a practice that can result in a conflict of interest. One example is the corporation that invited Arlie R. Hochschild (1997) to study it as a "family-friendly" company. The organization might even restrict the researcher from using particular words or phrases in the analysis. For example, one researcher wanted to study the ethical aspects of decision-making in a company and was given the go-ahead to do the research but was not allowed to use the word *ethics*! If you were to study work about the "tar" sands of Alberta, company officials might insist you call them "oil" sands, a term that sounds friendlier to ecological concerns.

Accessing government agencies can pose similar ethical dilemmas. Anthropologist Elliott Leyton (1978) provides a good example of how a researcher can resist the temptation to align themself with the interests of the agency under study. In his ethnographic study of the Workmen's Compensation Board in Newfoundland, "The Bureaucratization of Anguish" (1978), Leyton clearly aligned his ethical duties with his participants while meeting his moral obligation to accurately and fairly substantiate his findings. In the end, his study critiqued the government agency, revealing how incompatible the actions of the bureaucracy were with ameliorating the suffering of widows whose husbands had died of industrial disease.

More often, researchers are allowed to study government programs only within tight regulations set by the government. One such project, which was the subject of considerable ethical controversy, involved the United States Army's Human Terrain System (HTS) program in Iraq and Afghanistan. The program hired social scientists and combined scholarly research with military information-gathering (Institutional Review Blog 2009). The intent was to gather ethnographic information on local populations as a means of limiting the danger of war to those populations. In the end, however, the interests of the military came first.

Spending Time in the Field

The approach you take while spending time in the field can encompass a broad range of tones. Generally, the tone will depend on the character of the community or subculture to be studied and the personality of the researcher. Some researchers present themselves quietly while others have a more visible profile, either because of their outgoing nature or because their physical appearance—their age, skin colour, gender, and so on—stands out in contrast to the physical characteristics of the other members of the group. Whatever the tone of the participation, you must be aware of the effect your presence has on the community. While members of a group may accept the idea of your taking notes on their environment, they might (silently) object or find it irksome if you are too obvious. Thus, you should always respect the group's boundaries by not ostentatiously taking notes. As you spend time in the setting and get to know the culture of the community, you will learn the least obtrusive ways to publicly take field notes.

The longer you stay in the setting, the more informed you will become of its routines and activities and the more your participants will become familiar with *your* routines and activities. This familiarity has obvious benefits (for example, participants tend to be more open with individuals they recognize), but it also presents some ethical dilemmas. Sometimes, participants will become aware of your access to many corners of the setting, and they will try to get you to reveal information you have gained from others. You must exercise the utmost restraint in not revealing the sources of your information. Not only must you avoid directly naming the participants you have talked to, you must avoid conveying any details that would inadvertently reveal the source of the information. Your task is to safeguard the dignity of all of your participants. This can be quite challenging if the research setting is a small locale because almost everyone will know everyone else and whom you have talked with. Thus, anonymity is probably ruled out, but confidentiality remains a viable and important ethical dimension.

Close relationships with participants can provide additional ethical tensions. While many researchers form genuine friendships with their participants, you must be careful to avoid letting such friendships interfere with your ethical obligations to the other participants or to the community as a whole. In particular, initiating an intimate relationship with or even marrying a participant confounds many ethical issues—all of which must be resolved in a manner that fits the situation. Marrying a member of the research setting in advance of doing the research (and perhaps choosing the setting because of such an entree) casts the ethical issues in an entirely different light from starting a relationship once in the field. The ethics of fieldwork that involve intimate relations are very complex and contingent on a large number of factors. Given the almost limitless factors that affect interpersonal relationships, it is not feasible to set rules in advance, yet circumspection, caution, and consideration are watchwords that can apply to almost every field setting (see, for example, Bryant 1999).

Leaving the Field
As you will learn in Chapter 5, you should try to leave your setting as a good guest would leave his or her host. If you have established friendships with some participants, exiting the setting can be an intricate and delicate process. You do not want to suggest that the friendships were anything less than authentic, and you do not want anyone to feel betrayed by your departure. You may want to keep in contact with some participants, if only in a casual way. As a follow-up, you may also want to inform interested participants of your findings—passing along such information demonstrates your respect for the group and your appreciation for their participation. In some cases, you may wish to maintain a friendship, transmuting your status as "researcher" into a position of "friend." It is not uncommon for relationships formed in the field to flower into genuine friendships that sometimes last for a lifetime.

Conducting Covert Field Research

Covert research is not to be confused with "deception" in research. Deception involves lying, at least in the initial stages of research; covert research implies the need for protection from danger, both for the individuals under study and for the researcher. Thus, many researchers support covert research as an ethical option in a variety of closed settings. Some researchers, with support from their universities, might feel justified in conducting covert research in authoritarian or dictatorial countries, where the controlling regime would not otherwise allow research to be conducted, on the grounds that a study of the social life in that setting would benefit the wider population. Similar arguments are made by researchers interested in examining social situations of institutionalized individuals. For example, while the administrators of a nursing home might refuse a researcher open access to the environment, perhaps because they are worried that such a study could undermine their routines or reflect negatively on their practices, a study of residents' experiences could lead to reforms that would improve these individuals' daily lives. Many people—not just researchers—would argue that the ethics behind such research are sound.

As you will see in Chapter 5, the ethics of covert research are closely tied to the intent of researchers. If researchers act to support the welfare of a general population, the covert methods they use become highly justifiable. On the other hand, it is never honourable to use people as a means of pursuing a hidden, self-motivated research agenda. For this reason, many individuals have argued against secretive government-based intrusions into personal life for intelligence, police, or military purposes. Of course, researchers who do covert research on behalf of such agencies would probably argue that they *are* working for the good of the public.

The decision to carry out covert research is not an easy one. If you find yourself in a research situation in which you are considering using covert methods, ask yourself the following questions: Will the study focus on an important issue? Could the study bring to light a hidden injustice or give a voice to an under-represented group? Do you have a moral duty to conduct the research? Could the study help to improve the situation of a particular group? Has access to the setting been restricted by individuals who do not have a legitimate right to speak for the group? Could you be subject to physical or other harm if you were known as a researcher? If you can answer "yes" to all or most of these questions, covert research may be an ethically viable option.

Covert research is part of the history of social-science research, and some of this research has achieved notoriety. Among the most famous covert studies are Leon Festinger, Henry Riecken, and Stanley Schachter's 1956 study of a doomsday cult and Laud Humphreys's 1970 work on homosexual behaviour in public washrooms. Festinger was interested in the social dynamics of a cult whose members believed that the world would come to an end in the very near future. His students posed as "seekers" collecting information and making covert field notes of their experiences. One student was so convincing that they became one of the leaders! In their published account, the researchers were careful to protect the identities of those involved with the cult, and the resulting study contributed to our understanding of how cults operate. In Humphreys's case, he covertly observed men engaging in sexual acts in public washrooms, jotted down their cars' licence plate numbers, found their addresses in car records, and visited them at home under the pretext of doing another research project. Although he preserved the complete anonymity of the men he observed, and although his study contributed to improving the social and political climates towards gay rights, many objected to his methods as unethical because he observed and interacted with the men in his study under a false pretense.

Ultimately, the greatest argument in support of covert research is that it is the only way to achieve total anonymity—researchers do not reveal their name to the group being studied, and researchers do not reveal the name(s) of the group or its participants in the research (W.C. van den Hoonaard 2003). Any published report from the research cannot be traced back to members of the researched group.

Interviewing and Transcribing

The ethical considerations involved in interview situations are generally less ambiguous. Whether the interview is spontaneous or planned well in advance, you will always have the time and the opportunity to inform your participants of your research interest and to ask for their permission to be interviewed.

Seeking Consent

In private or face-to-face situations, researchers are expected to seek informed consent from participants. In medical and most quantitative studies, researchers use consent forms that participants must sign before the start of the research, and many research ethics boards require researchers to use consent forms, duly signed by the research participant. Typically, the form explains the purpose and the methodology of the study, informs participants that they can stop the interview at any time without any personal risk, and provides a guarantee of confidentiality and anonymity. The use of signed consent forms is a legacy of the biomedical approach, and some believe they protect researchers and participants. Many, however, contest their appropriateness.

First, there are certain settings in which it would be inappropriate or insensitive to seek individual written consent—for example, in cultures that nurture a sense of collectivity (and in which the individual's identity only makes sense insofar as it is part of that collectivity) or in a setting where illiteracy is the norm. Second, some collectives might interpret the researcher's seeking *individual* consent as an affront to the larger group. Third, some participants might want to protect their anonymity by not attaching their name to an "official" document. This is often the case when the research is focused on individuals living on the margins of society, those involved in illegal activities, or even those who occupy positions of power and prestige. Finally, some participants might see the need to sign a consent form as a serious betrayal of the trust that has developed over the course of previous interactions with the researcher. With the presentation of a formal consent form, what was initially a friendly soliciting of the perspectives and insights of a participant becomes a hopelessly unnatural relationship.

To overcome these obstacles, many qualitative researchers ask for their participants' verbal consent and provide an information sheet that contains the same information that would be found on a consent form. The information sheet does not require the participant's signature; more often than not, it is the researcher who signs the information sheet because the sheet entails promises made by the researcher.

Doing Content Analysis

Doing content analysis involves few ethical considerations, but you must be careful to avoid misrepresenting what you find. When studying the content of historical or even recent documents, you should always be mindful of **presentism**: that is, the belief that today's standards are a valid guide to studying older texts and social phenomena. For example, it isn't fair to criticize the lack of knowledge about sterilization in medical practice in the 18th century. Neither is it fair to analyze the frequency of the words *man* and *mankind* in pre-contemporary texts as a measure of lack of consideration for the social roles of women.

Similarly, you must not allow your own tastes and opinions to guide your analysis. If you do, you could misjudge the content or even entirely miss the point. For example, if a researcher who is generally uncomfortable with age disparity in sexual relationships were to watch the film *Harold and Maude* (1971) without making efforts to overcome their own biases, that researcher might easily misplace the film's intent. In addition to embodying major social and cultural concerns of its time, the film challenges ageism by depicting a touching, intimate relationship between a 20-year-old man and a 79-year-old woman.

The meanings we attach to words are so deeply embedded in our own culture and life experience that it is often difficult to step beyond the pale of personal experience. If you suspect that your analysis is too restricted by your own point of view, you might want to call upon a colleague or someone else involved in the research to conduct an independent content analysis. By comparing your own notes to those made by an individual with a different point of view, you may be able to identify and rule out the effects of presentism and bias in your work.

Analyzing Data

If faithfulness is a moral aim, then the ethical concept that will guide you through your analysis is faithfulness to data. Rather than contorting data to fit a theory or theories, you have an obligation to "listen" carefully to the data, much of which has been generously donated by research participants. William Least Heat-Moon, a Pulitzer Prize–winning author, powerfully describes the struggle between theory and data he faced when he was drawing together his observations for his study of a small Kansas county:

> For thirty months, maybe more, I've come and gone here and have found stories to tell, but . . . I had not discovered the way to tell them. My searches and researches, like my days, grew more randomly than otherwise, and every form I tried contorted them, and each time I began to press things into cohesion, I edged not so much toward fiction as toward distortion, when what I wanted was accuracy; even when I got a detail down accurately, I couldn't hook it to the next without concocting theories. . . . I was hunting a fact or image and not a thesis to hold my details together, and so I arrived at this question: should I just gather up items like creek pebbles into a bag and then let them tumble into their own pattern? (Least Heat-Moon 1991:14–15)

In the end, Least Heat-Moon surrendered to the data, trusting that it would "yield a landscape with figures" truly representative of the community he wanted to depict.

Acting Ethically in the Digital Age

There is no question that the digital age has had a profound impact on social relations. It has altered the ways in which we communicate with one another and the ways in which we perceive our place in the social world. As you will see in later chapters, the digital age has also brought new possibilities to the ways in which we can conduct qualitative research. Yet it has also called into question some of our basic understandings of ethical research practices. In recent years, many researchers have debated whether core ethical principles are still relevant in light of the widespread acceptance of new communications technologies that are undermining our privacy and, some might say, our dignity. Some, including Heather Kitchin (2002), suggest that the application of ethical principles should vary according to the relative accessibility of individual web pages. This argument generally states that postings on freely available web pages should be treated in the same manner as printed materials in magazines, while a higher threshold of ethical circumspection is needed when dealing with information available from web pages that are accessible only through private membership.

At the centre of this debate are issues of anonymity and informed consent. With the rise of Facebook and other new media that reveal so much private information, one may well wonder whether researchers' commitment to maintaining the anonymity of their participants at all costs is not anachronistic. Similarly, many have questioned why researchers should have to fully inform individuals of their role in a research project when hosts of other agencies, both governmental and private, regularly make incursions into citizens' private lives.

At this time, there are no clear responses to such speculations, and the debate may never be resolved. Yet we would argue that no matter how much technology affects our lives, there will always be the need for us to use a moral compass to foster human dignity, ensure the welfare of the people we study, and promote justice.

Writing Up Research

The process of writing up data requires a great deal of ethical reflection. In many ways, your writing reveals your ethical stance. As you are deciding what to include in your write-up, you will have to consider the extent to which you will address ethical aspects of your research methods and findings. Many of these aspects could have the power to raise awareness of issues central to your study. They might also be useful points of consideration for other researchers.

When you are writing up your report, remember that your task is to communicate your findings to your readers, who might include your professor, classmates, other researchers, or members of the general public. As one who has thought a lot about writing, I, as author of this chapter on ethics, sum up my goal as "protecting the dignity of the reader." You can accomplish this goal in several ways.

Writing Concisely and with Clarity

While Chapter 10 will explain the importance of clear and concise writing, a few points on the ethics of writing are in order. Avoiding jargon and using short, straightforward sentences in your write-up will show your reader that you are not trying to confuse the issues, that you have nothing to hide. Using the active voice and the first-person perspective will also help you to accomplish this goal by forcing you to unambiguously state who conducted the research, who led the interviews, who did the coding, and who did the analysis. Consider the ambiguity in this passive sentence: "The interview was conducted." Upon reading this sentence, the reader has no sense as to who conducted the interview. Why not clear up this confusion and take responsibility for your own actions: "I conducted the interview"? Similarly, instead of stating "The research was done in this village," say "I conducted research in this village."

Offering a Balanced View

When you are writing up your research, it is critical that you focus on presenting a balanced view of your findings. Having researched a topic extensively, passionately, and with a great deal of sacrifice of resources, time, and effort, you may have developed your own moral or ethical judgments, but you must be careful to avoid overtly supporting or criticizing any side of an issue in your report. You must also avoid assigning blame; there is no room for ad hominem statements in balanced writing. Offering a balanced view fulfills the principle of fostering human dignity on behalf of both research participants and readers.

By offering a balanced view throughout your written account, you allow the reader to make up their mind about your data and your findings. You are obligated to present data and findings in as convincing a manner as possible but also in a way that does not take away the reader's ability to decide, on their own terms, what the research means. This approach shows that you respect your reader as an intelligent individual. To illustrate the effect a writer's slant can have on the reader, I refer to my experience of reading a study of the sealers who hunt in the St Lawrence River (see W.C. van den Hoonaard 1987).[4]

In 1979, anthropologist Guy Wright decided to accompany a group of sealers on their hunt in order to study their lives. He published his account of this voyage in *Sons and Seals: A Voyage to the Ice* (1984). I approached the topic with an open attitude: I sided neither with the sealers nor with the anti-sealers. As the text unfolded, I noted that the study was well done and that the writer was able to pull me into the narrative and offer me a glimpse into the lived reality of the sealers. In his initial narrative, the writer achieved the researcher's goal of offering the readers the dignity of being able to make up their own minds. The writer's powerful writing moved me, and I felt an appreciation for the life of sealers. Then, in the last third of the narrative, the writer changed his approach. In no uncertain terms, he began to write disparagingly of the anti-sealers. This sudden shift had the opposite of the intended effect on me—my interest in the sealers' lives, which the writer had so carefully built up, dissipated, and I began to feel a loyalty towards the anti-sealers. What had happened? The writer had stopped offering a balanced view of the topic. He did not allow me to make up my mind about the seal hunt, and I felt that he had betrayed my dignity as a reader by trying to make up my mind for me. As a result, I felt disinclined to agree with his strongly opinionated assessment.

Summary

As you have learned in this chapter, conducting qualitative research involves many ethical considerations. Table 4.3 offers a list of some of the main ethical principles that can guide you in the various stages of research. This list is not meant to be exhaustive. Rather, it conveys how researchers rely on a diversity of ethical principles at each stage of research. Qualitative researchers are well aware that, once the research gets underway, questions of ethics can fluctuate in unpredictable ways. Yet this does not mean that you should abandon ethical principles—far from it! Rather, you must put great efforts into determining the ethical principles that fit the circumstances. Of course, not everyone will agree on what is ethical in any given situation, and ethical contradictions and paradoxes will always persist. For example, does the safeguarding of human welfare mean that anonymity be maintained even if research participants insist that their names be disclosed in research? Although there are no clear answers to these sorts of questions, you would do well to consider the dignity of your participants as your foremost goal when making ethical decisions.

Table 4.3 The Diversity of Ethical Principles That Can Guide You in Various Stages of Research

Developing a research question	Remain open-minded.
Fieldwork	Spending a long period of time will require researchers to be open to unexpected ethical dimensions.
Gaining access to the field	Be frank in explaining your research.
Spending time in the field	Be aware of the effects of your presence in a given community or population.
Leaving the field	Leave as a good guest.
Covert field research	Bear in mind that sometimes harm or danger can be avoided when doing covert research.
Interviews and transcriptions	Inform participants of the intentions of your research.
Consent	Typically ask for verbal consent.
Content analysis	Avoid presentism.
Analyzing data	Be faithful to your data.
Ethics in the digital age	Determine the difference between public and restricted access to data and information on the Internet.
Writing up research	Respect the readers of your report, and be careful to maintain your participants' anonymity.
Writing concisely and with clarity	Avoid jargon and the passive voice.
Offering a balanced view	Understand the challenge of being analytical and yet fair.

Key Terms

ethics code   research ethics board
presentism   vocabulary of motives

Questions for Critical Thought

1. What are the advantages of doing covert research? What are the disadvantages? Are there ethical principles that could sustain the choice of covert research?

2. Is it possible for a researcher to do away with concerns of anonymity and confidentiality and still be ethical in their approach? Why or why not?

3. How might research participants interpret ethical dimensions of research differently from the way researchers interpret them? Should such differences affect the way research is carried out?

4. What are some of the noteworthy aspects of doing ethical research involving Indigenous communities?

5. What may be some instances when consent forms are inappropriate? When might they be useful?

Exercises

1. Think about a research assignment that you have recently completed or one that you are planning to undertake. Make a list of the ethical issues that could be relevant to your study.

2. Read one Canadian ethnography that predates the first TCPS (that is, one that was published before 1998) and one that is contemporary. Try to select ethnographies that examine the same type of social setting. Are they different in terms of how they address ethical issues?

In-Class Exercise

Try to fairly describe the clothes your classmates are wearing. Can you do that without privileging your own tastes and preferences in clothes? You can try the same thing by describing the clothes an actor is wearing in an ad for a TV or online streaming service original series.

Suggested Readings

The following five scholarly journals, each of which is available online, deal with ethics in research. Increasingly, qualitative research journals are publishing articles on ethics and research:

Ethics and Information Technology
    www.springerlink.com/content/1388-1957
International Journal of Ethics
    www.novapublishers.com/catalog/product_info.php?products_id=1676

IRB: Ethics and Human Research
   www.thehastingscenter.org/Publications/IRB
Journal of Academic Ethics
   www.springerlink.com/content/111139
Journal of Empirical Research on Human Research Ethics
   www.csueastbay.edu/JERHRE

I also draw the reader's attention to a book on the subject of ethics and research:

Will C. van den Hoonaard and Deborah K. van den Hoonaard. 2013. *Essentials of Thinking Ethically in Qualitative Research*. Walnut Creek, CA: Left Coast Press. This book discusses the ethical dimensions of qualitative research in more depth. If you want to delve more deeply into these issues, you will find this book quite engaging.

Related Websites

Canadian Sociological Association Statement of Professional Ethics
www.csa-scs.ca/files/www/csa/documents/codeofethics/2012Ethics.pdf
This statement deals with a variety of ethical issues pertaining to being a member of the Canadian Sociological Association, including research.

American Anthropological Association Statement on Ethnography and Institutional Review Boards
www.aaanet.org/stmts/irb.htm
This statement pertains to research by American anthropologists.

Institutional Review Blog
www.institutionalreviewblog.com/2009/12/after-human-terrain-will-aaa-debate.html
This site is devoted to discussing the latest developments in ethics in the social sciences.

Panel on Research Ethics
https://ethics.gc.ca/eng/home.html
This is the portal to the website of the Interagency Advisory Panel on Research Ethics (PRE). Here, you will find links to the revised *Tri-Council Policy Statement*, a tutorial on the *TCPS*, and additional information on and publications from PRE.

Canadian Association of Research Ethics Boards
www.careb-accer.org
You may wish to subscribe to the listserv of the Canadian Association of Research Ethics Boards. Although the topics are primarily about biomedical research, there are occasions when sociological issues are raised.

Indigenous Research
www.fnigc.ca/ocap.html
The First Nations principles of OCAP are a set of standards that establish how First Nations data should be collected, protected, used, or shared. They are the de facto standard for how to conduct research with First Nations.

"The Intersection of People, Policies, and Priorities in Indigenous Research Ethics." Keynote speech by Julie Bell.
www.youtube.com/watch?v=rNSgFB8CTDU
This fascinating talk provides an overview of the challenges of and the promise of carrying out ethical research with Indigenous communities.

Notes

1. I wish to thank Julie R. Bull for her review and comments on this particular section of Chapter 4. Responsibility for its content rests with me.
2. Immediately after World War II, the Levitt brothers came up with the idea of expanding cities into suburbs with affordable homes using one of four or five blueprints (which made the homes inexpensive). This architect-accountant pair built three "Levittowns": one on Long Island (New York), one in New Jersey, and another in Pennsylvania. The street plans, street names, and house numbers are similar in all three suburbs.
3. Traditionally, some would argue that a minimum of two years is required to understand a new (sub) culture, although others would say that three or four months is sufficient in some cases. Vicki Smith (2002:228) looked at the fieldwork behind 50 research monographs and discovered that it took 8.14 years on average after the start of fieldwork to see its appearance as a book. Arlie R. Hochschild's study *The Second Shift* (1989), which is about how couples share housework, took 13 years of fieldwork and an additional six years of writing and preparation before it was published. Daniel R. Wolf took three years to do field research among outlaw bikers, and it took 15 years before his book, *The Rebels* (1991), appeared in print. Studying student culture took Cheryl and Daniel Albas (see, for example, 2009) more than 25 years of detailed observation and recording.
4. As you probably know, seal hunting was (and still is) quite controversial in Canada. A quick Internet search will provide you with a great deal of information on the current state of the debate. In particular, you might be interested in viewing the following news clip, which is related to some people's virulent opposition to Sara Green, former Miss Newfoundland and Labrador, for wearing a seal coat: www.youtube.com/watch?v=zvooeJY7S_c.

5

Observing Social Life through Field Research

Learning Objectives

- To learn about the development of ethnography in North America
- To learn how to prepare for and implement a fieldwork study
- To understand how to write good field notes
- To examine the development of virtual ethnography

Introduction

So far, we have discussed the basics of qualitative research, we have noted how qualitative research differs from quantitative work, we have looked at how to go about designing a study, and we have discussed research ethics. Now we have come to the point of actually carrying out research—it is time to get our hands dirty. In this chapter, we will learn about the history of **ethnography** (ethnographic field research) and the stages involved in carrying out a field study. A field study might tackle a setting as broad as a neighbourhood (see Gans 1967) or as small as a hair-dressing salon (see Furman 1997), and the studies are as varied as the social settings they examine.

Before we begin, we must understand the purpose of field research. In conducting a field study, a researcher attempts to understand everyday life from the perspective of the participants. The researcher strives for "intimate familiarity" (Prus 1993) with the group they are studying. Thus, fieldwork requires the researcher to immerse themself in a social setting. It involves "observing people *in situ*, finding them where they are, [and] staying with them in some social role," which allows the investigator to observe their behaviour, analyze it, and report on it in ways "useful to social science but not harmful to those observed" (Hughes 1960/2002:139).

By observing people in their everyday settings, researchers can avoid the distortion that may occur in interviews because people do not always have an accurate view of their own behaviour (Becker and Geer 1957). Carrie B. Sanders and Samantha Henderson (2013) demonstrated this advantage when they both interviewed and observed police officers about their use of information technologies. They found that although the designers of such technologies describe them as "objective, 'standardized' classification systems," *in situ* the use of these technologies is subject to "organisational contexts, which can change their intended use and function" (2013:256, 257). If the researchers had not gone on patrol with the police officers, they would have had no way of finding out how they used the technologies any differently from the designers' assumptions.

The most common method of fieldwork is participant observation, which involves becoming a participant in the setting while retaining some distance as an observer. We will examine the levels of participation a researcher can choose later in this chapter. For now, let's take a brief look at the evolution of ethnographic fieldwork across history.

Historical Antecedents of Contemporary Fieldwork

Ethnographic fieldwork has a long history that dates back to the fifth century BCE when the ancient Greek writer Herodotus, generally regarded as the first Western historian, recorded descriptions of the Persians and the Scythians. Herodotus travelled widely and gathered "legends and anecdotes" about the peoples he visited (Lateiner 2004:xvi). He was fascinated by the influence that the natural environment had on cultural forms. For example, as he observed, the Scythians used animal bones and fat as cooking fuel because there were few trees in their environment (Waterfield 1998: xxxviii).

Before the latter half of the 19th century, most ethnographic reports were made by travellers—explorers, missionaries, merchants, and colonialists—who recorded their observations of the peoples they met on their voyages. Often, these reports offered voyeuristic accounts of life in societies culturally and geographically distant from Western Europe. While many early travellers' accounts were highly insightful and informative, others were very provincial, ethnocentric (see **ethnocentrism**), or biased. Much of the research that took place at the height of the colonialist period presented Indigenous peoples as "primitive" and "other." These accounts often tell us more about the writers and their social backgrounds than about the cultures about which they were writing.

In the 19th century, there was increased interest in domestic ethnographies as investigators wrote about conditions in their own societies to promote social change. John Howard, for example, wrote about the conditions of prisons in 18th-century Britain, which included "the meticulous recording and reporting of what he saw, in order that the general public might be made aware" of the terrible conditions (Hay 2010). In 1883, Beatrice Potter, a social reformer, did participant observation among the underprivileged. She disguised herself as "Miss Jones, a farmer's daughter," to bring attention to the plight of the poor in Britain (Berg 2009). The same motive inspired English businessman Charles Booth to undertake a massive "survey" (door-to-door visits, interviews, neighbourhood observation, etc.) of the living and working conditions of the inhabitants of late 19th-century London. Booth published his account, *Life and Labour of the People in London*, in multiple editions between 1889 and 1903. Today, these 17 volumes are counted among the founding works of British sociology, and they have had a substantial impact in North America.

Ethnographic reports became more scientific during the late 19th and early 20th centuries as anthropological ethnographers began entering the field. These researchers went to "exotic" places to document the cultural practices of what were then thought of as primitive peoples. Most influential was Franz Boas (1858–1942), the father of modern cultural anthropology (Prus 1993), who studied Kwakiutl (Kwakwaka'wakw) peoples on Canada's west coast.

George Dawson, the "father of Canadian anthropology," established the "paradigm of **salvage ethnography**" (Harrison 2009), based on the then-prevalent belief that Indigenous cultures were moribund and would soon "vanish" (Nurse 2006:52). His work led to the establishment of the National Museum, which collected a "documentary and photographic record" of Indigenous peoples as well as "folk" cultures of Quebec in the early 20th century (Harrison 2009). This approach led to the legitimation of practices that included "commercialization and plain and simple theft" (Smith 2012:64).

When early anthropological studies were carried out, Indigenous voices and world views were "predominantly silenced" in ethnographic research (Battiste 2000:xvii). The history of Canadian research "on" Indigenous peoples created a situation that calls for reflection and sensitivity, as noted in the *Report of the Royal Commission on Aboriginal Populations* (Erasmus and Dussault 1996) and the more recent *Final Report of the Truth and Reconciliation Commission of Canada*, which states the following:

> By establishing a new and respectful relationship between Aboriginal and non-Aboriginal Canadians, we will restore what must be restored, repair what must be repaired, and return what must be returned. (2015:1)

In response to this growing awareness, contemporary anthropologists work in partnership with Indigenous communities using their notions of culture. Any other approach would be considered unethical today. The resulting partnerships form the core of Canadian anthropology (Darnell 1997:277).

Fieldwork in sociology, although contemporaneous with the development of cultural anthropology, developed "somewhat independently" (Prus 1993:6). Though a handful of studies were carried out around the turn of the century, ethnographic research in sociology first became truly prominent in the 1920s at the University of Chicago.

The Chicago School of Sociology

The early ethnographies from the **Chicago School of Sociology** focused on social processes and problems that sociologists associated with urban life. Chicago sociologists regarded the city as a "laboratory" for social research (Faris 1967:52) and concentrated on two, often interrelated, sets of phenomena—"race" and ethnic relations, and crime and deviance—by doing careful studies of institutions, neighbourhoods, and zones of the city. The early 20th century was a period of massive immigration to the United States and to large urban centres. Chicago sociologists took advantage of the opportunity to study first-hand the social processes by which culturally diverse newcomers adjusted not only to one another but also to the more established social groups and cultural practices they encountered in America. At the time, the common perception was that poverty, crime, and suicide among slum dwellers reflected innate biological qualities of the population. The early studies of the Chicago School demonstrated that the problems of poor people were not a result of individuals' innate weaknesses but rather were a "consequence of the experience of social disorganization" (Faris 1967:62–3). In other words, the issues associated with poverty grew from the social context, not from individual deficiencies or problems.

Ethnographies from this period include *The Hobo* (Anderson 1923), discussed in detail in Box 5.1; *The Jack Roller* (Shaw 1930), which deals with the experiences

Box 5.1 The Hobo

One of the earliest and most important studies to develop out of the Chicago School was Nels Anderson's *The Hobo* (1923). Anderson had been a "hobo" himself and had intimate familiarity with the way of life. The study provided insight into the "lived experience of homeless men" as well as the urban environment in which they lived (Prus 1993:11). In particular, it was the first study to identify the concept of "killing time" as a problem for the homeless:

> "Killing time" is a problem with the homeless man. . . . For the vast majority, there is no pastime save the passing show of the crowded thoroughfare. . . . The homeless man, as he meanders along the street, is looking for something to break the monotony. He will stand on the curb for hours, watching people pass. He notices every conspicuous person and follows with interest, perhaps sometimes with envy, the wavering movements of every passing drunk. If a policeman stops anyone on the street, he also stops and listens in. If he notices a man running down the alley, his curiosity is aroused. Wherever he sees a group gathered, he lingers. He will stop and listen if two men are arguing. He will spend hours sitting on the curb talking to a congenial companion. (Anderson 1923:215)

The concept of "killing time" continues to have resonance, as Leslie D. Harman (1989) discovered in her study of homeless women. More recently, Amy Cooper (2015:167–8) observed that homeless women in Chicago have to learn how to kill time to fill "empty time" that alternates with "urgent demands" to be at certain places at "specific times" to receive social services.

of young offenders; and *The Taxi-Dance Hall* (Cressey 1932), which explores halls where "male patrons would dance with the woman of their choice for a 'dime a dance'" (Prus 1993:12). These books were ground-breaking in that they depicted the social worlds of members of so-called deviant groups. For example, Shaw discovered that, in every case, boys were led into delinquency by experienced delinquents and, therefore, were conforming to the expectations of a **primary group**. This finding moved the understanding of deviance from an individualistic conception of youth problems to acknowledgement of the social circumstances of the boys' lives (Faris 1967:76).

During the 20th century, the ethnographic tradition—made popular in sociology by the Chicago School—developed through a series of American field studies, including *Street Corner Society* (Whyte 1955), *Boys in White* (Becker, Geer, Hughes, and Strauss 1961/2009), *Asylums* (Goffman 1961), *Outsiders* (Becker 1963), *Passing On* (Sudnow 1967), *Talley's Corner* (Liebow 1967), *The Levittowners* (Gans 1967), and *Making the Grade* (Becker, Geer, and Hughes 1968).

Ethnography in Canada

The development of ethnography in Canada was heavily influenced by the Chicago School sociologists of the early 20th century (see Box 5.2).[1] Yet even before the Chicago movement arose, Canadian researchers had already shown an interest in sociological ethnography and had begun to engage in fieldwork to study—and in many cases to try to assist—underprivileged social groups. In the late 19th century, businessman and social reformer Herbert Brown Ames carried out a thorough study of the living and working conditions of 38,000 people who inhabited a working-class neighbourhood in Montreal that contained deep pockets of poverty. Ames believed that he had a moral obligation to press for social change that would alleviate the social problems—slums, poverty, crime, etc.—that had developed in the wake of massive immigration, rapid urbanization, and unregulated industrialization (Allen 1971). Ames's published account of his study, *The City below the Hill* (1897/1972), is one of the most important early sociological ethnographies in Canada.

There is also a long tradition of ethnographic research among French-language researchers in Canada. Key early researchers include Charles-Henri-Philippe Gauldrée-Boileau, who wrote *Paysan de Saint-Irénée* (1875), which was published in Quebec in 1968; Léon Gérin, who published *L'Habitant de Saint-Justin* (1968); and Horace Miner, who produced *Saint-Denis: A French Canadian Parish* (1930). Everett C. Hughes (see Box 5.2) was also influential. His book *French Canada in Transition* (1943) was translated into French as *Rencontre de deux mondes: La crise d'industrialisation du Canada français* (1972).[2]

Many consider William (Billy) Shaffir the principal interpreter of the Chicago School tradition in Canada today (Low 2020). Shaffir graduated from McGill with its first doctoral degree in sociology in 1972 and recently retired from McMaster

Box 5.2 The Chicago School and McGill: Carl Dawson and Everett C. Hughes

Without a doubt, it was the efforts of sociologists Carl Dawson and Everett C. Hughes at McGill University in Montreal that did the most to establish the practice of ethnographic sociological research in Canada in the first half of the 20th century. Dawson, a Canadian from Prince Edward Island, and Hughes, an American born in Ohio, had earned their PhDs in sociology at the University of Chicago. Both were deeply influenced by Robert Park, one of the principal founders of the Chicago School, and are widely regarded as having established an "outpost" of Chicago sociology at McGill (see, for example, Wilcox-Magill 1983:1–10).

Dawson was appointed to McGill University in the 1920s and founded the first independent sociology department in Canada. While at Chicago, he had adopted the human ecology approach, and it was this orientation that contoured the research program that he and Hughes developed at McGill during the 1920s, 1930s, and 1940s (Wilcox-Magill 1983:1–10). Indeed, with Warner E. Gettys, Dawson wrote *An Introduction to Sociology*, a textbook modelled directly on Robert Park and Ernest W. Burgess's "green bible" of Chicago sociology. It played a legitimating role for the sociology program at McGill (Helmes-Hayes 1994:474) and incorporated "a generic interactionist social psychology" that stressed concepts of interaction and process rather than structure (p. 470).

Hughes was regarded by many prominent ethnographers as a—if not the—master fieldworker in the Chicago tradition (see, for example, Riesman and Becker 1984; Riesman 1983; Chapoulie 1987, 1996; Helmes-Hayes 2010; Low 2020). Recruited to McGill in 1927, Hughes played a central role as a champion, teacher, and practitioner of ethnographic research. He had a background in both anthropology and sociology and was deeply familiar with the fieldwork traditions in both disciplines. During the 1940s and 1950s, he taught the fieldwork course at the University of Chicago and helped to put together two versions of a fieldwork guide and source book (Hughes, Junker, Gold, and

University. A key figure in the annual Qualitative Analysis Conference, Shaffir has spawned more than one generation of interpretivist, interactionist practisers of ethnographic methods. In a recent *festschrift* (a volume published in honour of someone) dedicated to Billy Shaffir, his former and recent students demonstrate his core teachings concerning ethnography. He stresses the importance of getting out in the world and doing hands-on field research (Etoroma 2020; Low 2020), that research relationships are important and take time (Grills 2020), and that researchers must attend to academic status and power dynamics and work to minimize their impact (Grills 2020; McLuhan 2020). In particular, he advises his students not to overcomplicate their analyses and to stay involved with colleagues while analyzing and writing by editing each other's work (Kleinman 2020).

Ethnographic research developed later in Atlantic Canada. With the growing interest in anthropological fieldwork, Memorial University of Newfoundland

Kittel 1952; Junker 1960) that were used by generations of students at Chicago, McGill, and elsewhere. As well, during his time at Chicago, he taught and/or worked with some of American sociology's most prominent fieldwork researchers—Anselm Strauss, Blanche Geer, David Riesman, Howard S. Becker, and Erving Goffman, to name a few (Helmes-Hayes and Santoro 2010). Since his death in 1983, his influence has spread from North America to Europe, France, and Italy in particular (see Chapoulie 1996; Helmes-Hayes and Santoro 2010).

Hughes helped to carry out a number of important American ethnographies, but his most important and influential Canadian ethnography was *French Canada in Transition* (1943), a detailed analysis of the process of industrialization as it took place under the control of British and American capital in a small Quebec town during the 1930s. Though Hughes left McGill to return to Chicago in 1938, he continued to have a major impact on Canadian sociology. He maintained direct links with McGill's sociology department and, through Jean-Charles Falardeau, a key figure in Québécois sociology, forged a strong and long-lasting connection with Laval University (see, for example, Falardeau 1953). Indeed, through to the 1970s, dozens of Canadian students made the trek south to do graduate work in Chicago (and later at Boston College and Brandeis) with Hughes. A number of the early ones, Aileen Ross and Jean Burnet among them, returned to Canada to become faculty members at McGill, Toronto, Laval, and elsewhere. This group published important fieldwork-based research (see, for example, Ross 1952, 1953, 1954; Burnet 1951) and stewarded the fieldwork culture until the 1960s and 1970s when it finally became a part of mainstream sociological practice.[3]

As Chicago-style ethnographic research became more common in Canada, McGill began to lose its stature as the epicentre of interactionist sociology and ethnographic research. By the late 1970s, most of the faculty employing Chicago-style research methods had retired or moved on. McMaster University then emerged as the primary ethnographic research and training centre in Canada (Milne and Helmes-Hayes 2010).

Source: The text for this box was carefully researched and written by Canadian sociologist Rick Helmes-Hayes (University of Waterloo) and Emily Milne (McMaster University).

established the Institute for Social and Economic Research (ISER) in 1961 to foster research into the many social and economic questions arising from the particular historic, geographic, and economic circumstances of Newfoundland and Labrador (ISER 2010). Many of the resulting ethnographic studies required social researchers to move to local communities and spend considerable time doing participant observation. A few researchers even "married into" the community. Some of these studies have become enduring classics, and their titles express the researchers' engagement with the communities' vital concerns: *Fisherman, Logger, Merchant, Miner* (Philbrook 1966); *Brothers and Rivals* (Firestone 1967); and *Marginal Adaptations and Modernization in Newfoundland* (Wadel 1969).

Now that we have briefly explored the historical influences that have led to contemporary practices, let's consider how you might go about conducting your own fieldwork.

Conducting a Field Study

The first steps in your field study will begin when you are at the research-design phase (discussed in Chapter 3): as you develop your research questions, identify your participants, and assess the nature of the setting. You will need to choose your setting carefully. Recall that some settings are easier to get into than others. If the setting is a public place, such as a zoo or a park, then getting in should not be a problem. You simply have to show up. If the setting is restricted or exclusive, however—say, a prison, the offices of a corporation, or the meeting place of a secret society—you may find it more difficult to gain access. In addition, some settings may be dangerous, and you may need to take specific precautions to protect your own safety.

If you are considering an Indigenous setting, remember that it is essential that elders be involved from the beginning (Lavallé 2009) and that the research be "with" Indigenous peoples, not "on" them (Gaudry 2015:245). Indeed, ethnographic studies involving Indigenous settings and issues should involve collaboration between university-based researchers and the communities involved. It is the Indigenous community, itself, that determines the level and extent of its involvement in the research (Bull 2019:211). For example, Tang, Brown, Mussell, Smye, and Rodney (2015) conducted an ethnography that looked at the experience of Indigenous people in an emergency room in Alberta. The study showed how the way they are treated by staff creates a hierarchy that leads to their being an underclass and receiving unequal access. The study was a collaboration that involved scholars in Aboriginal Health and an Aboriginal Community Advisory Committee (Tang et al. 2015). This research also had the goals of improving conditions and locating the problems imposed by the institutional arrangements rather than in an imagined deficit of Indigenous people.

As soon as you decide on a topic and a setting, you should begin taking notes. If you do not write down your ideas, you will likely forget them. To start, keep a notebook or a computer file in which you can record your initial musings, observations, and encounters. When she began planning her study, Lisa-Jo started a notebook to help her remember stray thoughts and comments. As she was doing this, she noticed that people often talked about a particular woman's home and what she had done with her walls. When Lisa-Jo started her study, she made sure to contact this woman to get her story.

As you decide on your ethnographic field site, remember that many researchers follow up time in the field with interviews or combine other methods with ethnography. Although we will take each of these in turn over successive chapters, you may want to remain open to complementing your ethnography with other qualitative methods. Peter Grahame (2018), for example, used visual methods as part of his ethnographic work looking at whale-watching, and Jesse Smith (2017) followed up his ethnography of secular congregations by conducting interviews with participants to learn about what he calls *communal secularity*, the ways in which secular people form a group sense of belonging.

Preparing to Enter the Field

Before you enter the field, you must plan how you will approach your intended research setting and the participants in that setting. For some studies, this preparation begins with reading. If there is literature about the setting or if members of the organization have published pamphlets, articles, or books about it, you would be wise to read these documents. This background research will give you information about who the participants are and the nature of the setting (Berg 2009). In addition to reading, you should spend some time hanging out at the setting until you develop a firm research plan (Rossman and Rallis 1998:95). "Case the joint" (Schatzman and Strauss 1972:9), if possible, to familiarize yourself with the "routines, realities of factionalism, and the social structure" of the setting (Shaffir, Stebbins, and Turowetz 1980:23). This preparation will help you to decide if the setting you have chosen is an appropriate place to study your topic.

This is a good time to define the boundaries of your field setting and think about who you are in relation to the site. You should also think about any connections to the setting that you might already have in preparation for deciding on your level of participation and developing your story line.

Levels of Participation

Once you have gotten the lay of the land, decide how you want to participate in your setting, what role you will take. In 1952, Buford Junker suggested a typology of roles from which the field researcher can choose: **complete participant, participant as observer, observer as participant**, and **complete observer** (Junker 1952 as cited in Gold 1958).

When taking the role of the *complete participant*, the researcher attempts to become a full-fledged member of the group they are studying. The researcher, in this case, conceals their intent to study the group. Daniel R. Wolf (1991) discovered right away that he would not be able to study outlaw bikers if he explained his goal at the outset. So, before he asked the group's leaders for permission to conduct his study, he "establish[ed] contact with the Rebels as a biker who also happened to be a university—anthropology—student" (pp. 13–14). Wolf rode with the Rebels for three years before telling them that he was doing a study.[4]

The *participant as observer* makes their presence as a researcher known to the group and attempts to form relationships with the members of the group. This is the most common strategy that researchers use in field research, and it is most appropriate when the researcher has something in common with the members of the group. For example, Claudia Malacrida (1998), who lost a child to stillbirth, was both participant and researcher in the support groups she attended as part of her research on how parents cope with the loss of a baby.

The *observer as participant* also informs the members of the research setting that they are doing research but carries out a less involved role. If the investigator is visibly different from the participants in meaningful ways, this may be the only participatory role available. When Deborah was doing her research on retirement communities, she was in her 30s. Even though she participated in many social activities, Deborah was too young to be accepted as a member of the community. Lisa-Jo carried a notebook occasionally in her field site to purposefully remind those around her that she was not only a friend but a researcher as well.

In the role of the *complete observer*, the researcher does not interact with the members of the setting and might not tell anyone that they are doing a study. The researcher simply tries to be accepted or "tolerated as an unobtrusive observer" (Marshall and Rossman 2006:98). Deborah took this role when she observed a wetland preserve in south Florida. As she walked around and made observations, Deborah blended in with the many people who took regular walks on the boardwalk. In general, the role of the complete observer is most useful in research involving public places or public sites on the Internet.

These four roles are not mutually exclusive—they are **ideal types**, and researchers often straddle the line between two roles. The line between observer as participant and participant as observer is particularly fuzzy. As well, researchers often move from one role to another as they carry out their research. Wolf, for example, continued to ride with the Rebels after he told them about his study, but he was no longer a full participant. In his new role as participant as observer, he experienced what Shaffir, Dietz, and Stebbins (1994) have referred to as the "marginality" that all researchers who reveal their identity as a researcher experience.

All four roles have advantages and disadvantages. Complete participation offers an unobstructed view into participants' lives, but there are obvious ethical issues associated with this approach. In addition, the complete participant risks identifying so strongly with the group members that they lose the ability to look at the situation analytically. In some settings—particularly, those involving cults, gangs, and radical political groups—the members may "actively seek to convert the researcher" (Warren and Karner 2010:98). In the role of participant as observer or observer as participant, the investigator has the advantage of being a "known incompetent"; as a result, insiders (i.e., group members) will "teach [them] things [and] tell [them] things they would never tell one another" (Schwartz and Jacobs 1979:55). Adopting the role of the "ethnographic stranger" (Fine 2019) rather than passing as a group member allows for some analytic distance. The disadvantage of these roles is that the very marginality that allows the researcher to appear as incompetent prevents them from gaining an insider's experience of the group. Finally, because the complete observer has to rely on what they notice and overhear in the setting, they may misinterpret the meanings that behaviour and interactions have for the participants.

Whichever guise you adopt to do your research, it will take careful navigation of your relationship with your field site and participants. Gary Alan Fine (2019) argues for a *skeptical ethnography*. He encourages us to be upfront with ourselves in admitting to ourselves that we are first on the side of knowledge and learning. An ethnographer "desires to uncover *patterns of social life*" (Fine 2019:830), to discover generic social processes. He argues that one should "not select a group one wishes to help, but a group that one wishes to understand" (Fine 2019:837), while balancing that with an epistemic generosity which never belittles or judges the world views of participants. Others, such as Staci Newmahr, argue for closer relationships with participant groups. You will have to think about how to approach your participants and what kind of stance you will take in relation to them. Those involved in research with Indigenous communities may find that historical, and often contemporary, relations with researchers have created a situation in which epistemic generosity is not enough. Trust-based relationships and collaborations remain vital components of work with Indigenous groups—we do not, however, want to exclude Indigenous groups as we construct human knowledge through dense accounts and thick descriptions of social worlds.

Once you have decided what level of participation you will start with, it is time to prepare to interact with your setting. If you are doing overt research, you will need to develop a storyline.

Storylines

Your storyline is the explanation you provide to individuals in the setting about the purpose of your research and how you would like to participate. As you are preparing to enter the field, take the time to develop a standard storyline. If you try to tailor your explanation to the interests of each person you encounter, you will likely lose track of what you have told each person, and you may undermine your credibility. Unless you have a compelling reason to do otherwise, be truthful about your work. Always answer questions about the research as honestly as possible and avoid being condescending.

Keep your explanation simple. The story should not be too detailed or it could commit you to a focus that is too narrow (Schatzman and Strauss 1972:24). As Lofland and Lofland (1995:39) recommend, your explanation should be "brief, relatively straightforward, and appropriate to the audience." Most people are interested in a broad overview of your study rather than a long, technical explanation. Often, just telling people that you are interested in them or their organization is sufficient.

Gaining Access

As Adler and Adler (1987:12) note, the Chicago School researchers, whose early activities entailed "hanging out" and building up to asking "What's going on?" had little difficulty in gaining access to their research settings. Based on this precedent, the Adlers suggest that field researchers should simply "enter their settings, announce their intentions, and begin to interact with the people they encounter" (1987:12). In recent years, partly in response to ethical concerns (see Chapter 4), this approach has waned, but it has not disappeared, and in many cases, it can be quite successful.

William Shaffir and Samuel Heilman, who conducted separate studies of religious Jews, both describe an entry process that includes hanging around, getting to know some people, and frequenting synagogues. Shaffir (2009:214) struck up conversations with young Hassidic men who were as curious about his world as he was about theirs. Heilman's approach (2009: 203) was "deceptively simple": he began to go to synagogues, spend time in yeshivas, and wander along the streets of ultra-orthodox neighbourhoods.

Many groups appreciate the interest of the researcher, particularly if the study deals with an issue that the members feel does not get the attention it deserves. In such cases, the group will likely welcome the researcher into its community. Karen March, in order to gather research for *The Stranger Who Bore Me*, attended self-help groups of adoptees who were seeking information about their birth parents. She recounts such an experience:

> Entering the field . . . I found little difficulty. . . . The two self-help groups . . . were members of [a] larger Canadian self-help search organization [and had] monthly meetings which were open to the public. Non-members attend meetings frequently. . . . Thus, when I contacted both groups . . . I was told to "just come, mingle with the members, and see what happens." . . . When I arrived at my first meeting, I found that most group members accepted my presence. (1995:88)

Establishing Relationships with Gatekeepers

Often, you will need to obtain permission to conduct your study from a **gatekeeper**, a leader within the group. Gatekeepers are individuals who have the power to deny or grant access to a social setting (Berg 2009). In many cases, they have formal authority, and their position as a recognized leader is clear. In other cases, their power may be informal, and their position may not be immediately obvious. You may need to hang around to discover who has the status to influence other members in accepting or rejecting your presence within the community.

In Indigenous communities or settings, the community is the gatekeeper. In most cases, the chief and council or elders give approval for a study to begin. In other cases, a community research arm or traditional governance body has authority over community-based research concerns. Many Indigenous communities have formal protocols that researchers adhere to when asking the gatekeepers for permission to begin a study. Before Lisa-Jo began her study in Nunavut, she had her research approved by the Nunavut Research Institute, which circulated her proposal within the local community. On the local level, Lisa-Jo appreciated key members of the community who essentially vouched for her proposal based on the previous trust-based relationships she had developed. When you approach the community and elders, you should put the elders' and community members' needs first. For elders, this means travelling to their preferred location and paying them consultants' rates (Assembly of First Nations 2009).

The way you present your storyline to a gatekeeper is very important. If gate-keepers believe that the research will make their organization or themselves appear in a positive light, they will be more likely to give you access. If they suspect that you are a muckraker or plan to evaluate their organization or threaten their posi-tion, they may turn you down. In some cases, it might be useful to build on pre-existing relations of trust to remove barriers (Lofland and Lofland 1995:38), but a gatekeeper will not always grant you access simply because they know you. In fact, some gatekeepers might even be hostile to your efforts because of a past relation-ship. Lisa-Jo found that the most accommodating participants were "close, but not too close" (van den Scott, 2018).

Deborah approached such a gatekeeper when she was doing her research on widows. Deborah wanted to observe a support group that happened to be facilitated by a former student. However, when she phoned to ask for permis-sion, the facilitator was immediately wary of Deborah's coming. Eventually, the gatekeeper gave Deborah permission to attend one meeting, with the stipulation that she could continue to attend only if the group approved. When the facilita-tor invited Deborah to attend a meeting, she gave her an incorrect time. So when Deborah showed up at what she thought was the correct time, she was actu-ally half an hour late. Thus, Deborah began with the group on the wrong foot. After the meeting, the gatekeeper told here that the members were uncomfort-able with her presence because she was not a widow, but the facilitator suggested that Deborah could help them with a monthly tea they put on for "seniors." After a few months, the gatekeeper told Deborah she was no longer welcome to help with the teas because she made the women uncomfortable. Later, when Deborah ran into a member of the group at a social event, she told her that the members of the group missed her.

In retrospect, our guess is that this gatekeeper saw Deborah as a potential threat to her status as leader because she had been her professor. Had Deborah been clearer that she just wanted to sit in and listen, things might have turned out dif-ferently. Or they might not have. Deborah will never know. The moral of the story is to be very thoughtful in your approach to any gatekeeper. If you do find yourself in a situation in which the gatekeeper shuts the door to the setting, you should be flexible enough to figure out another way to conduct your research. Deborah organ-ized a six-week workshop for widows that was facilitated by other widows. Both the participants and she benefitted greatly.

In contrast to that experience, a gatekeeper who already trusts you may let you in with the briefest of explanations. For example, Frida Furman (1997:9) describes what happened when she presented her idea for studying beauty-shop culture to the owner of the beauty salon:

> I asked [Julie] permission to conduct an ethnographic study of her salon. She hap-pily agreed, suggesting that she herself had more than once thought her custom-ers' stories would make a good read. While Julie may not have known exactly what

an ethnographic study entails, she seemed flattered by my interest in her work and her world. She was a fine advocate of this project from the start. (1997:9)

As you may recall from Chapter 3, Furman had been a regular customer of the salon for several years, and her relationship with Julie made it easy to ask for permission.

You may also need to consider making a **bargain** with the gatekeeper. This bargain often entails a promise of confidentiality. As with any study, you must also protect the confidentiality of your participants. In making a bargain with a gatekeeper, avoid promising to report back to the gatekeeper or to disclose information that could have a negative impact on any participants, especially if they are subordinate to the gatekeeper. The gatekeeper might also insist on hearing about your eventual findings. Occasionally, a gatekeeper will want to approve your analysis before you publish it. Most researchers avoid agreeing to such a condition. However, it is possible that the researcher would agree in rare situations, particularly if the gatekeeper had commissioned the study. There are alternatives. For example, Elliot Liebow, in *Tell Them Who I Am* (1993), a field study of women's homeless shelters, shared his analysis with one of the women as well as a manager of one of the shelters he studied. He included their response to his analysis in his book, but he did not change his analysis.

Gaining Support from Sponsors

Sponsors are individuals who have deep ties to the community and can provide access to certain settings and populations in informal ways.[5] For example, Elliot Liebow (1967), in *Talley's Corner*, explains that after hanging around with young African-American men in a poor neighbourhood, he developed a friendship with Talley, who "vouchsafed" for him, introducing him to a circle of friends and acquaintances.

Often, a sponsor will be more willing to facilitate your entry into a group if you show a genuine interest in their social world. Michael Atkinson (2003) describes how he got support from a local tattoo artist in Calgary (see Box 5.3). Notice that Atkinson hung around and became familiar with the rhythms of work in tattoo shops before he approached his potential sponsor.

In areas where there is conflict or social unrest, finding a sponsor can be particularly challenging. Christine Leuenberger (2015) conducted research on the impact of the separation wall on Israelis and Palestinians. Her research focuses on the social process of fear creation. She asks these questions: How is fear created? Who creates fear? Whom do we fear? Getting access to Palestinians was one of the major challenges she faced because, as a marginalized group, they exhibited distrust and hostility. When conducting one of her first interviews with A'mar, she mentioned that she was from Cornell University and was a Swiss national. He became friendlier because the Swiss government funds development projects in Palestine. After a number of conversations, A'mar offered Leuenberger the use of an empty office. Through this simple gesture, A'mar communicated his trust and

---

Box 5.3 Connecting with a Sponsor to Gain Access

Before attempting to access the wider world of Calgary's tattoo scene, Michael Atkinson decided to find a sponsor who could help to ease him into the setting. Atkinson was not entirely a newcomer to the community, and he had even briefly encountered his potential sponsor, Jack, in a previous trip to the tattoo shop in which Jack worked. Atkinson used his background knowledge and experience to approach Jack in the most appropriate way:

> I knew that Wednesday was often a slow workday . . . and thought it would be an ideal time to re-introduce myself to [Jack]. . . . With some nervousness I approached Jack . . . and asked him if he remembered me, . . . He nodded . . . and we began to talk about tattooing. . . . I showed him some of my existing tattoo work. . . . Showing your tattoo work . . . buys a certain amount of street credibility. (Atkinson 2003:74–5)

After discussing each of his tattoos, Atkinson revealed the purpose of his visit. Jack was amazed that someone wanted to do research on tattooing and tattoo artists and was even more surprised that Atkinson had received funding to do the study. Jack's enthusiasm was apparent:

> [Jack] rushed to the back room, then brought back an armful of articles, books, and historical pieces on tattooing . . . and for about an hour and a half we pored through the texts. . . . I left the studio feeling that . . . I had found a potential site to begin my venture into tattooing in Calgary. (2003:75)

Source: M. Atkinson. 2003. *Tattooed: The Sociogenesis of a Body Art* (pp. 74–5). Toronto: University of Toronto Press. http://site.ebrary.com/lib/unblib/Doc?id=01218915&pp=9-10.

---

support and became her mentor. She comments, "the day A'mar opened the door to an empty office, he opened for me the doors to Palestine" (Leuenberger 2015:28).

There is one caveat regarding sponsors. Individuals who are immediately welcoming to newcomers are often outsiders in their own social circle. You should therefore be cautious of aligning yourself with any individual who offers you an overly warm welcome. Becoming associated with a marginal member of a social group may make others wary of you and close off association with central members of the group (Warren and Karner 2010:77).

Entering the Field

Once you have received permission to do your study, you will need to think about how to approach your setting for the first time. If you have been hanging around, the participants will already know and recognize you. Some of this advice, therefore, applies equally to earlier stages, particularly when doing research with Indigenous groups because you would have been building relationships with them long before it was time to begin the research.

First impressions are important. If you have made an appointment with a gate-keeper or a sponsor, make sure that you are punctual. Also, remember that your dress and your demeanour should be appropriate to the setting. If the participants dress informally, you should too. Don't try to mimic their dress too closely if they are noticeably distinct from you, however. For example, if we were studying teenage girls, we would look ridiculous if we tried to dress like them; at the same time, we might dress less formally for such a setting than we would if we were studying an adult population.

It is quite common for researchers to feel anxious about entering their set-ting for the first time, especially if they have never been in the setting before. Staci Newmahr conducted a field study of a sadomasochist organization. She notes that all she needed to do was to "pay dues and attend functions" (2011:11). Nonetheless, it is not surprising that she was nervous about her safety because of the stigma of sadomasochism (SM) and her own initial ignorance. You can almost feel the tension as she explains:

> My heart pounded as we neared the street I would need to cross to get to the building [where the function was taking place]. As long as they hadn't seen me . . . I could change my mind. Nervously, I crossed the street and began my field work. (Pp. 11–12)

Even when entering less stressful settings, it is quite common for researchers to be nervous about their first entry into a field site.

Gaining the Group's Trust

When you first enter your research setting, you will likely be seen as an outsider. If you have gained entree through an individual who is not trusted by the ma-jority of the group, some people in the setting may worry that you are a spy. For example, if you have been granted permission by a top-level gatekeeper—such as an employer—some participants, particularly those in positions subordinate to the gatekeeper, may be leery of you. If this is the case, you need to figure out how to gain the group's trust and convince them that you have not been sent by management to spy on them. Box 5.4 illustrates one researcher's successful attempt to gain the trust of his participants.

An effective way to gain trust and build rapport is to adopt the attitude of a learner or take the role of an "incompetent" (Lofland and Lofland 1995:40). Asking questions at this stage will show that you respect the knowledge of your partici-pants and communicate your genuine interest in their affairs. It demonstrates that you are there to learn from them. Of course, it will also help you to gain an under-standing of the group and the environment.

Box 5.4 Building Trust in the Research Setting

|||||||||||||||||||||||||||||||||||||||||||||||||||||||||||||||||||||||||||||||||||||||||||||||||||||||||||||||||||||||||||||||||||||||||||||||||||||||||||||||||||||||||||||||||||||

When Gary A. Fine (1996) wanted to gain access to restaurant kitchens, he had to approach the managers of the restaurants for permission. With the managers' consent, he entered the environments, but the kitchen workers were concerned that he might be a spy or conducting a time-use study that would result in lost jobs:

> Because [restaurant kitchens] are not public arenas, access is provided through management; as a consequence, researchers will have, even in the most optimal circumstances, a burden of trust to overcome (Burraway 1979). Whose side are we on (Becker 1967)? As a result, who I really represented was an issue, although one that became muted when it grew clear that I was not reporting to the management. . . .
>
> [O]ften, my role emerged in the context of joking and teasing but always with an underlying concern. . . . This [concern] became salient when I observed minor deviance, especially among low-status workers, who feared my power over their careers. (1996:234)

Eventually, the workers became more comfortable with Fine's presence and were less inhibited in their actions. In order to be accepted, Fine had to prove that he was aligned with their interests by establishing a reciprocal relationship:

> These workers trust[ed] that I [would] place myself on their side as a true, if limited, member of their group, embracing its under-side. . . . As I gave them leeway, they returned the favor. (1996:234)

Establishing Your Place in the Group

In the early days of your study, you will need to establish your role in the setting. You will have some control over your level of participation, but the members of the group will define where you fit in and "accord [you] a particular role or social place in that setting," a process of **incorporation** (Warren and Karner 2010:85). This process involves negotiation between you, as the researcher, and the participants in the setting.

As you spend more time in the setting, your role may change. Gary A. Fine (1996), mentioned earlier, started out his research in restaurant kitchens by standing in a place that was out of the way. As time went on and the cooks got to know him, they allowed him to perform small tasks, such as peeling potatoes. Similarly, Izabella Ślezak (n.d.), who carried out an ethnography of sex work in escort agencies in Poland, noted that sex workers tested her loyalty by talking about ways they had broken the rules of the agencies to observe whether she would keep the information to herself.

Michael Atkinson (2003:76–7) recounts that his initial encounter with Jack, the tattoo artist, had "a profound impact" on the role he adopted as he continued his study. In response to Jack's fervent interest in literature on tattooing, Atkinson chose

Box 5.5 Addressing Gender in Establishing a Research Identity

Ross Haenfler (2006) and C.J. Pascoe (2012) used complementary strategies to establish their research identities. Haenfler, a man, studied the "straight edge scene" (sXe), and Pascoe, a woman, studied the process through which teenage boys establish a masculine identity at high school. They demonstrated creativity in dealing with the challenges of incorporation in highly gendered settings.

Haenfler had to find a gender identity that would allow him to interview sXe women, particularly about "awkward topics such as sex, female oppression, and . . . their marginal position in the scene." His strategy included "[c]onstruct[ing] a very non-threatening and . . . nonmasculine role in the setting by refusing to act 'tough,' wearing shirts with anti-sexist slogans, and trying to make women feel welcome in the scene" (2006:26). He notes that although he might have gotten more nuanced responses if he had been a woman, his female participants "seemed appreciative that a man would listen to their frustrations" with some aspects of the scene.

C.J. Pascoe faced the opposite challenge in her ethnographic research. She observed that, for teenage boys,

[s]exuality is not just a set of behaviors . . . but . . . mediated, complicated and illuminated researcher-respondent interactions. As a female researcher, I was drawn into a set of objectifying and sexualizing rituals through which boys constructed their identities . . . as masculine. . . . I tried to . . . creat[e] a "least-gendered identity," positioning myself as a woman who possessed masculine cultural capital. I carefully crafted my identity and interactional style to show that I . . . knew about "guy" topics and could engage in verbal one-upmanship so common among boys. (pp. 175–6)

to establish himself as "a provider of academic information on tattooing and [an] avid tattoo client" (2003:76). Because Jack accepted him in this role, others within the community likewise accepted him and treated him as an informed participant.

Gender can also provide challenges in finding a role in your setting. Box 5.5 demonstrates how two researchers attempted to tone down their gender identities to establish appropriate roles in their settings.

Making Observations and Taking Field Notes

Once you are in the field, you must be very attentive to your surroundings. Keep in mind that you are the research instrument—you must depend on your observations, on what you see and hear, to produce results. If you have not been in your setting before, you may want to begin by mapping the location and identifying the subgroups and central figures within the population. As Goffman has commented, your initial observations in the field are particularly important: "The first day you'll see more than you'll ever see again. And you'll see things that you won't see again. So, the first day, you should take notes all the time" (1974/2004:152).

As you spend time in your setting, you should keep an eye out for possible sources of data. Li, Moore, and Smythe (2017) studied how the annual "Heart of the City Festival" in Vancouver's Downtown Eastside contributed to a sense of community and disrupted its negative media portrayal as a "rough environment" (2017:6). Their data included not only what they observed by attending festival events over a period of three years but also "artifacts of social media on the Festival (e.g. videos, photos, blogs) . . . visual artifacts and media texts . . . the Festival website, program guides . . . and other related documents" (2017:6). The resulting article provides a fascinating and uplifting demonstration of how the Festival brings together residents of diverse backgrounds and allows them to "experience a sense of hope and dignity" (2017:21).

As you get to know people, you will begin to ask questions. Although you will have collected a lot of information about your setting and the people in it before you entered the field, the participants know a lot more about what is going on than you do. The people you are meeting are the experts in their own lives; they know what is going on and can help you to understand. They are the only ones who truly know what things mean to them.

During these early days, you will be able to ask questions about what is going on as a naive, new participant. This is the easiest time to ask questions about things that are obvious or invisible to participants. After a while, the people in the setting will expect you to have learned these obvious things. You should also show interest in the participants and their lives and demonstrate reciprocity by listening to stories and helping out with some simple tasks.

It will be impossible to remember everything you learn in the field. Therefore, you will have to keep detailed records of what you see, hear, feel, and do. These records are called **field notes**, and they are absolutely essential to field research. Field notes are so important that Emerson, Fretz, and Shaw (1995:1) refer to their production as "one of the core" activities of ethnographic research.

Writing field notes will also help you to organize your thoughts. As Esterberg (2002:73) observed, "writing is a way of making meaning." As you write your field notes, you will begin to make sense of what you see because putting experiences into words inevitably requires some interpretation. Although consistent note-taking requires a lot of time and discipline, the process will become exciting when you begin to make meaningful connections within your setting.

The next two sections explain the two stages involved in creating good field notes: (1) making **jottings** in the field to help you remember details and (2) writing up your full field notes based on your jottings.

Making Jottings

When you start observing at your research setting, direct your mind to remember things at a later point. With practice, you can become quite good at this, but you will never be good enough to remember everything. For this reason, you should

---

Box 5.6 Advice for Making Jottings

- Record what you know has happened versus what you think has happened.
- Record your observations during or immediately after the event.
- Abbreviate your words and consider using standardized coding forms. (We will discuss coding in detail in Chapter 9.)
- Use a grid to represent different areas within the setting, and, to save time, make jottings in the appropriate section of the grid on what happened in each area.
- Record even seemingly unimportant things.
- Use concrete words.
- Compile a lexicon of local terms used by participants.

---

carry a notebook or your cellphone (on airplane mode) with you so that you can make jottings at any time. Jotting down brief notes—phrases, quotes, and key words—at your field site will help to jog your memory when you write your full field notes later on. If you want to remember longer dialogues, you can make more extensive jottings to preserve the actual words that you hear. (See Box 5.6 for tips on making jottings.)

There is no single correct way to take jottings. As you practise, you will develop your own style. Your jottings are not for anyone else to read, so the most important thing is that they work for you.

When, where, and how to write jottings depends on your research site. In some settings, you won't have any problem with overtly taking notes. If you are sitting in a coffee shop, no one will feel uncomfortable if you occasionally write things down (although, if you seem to be staring and writing, staring and writing, you may make people uncomfortable). In other places, taking notes while the action is going on may be rude or inhibit natural social interaction. At a party, people might think it weird if you take notes. The general rule is to take notes in a way that fits with your setting. Often, researchers withdraw to a quiet place to write jottings and then return to the scene. There is an old joke about ethnographers' needing to take frequent trips to the washroom to write their jottings (Hammersley and Atkinson 1983:147).

If you are in a setting where writing in a notebook fits in well, you may be tempted to write full field notes while you are observing, but it is impossible to write and pay full attention to what is going on at the same time. If you are too involved in writing about one event, you may miss something else that is happening—just think about when you missed something your professor said because you were taking extensive notes on a topic that was just covered. Wait until you have left the field to write your full field notes.

Writing Up Full Field Notes

One of the most common questions students ask about writing field notes is what to include. The short answer is "Everything you can remember." It is probably impossible to have too much detail.

Recording as many details as possible is important because you never know what might be relevant later on. When Deborah was studying the retirement community, she noted that people often referred to "ring around the collar" to make note of grease marks in the pool. Deborah wrote the phrase down even though it did not seem important at the time. Later, Deborah realized that the comment was representative of the residents' strong sense of ownership of the common areas in the community, and her notes about that phrase became important. Similarly, in her study of Inuit housing, Lisa-Jo noted many times participants' mentioning their nieces or nephews' sleeping over and only later realized how that connected to issues of overcrowding. She coined the term **spatial fusion** to refer to practices that enable multiple houses to be envisioned as part of the same home.

As you write your notes, avoid making statements that characterize what people do in a general way. Be precise. Avoid "opinionated words which lend themselves [more] to [evaluation] than to detailed, textured descriptions" (Emerson et al. 1995:32). If you are observing the checkout point at your university's cafeteria and someone pushes into the line, do not write that the person was very rude. Instead, write exactly how the person moved into line. Did they walk in front of someone while looking off to the side or avoiding eye contact in some other way? Did the person say anything to the individual they cut in front of? Did they seem to know one another? What did other people do when this event occurred? By providing concrete details, you focus on what people do rather than on what you perceive them to be doing.

This is not to say that you shouldn't record your own ideas and reactions to what you observe. Just remember to clearly distinguish between what you actually observed and what you think or feel about it. Some researchers find it helpful to keep two different files: one for field notes and one for personal memos. Others like to separate field notes and memos into two separate columns in the same file. Deborah and Lisa-Jo both put their reactions in brackets within the field notes because this allows them to see their thoughts in direct relation to their observations.

Similarly, when you write about what people say, be sure to distinguish between the words they actually use and your paraphrased notes. You can use quotation marks to note when you are writing down people's words verbatim. This distinction is important, for the terms people use to refer to events or to others may provide clues that will help you to identify concepts when you are analyzing your data.

What you write in your field notes will change over the course of your project. During the early days, your notes will be fairly general. You will likely focus on recording your first impressions, providing a physical description of your site, and describing the cast of characters you meet. As you get to know your setting better, issues and questions will emerge from your observations, and your notes will become more selective to reflect your growing understanding of what is going on. As time passes, you will come to recognize the events that are most important to the people who are in the setting. Notice what they stop to look at and what they talk and gossip about (Emerson et al. 1995:28). Keeping good notes will help you to discern what is meaningful to those in your setting.

Another common question that students ask is when they should write their field notes. Often, in the early days of your study, you will find it difficult to allocate time to write because you will be worried that you might miss something important in the field. If you find yourself in this position, you need to begin by accepting that you cannot observe everything at all times. In addition, spending too much time in the field can lead to fatigue, and you may miss things even if you are physically present in your setting. As your study progresses, you will find the rhythm of the setting and identify the periods with the least amount of action. These relatively quiet periods will likely be the best times for you to withdraw to write up your field notes.

It is important to write your field notes as soon as possible after leaving your setting. Once you have left the field, go directly to your computer and do not talk to anyone about what happened until your field notes are complete. As time passes, the "immediacy of [your] lived experience fades, and writing field notes becomes a burdensome, even dreaded experience" (Emerson et al. 1995:41). In contrast, when you write your notes soon after you return from the field, you will be able to include the "idiosyncratic, contingent character" of what you observed (Emerson et al 1995:14), and the writing process will be much easier. Writing your notes without delay helps you to avoid the "homogenizing tendencies of retrospective recall" and allows you to record "vivid memories and images" (Emerson et al 1995:14). Writing up your notes after each session will give you an overview of your day's progress and help you to plan for the next session in the field. If you act promptly and take the time to write thickly descriptive field notes, you will end up with the data you need to find patterns in your social setting.

As you are writing up your field notes for the first time, remember that every researcher has a different system for organizing their observations. We have included a sample of Deborah's own field notes in Appendix B for your reference, but you can develop a system that works for you. You will almost always want to structure your field notes so that they provide a running chronology of events, people, and conversations. This means that you should record the precise time, date, and place that you made your observations. Also, try to use complete sentences to describe your experiences. This will force you to form complete thoughts on your observations and help you to ensure that you have not left out any important details.

Keep in mind that your writing must be clear—a reader should be able to visualize your experiences in the field after they have read your full field notes.

Warren and Karner (2010) refer to writing full field notes as drudgery. We would not go that far, but writing up your field notes does take discipline and effort to overcome the pull of procrastination. It also takes a lot of time to write good field notes. You should plan to spend at least as much time writing up your field notes as you did observing. Michael Atkinson (2003:76) notes that he spent three to six hours writing up his field notes after each period of observation. Because this process is so labour-intensive, always keep back-up copies of your full field notes. This will prevent you from having to go back and recompose your notes if you happen to lose the files as a result of a computer problem.

At some point, you will likely find that you have become too familiar with your setting and that you cannot make any observations that you have not already made. When you can no longer learn anything new from your setting, it is time to leave the field.

Leaving the Field

No project can go on forever, and you will eventually have to withdraw from your study. Conventional wisdom suggests that you should leave the setting in a manner that would not make the entrance of a future researcher difficult. In some situations, you can simply stop going to the site. However, if you have established relationships with your participants, you must take more care in deciding how to leave the field. Think about how a good guest would leave. Express your appreciation for your participants' hospitality; do not simply disappear. In some situations, you may want to promise to share your findings or plan a return visit. If you make these promises, make sure you fulfill them. You want to leave your participants feeling positive about their experiences in your study.

Innovations in Virtual Ethnography

Conspicuously absent from our discussion so far has been the impact of the Internet on ethnographic research. **Virtual ethnography** is the in-depth study of a group or culture that exists in an online environment. The discipline emerged in the 1990s when sociologists and others noticed that virtual environments provide spaces in which online communities develop. Virtual ethnographers use various media, such as email, message boards, blogs, and wiki spaces, to study these communities. The ethnographer's sense of what is appropriate and meaningful in a particular site or online community guides the form and types of engagement they will use in the study (Hine 2008). Virtual ethnography requires the same labour-intensive, systematic approach as all qualitative research, and, as with any ethnography, the researcher has the goal of discerning the distinctive characteristics of the particular culture, its norms, and its social hierarchies. They also seek to learn the jargon and how the community recognizes and identifies insiders and deviants and establishes its boundaries.

Virtual ethnography also presents challenges unique to the online environment. First, deception by participants is fairly common online. Therefore, the researcher cannot be sure that what people say about themselves bears any resemblance to their reality offline. Yet, when the researcher's goal is to study an online culture, what matters is the definition the members of the culture have of each other. Second, the researcher must decide whether to "lurk" or to participate. It is quite common for many members of a list to lurk, to read messages without ever being visible. If the virtual ethnographer decides to participate, they must also consider how to develop an appropriate online persona. This step might include creating a signature, an avatar, or even a website (Hine 2008). These preparations mirror those that any ethnographer must consider before approaching a social setting or community.

Nancy K. Baym (2000) carried out an early virtual ethnography of an online discussion group organized around watching soap operas. Baym, a soap opera fan herself, did participant observation of this discussion group for three years in the early 1990s. At the centre of her study was the question of how soap opera viewers "use the mass media to structure and articulate [their] relations with one another and to make the world intellectually meaningful, aesthetically pleasing, and emotionally compelling" (Jenson and Pauly 1997:163 as cited in Baym 2000:9). She writes that two methods drove the research: discourse analysis and online surveys. Her approach was careful and systematic.

Baym collected more than 32,000 messages in a 10-month period. She quickly decided that she needed to refine her focus, so she chose to examine a subgroup that was made up of fans of the soap opera *All My Children*. Participants were eager to share their insights with a fellow viewer. She observes that the members she studied defied the stereotypes of soap opera fans as bored, uneducated women with nothing better to do with their time than sit around and watch television. Rather, she discovered that many of the members were educated professionals who participated in meaningful, analytical discussions on the topic of soap operas.

Ten years later, as online forums developed and grew, Krista Whitehead (2010) carried out a virtual ethnography of an online pro–eating disorder (ED) community. Her approach approximates the role of complete observer in traditional ethnography. She visited only those parts of the website that were publicly available and did not become a member. She began by looking for the online presence of pro-ED groups by googling the terms *pro-ana* and *pro-mia* (referring to "pro-anorexia" and "pro-bulimia," respectively). As a result of her search, Whitehead found the site ProAna[DOT]US,[6] which she used as her main data source. She spent two weeks exploring all the sections of the website to get a general sense of the setting, and she took field notes. Similar to the way other ethnographers hang around their field sites, Whitehead visited the site daily for several hours over a six-month period. She explains that these visits are an "adaptation of face-to-face ethnographic methods [and] approximate the visiting habits of individuals most involved" in the community (2010:597). After careful analysis of her data, Whitehead found that the community sought to draw boundaries between those who have eating disorders and those who do not. Members used gendered practices, such as equating beauty with self-worth, "to establish a bounded eating-disordered identity" (2010:604).

More recently, Casey Scheibling (2019a, 2019b) used **cyber-ethnography** to explore the culture of dad bloggers who make up the "Dad 2.0 community" (2019b:478) that critiques laws and policies associated with patriarchy (2019a). He explored and compared data from "both online and offline worlds" (2019a:5), combining his cyber-ethnography with in-person field work. Scheibling attended Dad Summits in person for about three years where he took extensive field notes. He then analyzed 201 blog posts written by 40 dad bloggers and conducted interviews. He found that the bloggers functioned as a "**tiny public**" (Fine 2012) in that they developed a collective way of conceptualizing fatherhood that included and used their blogs to "publicly document how . . . role models and turning points shaped their identities . . . shared advice on how to 'do' fathering in everyday life . . . challenge[d] older fatherhood ideologies that . . . men are not nurturing parents . . . and . . . brand[ed] involved fathers as 'superdads'" (Scheibling 2019b: 485). Scheibling argues that the dad bloggers are working collectively to construct an ideology of "normalized involved fatherhood" (2019b:486). He was able to blend online and offline observations, demonstrating that we can be creative in how we incorporate and account for the intersection of our everyday online lives and our everyday offline practices.

Summary

In this chapter, we have explored aspects of field research. We looked at the development of ethnographic studies, primarily in North America in the past century. We discussed how to plan and prepare for a field study. We examined the four main levels of participation that researchers use in their participant-observation studies, and we learned the importance of creating a coherent storyline and of establishing relationships with gatekeepers and sponsors. We explored what to do once you are in the field—how to interact with participants, take jottings, and transform your jottings into field notes. Finally, we looked at the development of virtual ethnography. We saw that it is very similar to face-to-face fieldwork in that it entails careful, systematic observation of online communities and making decisions about one's role in the setting—just as when researchers study more traditional communities. In Chapter 6, we will look at another form of data collection: the qualitative interview.

Key Terms

bargain

Chicago School of Sociology

complete observer

complete participant

cyber-ethnography

ethnocentrism

ethnography

field notes

gatekeepers

ideal types

incorporation

jottings

observer as participant

participant as observer

primary group

salvage ethnography

sponsors

spatial fusion

tiny publics

virtual ethnography

Questions for Critical Thought

1. If you were conducting field research in your own city, what groups do you think you could easily get access to? What groups might be the hardest for you to access? How might you go about gaining entry into some of these groups?

2. Which research role from the participant–observation continuum would you prefer to adopt in your own studies? What advantages and disadvantages are involved in the role you chose?

3. In ethnographic field research, can friendship ever be genuine? Are there any boundaries of friendship that should not be crossed?

4. Say you were studying your class. How might you gain or be limited by being an insider? How might you gain or be limited if you were approaching as an ethnographic stranger?

5. What is the role of compassion in the field? How might that conflict with the integrity of your work? How might this be different if you are doing participant observation and/or work with an Indigenous group?

Exercises

1. With a partner, go to a public site, and begin making observations. Alternately, you could watch some commercials together (try collections of Super Bowl commercials on YouTube. com). Without consulting your partner, make jottings on what you see and hear. When you have finished observing, compare notes with your partner's. Identify any differences between the notes, and think about why you might have missed something that your partner noted.

2. With a partner, observe a setting, or those Super Bowl commercials, without making any jottings. Wait an hour and then write down everything you can remember. When you are finished, trade notes with your partner. Were there any significant details that you had forgotten about?

3. Think of a setting that might be difficult to gain access to—say, a prison. Write a few paragraphs about how you might go about gaining access to this setting.

In-Class Exercise

With a partner, have a five-minute conversation without taking notes. Share with each other how much you remember from the conversation.

Suggested Readings

Robert M. Emerson, Rachel I. Fretz, and Linda L. Shaw. 1995. *Writing Ethnographic Fieldnotes.* Chicago: University of Chicago Press. This book provides very practical advice for novice ethnographers. It focuses on how to take jottings and field notes.

Gary Alan Fine. 2015. *Players and Pawns: How Chess Builds Community and Culture.* Chicago: University of Chicago Press. Gary Alan Fine has written numerous fascinating ethnographies about a wide variety of social contexts including Little League, restaurant kitchens, and mushroom collecting. As with all his work, this book is a model of ethnography.

C.J. Pascoe. 2012. *Dude, You're a Fag: Masculinity and Sexuality in High School.* Berkeley: University of California Press. This engrossing ethnography demonstrates how Pascoe dealt with the challenges of gender and age in her study of compulsive hegemonic masculinity in high school.

Staci Newmahr. 2011. *Playing on the Edge: Sadomasochism, Risk, and Intimacy.* Bloomington, IN: Indiana University Press. This fascinating ethnography involves a subculture most of us will never experience. The author spent four years immersed in her field site and communicates the recreational and gendered nature of the setting in a book that is a page-turner.

Related Website

The Qualitative Report
http://nsuworks.nova.edu/tqr/
This website, maintained by Nova Southeastern University, includes links to an online journal for qualitative research (*The Qualitative Report*), a weekly qualitative report with a list of notable new articles, and other useful qualitative research resources.

Notes

1. Before the field of sociology gained prominence in Canada, early interest in field research was rooted in developments in anthropology. Early anthropological studies tied to the Victoria Memorial Museum in Ottawa, with an anthropological division headed by the famous American linguist and anthropologist Edward Sapir, led to detailed and influential ethnographic studies of First Nations peoples. In addition, the Royal Ontario Museum in Toronto took a deep interest in cultural diversity throughout the world (Darnell 1997).
2. See the Companion Website for a list of recent qualitative studies by Canadian researchers and Jean (2006) for a history of the development of field research in Quebec.
3. A rough outline of the institutional spread of interactionist-type sociology in Canada during the 20th century has been put together by Fatima Camara and Rick Helmes-Hayes (2003) and Emily Milne and Rick Helmes-Hayes (2010).

4. In one of the highest ethical stances recorded in the literature, Wolf (1991:18-19) was prepared to abandon his project and destroy his field notes if the Rebels refused him permission to write up the study. Fortunately, they agreed to let him publish his results.
5. The most celebrated sponsor in the annals of ethnography is "Doc," the individual who helped William Foot Whyte (1955) in his study of "corner boys" (Hammersley and Atkinson 1983:58). Doc has become so famous in the history of ethnography that many researchers talk about finding their Doc as an important early step in their fieldwork.
6. This website was devoted to the pro-eating disorder community. It was quite active when Whitehead conducted her research. As Whitehead notes in her article, pro-eating disorder websites are often taken down, possibly because they are so controversial.

6 In-Depth Interviewing

Learning Objectives

- To recognize the limitations of standardized interviews
- To understand the strengths of in-depth, qualitative interviews
- To discover ways of identifying participants for a qualitative interview study
- To learn how to construct an interview guide and conduct an interview
- To learn how to transcribe interviews

Introduction

In the last chapter, we explored field research. In this chapter, we move on to another form of data collection: in-depth interviewing. First, we assess **standardized interviews**, or surveys, to better understand their limitations and the reasons why qualitative researchers prefer to conduct **in-depth interviews**. Then, we take a brief look at different types of and approaches to in-depth interviews. Finally, we learn how to design and conduct an in-depth interview study.

Interviews have become so common in everyday life that sociologist David Silverman (1997, 1993) has dubbed our society the "interview society." He points out that interviews are a centrepiece of mass media, of market research, and of political polling. It is the rare person who has escaped being interviewed about some aspect of their life. Most of the time, the type of interview we encounter in our personal lives is the standardized interview, or survey.[1] As qualitative researchers, however, we are more interested in conducting *in-depth* interviews. To understand this preference, let us look at the assumptions underlying the use of standardized interviews and the inherent limitations of this type of data collection.

Standardized Interviews

Your telephone rings, and when you answer it, the person on the other end asks you to participate in a survey. If you say yes, you spend the next several minutes answering questions that require you to agree or disagree with a particular opinion, to rate things on a scale of one to five, or to select an option from a list of predetermined responses. You have just experienced being an interviewee in a standardized interview.

In general, standardized interviews reflect a positivist approach to research. Investigators use them to collect "standardized information about a large number of respondents relatively cheaply" (Fontana and Prokos 2007:21), often to test hypotheses. Standardized interviews are most useful when the researcher wants information that is unambiguous and knows the "very thing" that they want to uncover (Schwartz and Jacobs 1979).

This type of interview assumes that the researcher can minimize or eliminate bias by making everything in the interview uniform. It functions on a stimulus–response model that suggests that if you standardize the stimulus (that is, the questions and the way that the interviewer reads them), the variations in answers represent a true measure of what you are investigating (Mason 2002:65). As such, a standardized interview consists of a standard protocol or a questionnaire that the interviewer always reads in the same way and in the same order so that the "stimuli" will be the same across all interviews; even the introduction at the beginning of the interview is scripted. The interviewer is trained to treat every situation in a like manner (Fontana and Prokos 2007). If the respondent does not understand a particular question, the interviewer is not permitted to rephrase it. Typically, they will simply repeat the question (Esterberg 2002).

Questions in this type of interview are worded to collect structured data. Therefore, the questions are usually what we call **closed-ended** or **forced-choice questions** for which the respondent must choose their response from a list of answers provided by the interviewer. Ideally, the researcher tries to offer answers that are as exhaustive and mutually exclusive as possible. In other words, the researcher designs the answers to include all possibilities and avoid any overlap. Therefore, a question meant to discover a respondent's age cannot present the options as "20 to 40 *or* 40 to 80"—anyone under 20 or over 80 would be excluded, and a 40-year-old would not know which category to choose.

Limitations of Standardized Interviews

Qualitative researchers have objected to the use of standardized interviews in sociological research. (Box 6.1 discusses some objections from the perspective of feminist researchers.) Standardized interviews provide only a rough sketch of respondents' true situations and cannot uncover any unexpected data. They further note that the basic assumptions of standardized interviews—those assumptions that make these interviews useful when conducting quantitative research—stand in direct opposition to the qualitative researcher's goal of obtaining complex, participant-defined data.

To begin with, the standardized interview takes for granted that all respondents will understand and relate to the questions in the way in which the researcher intended. In other words, it assumes **validity** across various social contexts (Mishler 1986). Yet, as we have learned, every person interprets language based on their personal knowledge and experience. As Elliot G. Mishler (1986:22) has noted, "survey

Box 6.1 Feminist Critiques of Standardized Interviews

Feminist researchers have long questioned the effectiveness of standardized interviews to shed light on individuals'—especially women's—lived experiences. Ann Oakley (1981), for example, challenged the stance of the distant, neutral interviewer who does not spoil the stimulus–response model of the interview by deviating from the script. "Feminist interviewing" should strive for openness and engagement on the part of the interviewer and recognize the possibility of developing a relationship between the interviewer and the interviewee (Reinharz 1992). More recently, Oakley (2016: 209) has suggested that we think of researchers' dependence on what research participants are willing to contribute from "the memories and stories of their lives" as a gift, since they have the "ability to choose to answer the researchers' questions" (p. 208) or not.

Marjorie DeVault (1999) challenged the taken-for-granted categories that researchers use in standardized interviews. She suggested that their language often does not capture women's experiences. This is especially evident in words such as *work* and *leisure*, which do not relate easily to women's lives because women's activities do not always fit into one or the other category and because much of the work women do is invisible.

Similarly, Linda Caissie (2006), who carried out a study of the Raging Grannies (a group of older women activists who use street theatre, outrageous costumes, and satirical songs as methods of protest), discovered that although academic literature would identify their activity as serious leisure, the Grannies disagreed. The Grannies' definition of leisure included relaxation and rest, play, entertainment, recreation, unstructured free time, frivolous activity, choice, and social activities—the opposite of work. In contrast, they defined activism as unpaid work, self-expression, a calling, a way of life, political protest, commitment to justice, fun, social action, resistance, and volunteering (Caissie 2006:145–6).

Tricia Agocs, Debra Langan, and Carrie Sanders (2015) have pointed out that standardized interviews often use gender as a variable that simply looks at statistically significant differences between women and men. In contrast, in their study of police officers who are mothers, they conducted in-depth interviews that asked broad questions such as "How does your role as a police officer both benefit and create challenges for you as a mother?" (2015:272). This approach allowed them to identify the "arduous and complex home lives of police mothers" (2015:273) rather than to simply compare them to male police officers.

research is a context-stripping procedure" in which researchers "pretend" that diversity in social contexts and meanings does not exist.

The standardized interview also presumes that the response options provided by the researcher will be exhaustive and that they will not inadvertently exclude other valid answers that the interviewee might provide (Schwartz and Jacobs 1979). Yet, given the opportunity, most individuals will offer an opinion that is more complex than the ones predetermined by the researcher. Consider the following question, which appears in a textbook as a good example of the simple and direct wording that standardized interviews use: "Sugar is bad for health. Do you agree or disagree?" (Bouma, Ling, and Wilkinson 2009:77). Notice that the wording of this question assumes that it has a straightforward answer. Yet few of us would agree that *all* sugar is bad for *everyone's* health at *all* times. The respondent has no way to indicate a more detailed, middle-of-the-road opinion.

Similarly, standardized interviews assume that the researcher can construct mutually exclusive responses to the survey questions. While this might be possible when the focus is on determining simple facts—a person's age or the party an individual voted for in the last election—it is less feasible when dealing with complex issues. For example, a survey on equality in the workforce might ask whether respondents think that women make less money than men because women work in lower-paid occupations or because of discrimination. The wording of the question implies that the two possibilities are mutually exclusive. Yet both factors could, and sometimes do, work together to contribute to women's making less money.

Standardized interviews assume that it is possible for an interviewer to present the script in a manner that is neutral and consistent across multiple interviews. Yet no two interviews can ever be exactly the same because no interviewer can control every aspect of their tone and body language. In many cases, the interviewer may make a mistake when reading the script or add details that are not included in the script. In fact, research has shown that interviewers change the wording of up to one-third of questions on an interview script (Bradbury, Sudman, and Associates 1979 as cited in Fontana and Prokos 2007:21). A few years ago, Deborah was a respondent in a phone survey. When the interview was almost done, the interviewer asked if Deborah was Professor van den Hoonaard and then told her that they had been a student in one of her classes. Deborah is quite sure that these comments were not part of the interview script!

Indigenous researchers have also addressed the shortcomings of interview practices that reflect Western cultural bias. Standardized, questionnaire-type interviews are "top down . . . and mirror the worldview of the researchers and their perception of the topic to be covered" (Bagele 2012:78). The measures and questions have usually been developed with non-Indigenous people (Smith 2012:141) and, as a result, adhere to individualistic, Western assumptions (Bagele 2012:204). Interview research with Indigenous people recognizes that their stories have previously been told through "outsider research" (Kovach 2015:50). As we move forward, it is essential that researchers include "receptivity and relationship" as an intrinsic part of their research and, therefore, learn about how respect is offered in Indigenous cultures (Smith 2012), for example, by recognizing the centrality of elders. By listening with an attitude of learning, researchers can find out how Indigenous communities and individuals have survived centuries of marginalization (Strega and Brown 2015). As Karen L. Potts and Leslie Brown eloquently put it, "Through paying attention and listening, research is deconceptualized and becomes an emergent, unfolding process rather than a trip to a predetermined destination" (2015:24).

Lisa-Jo (van den Scott 2016) provides an example of interview research with Inuit participants in Nunavut concerning how they have engaged with permanent walls, which were only introduced in the 1960s when Inuit of that area were forced off the land into permanent settlements. Previously, they had lived "a nomadic lifestyle with ingenious and creative survival-based technology," including *iglus* and caribou-skin tents (2016:38). In her study, Lisa-Jo focuses on the creativity and ingenuity with which Inuit engage with their walls after learning to live indoors and becoming visitors to the land, "the locus of their identity" (2016:39). Lisa-Jo had lived in Nunavut for five years prior to conducting her study. She knew that storytelling had value in Arviat and, therefore, encouraged storytelling. Lisa-Jo also understood the importance of elders. She strove in every aspect of this research to respect the Inuit culture and world view. As you will discover in the following sections, in-depth interviews allow the researcher not only to overcome some of the difficulties associated with standardized interviews and to work within Indigenous contexts but also to use the interview process itself as a source of data.

In-Depth Interviews

Unlike standardized interviews, the purpose of in-depth interviews is to allow people to explain their experiences, attitudes, feelings, and definitions of the situation in their own terms and in ways that are meaningful to them. To get a sense of what an in-depth interview can accomplish, consider the following example, which we have taken from Deborah's study of women's experiences as widows:

> On a warm spring day, as I make my way up the driveway to the house of my first participant, I see that the mailbox lists both the husband's and the wife's names on it. I make a mental note to ask the woman I am about to interview about the mailbox. Adding a new question would be a problem were I conducting a standardized interview. Fortunately, I am not.
>
> When I reach the door I knock, and my participant welcomes me into her home. We chat a bit as I set up my recording equipment. Once we are both ready to begin, I turn on the tape recorder. I explain that I am interested in hearing about her experiences of being a widow:
>
> > What I would like you to do now is tell me about your experience with losing your husband. You can start where you want and end where you want. Put in what you want and leave out what you want. I'm just interested in hearing about your experience.

After a few moments of thought, the woman responds:

> What was it like to lose him? I suppose first of all, you have to say what
> it was like to have him . . . he was a very supportive person. He was quite
> romantic, in a way. We met in a romantic manner . . . during the war in
> London. We did our courting during the Blitz, so he actually saved my life
> once in the Blitz at some risk to himself. And then he was overseas, too.
> (van den Hoonaard 2001:8)

In the first moments of the interview, this woman communicated the impact of the history of her marriage and relationship with her husband on her experience of being a widow. Had Deborah designed a questionnaire based on the literature and her own hypotheses, she would never have thought to ask about the way this widow met her husband. Deborah would have missed out on hearing about something that her participant felt was central to her experience.

This recognition of the importance of the participant's perspective is the hallmark of qualitative interviewing. In the next section, we look at several types of qualitative interviews and some approaches researchers take when thinking about the interview process itself. We then talk about how to plan and carry out an in-depth interview study.

Types of Qualitative Interviews

Qualitative interviews take several forms. Some include "a series of predetermined but open-ended questions" and "use a variety of probes that elicit further information" (Ayres 2008:810). Others are more flexible, and "the interviewee determines the direction the interview will take" to allow the researcher to "discover [the interviewee's understanding of] the topic of interest" (Firmin 2008:907). Many researchers refer to the former type of interview as "semi-structured" and the latter as "unstructured," but, as Hammersley and Atkinson (1983:112–3) have pointed out, all interviews have some structure. Just as all social interaction is structured by the individuals involved, interviews are structured by both the interviewer and the respondent.

Researchers design different kinds of interviews depending on their proclivities and projects. Some design an **interview guide** that encourages the participant to develop a chronological account of their life. Others may create a list of areas that they want to cover and provide little direction to the person they are interviewing. Still others may start with one opening question and let the participant lead the researcher where they will. For example, when Deborah interviewed an acquaintance to discover more about the experience of being a vegetarian, she started with a simple question: "How did you happen to become a vegetarian?" His answers led to other questions, and they talked for over an hour. When it was over, Deborah's interviewee told her that he had not realized how much he knew about vegetarianism.

Jesus Reyes

Figure 6.1 Spontaneous interviewing

Interviews that take place in the throes of a field study tend to be highly informal and happen on the spur of the moment. Harry F. Wolcott (1995:106) suggests that even a "casual comment or inducement such as 'what you were telling me the other day was interesting'" can initiate an informal interview. In some situations, these on-the-fly interviews or "incidental ethnographic encounters" (Pinsky 2015:292) are the only possibility. For example, when Will C. van den Hoonaard (2000) was on a lunch break at a cartography conference where he was gathering information for his study on women's experiences of becoming cartographers, he unexpectedly encountered a woman who was on the team that mapped the far side of the moon (see van den Hoonaard 2013). Not wanting to miss an opportunity to gather information from this woman, he quickly improvised an interview. Figure 6.1 shows this encounter. Note that van den Hoonaard is making use of the only recording devices he had at hand—a pencil and a paper plate!

Regardless of how formal or informal the encounter is, the qualitative interview is "a directed conversation that elicits inner views of respondents' lives as they portray their worlds, experiences, and observations" (Charmaz 1991:385). Such interviews are characterized by a relatively informal style in which the interviewer encourages "people to describe their [social] world in their own terms" (Rubin and Rubin 1995:2). Interviews, however, diverge from conversations in three important ways. First, the interviewer has the task of bringing the discussion back to the topic of the interview when it veers off track. Second, the discussion is lopsided—the researcher says much less than the participant says. Third, the investigator can never engage in passive listening. The interviewer must listen intently because they need to identify ideas or potentially useful concepts to ask about in subsequent questions. Elaine Brody (2010) calls this "organized listening."

Approaches to Qualitative Interviews

Traditionally, in-depth interviewers saw the interviewee as a vessel full of answers that the interviewer could access with a sympathetic demeanour and skilful questioning (Gubrium and Holstein 2001:13). Thus, Firmin (2008:907) writes that an "unstructured interview . . . is designed to draw from the interviewee constructs embedded in [their] thinking." Others have suggested that the in-depth interview "centres on the meanings that life experiences hold for the individuals being studied" (Warren and Karner 2010:127). With this understanding, researchers approach in-depth interviews as a way to "help to uncover the participant's views," to allow their perspective to "unfold as the participant views it . . . not as the researcher views it" (Marshall and Rossman 2006:101).

In-depth interviews do, indeed, help researchers to appreciate how participants understand their social worlds. However, they are also social events that do more than simply extract data that already exist inside individuals. In fact, in-depth interviews often encourage participants to think about their experiences in new ways and to formulate ideas and opinions that they did not possess before the interview began. Thus, an in-depth interview is an interactional process more accurately described as "generating data" than "collecting data" that are already inside a research participant, waiting to be mined (Mason 2002).[2] This approach to in-depth interviewing has been conceptualized as the **active interview** (Holstein and Gubrium 1995).

The Active Interview

Qualitative researchers are very aware that social reality is constructed through interpersonal interactions as much as words. Therefore, when conducting in-depth interviews, we pay close attention not only to what participants say but to how they say it and how they behave in relation to the interviewer. As James A. Holstein and Jaber F. Gubrium noted in their influential book *The Active Interview*, interviews are "meaning-making occasions" that allow us to "reveal both the substance and the process of meaning making" (1995:76–7). As such, Holstein and Gubrium encourage researchers to take the approach of an "ethnographer of the interview" and analyze the interactional process through which the interview takes place (1995:78). By recognizing the interview as an active social process, we take into account the importance of the strategies that participants (and researchers) use during the interview. Thus, we can view the interview process itself as a source of data. Let us look at examples that illustrate what we can learn by actively analyzing the interactions that take place during interviews.

When Deborah was conducting her study of older widowers, the men she interviewed behaved in an overtly assertive manner. They interrupted her questions, referred to Deborah as "girl" or "dear" or by a diminutive of her first name and lectured her about a variety of topics (van den Hoonaard 2009). Although the men did not express their motivations in words, their behaviour demonstrated that they were trying very hard to display their masculinity to make sure that Deborah understood that they were still "real" men.

In contrast, when Deborah interviewed older widows, the women took on a more submissive role. They questioned whether they were "doing it right" and worried aloud that they might be talking too much or "gabbling," talking nonsense. The women also offered Deborah tea to enact the hostess role with which they were familiar and comfortable. Their actions revealed their unspoken fear of being perceived as incompetent in their everyday lives (van den Hoonaard 2005).

Deborah was able to gain a deeper understanding by observing how participants interacted with her in the interviews. In addition, she learned a lot by comparing the behaviours of the widowers to those of the widows. The differences in the ways the participants communicated and managed their discomfort told Deborah a lot about what it means to be a member of each of these groups and the gendered social meaning of an individual's status as an older widowed woman or man.

When visiting participants in Nunavut, Lisa-Jo found that both women and men often used the phrase "us Inuit" when they were helping her learn more about their lives. Paying attention to these interactional signals helped Lisa-Jo to better understand their desire to express a collective Inuit identity. By approaching each situation as an active interviewer, we were able to use the social process of interaction that took place during the interviews as a source of data, which helped us to understand the way our participants experienced their everyday lives.

Conducting an In-Depth Interview Study

We are now ready to think about how to actually go about conducting an in-depth interview study. Once you have decided on a research question to be addressed through in-depth interviews, you need to decide whom to interview, and you need to design an interview guide.

Identifying Participants

If you are familiar with quantitative research methods, you may know that researchers who conduct surveys and do statistical analyses have developed sophisticated techniques to identify a random sample (see **random sampling**) of the population. This method makes sense when a researcher wants to interview a large number of people and has a goal of generalizing the study's findings to a wider population. In contrast, qualitative researchers are more interested in learning a lot about a relatively small number of people, so random sampling is not an effective way to identify participants for a qualitative interview. How, then, do researchers decide whom to interview?

First of all, qualitative researchers choose people who can provide the greatest insight into the topic at hand. For example, Deborah was interested in finding out the social meaning that being a widow has for older women. She therefore decided to recruit women over age 50 who had been widowed between one and 10 years. Deborah also wondered if the experience of women who live in urban areas would be different from the experience of women who live in rural areas. In the end, she sought a "sample" of women that was split, approximately 50–50, between urban and rural widows over age 50.

Simone Ispa-Landa and Sara Thomas (2019) were interested in the **feeling rules** and emotion work done by novice women principals. They looked for a racially diverse sample to avoid "position[ing] white women as the 'universal female subject' (Glenn 1999)" (p. 388). They found that white women began by establishing themselves as emotionally supportive leaders, experienced a tension between authority and emotional support, and felt a need to balance the two approaches. In contrast, women of colour started with a more directive approach and viewed the emotional labour involved in showing support as "blended" rather than in tension. By intentionally interviewing their diverse sample, Ispa-Landa and Thomas were able to discover how race intersected with gender in the "relationship of care and authority for women leaders" (p. 394).

When you are deciding whom to interview, keep in mind that you want to undermine the "hierarchy of credibility," as we discussed in Chapter 3. You will learn more about people's lives if you avoid interviews with experts and instead interview the people whose lives you want to know about. Hence, when Timothy Ross and Ronald Buluing (2019) studied the adequacy of school parking for parents of disabled children, they talked to parents and their children with disabilities, themselves, rather than with planners and designers. They asked them to take photos of their morning school travel and then interviewed them about the challenges they faced. They found that although some sites had "technically accessible parking spaces," they were "rendered functionally inaccessible due to designs that discount how the spaces are actually experienced" (p. 298).

Once you have identified the types of individuals you want to interview, you must spend some time searching for participants who meet your criteria. One strategy that can help you find members of your target group is **snowball sampling**. When an investigator uses this strategy, they locate initial participants and then ask them if they know anyone who fits the criteria and who might be interested in participating in the study. For Deborah's study of widows, she started by identifying a few participants and then asking them to approach other potential participants on her behalf. If the potential participant was interested in being contacted, Deborah phoned her to talk about the study and to invite her to participate, and to protect their confidentiality, she did not report back to the original participant who had recommended them.

Sometimes, you can approach an organization to help you find your sample. Even if you do not have an established connection to the organization, you may find this approach useful. As a note of caution, if you choose this route when identifying participants, you may miss potential participants who do not belong to the organization you have chosen, and you may end up with a sample group that is too narrow in focus.

In other cases, you may need to contact a person in a position of power—for example, a warden in a prison or a supervisor in a nursing home—to gain access to participants. In such a situation, it may be challenging to ensure that your participants are involved voluntarily. A resident of a nursing home or an inmate of a prison might not feel free to refuse participation even if you assure them that participation is voluntary. In addition, these participants may not feel that you will be able to follow through on your promise of confidentiality. This sense of insecurity may have an impact on how they answer your questions. These potential complications need not prevent you from carrying out your research, but you should consider them in the planning of your study and in the analysis of your data.

Of course, some groups are easier to find than others. When Deborah wanted to study older urban and rural widows, for example, she found a journalist who was willing to write an article about her research for the local newspaper. By nine o'clock the morning after the article appeared, Deborah had already received five phone calls from women who were interested in participating. Within a week, she had 18 volunteers! This is quite a lot, considering that in-depth interview studies often have samples of 30 or fewer (Deborah ended up with 27). As time went on, she strategically recruited from rural areas to even up her sample.

Recruiting older widowers was more difficult. Deborah knew that she would be recruiting from a much smaller population. In addition, based on her past experience, Deborah knew that older men are less likely than older women to volunteer as research participants. She therefore spread as wide a net as possible. Deborah used newspaper, radio, and television publicity. She asked friends and colleagues if they knew a widower to whom they could refer her. She also tried snowball sampling, which had worked with widows. As others have discovered (for example, Davidson 1999), snowball sampling is not an effective way to recruit older widowers. Deborah did not find a single participant using this method.

Today, many researchers use social media to recruit participants for their research. For example, when Lynne Gouliquer, Carmen Poulin, and Jennifer McWilliams (2020:54) wanted to interview women firefighters from all over Canada about their experiences with being "othered" as full-time and volunteer firefighters, they used ads that appeared on a "Women in Fire" web page as well as newsletters and discussion forums.

As you can see, there are many ways to go about finding people to participate in your interview study. Yet there are always some people who will not take part in research. We know that women are more likely than men to agree to participate and that higher levels of education correspond to greater willingness to participate. But it is likely that there are other consistent factors that lead to refusal to participate in a study. It is therefore useful to think about who refuses to participate and what you might not learn because you do not have the opportunity to talk to those people.

Nonetheless, whether finding people to interview is easy or difficult, you will locate enough people if you are persistent and creative. Next, we talk about the interview guide, which you will develop during the processes of defining your research question and recruiting your participants.

Designing an Interview Guide

When discussing qualitative interviews, we use the term *guide* rather than *script*, *questionnaire*, *schedule*, or *protocol* to refer to our written plan. The term *guide* reflects the flexibility of our approach. We can rearrange questions to suit a particular interview, and we can choose to add or omit questions depending on how appropriate they are for a particular situation.

The first step in designing your interview guide is to list the broad categories that are of interest to you in your study. The second step is to develop the **open-ended questions** that are relevant to these categories. These questions will be the most significant questions you ask during the interview process. When you are designing your questions, keep in mind that you should address only those themes that are directly related to your research topic. Avoid asking questions on topics that are simply a matter of personal curiosity.

The next step is to compose your draft guide. Think about the order of your questions. Do they flow from one to the other? Although the order may change during each interview, listing the questions in a logical order in the guide will help to keep you on track. Be careful not to include too many questions. Remember that the participant may give long answers to your questions. A 10-question guide may result in an interview that lasts 30 minutes or one that takes three hours. Too many questions may lead you to rush through the interview instead of listening closely to responses and asking good follow-up questions.

Follow-up questions, or **probes**, ask the participant to elaborate on, explain, or provide a story or example of what they have said. During the interview, you should listen intently to every answer and plan potential follow-up questions. A probe might be general (for example, "Can you tell me more about that?"), or it might be more specific (for example, "You mentioned that your friends treat you differently since you made the Olympic bobsleigh team. In what ways?"). Although you will devise most of your follow-up questions in response to what your participant says during an interview, try to anticipate some potential follow-ups and include these questions in your guide.

As you look over your guide, make sure that you have designed questions that you think your participants can answer. You can ask people about the following:

• Their experiences or behaviours
• Their opinions or values
• Their feelings
• Their factual knowledge

- What they saw, heard, or felt
- Their personal background

Keep in mind that people can only tell you about their own experiences. So, for example, you can ask a widow how her relationship with her friends has changed, but you cannot ask her how widows, in general, feel about their friends.

Plan to start your interview with questions that the participant will find relatively easy to answer. Many people are nervous when they are being interviewed, so putting your participants at ease will help to build rapport and make the interview both more informative for you and more enjoyable for the person you are interviewing.

We cannot always anticipate what things a participant may find important or meaningful. Therefore, it is both useful and respectful to include questions that invite your participants to add anything that they think is important that you have not asked in the interview. When we conduct interviews, our last planned question is always "Is there anything that I haven't asked you about that I should have?" This question has often opened an entirely new line of inquiry. In addition, because data collection is emergent, you should always be open to adding questions during the interview itself.

To help guide you through the process of creating your first interview guide, Deborah has included an example from her own work in Box 6.2. Notice the conversational tone she uses in phrasing her questions. Also notice that the questions encourage the participant to give expansive rather than short or categorical answers. In the next section, you will find advice on avoiding some common mistakes that can negatively affect the quality of your interviews.

Common Pitfalls

There are a few errors that novice researchers often make when they write their guiding questions. If you are aware of these potential mistakes, and if you pay close attention to the tone, wording, structure, and content of your questions, you should be able to avoid them. The following advice will help you with this task.

Don't make your participants feel as though they are being interrogated. The tone of your questions should be open and inviting. As we noted above, you should use conversational rather than technical or formal language to establish your tone. Most of the time, you do not want the wording of your questions to make the interview participant feel defensive or put on the spot.

Avoid using questions that begin with the word *why*. Rather, ask participants *how* they came to think or do certain things. "Why" questions are likely to elicit answers that focus on motivation, and research shows that many people respond defensively to being asked *why* they did something. In contrast, "how" questions are more likely to draw out answers that capture both motive and process.

Never ask leading or loaded questions. Choose your words carefully to avoid encouraging the participant to give a particular response. For example, a question

Box 6.2 Sample Interview Guide

This is the interview guide Deborah used for her interview study of women's experiences as widows. During the interview itself, she followed up, or probed, whenever appropriate and skipped questions that the participant had already answered in response to a previous question. The list of topics towards the end of the guide is there to remind Deborah to ask about these topics if they do not come up as responses to earlier questions.

Guiding Questions

- Where and when were you born?
- How long were you married?
- What I'd like for you to do now is tell me about your experience with being a widow. You can begin wherever you like and include or leave out whatever you choose. I'm just interested in finding out about your experience. Could you tell me about this?
- What are your most vivid memories from the first few days after your husband died?
- How would you say your life has changed since your husband died?
- What has been the most difficult aspect of your life since his death?
- Is there anything that particularly surprised you?

that begins with "Don't you think . . .?" leads the participant to believe that there is a "correct" response. Naturally, the participant will try to supply you with the answer they think you want to hear. A loaded question is an emotionally charged question that makes an unqualified assumption about an individual. For example, if you ask "How many times have you done an illegal drug?" without establishing that the participant has ever taken an illegal drug, you have asked a loaded question. Often, loaded questions imply guilt, and they may cause participants to feel that they are being accused of wrongdoing.

Another type of question to avoid is the **double-barrelled question**. This type of question asks more than one thing at the same time: for example, "Do you respect your mother and your father?" In actuality, this question has combined two separate questions: "Do you respect your mother?" and "Do you respect your father?" Even more difficult than double-barrelled questions are complex questions that are long, with several phrases. By the end of hearing the question, the participant will have little idea of what you are asking. Remember that the structure of interview questions should be simple and direct so that the participant knows what you are asking.

Finally, avoid closed-ended questions (mentioned earlier), especially ones that lead to one of only two possible answers. Examples include "yes/no" questions and "either/or" questions. These types of questions are likely to shut down the participant. The exception to this rule is that you may use closed-ended questions when

- Have you ever lived alone before? What is it like?
- Has your relationship with your children changed since your husband died? How? What about your relationship with your friends?
- How would you say you have changed since your husband died?
- Do you remember the first time you thought of yourself as a widow?
- What are the most important things other people should know about the experience of being a widow?
- Are you doing okay financially?

Additional Topics

- Decisions
- Relations with men—wedding rings
- Weekends; difficult times
- Mothers as widows
- Church support

Final Question

- Is there anything that I haven't asked you about that I should have?

you plan to follow up with a more open-ended question, such as "How so?" You could, for example, ask members of a bobsleigh team if their parents supported them in their quest to make the Olympics and then immediately follow up with "How so?" or "What kinds of things did they do?"

Once you have located participants and written your interview guide, it is time to carry out your first interview. The next section provides some ideas about how to conduct the interview. Although you may feel a little nervous about conducting your first interview, interviewing participants can be the most pleasant, exhilarating, and fascinating part of doing qualitative research.

Doing Interviews

Thinking about the distinctive characteristics of in-depth interviews will help you to prepare for your first interview. To begin with, there is an intrinsic sense of reciprocity between the interviewer and the participant in an in-depth interview. So, in exchange for the stories and insights your participant offers, you should feel free to share your own ideas and details about yourself if your participant is interested. Next, the interview process carries with it a fundamental understanding that your participant is the expert on their own lived experience. Therefore, you should always ask for clarification if you think that you have misunderstood something that your participant has said or if you believe that your participant's meaning differs from your own. Finally, the structure of an in-depth interview is highly flexible. This flexibility is a particular strength of qualitative interviews because it allows you to deviate from your guide and probe into interesting topics as they surface.

When you are getting ready for an interview, you should focus on making a good impression. First, as when conducting a participant-observation study, make sure that you are dressed appropriately for the circumstance. For in-depth interviews, you want to look professional but unintimidating.

Second, always be on time. If you are unfamiliar with the interview location, get directions and use a map, an Internet resource, or GPS to plan your route. Give yourself plenty of time to travel. If you are using an online medium, be sure you have taken the time to figure out the technology in advance.

Third, ensure that you allot enough time for each interview. The conversation may last 30 minutes or three hours, and you don't want to make your participant feel rushed. Remember that your participant is giving you their time to share information, so you must reciprocate by giving them as much of your time as it takes to complete the interview.

Fourth, check that you have everything that you need. This may include an information letter or a consent form, a copy of the interview guide, and recording equipment. Make sure that you know how to use your equipment and that it works. Bring extra batteries or an extension cord as well as a pad of paper and pens in case your participant does not agree to be recorded.

Once you get to the interview location, focus on setting your participant at ease and making them feel confident that you know what you are doing. Deborah usually hands her information letter to her participant to read (which she will usually summarize if participants cannot read it themselves), and she makes small talk while she is setting up her recording equipment. Make sure to place the equipment where it will pick up both sides of the conversation—you will look unprofessional if you have to adjust the microphone once the interview begins. In addition, always accept tea or coffee when it is offered whether you want it or not. This provides a feeling of balance and informality to the interview. Once everything is ready, and you have discussed the contents of the information letter, the interview begins.

There are a number of things that you can do during the interview to encourage your participant to enjoy the encounter and to give you expansive answers. You should try to communicate your interest through your body language. Sit forward and look engaged. You want your participant to know that you think that their comments are important. In contrast, sitting back with your arms folded, listening with a blank expression on your face, or speaking in an uninflected voice communicates a lack of interest.

Nodding, saying "hmm," and repeating part of an answer or summarizing it will encourage the participant to elaborate or provide an example. You can also express genuine ignorance about what the person said, particularly in the case of jargon or a phrase that you are not familiar with. For example, one of the widows Deborah interviewed told her that she appreciated the support of her "church family." Deborah was unfamiliar with the term and asked her to explain it. She not only clarified her definition of the term as referring to the members of her congregation but also went on to explain how that group symbolized family to her.

Lisa-Jo, on the other hand, had spent five years living with participants by the time she engaged in formal interviews. When conducting interviews about air travel (van den Scott 2009), the participants knew that she was already familiar with the airport. Lisa-Jo, therefore, asked her participants to describe the airport to her as if she had never seen it before. Participants included many social interactions in their descriptions, and Lisa-Jo learned about how these conversations bracket, or begin and end, time spent out of the community.

You can also show that you are engaged in what your participant is saying by asking appropriate follow-up questions. To do this, you have to actively listen and think at the same time. It takes a great deal of concentration to conduct a rich interview, but the results will be well worth your effort.

Remember that it is your job to keep the interview on topic. Your participant may go off on a tangent that does not seem relevant, and you should be willing to listen when this happens, but it is always your job to bring the discussion back to the question at hand.

When you have run out of questions on a topic and plan to introduce a new one, use a transition to help your participant follow the development of the conversation. This transition may be as simple as "Moving on to another topic" or "Now I'd like to ask you about. . ."

Finally, don't fear pauses. Although many of us are uncomfortable with silence during a conversation, silence can give your participant a chance to compose their thoughts. Hence, when a participant stops speaking or takes a few moments to respond to a question, it often helps to simply wait longer than you ordinarily would before speaking. Avoid the impulse to jump in and clarify your question. Often, this will only cause confusion because you are likely to come up with a rewording that is more complex and convoluted than your original question. Only offer to reword the question if your participant asks for clarification.

What You Should Do after the Interview

After you have given your participant time to answer the interview's final question, it is time to thank the participant and put the equipment away. Participants often want to chat for a while after the interview. Always make time for post-interview discussion. Sometimes, participants bring up an entirely new, but important, topic after the recorder is turned off. When this happens, we usually ask permission to turn the equipment on again to record the comments. In the days following your interview, you may want to send a thank-you note to your participant. If you promise to send a copy of the recording or a transcript, make sure that you follow through.

As soon as possible, write your field notes. Include your thoughts on the interview process, comments on the participant's demeanour, and descriptions of anything they did. If your participant offered to give you a tour of their home, describe the incident in your field notes. Of course, do not include any details that the person asked you not to record. You will also want to transcribe your interview in full.

Transcribing Interviews

Researchers have different approaches to creating interview transcripts. Some believe in transcribing the whole interview, word for word, while others transcribe only what seems applicable to their own study. We belong to the first group. After all, how can you know what you need to transcribe before you have done your analysis? We even transcribe pauses, laughter, crying, and significant changes in pitch and volume. In addition, we include our own words to contextualize what the participant has said, since context can provide deeper meaning for analysis. For example, if Deborah asks a widower if he is interested in remarriage and he answers "yes," her question has elicited his answer. If she ask a widower a more general question such as "What is it like to be a widower?" and he says that he is interested in remarriage, he has revealed that he associates remarriage very strongly with the concept of being a widower.

Transcribing can be a very time-consuming, tedious process, but it also bears the fruit of deep familiarity with your data and can include euphoric moments of discovery. One hour of an interview may require four to seven hours to transcribe, depending on the available equipment and the skill of the transcriber. There are also transcribing apps that you might find useful. As with field notes, it is essential that you always keep at least one back-up copy of your interview transcripts in case you run into any unforeseen glitches. Deborah learned the importance of backing up her transcripts when, not too long ago, she had a computer problem and lost her digital files. Because she had printed out hard copies of the transcripts as she went along, Deborah was able to scan the pages and reconstruct her files. Had she not made a back-up copy, she would have lost hundreds of pages of data.

If you are lucky enough to have funding to pay for a transcriptionist or if you use a transcribing app, it is essential that you correct the transcripts yourself. This entails listening to the interview with the transcript in front of you, either in hard copy or on the computer screen, and correcting any errors that appear. This process will help you to become familiar with the content of the interview, which will in turn make the process of analysis easier. Deborah found that when she was writing *The Widowed Self: The Older Woman's Journey through Widowhood* (2001), she could "hear" the interviews whenever she read the transcripts because she had listened so carefully when she was correcting the pages.

Intimate familiarity is not the only reason to listen to the recording. Because the transcriber was not present during the interview and apps are not perfect, they may miss a subtle meaning that you picked up on. Hearing the recording for yourself can also help you to remember details that you forgot after you left the interview.

In addition, the transcriber might mishear or misinterpret what the participant said. For example, when Deborah was correcting one interview, she noticed that the transcript read, "I must have met a thousand Africans in my life." From what Deborah remembered about the woman whose transcript she was working with, she would have been surprised if she had met even one African. When Deborah listened to the interview, she discovered that what the widow had actually said was "I must have made a thousand afghans in my life." Now it made sense. A transcriber might also miss a small word, such as *not*. This is a simple error, but the loss of such an important word could change the entire meaning of your interview.

Listening to a recording of your interview will also give you a chance to revise your interview guide to prepare for your next interview. You should include topics that unexpectedly came up and remove or edit questions that did not work well. It is not unusual to develop several versions of an interview guide during the life of a study.

There is one final benefit to listening to the interview—it will help you to identify your strengths and weaknesses as an interviewer. This is a very important step to take when you are conducting your first interview study. In reviewing the session, you are likely to hear double-barreled questions, missed opportunities for follow-up, and times you spoke too soon to fill an awkward silence. As you do more interviews and critique your own performance, you will hone your skills and get better and better as an interviewer.

Innovations in Interviewing

Online Interviewing

Over the past 20 years, some researchers have conducted interview studies via email. These studies are different from the online surveys you may be familiar with because they entail a series of back-and-forth communications rather than a respondent answering a series of question in one go (Meho 2006). This type of study has some obvious advantages: it costs less to administer and does not need to be transcribed (Meho 2006); email interviews allow participants an opportunity to reflect on and edit their responses and give the researcher time to think about the response before sending follow-up questions or continuing on to the next question (Gibson 2010); and they allow researchers to collect data from people who are very busy, are geographically dispersed, and/or have a disability that might make it difficult for them to participate in a face-to-face interview.

Although on the surface conducting email interviews in our "email society" (Burns 2010) may appear easier than doing face-to-face interviews, there are some things to take into account before deciding to carry out an email-interview study. First of all, the study may take longer to conduct. Some participants will respond immediately to a follow-up question, while others may take days or weeks, and it can be challenging to discern the reason for a delay. When Sarah Hodgson (2004) conducted an email-interview study with self-injurers, she didn't know if someone who was taking a long time to reply was busy, thinking about a response, or in trouble. As well, emails are often "clipped conversation" (Burns 2010:11.7). The researcher often needs to find ways to encourage participants to write expansively. Finally, as you already know, without the non-verbal cues or tones of voice, it is easy to misunderstand the meaning of an email. Some researchers encourage their participants to use acronyms (such as *lol*) or emoticons (Meho 2006) to lessen the potential for misunderstanding.

In an email-interview study, some researchers send the entire interview guide in one email and leave spaces for responses, while others send one or two questions at a time. Bampton and Cowton (2002) suggest that when you send one question at a time, the interview is more interactive. They also note that it can be challenging to know when an interview is nearing an end, when the participant wants to be finished with the interview. Possible clues include longer intervals between your sending a question and receiving a response, shorter responses, and a decline in the "quality of responses."

Face-to-face interactions are sometimes impossible due to health risks, geography, or other barriers. In these cases, many researchers have moved interviews online. Interviews over online video platforms, such as Facetime, Zoom, Skype, or Messenger, naturally spiked during the global COVID-19 pandemic. While moving interviews online may seem an easy fix, there are still a number of things to consider beyond technological compatibility. It will be difficult to fully understand the context from which your participant is talking. Are there people off-screen? Is your participant being distracted by children or pets? How freely might a participant talk within their context? In addition, it may be challenging to read their body language and for them to read yours. You will have a kind of interaction different from what you otherwise might have, which may mean you gain information, but also may mean that you lose a fair bit of information. It takes practice to develop a rapport when in face-to-face situations, and those skills have to be tweaked for online interactions in which rapport may be more difficult to establish.

In some cases, you might want to combine in-person interviews with email, phone, or online interviews. Doing so would provide a wider range of participants. It does require the researcher to think carefully and adapt each interview to the method of conducting the interview.

As with adopting other technologies, it is worthwhile to hone your skills in face-to-face interviews before trying a method that mediates between you and your participants.

Photo Elicitation

Photo elicitation is a method of data-generation that combines aspects of visual sociology and interviewing. In this method, researchers display photographs and ask participants to comment on what they see. Sometimes researchers take the photographs themselves, but, as Marisol Clark-Ibáñez (2004) observes, this practice is more useful for deductive, theory-driven research than for inductive research because the researcher may take photos that grab their attention but are not particularly meaningful to the participants.

For qualitative researchers, it is more productive to ask the participants to take photographs that they find meaningful. Often, the researcher will ask participants to take photographs either of anything they find interesting or that focus on a particular aspect of life that relates to the research question as Ross and Buluing (2019) did for their study of the work involved with school parking access for families living with childhood disability that we looked at earlier in the chapter. Asking participants to take photographs serves two purposes: (1) it starts the participants thinking about the topic; and (2) it allows them to bring into the research what is meaningful to them (Keegan 2008). After the participants have taken the pictures, the researcher sits down with each participant to talk about how they decided to take each picture and what it means to them. This method is sometimes referred to as "photovoice" because the photos help participants to express what they want to say. Clark-Ibáñez (2004) explains that discussing photographs often leads to rich personal narratives.

John L. Oliffe and Joan L. Bottorff (2009) used photo elicitation in their study of men who had prostate cancer. They asked the men to take photographs as though they were mounting a photographic exhibition called "Living with My Prostate Cancer" and then discuss the pictures during an interview. Oliffe and Bottorff report that the "planning, introspection, and reflection" of the process led the men to develop fresh perspectives on their illness. The process also helped the men to overcome their reluctance to discuss their emotions by engaging them in a familiar activity and encouraging them to take charge as experts on the photographs.[3] Further, the photos elicited telling narratives about dichotomies, such as survivorship and mortality, that the men interwove with "details about fear, uncertainty, bravado, and hope" (2009:853). The process allowed the participants to set the agenda for the interview and thereby resulted in truly inductive research. Oliffe and Bottorff observe that a simple prompt, such as "tell me about this photograph," might result in a 20-minute commentary about the "meanings embedded in the photograph" (2009:853).

Elizabeth Mamali and Lorna Stephens (2020) wanted to find out what kinds of display same-sex couples used in their wedding ceremonies to negotiate wedding rituals that were rooted in heteronormative meanings and traditions (p. 1). They interviewed recently married couples together to produce "collaborative accounts" of their weddings. They also asked the couples to share photos from their wedding day, which "became an additional device for couples to communicate their experience and to share their story behind the picture" (p. 6–7) and provided a more nuanced view of the couple's meanings and experiences.

Box 6.3 describes a study that Heather Castleden carried out in partnership with the Huu-ay-aht First Nation of British Columbia. She adapted the method to a more appropriate process for working with Indigenous people. As she comments, by adapting the usual photovoice approach, she avoided the "academic trend of doing 'parachute'" research. Her study lasted six months, which allowed her to "establish rapport and build trust" (Castleden, Garvin, and Huu-ay-aht First Nation 2008:1401).

Box 6.3 Photovoice in Indigenous Research

II

Castleden et al. (2008) adapted photovoice to carry out research on the "meanings Indigenous peoples attribute to particular 'resources'" (Castleden 2007:105).
Heather Castleden wanted to avoid the mistakes Western researchers have previously
made (discussed earlier in this chapter). She, therefore, used a community-based
participatory research model to ensure that she would work in partnership with the
First Nation involved in the research. The community helped her to plan the research,
analyze her data, and keep the community informed of what she was finding.

Castleden (2007) provided community members with cameras and asked them to
take photos of the environment that were meaningful to them. She then asked them
to explain what the photos meant to them and which ones were the best representations. A particularly useful aspect of the research was the creation of posters and the
holding of potluck dinners when the community could find out about and discuss the
research as well as have ownership of the knowledge that resulted. In her write-up of
the research, Castleden shares a moving story:

> At the third potluck dinner, the research team displayed their third poster.
> One of the photographs on the poster was of the village's fire hall defaced by
> graffiti. The photographer's concern was not about the graffiti but about the
> need for more activities for Huu-ay-aht youth. Later that evening five youth
> were spotted in the cold winter rain with rags in their hands. They had been
> "caught" *cleaning* the graffiti from the fire hall. When asked why they were
> doing it, their response was "we saw the poster." Their actions were cap-
> tured on film and appeared on the fourth research poster along with a cap-
> tion indicating a sense of pride in the youths' actions. Community concerns
> became visible through the posters and were, in this case, catalysts for change.
> (2007:38)

At the time Castleden wrote her PhD dissertation, the Huu-ay-aht Council had already begun to use the findings to plan land-use protocols and in treaty negotiations.

Source: H.E. Castleden, 2007.

Summary

In this chapter, we looked at the distinctive aspects of qualitative interviews. We
delineated the differences between standardized and qualitative interviews and
saw how their different underlying assumptions suit them to uncovering different
types of data for different purposes. As well, we talked about how to conduct in-
depth interviews, including how to identify participants and design an interview
guide. As we learned, the participant is central to generating data in the interview
process. Once you have interviewed all of your participants, written up your notes,
and transcribed your interviews, the next step is to analyze your data—a process

we will discuss in Chapter 9. In Chapter 7, we will look at a method that combines attributes of interviewing and observation: focus groups. In the same chapter, we will also discuss talking circles, which are more appropriate to research with Indigenous peoples.

Key Terms

active interview
closed-ended (or forced-
    choice) question
double-barrelled question
feeling rules

in-depth interview
interview guide
open-ended question
photo elicitation
probes

random sampling
snowball sampling
standardized interview
validity

Questions for Critical Thought

1. Is there any group that you would like to examine in an in-depth interview study? How would you go about identifying individuals to participate in your study?

2. What would you do if you were presented with a sudden opportunity to conduct an interview "on the fly"? What strategies might you use to guide your interview?

3. How would you establish yourself as a professional in an interview setting? How might your approach differ if you were interviewing someone significantly older or younger than you are?

4. Some ethics committees insist on signed "informed consent" forms. Is there a time when it is not advisable or possible to use signed forms? How might you go about being confident that your participants are voluntarily and knowledgeably allowing you to interview them?

5. What might some of the advantages and disadvantages be in using alternatives to face-to-face interviews, such as email or video chatting? When might you choose one of these alternatives? What would you do to compensate for the fact that technology would be mediating your interactions?

Exercises

1. Visit the website for CBC Radio (www.cbc.ca/radio), and listen to a podcast of an interview. Think about what makes it a good or a bad interview. Identify good questions, double-barrelled and complex questions, leading questions, and loaded questions.

2. Develop a brief interview guide on a topic related to student life.

3. Interview a friend using the guide you developed in the previous exercise. Ask the friend which questions felt like good questions and which were ambiguous or made them feel uncomfortable. Revise your guide based on your conversation and on your own sense of how well the questions worked.

In-Class Exercise

Interview a classmate for 10 minutes about their best or worst class experience. Listen carefully, and follow up or probe when the opportunity arises.

Suggested Readings

Marjorie DeVault. 1990. "Talking and Listening from Women's Standpoint: Feminist Strategies for Interviewing and Analysis." *Social Problems* 37:96–117. This seminal article illustrates the shortcomings of using standardized interview strategies when interviewing women. DeVault's arguments have relevance for anyone considering an interview study.

Lisa-Jo K. van den Scott. 2016. "Mundane Technology in Non-Western Contexts: Wall-as-Tool." Pp. 33–53 in *Sociology of Home: Belonging, Community, and Place in the Canadian Context*, edited by Gillian Anderson, Joseph G. Moore, and Laura Suski. Toronto: Canadian Scholars Press. This book chapter provides an excellent and fascinating example of interview research with an Indigenous group. It demonstrates an understanding of the importance of relationship and respect between researcher and research participants. The chapter also illustrates the creativity of Inuit of Arviat, Nunavut, in the face of colonialism that attempted to destroy their way of life and world view.

James A. Holstein and Jaber F. Gubrium. 1995. *The Active Interview.* Thousand Oaks, CA: Sage. This influential and accessible book argues for an approach to interviewing that recognizes that an interview is an interpersonal accomplishment. It uses examples to show how to use the "how" of the interview as well as the "what" to understand the phenomenon under question.

Kathleen Steeves and Deana Simonetto. 2018. "'Show and Tell': Using Objects as Visual Interview Guides in Qualitative Interviewing." Pp. 178–84 in *The Craft of Qualitative Research*, edited by Steven W. Kleinknecht, Lisa-Jo K. van den Scott, and Carrie B. Sanders. Toronto: Canadian Scholars Press.

Related Website

Robert Wood Johnson Foundation, Qualitative Research Guidelines Project, Interviewing
www.qualres.org/HomeInte-3595.html
This web page provides brief descriptions of different types of interviews and useful summaries of when and how to use each type.

Notes

1. As long ago as 1956, Mark Benney and Everett C. Hughes noted, "There is an enormous amount of preparatory socialization in the respondent role—in schools and jobs, through the mass media—more and more of the potential respondents of the Western world are readied for the rap of the clipboard on the door" (1956:139).
2. For this reason, qualitative researchers often use the term *participant* instead of *interviewee*. After all, we participate together to accomplish an in-depth interview.
3. Researchers have found that men are often reluctant to talk about emotional events or situations when they are in an interview situation in which they feel they are not in control (see, for example, Schwalbe and Wolkomir 2001).

7

Focus Groups

Learning Objectives

- To become familiar with how focus-group research developed from its use in market research
- To learn how to plan focus groups
- To understand the difference between Indigenous talking circles and focus groups
- To learn how to conduct focus-group research
- To enrich findings by including the interactions in focus groups as data

---

Introduction

In the previous two chapters, we discussed field work and in-depth interviewing. In this chapter, we talk about **focus groups**, which incorporate aspects of both observation and in-depth interviewing. In this chapter, we first look briefly at the history of focus groups. We then look at how to plan a focus-group study, how to choose participants, and how to implement the groups. Along the way, we examine some studies and think about how we might conduct similar studies with Indigenous participants.

Focus groups are a type of qualitative interviewing that involves group discussions moderated by a researcher on a specific topic. These groups do not require consensus; rather, the researchers seek to study the discussion that participants carry out (Morgan 2008) to explore how a specific group of people discusses aspects of their lives. We can learn not only what individuals think about a particular topic but also how they talk about the topic with each other. A focus-group study involves a number of groups, and each group usually includes between six and eight participants.

Box 7.1 provides an example of a focus-group study that Deborah carried out with students about student culture. It includes an interaction among participants that opened a door to understanding how students talk among themselves about skipping classes.

Sociologists have been using group interviews since the 1920s, but Robert C. Merton and Paul Lazarsfeld carried out "ground breaking work" just before and during World War II that resembles what we call focus groups today. They called

Box 7.1 Interactions in Focus Groups: An Example

||||||||||||||||||||||||||||||||||||||||||||||||||||||||||||||||||||||||||||||||||||||||||||||||||||||||||||||||||||||||||||||||||||||||||||||||||||||||||||||||||||||||||||||||||||||||||||||

A few years ago, Deborah's university was considering implementing a core curriculum. They had invited people from other universities that had implemented such curricula to tell them about the models they used and their experience in adopting them. The faculty had had a number of retreats to discuss the ideas and wrestle with both the practicality and desirability of making such a major change.

One thing they could not know, however, was how their students would react to the implementation of a new curriculum. As we discussed in Chapter 2, professors often ascribe thoughts and attitudes to students without actually asking them what they think. To avoid this mistake, the university asked Deborah to carry out a focus-group study with their students to discover more about student culture (van den Hoonaard 2001): What did they think was the purpose of a university education? How did they decide how much work to do for their classes? What did they see as important? How much did they take part in university life outside of classes? By carrying out focus groups, they learned what the students thought about these questions, and they also learned how students talk about other topics—for example, skipping classes—with each other. The interactions that they observed taught them a lot about student culture.

A particularly interesting exchange took place among the students when one participant mentioned that they were amazed at how many students skip classes:

> I will admit I've skipped classes . . . not very many. But the amount of people that literally don't go to classes. And don't do their assignments. And slack off. And it's like, you are paying to come here. It's not like high school. . . . And it just seems so unreal to me, how people can not even care. And they're paying to be here. That really shocked me. . . . And I cannot believe that because why would you spend all that money and come here *not* to get your education?

Another participant in the group, K., reinforced this comment:

> I want to respond. . . . I'm in a class which is . . . required. . . . There is so many people signed into the course that we barely fit into the room. The first, two, three weeks, it was packed. Now, we're lucky to have 15 people. . . . It's crazy. *Attendance is counting. You need to know this material. What's going on?* [emphasis in original]

them "focussed interviews," and they were used to develop propaganda materials, to create training manuals for soldiers, and to "investigate basic social issues such as racial segregation in the armed forces" (Morgan 1997:38). Following these studies, focus groups became an important tool of market research.

Although market researchers continued to use focus groups, after 1950 they practically disappeared in sociology until 1984 when David L. Morgan and Margaret T. Spanish published "Focus Groups: A New Tool for Qualitative Research." They wrote that they were interested in studying the role of

So, we seem to have a simple matter of agreement that skipping class is unacceptable. But wait. In response to K.'s comments, S. began to list legitimate reasons for not going to a class:

> If I am up all night doing a paper . . . or I have an appointment or something . . . It's not because, "Oh, I just don't feel like going today."

K. agreed that it was okay to skip if you have a legitimate excuse:

> The only classes that I've ever missed apart from having a legitimate reason are my 8:30s because I just find it too difficult. . . . I can go, but I'm going to be half asleep. . . . So, there's no point.

This discussion between two focus-group members provided a window into students' decision-making when they are thinking about missing a class. If Deborah had been conducting an interview study, she might have taken what the first student said about skipping classes at face value and assumed that they never missed a class, but the response of another member of the group gave a context to their comments. The students' interaction may have resembled the type of conversation students have among themselves. It identified several justifiable reasons for skipping classes: staying up late to work on a paper the night before it is due, having an appointment, and having an 8:30 class, which is, by definition, too early to expect students to be awake and aware. It is this sort of interaction that is the hallmark of a focus-group study. Perhaps you and your friends might have had a similar conversation when you were deciding whether it was okay to skip a particular class.

You may also find it interesting to think about how your experience compares to those shared by participants in Michale Adorjan and Rosemary Ricciardelli's (2019) focus-group study of youths' practices of "privacy management" when using social networking sites. These researchers chose focus groups because they wanted to "provide a forum for interconnection and mutual sympathy" (p. 13). Adorjan and Ricciardelli noted that an "interesting dynamic" (p. 19) emerged during the focus group. Some of the participants talked about the security of using Snapchat, while others challenged that it was really secure. The researchers concluded that their participants had sophisticated methods of managing privacy while, at the same time, holding an I've got "nothing to hide" mindset (p. 21).

Source: D. K. van den Hoonaard, 2001.

socialization in how people find out about foreseeable life problems, particularly heart attacks. They were trying to figure out a way to create groups to discuss the issue when "fate . . . stepped in: a friend with a background in market research pointed out that we were in the process of inventing the focus group" (Morgan and Spanish 1984:256). Serendipity brought focus-group research back into the academic sphere.

Morgan (2012), himself, has charted the growth in popularity of focus groups since he and Spanish wrote their seminal article. He conducted a search of "sociological abstracts" and "psychological abstracts" and found only a "handful" of publications that used focus groups in the 1980s. By the end of the 1990s, however, he reports that more than 200 published articles per year were based on focus-group research. A current search of the Sociological Abstracts database results in over 40,000 publications that mention focus groups since 2000.

Initially, both market researchers and sociologists used focus groups primarily to help them design surveys. The quantitative components made up the substantial aspect of the research while the qualitative part was used only in deciding on the questions to include in the surveys. Currently, many social scientists use focus groups as a stand-alone method that allows them to study the everyday understandings of group members as well as the social processes through which they agree on, disagree on, and often construct new understandings of the research topic. Now that we have some background in the origins of focus-group research, let's talk about how to plan and carry them out.

Planning Focus Groups

A number of years ago, the national governing body of the Bahá'í community of Canada was interested in finding out the community's progress in implementing the teachings about the equality of women and men, a core teaching of their faith. They asked Will C. van den Hoonaard and Deborah to carry out a survey to explore the issue. They were intrigued because such a project would give them the opportunity to study a contemporary community that sees the establishment of gender equality as "a joint mutual effort" of both women and men (van den Hoonaard and van den Hoonaard 2006:3).

Although neither of them normally does survey research, they began to contemplate what questions they would ask on such a survey. No one knows what true gender equality looks like, but Bahá'í texts do contain many guidelines. They began to ask friends what questions they would include on such a survey. Their answers were thoughtful and intriguing, but they still didn't know what questions to ask. It occurred to them that this research question, by itself, was perfect for a focus-group study. It involved a topic that Bahá'ís were familiar with, cared deeply about, and had attempted to put into action in their lives. They, therefore, carried out a focus-group study that explored how Bahá'ís understand and think about their experiences with putting the Bahá'í teachings on equality into practice. They asked participants to talk about what questions they would include on a survey about the equality of women and men.

Focus groups are particularly appropriate when you are interested in learning about how people understand things that occur in their everyday lives or that they have thought about. For this reason, you would use focus groups only if the topics you were exploring were familiar to the participants. Indeed, focus groups work best when the participants are knowledgeable enough or have had enough experience to carry on a free-flowing conversation about the topic under study.

As well, for each focus group, researchers recruit participants who have at least some common characteristics (Litosseliti 2003).

Focus groups may also be useful for topics that participants care deeply about and may find hard to talk about in individual interviews. For example, Martinez-Serrano, Palmar-Santos, Solis Muñoz, Álverez-Placa, and Pedraz-Marcio (2018) used focus groups when they wanted to understand midwives' experiences involving delivery care in the face of late foetal death. The researchers explain that the focus groups provided a supportive environment where "discourses that have been silenced can be aired because there is an understanding that is difficult to achieve in individual interviews" (p. 132). Through the discussion the midwives had during the focus groups, two themes emerged: That the midwives saw themselves as "professionals for life not death" and that they faced challenges "organizing the work without guidelines" (p. 129). Interestingly, the researchers also found that there was a gender bias that involved midwives' greater focus on the mother's loss than the father's rather than an equal focus on both parents.

Talking Circles

If you are considering doing research with an Indigenous community, however, **talking circles** may be more appropriate than focus groups. They avoid the possibility that a few assertive individuals may dominate the discussion (Bagele 2012:212). Talking circles originated among the Woodland Tribes in the midwest, where they were used as a parliamentary procedure, and they have a sacred meaning for many Indigenous communities (Lavallé 2009).

Today, talking circles have many uses, including healing interventions. If you have taken part in a talking circle, you know they involve passing around a small object, perhaps a stone or a feather, that has a symbolic and, sometimes, sacred meaning. Each group member who receives the object has the choice of responding to the topic or remaining silent and passing it on to the next member. No one is allowed to interrupt the speaker who is holding the object (Running Wolf and Richard 2003).

Chilisia Bagele (2012:213) writes that talking circles, based on the idea of participants' respect for one another, can serve as a "focus-group method derived from postcolonial Indigenous world views." When planning talking circles, researchers dialogue with the participants regarding the "cultural symbols to be used and the ground rules associated with the symbolism, which should guide the discussion" (Bagele 2012:221).

Box 7.2 describes how Rebecca Hall (2016) used talking circles as part of her research when she was studying the impact of diamond mines on the Indigenous peoples of the Northwest Territories.

Some researchers think that a focus-group study is an easy, short way to collect data from a number of individuals at the same time, but such studies require a great

Box 7.2 Using Talking Circles with Indigenous Communities

Rebecca Hall was planning a study of how diamond mines had affected the way Indigenous women in the Northwest Territories (NWT) provided caring labours to their families and communities. The Native Women's Association of the NWT helped her to design and carry out her research and provided both support and ongoing advice and insight. Hall, a non-Indigenous woman, recognized and valued their expertise. She had not originally planned to use talking circles because she was concerned that the women might be uncomfortable. However, the Native Women's Association and other community groups felt that hosting talking circles could provide learning and development for the community. Therefore, they held two talking circles that included between 15 and 20 people. Hall writes that "[m]ore than a focus group, these events were spaces for community members . . . to come together to share their experience of the diamond mines" (2016:223).

She and the Native Women's Association of the NWT cooked lunch for participants of the talking circles with "the aim of creating a warm and inclusive atmosphere" (2016:223). They followed the Indigenous tradition of having a community leader lead the circles. Indeed, rather than speaking during the groups, Hall made poster boards with the questions on them. She notes:

> Displaying the questions . . . rather than posing [them] orally and consecutively allowed the participants to respond to one another freely while personally reflecting upon the questions and voicing their thoughts at the time of their choosing.

The talking circles were very useful. They led to "richer insights and learning" because the participants were able to build on one another's thoughts. They shared approaches to dealing with hardship and community-building strategies "to move beyond (material and cultural) resource extraction dependency" (2016:224).

The findings from the talking circles, as well as other data Hall collected, allowed her to move beyond the deficit model that assumes that any problems Indigenous people have reflect some inner weakness or inferiority. This destructive and inaccurate way of thinking had characterized earlier approaches to Indigenous research. Hall notes that Indigenous women's social reproductive labour "holds within it both the violent colonial oppression and exploitation, and the *creative* labours of resistance, growth and possibility" (2016:228). Hall does not ignore the problems caused by colonialization; rather, she includes them and identifies how the Indigenous women she worked with have used their culture and strength to go forward.

Source: Rebecca Hall, 2016.

deal of thought, planning, and, sometimes, expense. David L. Morgan (1997:7) reminds us that we need to make these decisions: "Whom will you talk to? How will you recruit them? What questions should you ask? How will you moderate the groups? How will you analyze the data?" Let us think about each of these questions.

Whom Will You Talk To?

When Deborah and Will van den Hoonaard were carrying out their focus-group study on the equality of women and men, they wanted to get a sense of what was going on nationally, so they sought 12 groups from across the country. They wanted each group to involve participants who knew each other and to have groups that represented rural and urban communities, anglophone and francophone communities, youth, and Iranian Bahá'ís who had immigrated to Canada. These groups captured the diversity of the national community. Deborah and Will had also hoped for an Indigenous focus group but were unable to convene one.

Morgan (1997:67) calls poor recruiting the "Achilles heel" of focus groups because if the members of each group are not compatible, there will not be a rich discussion. Therefore, most focus-group researchers suggest that each group should be made up of participants with common characteristics because people are likely to share their personal views and disclose more to people they see as like themselves (Litosseliti 2003). Because the goal is to generate discussions that are free-flowing, the composition of each group should encourage active participation among all members. Hence, some researchers have separate groups for men and women because men tend to dominate in mixed-gender groups (Litosseliti 2003). In the case of Deborah's study for the university, she formed separate groups for first-year and fourth-year students to ensure members of each group had a similar level of experience as a university student.

In addition, it would be unwise to include participants who have different statuses in the same group. For example, you would not put supervisors and front-line workers into the same focus group because the front-line workers might be silenced by having their work superiors in on the discussion. Deborah and some colleagues discovered this when they were looking at how care workers managed lifting residents in a nursing home. Given the limited number of staff available, they often had to bend the rules to accomplish their work. The care workers were happy to talk about how they "worked around" the rules when necessary, but they became silent when their supervising nurses were in the room.

Similarly, issues of status might work differently in different cultural groups. Wooksoo Kim (2009), for example, carried out a study to explore drinking culture among elderly Korean immigrants in Canada. She understood that status and power and "modesty and respect for elders" (p. 342) would affect how participants interacted in the focus groups. Kim, therefore, was careful to exclude individuals who held a high position in the seniors' organization to which participants belonged. If she had wanted to find out what high-status individuals thought, she might have convened a group just for them.

There are situations for which it is appropriate to seek naturally occurring groups. In the 1990s, Jenny Kitzenger (1994) wanted to study how different audiences understood media messages about AIDS (acquired immune deficiency syndrome). She conducted this study at a time when there was a great deal of misunderstanding about AIDS and how it was contracted. Kitzenger decided to work with groups that already existed, "clusters of people who already knew each other through living, working or socialising together" (1994:105). By convening groups of those who might "naturally discuss" the topic, she felt they would be able to "tap into fragments of interactions" that might actually take place during the course of the participants' everyday lives.

How Will You Recruit Them?

As with in-depth interviewing, you will need to think about how you will go about finding participants for the focus groups. The recruiting is a little different because you are looking for people who know something about your topic. If you want to find out about diverse groups, as Deborah and Will van den Hoonaard did with their equality study, you will likely want to make each group homogeneous in some ways and each group different from the others.

When recruiting for focus groups, you can use the same strategies that we discussed in Chapter 6. You might, for example, use snowball sampling, whereby you locate one individual and ask that person to help you find others. If we wanted to do a focus-group study about book clubs, we might find a member of one club and see if that person might help us to recruit members of that club for a focus group.

You might have to try a few other methods to find participants. When Beverly Holbrook and Peter Jackson (1996) were looking for participants for their study of shopping, they wanted to talk to ordinary people rather than to experts. They initially used a traditional marketing-research method that involves calling potential participants. When they were unsuccessful, they turned to settings where people would ordinarily meet, talk, and socialize, including mother and toddler centres, seniors' homes, and job clubs.

When Deborah and Will conducted their equality study, they depended on the national governing body to identify appropriate communities that would have the demographic profiles they were interested in. They found individuals eager to participate. In some cases, this eagerness resulted in larger groups than they might have liked, but they had to be flexible. Michele Crossley (2002) had a similar challenge. When she was studying women's reactions to health-promotion strategies, she over-recruited for each group because it is common for potential participants to drop out at the last minute or not show up. Not only did all the women show up for her focus groups, one brought her sister and a friend along. Hence, the groups were larger than the ideal six to eight participants. In the crucial interest of maintaining rapport, she worked with the larger groups, one of which had 13 participants, and did not turn anyone away.

Attempts to recruit may give you information about your participants. When Deborah tried to recruit students using their university email addresses, she discovered that not only did few respond, but not very many recipients even opened the email invitation. This information was useful to the university, for it learned that using email was not an effective way to communicate with students at that time.

Once people have agreed to participate in the study, it is a good idea to send them a follow-up message that includes the date, time, and place that the focus group will take place. If you have offered to cover transportation, babysitting, or other costs, or if you are providing a modest honorarium, this message should remind the participants of these details. A brief agenda and your contact information would also be useful to include in the follow-up message.

What Questions Will You Ask?

Many of the principles of writing qualitative interview questions are appropriate for a focus-group guide. The questions should be open-ended and address the question(s) you are interested in answering. And, as in an interview study, it's a good idea to brainstorm relevant questions and how to sequence them (Litosseliti 2003). Ten questions are probably sufficient. As in interviewing, the questions should be clear, understandable, and not loaded. (See Chapter 6 to refresh your memory on designing qualitative interview questions.)

Because the goal is to develop questions that elicit spontaneous discussion among participants (Kidd and Parshall 2000), there are some differences in designing a focus-group topic guide. Focus groups "sacrifice details about each individual in favor of engaging the participants in active comparisons of their opinions and experiences" (Morgan 1997:33). The early questions, therefore, should get the participants talking. Simple, non-threatening questions will help them to feel relaxed. Litosseliti (2003:59) recommends using "uncued questions such as 'Tell me about . . .'" to get participants talking. Such questions are also useful for changing topics.

As with in-depth interviews, the guide should include transitional questions or statements, such as, "Changing subjects, let's talk about . . ." Then, as the session winds down, you may want to include a summarizing question, such as "What were the most important aspects of our conversation?" Finally, at the end of the focus group, it's a good idea to ask if you have missed anything or if there's something important the group hasn't talked about. As in interviews, the final question might open the door to a whole new aspect of the topic that you hadn't anticipated.

Box 7.3 provides the guide that Deborah and Will van den Hoonaard used in their study of equality of men and women in the Bahá'í community of Canada. Before launching into the questions, the **moderator** started by going around the table and asking participants to introduce themselves. The moderator also stressed that there were no right or wrong answers and that participants should feel free to respond to each other's ideas.

Box 7.3 Sample Topic Guide

If you were putting together a questionnaire to find out how the Canadian Bahá'í community is doing in its effort to implement the principle of the equality of men and women, what questions would you include that would tell us how we are doing?

1. What kinds of questions would you ask about families?
2. What kinds of questions would you ask about local Bahá'í communities? Consultation?
3. What kinds of questions would you include about children and youth?
4. What kinds of questions would you ask about the public face of the Bahá'í community?
5. How can men encourage women?
6. In what areas are we doing well in implementing equality? What do we need to work on?
7. What personal experiences have you had in the Bahá'í community that show equality? Inequality?
8. What are you doing personally to promote equality between women and men?
9. Is there anything else that we should be talking about that would tell us more about the equality of men and women in your Bahá'í community and personal experience?
10. Any final comments?

How Will You Moderate the Groups?

When you are planning your study, you will need to decide whether you will moderate the focus groups yourself or hire a professional, as many researchers do. Moderating focus groups requires skill and experience, and Morgan (1997) notes that although professional moderators do have valuable experience, it is a myth that you cannot carry out good qualitative research. Nonetheless, effective moderating is crucial to successful groups because it has a direct impact on the quality of the data.

Just as it is problematic if there is a power differential among participants, it is worthwhile to give some thought to possible power differentials between the moderator and the participants (Litosseliti 2003). It is for this reason that Indigenous community members often facilitate talking circles. When we were planning the focus-group study on student culture, for example, we decided that Deborah would not moderate the groups. We were concerned that if the moderator were a professor, the students might give answers that they thought would be acceptable to professors. We therefore chose a graduate student from a university close by who would not intimidate the participants.

The moderator needs to understand the culture and traditions of the focus-group participants as well as the research topic. Deborah and Will van den

Hoonaard discovered the usefulness of this knowledge when they were conducting their study on the equality of women and men. As mentioned above, they included a group composed of Iranian immigrants. The group was facilitated by an Iranian woman and in Persian. For whatever reason, she did not use the topic guide that they had designed from their own Western perspective. Her improvised moderation not only resulted in a successful group, it also shed light on Deborah and Will's own ethnocentric assumptions about the meaning of gender equality.

The moderator's job is to guide the focus groups with as little intervention as possible while maintaining the group's focus, ensuring that the major topics are addressed and that no one person dominates the conversation (Litosseliti 2003). Lia Litosseliti (2003:42) has provided a list of qualities and characteristics of a good moderator:

- Familiarity with moderating focus groups
- Affinity to the task
- Ability to listen sincerely and inspire people to talk
- Ability to maintain enthusiasm and interest
- Curiosity and respect for the participants
- Good interpersonal communication and managing skills
- Ability to appear neutral so as not to steer the conversation
- Confidence and the ability to be in control, while staying flexible and adaptable

Although this list of characteristics may seem daunting, if you take the time to practise and prepare, you will likely be an effective moderator.

As we saw with Rebecca Hall's (2016) research, it is useful for a respected community member to lead an Indigenous talking circle. The characteristics of that person should mesh with those recognized by the particular cultural group. Similarly, Ashely Goodman and colleagues, in partnership with an Indigenous community organization (2017, 2018), used talking circles to study the health care and research experiences of urban Indigenous peoples in Vancouver who had used illicit drugs and/or alcohol. They decided that the talking circles should be facilitated by board members of the community organization who were peers of the focus-group participants. These community researchers initiated the discussions by "sharing their personal experiences with research and as an Indigenous person who uses illicit drugs and/or alcohol, and who lives in the DTES [Downtown East Side of Vancouver]." During the talking circle, an eagle feather was held by the speaker "signifying a space to speak without interruption" (p. 4). Participants, who said that they had been "researched to death" found that the talking circles "provided a safe space to talk candidly about their personal experiences," in contrast to their usual experience with research, which usually resulted in telling researchers what they wanted to hear.

Having an assistant moderator or observer is also useful. This person is there to take detailed notes, operate equipment such as recorders, and make sure that the participants are comfortable. Because understanding the social process of interaction among focus-group participants is a fundamental goal of the study, the observer's notes regarding "revealing or eloquently expressed comments" and participants' non-verbal behaviour are crucial. The notes regarding gestures, laughter, posture, and so on will capture aspects of the conversation that participants found challenging, exciting, or disturbing. They may also capture the exhilaration of discovery of a new way of understanding an aspect of the topic that arises through the group's discussion. The notes also include the seating plan and link a quote to a particular speaker, which can be difficult if you only have an audio recording of the meeting (Kidd and Parshall 2000; Litosseliti 2003:68). If there is no observer, it is necessary to write detailed field notes immediately following the group to avoid forgetting these nuances.

Conducting Focus Groups

Now that you have chosen a topic, decided on and recruited the participants, designed a topic guide, and made decisions about whether you or someone else will moderate your focus groups, it is time to get ready to conduct the groups. Lia Litosseliti (2003) recommends convening a pilot focus group to try out your topic guide. The themes that members of the group bring up or focus on will help you to revise the guide and provide a sense of the interactions you can expect. Conducting the group also provides an opportunity to try out the practical logistics, such as where to place microphones and how to seat people around the table. Whether or not you conduct a pilot focus group, you will want to revise your topic guide after each group based on what you discover.

Doing Advance Planning

In advance of your focus groups, you need to make plans regarding logistics. Most often, researchers arrange for a room that has an oval table and comfortable chairs and that also accommodates serving refreshments. Your university likely has rooms that would fit the bill. The goal is to create a friendly atmosphere that encourages informality. Unless it's a seminar room, you would not be happy with a classroom, which would create a hierarchical atmosphere with the moderator at the front; as well, participants would not be facing each other.

Focus groups are most often audio-recorded. As the researcher, you need to decide where to place the recorder and microphones. The microphone should be visible but not in the way, and you might want to use more than one microphone to ensure that you can hear all the participants. If you know that someone in the group has a fairly soft voice, you will want that person to sit close to a microphone. It's also a good idea to think about where men and women will sit if you have a mixed-gender group. Men's voices are often louder, so men can be seated farther away from the microphone.

Experienced focus-group researchers recommend arriving 30 to 45 minutes in advance of the group to set things up (Litosseliti 2003; Morgan 1997). Often, some eager participants will arrive early, and the room should be ready when they walk in. Before the participants arrive, you should set up and check the equipment, make any changes necessary in the room to create the atmosphere you want, put name tags around the table, and have any handouts and refreshments ready. Greeting each participant in a warm and relaxed way as they arrive will encourage open and friendly participation (Litosseliti 2003:69–70). Such preparation gives the participants confidence in the process.

Getting Started on the Right Foot

The first few minutes of the focus group will set the tone for the rest of the discussion, so the early moments are important. At the outset, the moderator should explain that the participants have been invited to the group because they have something to say about the topic and that they have something in common, perhaps being first-year students. If the participants don't know each other, the moderator goes around the room and asks them to introduce themselves. The moderator should let them know that the purpose of the group is for everyone to exchange ideas in an informal and relaxed way. There are no right or wrong answers, and reaching a consensus isn't necessary. The moderator should also point out the ground rules of not interrupting each other and giving everyone an opportunity to say something. It's a good idea to ask people to turn off their phones and to put them away rather than place them on the table where they're likely to be distracting. It's also important to point out the recording equipment and explain that each person's contributions will be confidential (Litosseliti 2003:71). The moderator will want to edit their remarks so that they sound natural. Box 7.4 provides an example of what the introduction might look like.

Confidentiality among focus-group members is more complicated than in in-depth interviews, for which the interviewer promises not to divulge any information that would connect the participant to the research. Morgan (1997:91, 93) suggests that researchers take into account the appropriate level of self-disclosure among participants and set limits on how far the discussion should go. He advises that the researcher remind the participants that they already know each other (if they do) and that their contact will continue afterwards. Morgan also points out that a "useful way to set boundaries" is to encourage participants to imagine how they will feel about what they have said the morning after the discussion. The moderator should ask the participants to honour confidentiality for the focus group. Some research ethics boards may require the researcher to ask participants to sign a confidentiality agreement. If that's the case, it will be useful to think about a way to introduce the form without adding a layer of formality to the process.

Box 7.4 Sample Focus-Group Introduction

Welcome and thank you for taking the time to attend our focus group. The purpose of the group is to discuss your ideas, opinions, and experiences on the topic of
_____. Your discussion will be very helpful for my study, and, after the session, you
are welcome to ask me any questions you have about it and about our discussion.

You have been invited because you have something in common (for example,
you are all first-year students) and because you likely have thought about and have
experience with the topics we will discuss.

The idea of the focus group is to allow you to share your views in a relaxed and
informal environment. There are no right or wrong answers but, rather, different
points of view, all of which are important. What you say, how you say it, and how
much you say is up to you. Don't worry about what you are expected to say or
whether you agree with others in the group. We are not trying to reach a consensus
or find out a correct answer. Please make sure you allow others to speak, and don't
interrupt others.

I am recording our discussion so that I don't miss anything anyone says. I should
remind you that your contributions will be confidential and that I will not use your
name in any publications.

Our meeting will last about an hour. During that time, we will explore a number
of issues on the topic and listen to what everyone has to say about it. Please feel free
to ask questions relating to the topic during the discussion and to respond directly
to each other.

Let's start by going around the table, introducing ourselves.

Source: This example is based on Litosseliti, 2003.

Getting to the Heart of the Matter

Once the moderator has introduced the group and conducted any icebreaker exercises, it is time to get down to discussing the topic at hand. As the discussion gets
going, the moderator is looking to establish an informal, open atmosphere in which
all the participants feel comfortable participating and freely expressing their opinions. Hydén and Bülow (2003:311) suggest that the moderator encourage people to
talk as though they were on a coffee break. Litosseliti (2003:72) refers to this early
part of the group as the "forming stage."

Jocelyn A. Hollander (2004:620) has pointed out that "the first person to speak
or to speak at length" often sets the tone or the direction of the whole discussion.
This person often has higher status or power and will "tend to contribute more 'successful' topics," those that others will take up. Not surprisingly, in mixed-gender
groups the topics preferred by men tend to dominate, thereby making these groups
similar to all-male groups. This phenomenon is one reason that researchers often
prefer separate groups for each gender identity.

As the conversation continues, participants may be testing each other and trying to create an impression of the kind of person they are (Goffman 1959). Some may be attempting to establish themselves as leader of the group while others say very little. There are several strategies you might use to avoid having one person dominate the discussion. Holbrook and Jackson (1996:140) noted that when they had an established leader in the group, they would attempt to "co-opt" that person into the "process of leading the group without inhibiting" others from expressing their own points of view.

Lia Litosseliti (2003) provides concrete suggestions for dealing with "self-appointed talkers," "dominant talkers," and "ramblers" (Krueger 1994 as cited in Litosseliti 2003:74), who tend to take up a great deal of time and silence others. She suggests that the moderator might discourage them by avoiding eye contact, not acknowledging their contributions, calling on other participants, and asking others carefully worded questions about what they think. The moderator can address the opposite challenge of shy participants by making eye contact with them or nodding encouragingly. These issues would not be a challenge in Indigenous talking circles because each member has an opportunity to speak when they are holding the symbolic object and members do not interrupt each other.

To avoid the tendency of focus groups to produce conformity (Morgan 1997), the moderator can ask probing questions: "What do others think?" "Do others agree?" "Has anyone had a different experience?" "Does anyone see things differently?" As the conversation continues, the moderator should continually encourage the participants to explore how they are both similar and different from each other. Morgan (1997:12) writes that in the process of "sharing and comparing," the participants do much of the work for the moderator.

Litosseliti (2003) identifies the middle stages of the focus group as the "norming" and "performing" stages. She writes that during these two stages the participants work together as a team to address the issue and are interactive and productive. They value each other's points of view. During these stages, they are likely to come up with new ideas and ways of thinking about the issues under discussion. The moderator can say very little if the group is moving smoothly.

One of the moderator's goals is to avoid being too controlling. Each group has its own dynamic, and some groups will be more lively and enthusiastic than others. In Deborah and Will's study of the equality of women and men, for example, some groups were made up of people who knew each other well and had worked together before. They tended to be very relaxed and shared jokes and experiences freely. Groups that knew the researchers addressed some comments and laughter towards them even though they weren't there. Finally, groups in which the participants didn't know each other well tended to be more cautious, with the members being careful not to inadvertently hurt each other's feelings. As David Morgan (1997:10) has pointed out, "it's *your* focus, but it's *their* group."

As the group reaches what Litosseliti (2003) calls the "adjourning stage," it is time for the moderator to wind things up. They might summarize the discussion and ask if anyone has anything to add to the summary. The last question, as always, requests the participants to bring up any topics the group has not addressed. If a response leads to a rich discussion, it might be a good idea to add the new topic to the discussion guide for future groups. Finally, the moderator can invite questions the participants might have about the research itself.

As the participants are leaving, the moderator and observer should thank them for attending. The objective is for the participants to feel satisfied that their viewpoints have been heard and that they have had an opportunity to think about the issue in a new way. At the end of several of the focus groups on gender equality, the participants were so enthusiastic that they asked the researchers to consider conducting a similar study on racial harmony, another principle of their faith.

When a focus group is working well, the moderator has little to do besides sit back and listen. Indeed, Holbrook and Jackson (1996:139) noted that there were times during their focus groups about shopping that it "felt as if they were eavesdropping" rather than leading the groups.

Analyzing the Data and Group Interactions

As editors and reviewers for academic journals, both Deborah and Lisa-Jo have read a lot of manuscripts, many based on focus-group research. We agree with Jenny Kitzenger (1994:104), who notes that when you read some of these reports, "[I]t is hard to believe there was ever more than one person in the room at the same time." The distinctive characteristics of focus groups are lost when researchers analyze the data as though the interactions among members of the groups were not meaningful.

In Chapter 6, we discussed the underlying premise of the active-interview approach (Holstein and Gubrium 1995) that interviews are a social process through which participants make meaning. Similarly, Hollander (2004:611) argues that participants in focus groups do not come into the groups with "stable underlying attitudes and opinions." Rather, they are socially constructed through interaction. Hence, the interactions that include "conformity, group think, and social desirability" are the data in focus-group research. Let's look at some examples of how researchers have included interactions within focus groups in their analysis.

Jenny Kitzenger's (1994) focus-group study examined the effect of media messages about AIDS. As we discussed earlier, her focus groups comprised people who knew each other. She found that the participants developed their points of view in relation to others' perspectives. In addition, her analysis showed how people used their own ideas, how their personal stories operated and were mobilized in interaction, and what those stories achieved. By carefully analyzing these interactions, Kitzenger was able to understand how people challenge each other's assumptions through questioning and what kinds of evidence they use to support their own ideas and to sway others.

Through looking at these aspects of interaction and "turning points" in the discussions, Kitzenger concluded that people changed their minds in response to personal evidence communicated through anecdotes or the behaviour of professionals rather than evidence from leaflets or advertisements (1994:115). The interaction brought to light a "hierarchy of credibility" among different types of sources of information.

Based on her experience, Kitzenger suggests that researchers include codes in their data analysis for different types of interaction. Such codes could be questions, cited sources (by participants), deferring to others' opinions, and changes of mind. Using codes allows the researcher to capture both the substance of what is said and the interactions among participants.

Wooksoo Kim (2009), in her study of drinking among Korean immigrants, shows how members of a focus group can reinforce one member's idea and construct a new understanding among the participants. She cites the following exchange:

> I think all of us [who are drinking] are probably addicted. . . . I feel empty without alcohol . . . that is already an addiction.
>
> Yes, you are right. . . . We all are light addicts.
>
> Yeah, that's right. If we go through close examination, I am an addict. (2009:347)

This excerpt demonstrates not just agreement but also how, as the discussion unfolds, the second and third participants seem to be developing the idea that anyone who likes alcohol has addictive tendencies.

Hollander (2004) takes this approach one step further by suggesting that we ask of the data not only what is said by whom but also what is not said and who is silent in the group. These absences can be as informative as what is said. Hollander (1997) had conducted a study on how people experienced and understood violence that included 13 focus groups, a third of which were all male, all female, and mixed, respectively. She tells a story of running into one of the group members some time later who told her that she had not disclosed having been raped because her group was composed mostly of men and she thought it would make them uncomfortable if she raised the issue. In addition, the group took place at the woman's workplace, where, she felt, bringing up her experience would be awkward. This conversation led Hollander to think more deeply about how the social and relational contexts affected the discussion in the focus groups.

Hollander also identifies the issue of participants' "invention or exaggeration of experience" in a group (2004:622–24). This phenomenon occurred in a focus group made up of members of a university fraternity who lived together and knew each other well. This group's discussion was different from that of any other group. The first participant who spoke in the group talked about violence between him and his father; they had gotten into a fistfight. Hollander notes that this story set the tone for the rest of the session. Other participants followed by telling stories about violence that they had been involved in. This was the only group in which a theme was commission of violence. In every other group, the discussion revolved around victimization, fear of victimization, and how to avoid becoming a victim. Interestingly, participants had filled out a survey before the groups started, and none of the incidents that came up during the discussion had been mentioned on the surveys. Hollander suggests that a combination of the gender and associational and conversational contexts "encouraged the men to exaggerate their violent exploits and mute their experiences of victimization and fear" (p. 624). As Deborah read the report of this group, she was reminded of how men might try to outdo each other in tales of sexual conquest. Hollander suggests that the pressure on young men to differentiate themselves from women to demonstrate their masculinity "encouraged narratives that would boost participants' apparent conformity to hegemonic masculine experiences" (p. 625). As we discussed above, when the first participant sets a particular tone, it creates a precedent for what follows.

A last example comes from the focus-group study of the equality of women and men in the Bahá'í Community of Canada. There are two aspects of the interaction that stand out. The first involved the gender dynamics of the discussion. The second involved the **career** of the discussion.

As we have noted, in mixed-gender groups men are likely to dominate the discussion, to talk more than women (Aries 1996), and the topics they bring up tend to be taken up by the group. Therefore, when Deborah and Will analyzed the focus-group discussions, they paid attention to who talked the most, who responded first, who interrupted whom, whose statements were affirmed or not affirmed and by whom, who diverted attention away from the topic, who asked for clarifications, and who made statements that would close off the discussion of a particular question.

Some of the dynamics were similar to what others have found. Women were most likely to interrupt other women, and men were least likely to interrupt other men. Men were also more likely to divert the discussion onto another topic, to express puzzlement about a topic, and to make a summary statement that indicated they thought it was time for the group to move onto another topic.

Although these dynamics fit the patterns others have noticed, Deborah and Will also found aspects of the interaction that indicated a more equal approach. Women were likely to be the first speaker in response to a question, the pattern of men's and women's not affirming each other's statements was low, and men were as likely to affirm statements made by women as those of other men (van den Hoonaard and van den Hoonaard 2006:239).

When they were analyzing the focus-group transcripts, Deborah and Will noticed that the discussions tended to have a career that was consistent across groups. Career, in sociological terms, refers to the stages a social group passes through. In this case, the focus groups often started with the assertion that there was no problem with the principle of the equality of women and men in the Bahá'í community. When this claim was contradicted by some members of the group, the discussion moved on to statistical measures: What is the percentage of women and men on the elected governing bodies or who acted as public speakers at meetings?

As the discussion continued, the groups began to think more deeply. At this point, the discussions centred on equality in the family or in other aspects of life. There were pauses and silences as the groups struggled with gaining a deeper awareness. Then, suddenly, one member of the group recalled an event that seemed to involve inequality. The impact of that insight was profound. In each instance, the group then recognized aspects of gender inequality it had not observed. This pattern was so common that when they were reading the groups' transcripts, Deborah and Will would anticipate such moments and write "Bingo!" on the transcript where it occurred. Their concentration on the interaction led to insights that they would not have had, had they looked only at the substance of each person's comments.

Summary

In this chapter, we looked at how to plan and implement focus-group research. We saw how focus groups combine the attributes of field research and in-depth interviews and how talking circles may be more appropriate for Indigenous research. We discussed the decisions researchers make about whom to include in their focus groups and how to recruit members. We then looked at the characteristics of good moderators and how to carry out rich focus-group discussions. Finally, we looked at some examples of how some researchers have used the interactions in focus groups to enrich their findings. Chapter 9 explains, in detail, how to go about analyzing qualitative data. But before we learn about data analysis, let us examine methods of data collection that do not rely on direct interaction with participants. Chapter 8 will discuss unobtrusive research.

Key Terms

career
focus groups

moderator
talking circles

Questions for Critical Thought

1.   What do you see as the major advantages of focus groups? What are the disadvantages?

2.   If you were to do focus-group research, do you think you would moderate the focus groups yourself? What characteristics do you have that would make you a good or a poor moderator?

3.   Do you think it's a better idea for the composition of focus groups to be mixed or the same gender? What are your reasons for this opinion?

4.   What are the main differences between focus groups and talking circles?

5.   What are some situations that might intimidate participants in a focus group or talking circle? How can those situations be avoided?

Exercises

1. Try your hand at designing a discussion guide for a focus-group study of student culture at your university.

2. Decide whom you would recruit to be members of your focus-group study on student culture. Think about what the composition of each group should include.

3. Organize and moderate a focus-group discussion on student culture. Discuss the challenges you encountered as well as what you learned. If it's practical, each student in the class might moderate one group and then compare their experiences.

In-Class Exercise

Create breakout groups of three or four, and have a discussion about the pros and cons of using a computer to take class notes. Every five minutes, take turns sitting out the discussion, and have the person sitting out take notes on the interaction and how it influences the opinions of the group members.

Suggested Readings

Lynn F. Lavallé. 2009. "Practical Application of an Indigenous Research Framework and Two Qualitative Sharing Circles and Anishnaabe Symbol-Based Reflection." *International Journal of Qualitative Methods* 8(1): 21–40. This article is an excellent resource for those considering talking circles.

Lia Litosseliti. 2003. *Using Focus Groups in Research.* London: Continuum. This book contains practical and constructive advice about conducting focus groups. It includes discussions of decisions researchers have to make in the planning and carrying out of the research.

David L. Morgan and Margaret T. Spanish. 1984. "Focus Groups: A New Tool for Qualitative Research." *Qualitative Sociology* 7(3):253–70. This old article takes us back to Merton's and Lazarsfeld's serendipitous discovery of the usefulness of focus groups in sociology. It includes Morgan and Spanish's rationales for using focus groups in qualitative research.

Jocelyn A. Hollander. 2004. "The Social Context of Focus Groups." *Journal of Contemporary Ethnography* 33(5):602–37. This fascinating article demonstrates how the membership and social context of focus groups can influence the research.

Related Website

How to Use Focus Groups in Research: An Overview of the Method by Ashely Crossman
www.thoughtco.com/use-focus-groups-in-research-3026533
This site provides a brief overview of how to organize and run focus groups. It includes step-by-step advice on how to organize and conduct groups and can serve as a checklist.

8 Unobtrusive Research

Learning Objectives

- To become familiar with unobtrusive methods of research
- To understand the difference between manifest content and latent content
- To become familiar with the variety of ways in which sociologists use content analysis

Introduction

Imagine that you wanted to identify the most popular exhibit at a museum. You could set up a field study in which you station observers throughout the museum to note how many people are at each exhibit and to record how long each person stays in each location. This might work, but it would be a complex procedure and it would take a lot of time to gather enough data at each exhibit. You could also conduct a survey or set up in-depth interviews to ascertain visitors' opinions on which exhibit they found most interesting, but this method would also take up a lot of time and it might be difficult to convince enough people to participate in your study. Webb, Campbell, Schwart, and Sechrest (1966) report a much more creative approach, which was used at the Museum of Science and Industry in Chicago: researchers noted that the floor tiles around the chick-hatching exhibit needed to be replaced very often—about once every six weeks—while the tiles around other exhibits did not need to be replaced for years at a time. Hence, by taking the unobtrusive measure of looking at differential rates of erosion of floor tiles, researchers were able to ascertain that the chick-hatching exhibit was by far the most popular.

In this chapter, we look at a variety of **unobtrusive methods**—ways of amassing data without interacting with research participants—that researchers can use to carry out qualitative research. Unlike the qualitative methods we have discussed so far, unobtrusive methods do not involve interaction with participants. This can be a good place for new researchers, such as students like you, to get their feet wet. The researcher simply analyzes materials that already exist, and the process of collecting data does not affect the materials that are studied (Reinharz 1992:147). Most often, unobtrusive methods are used in conjunction with other more interactive methods.

Almost anything that has been created or modified by people can be a source of data. Many researchers have gained valuable insight into their research topics by examining materials as diverse as maps, archival records, letters, photographs, movies, advertisements, books, and even trash. Shulamit Reinharz (1992:146–7) provides a list of "cultural artifacts" that feminist researchers have used as "texts" for research: children's books, fairy tales, billboards, works of fiction and non-fiction, children's artwork, fashion, postcards, Girl Scout handbooks, works of fine art, newspaper articles, clinical records, research publications, textbooks, and academic citations. In our own work, we have analyzed the contents of monthly newsletters, autobiographical writings, novels, movies, children's books, students' essays, photographs on display, and reality television. When searching for materials for content analysis, you are bounded only by the limits of your own imagination.

Researchers who engage in unobtrusive research understand that cultural artifacts contain meaning on two levels: one that is obvious and one that is subtle. When analyzing **manifest content**, the researcher looks at content that is easily observed and immediately evident. When analyzing **latent content**, in contrast, the researcher focuses on uncovering implicit meanings. Most often, latent meanings provide the researcher with the deepest understanding of an artifact. Consider the following example from Manning and Cullum-Swan's (1994) analysis of the menus at a McDonald's restaurant. Part of their study involved analyzing the manifest content of the menus: the ways the food items were described, the ways the items were organized into different categories, and the way the items were listed within each category, in order from most to least popular. Once they had assessed the manifest content of the menus, the researchers interpreted this content to uncover latent meanings. Through this analysis, they concluded that the menus "convey messages that enable fast decisions and increase turnover" and that the categories of items, such as "Value Meals" and "Happy Meals," "raise per person expenditure and minimize complex, ad-hoc item selection"; in short, the menu's design reflects an "efficient, routinized, fast transaction-based food service" industry (1994:471).

Kayla Preston (2020) analyzed social media posts of three Canadian right-wing extremist groups. Her manifest analysis found that these groups make "mundane claims" about the importance of immigrants' assimilating and the untrustworthiness of the media and the Liberal Party of Canada. When you combine their claims, the latent content emerges and provides a "more worrying message about Canadian identity and belonging" in that "Canadian identity is equated with being white" and that "Canadian values are synonymous with traditional values and that both are under attack." These two claims combine to support their arguments about "social decay" and the need for "authoritarian governments" (p. 75–6). Preston refers to this latent content as the "bigger story" of her findings.

The structure of this chapter differs from that of the previous two chapters. Rather than go into depth about how to carry out research using unobtrusive methods, the chapter demonstrates through examples from a wide variety of sources to indicate the range of possibilities. As we examine the striking variety of types of content that sociologists and others have studied, try to imagine other possibilities.

Analyzing Pre-existing Documents

Many researchers argue that it is essential to include documents in our studies if we are to understand contemporary society. After all, individuals and groups represent themselves, both to themselves and to others, through the documents they produce (Atkinson and Coffey 1997:45). We can learn much about the people who created a document by analyzing what they chose to represent in their creation. As Howard S. Becker (1986:127) has noted, representations are a translation of reality "into the materials and conventional language of a particular craft." In addition,

> [s]ince any representation always and necessarily leaves out elements of reality, the interesting and researchable questions are these: Which of the possible elements are included? Who finds that selection reasonable and acceptable? Who complains about it? [And who does not?] What criteria do people apply in making those judgments? (Becker 1986:126)

While these questions could easily apply to analysis of any cultural artifact, they are especially salient in relation to document analysis.

In highly literate societies, written texts provide particularly telling windows into social worlds. Think about how much statistical records, survey forms, letters, autobiographies, articles in professional journals and magazines, and even works of fiction can tell us about the interests and concerns of the individuals who created them. Glaser and Strauss (1967 as cited in Pawluch 2009) have referred to such documents as "voices in the library" waiting to be heard and used for our analyses. Let us look at ways that researchers can gather valuable information from such voices.

Statistical Records

When conducting a study, researchers often consult pre-existing statistical records to get a general sense of a topic. In addition, many researchers have repurposed or reinterpreted existing statistics to reinforce their own findings or theories. Émile Durkheim (1897/1951), for example, used official statistics related to suicide rates to demonstrate his idea that lack of social cohesion rather than mental illness led to an increase in unhappiness. This example illustrates a very traditional approach to the use of statistical records in sociological research.

More recently, we have realized that *sources* of statistical data can reveal as much about a social group as the statistics themselves. For example, when someone kills themself, individuals might choose to report the death as resulting from natural causes or from an accident for a number of reasons, such as burial rites, insurance claims, or protecting the reputation of prominent members of society.

Often, these reports make their way into official records and affect the statistical rates based on these records. Thus, an examination of the documents behind suicide rates could reveal much about the social stigma a society attaches to suicide. A study of the documents behind the statistics may reveal that these statistics are not as objective as they seem.

Joel Best (2020) points out that in looking at statistics we need to remember that "labelling something a fact always occurs within a particular context" (3). Best examined the challenges involved in measuring numbers of cases of COVID-19 and the resulting death rates. He points out that counting is determined by a series of choices, what he calls "messy procedures" (p. 4). For example, in many places only people who were admitted to hospital were counted as COVID cases, but this practice "inevitably undercounts" (p. 6) because it misses people who might have had the virus but were not sick or who had moderate cases. In countries, like the US, where people pay out of pocket for health care, some who were very ill may not have had the health insurance to seek treatment or even get tested.

Researchers can also gain insight into the ideologies behind previously conducted studies by analyzing the design of the forms used to collect statistical data. To understand what such analysis can reveal, let us compare how questions of "race" and ethnicity are treated on the American census (US Census Bureau 2010) to how such questions are treated on the Canadian census (Statistics Canada 2017). The American form first asks if the person who is filling out the form is of "Hispanic, Latino, or Spanish origin"; it then asks, "What is [this person's] race?" followed by a list of options. In contrast, the Canadian form does not use the word *race*. Rather, it has three questions about *identity*: "What were the ethnic or cultural origins of this person's ancestors?"; "Is this person an Aboriginal person, that is, First Nations (North American Indian), Métis or Inuk (Inuit)?"; and "Is this person . . ." (followed by a list of racial, ethnic, and geographic designations). In addition, the Canadian form provides rationales for asking about ancestry and identity ("This question collects information in accordance with the Employment Equity Act and its Regulations and Guidelines to support programs that promote equal opportunity for everyone to share in the social, cultural, and economic life of Canada"). The American form simply asks about "race."

Because these studies were designed to address national interests, we can interpret differences in how the two countries think about ethnicity and race. These differences tell us much about differing national identities. The focus on "ethnicity" and the rationales on the Canadian census questionnaire suggest that Statistics Canada seeks to represent Canada to Canadians as a multicultural society that appreciates its diversity and seeks full participation from its diverse population. The explanations suggest that Statistics Canada respects respondents as intelligent partners in the information-gathering process. In contrast, the American form focuses on "race," a category loaded with meaning across the history of the country, and does not offer any explanation as to why the census is being conducted.

We can also see similarities in the way questions of identity are presented. Both forms expect individuals to identify with at least one "race" or ethnic heritage. Both forms also invite the respondent to check one or more boxes for racial or ethnic identity, which reflects social changes associated with increased rates of intermarriage among diverse groups. In the past, the forms asked each person to check only one box. At the same time, the Canadian form instructs Indigenous individuals to skip the question on heritage, suggesting that the creators of the form do not think that the possibility of a mixed heritage applies to them. The American form also makes assumptions about how individuals understand their own identity. It states that, for the purpose of the census, Hispanic, Latino, or Spanish origin does not designate "race." These observations relate to only a few questions on the forms; a full analysis would surely yield fascinating conclusions.

The marital status question on the Canadian census (Statistics Canada 2017) asks if a spouse is "opposite sex" or "same sex," reflecting the legalization of same-sex marriage. The form, however, asks only if the respondent is male or female. It does not allow for transgender, transsexual, or other varieties of gender identity that have entered public discourse. It will be interesting to see if this question changes in the next census as a reflection of social change.

Maps

Maps provide a strong example of the sort of documents that represent not "reality" itself but a translation of reality. Think of how your city is depicted on a road map, and compare that representation to the geographical reality you encounter every day. Howard S. Becker (1986) uses the example of San Francisco to illustrate this point. He notes that San Francisco is a very hilly city. Yet, despite cartographers' ability to indicate hills on a map, these hills are absent from the road maps most tourists pick up to navigate the city streets. Becker points out that we can determine the intended user of these maps based on this omission. These maps are designed for people in cars who are not worried about having to hike up and down steep hills. They are not designed for pedestrians, who might be quite chagrined to discover that the short walk they had planned entails walking up and down very steep hills.

Christian Leuenberger and Izhak Schnell (2010) demonstrate how mapmakers construct maps in a particular way to accomplish political goals. They studied how Israeli groups used maps to "invoke authority, appeal to particular audiences, elaborate social concerns and make political statements" (p. 94). They analyzed how maps of Israel had changed over time, from the 1950s to the present, to serve as "tools in territorial power struggles and have been visually powerful means for silencing a population by designifying its presence on the maps" (p. 32). Early maps emphasized the threat Israel felt from its Arab neighbours, while more recent maps seek to make the Palestinian territories appear insignificant. It is also likely that we would see changes in Palestinian maps over time as their relationship with Israel has changed.

Letters and Autobiographies

Personal letters and autobiographical accounts can provide insight into individuals' lived experiences. W.I. Thomas and Florian Znaniecki understood this when they were gathering information for their in-depth study of Polish immigrants, *The Polish Peasant in Europe and America*, a five-volume work that they published beginning in 1918. In developing this ground-breaking study, Thomas and Znaniecki used a biographical approach that involved analyzing autobiographical materials, including letters between peasants in Poland and their relatives in the United States, in conjunction with public documents, such as newspaper files and institutional records. Ultimately, this approach led the researchers to understand immigrants' lives with greater depth than had ever been accomplished before, and this deep understanding led the researchers to identify the concept of **social disorganization**. This concept, which suggests that rapid social change can lead to the loss of norms and values, had an enormous effect on the development of sociological research. At this time, scholars began to distinguish between what C. Wright Mills (1959/1976) would later refer to as "private troubles," which we can address on an individual basis, and "public issues," which require social solutions. (See Chapter 3 for a discussion of private problems and public issues.)

More recently, Terry Williams (2017) carried out what he calls "an ethnography of self-harm" by analyzing teenage suicide notes and diary entries. He augmented his data by talking to the writers of the notes or to their close friends (when the writer had committed suicide). In these notes and diaries, he identifies recurring themes of a breakdown in family structure and the sense of being different. Williams concludes that "understanding teen suicide requires respect for teens' insights and an understanding of history and culture" (p. 190).

As Hammersley and Atkinson note (1983:130), autobiographical accounts can also help researchers to identify sensitizing concepts. Deborah found this to be the case when she analyzed published autobiographical accounts of women's experiences of widowhood. These texts made her aware of the concept of **identity foreclosure** and that the women were experiencing "identifying moments" (van den Hoonaard 2013, 1997). Deborah was then able to address issues related to identity foreclosure when she carried out interviews. In addition, she noticed that the more recent autobiographies had an advice-giving tone, indicating a societal shift towards an increasing desire for self-help resources.[1] Understanding social changes can help us, as sociologists, to understand our research participants within a broader context.

Professional Publications

Journal articles and scholarly publications can provide broader coverage of a topic than a single researcher might otherwise be able to accumulate on their own. By analyzing ongoing discussions and controversies in professional publications, researchers can also follow changing social trends. For example, Dorothy Pawluch (1996) wanted to trace changes in pediatricians' self-perceptions and understanding of their profession. Her initial intention was to base her study primarily on interviews, but she found that published materials provided more insight into the topic. By examining "articles, discussion, and debates in their professional journals," she identified changes in what pediatricians did and the medicalization of broad aspects of children's lives. Box 8.1 describes the approach she took and the excitement of discovery she experienced as she read these periodicals.

Similarly, Monica Stelzl and her colleagues (2018) carried out an analysis of how psychology textbooks on human sexuality characterize sexual problems. They were interested in finding out how these texts "represented the notion of 'sexual problems'" itself (p. 150). This research team systematically went through 16 textbooks. They found that most presented uncritical discussions of sexual problems using a biomedical approach, which "conveniently leads to biomedical treatment as the logical solution" (p. 156). Only a couple of textbooks included alternative explanations, perhaps introducing social context and gender issues. Hence, the biomedical approach that transforms sexual problems into disorders was reinforced and promoted in these textbooks.

Box 8.1 Discovery in the Library

At the time that Dorothy Pawluch was doing her study, pediatricians were starting to expand the territory of their practice by defining more aspects of childhood—for example, sibling rivalry—as having a medical explanation. Yet not all pediatricians were comfortable with this new direction, as Pawluch's research quickly revealed. Pawluch describes her process of analyzing articles and letters in professional journals using a "crude but effective" system involving "a series of margin notations" (2009):

> Where I was able to articulate why I thought the observation was significant . . . the notation would be accompanied by a conceptual note. . . . I would [later] try to "translate" . . . what I had found into more analytical language. . . . The note was probably attached to a letter that a pediatrician had written . . . complaining about . . . a discussion of some subject [perhaps sibling rivalry] . . . about which the letter writer did not think pediatrics ought to be concerned. . . . With growing conviction, I [realized] that I would find the story behind pediatricians' involvement with medicalization of childhood in these documents. There was no "eureka moment," only a growing sense that "the field," as it were, lay in the pages of the materials I was reading. (p. 318–30)

Thus, Pawluch's "exciting discovery"—the existence of widespread controversy surrounding the changes in the profession—lay in the letters to the editor and articles in the professional journals of pediatricians rather than in her interview transcripts or field notes.

Analyzing Documents of Social Institutions

Social institutions produce masses of documents—including mission statements, strategic plans, forms, and letters—that researchers can use as sources of data. Dorothy Smith, in developing a research method called **institutional ethnography** (IE), has argued that such documents can "produce and sustain standardized practices" and establish "relations of ruling" (Smith 2005 as cited in McCloskey 2008:44). In other words, bureaucratic forms "represent people, establish priorities, and dismiss specific events or individuals" (McCloskey 2008:44). To see how bureaucratic documents "rule" the experiences of individuals who live and work in institutions, we will look at two IE studies that combine document analysis with participant observation to examine social life in nursing homes.

First, let us revisit Timothy Diamond's (1992) study of life in nursing homes, which we first encountered in Chapter 3. In one component of his study, Diamond examined the process of charting (1992:130–67). He used a combination of participation and analysis of residents' charts to demonstrate how these texts misrepresented the actual work that nursing assistants did. Along with their "official" work—the physical tasks that authorities monitored through the charts—nursing assistants talked to, comforted, and cajoled residents. Diamond describes how this complex relational work was reduced to a tick mark on a chart. Officially, "if it wasn't charted it didn't happen, but much more happened than got charted" (1992:137). Hence, the documents rendered invisible much of the work the nursing assistants did in the institutions:

> The chart demanded that whatever happened as a human encounter be eliminated from the recording of the event. Recording the work in the charts came to be no more than jotting down numbers and check marks, transforming it out of social contexts into a narrative of tasks. . . . [The work] became simply menial and mechanical as recorded. (1992:164)

Diamond's juxtaposition of the actual work the nursing assistants did with the way it had been minimized as unskilled labour in official documents provides a powerful picture of the social world of nursing homes.

Next, let us turn to Rose McCloskey's (2008) Canadian study on the transfer of nursing-home residents to hospital emergency rooms (ERs) via ambulance. Like Diamond, McCloskey used a combination of first-hand observations and document analysis to complete her study. McCloskey notes that her analysis of the patients' "care plans" revealed a greater interest in demonstrating "the facility's ability to identify residents' needs" than in actually addressing those needs (2008:114). In addition, the standardized forms that ambulance personnel complete and the standard ER records showed the system's interest in bureaucratizing the care of patients. As McCloskey observes,

[s]tandard texts and protocols provide ER practitioners with the legitimacy necessary to think and act in a mindless fashion. Mindless strategies satisfy the ER's
need for timely responses to complex circumstances and help to ensure objectivity
is upheld. (2008:119)

McCloskey's findings regarding the use of forms to selectively record aspects of experience are similar to Diamond's. Her study, like Diamond's, captures how documents of social institutions can contribute to "relations of ruling" and establish the
dominance of bureaucracy in the nursing-home setting.

Analyzing Media Content and Reflections of Reality

News Media

News coverage can frame our understanding of our social world and can communicate the importance, or lack of importance, of issues, people, and events.
Therefore, it is not surprising that researchers use material from the news media as
a source of data. In this section, we will examine some examples of how researchers
have analyzed articles from popular newspapers and magazines.

If you pay attention to the news, you may be under the impression that we are
in the grip of a crime wave. There is heavy coverage of violent crime, and many
politicians are promoting a "tough-on-crime" agenda that only makes sense if the
incidence of crime is increasing. But if you look at actual statistics, you will discover that the crime rate has been falling for years. What is going on? Altheide and
Michalowski (1999) provide a possible explanation in their study on the use of the
term *fear* in a daily newspaper, *The Arizona Republic*, from 1987 to 1996.

Altheide and Michalowski (1999:478) used the concept of **frames** to conduct
their analysis. As they note, frames shape media articles by determining "what will
be discussed, how it will be discussed, and above all, how it will not be discussed"
(1999:478). These frames contribute to particular definitions of the situation,
which, as we have seen, have consequences for individuals and societies.[2] Altheide
and Michalowski observe that media reports frequently use a "problem frame,"
which they describe as "a secular alternative to the morality play" and characterize as having a "narrative structure, universal moral meanings, specific time
and place, and an unambiguous focus on disorder" to "satisfy the entertainment
dimension of news" (1999:479). They further note that this frame often generates
reports about fear.

Altheide and Michalowski describe their method as both a "mapping" of
"where the word and related references to fear occur throughout news reports" and
a "tracking" of "changes in usage, particularly with different topics and issues, over
time" (1999:477). Through this mapping and tracking, the researchers were able to
identify the top three topics associated with fear in newspapers: children, crime,

and schools. Tracking the use of the term over time revealed that *fear* was more prevalent in the news at the time of their study than it had been a few years earlier. In their conclusion, Altheide and Michalowski comment that "fear is a larger part of our symbolic landscape at a time when the social terrain is comparatively routine, predictable, and safe" (1999:500).[3]

Clarke and Binns (2006) also used the concept of frames in their analysis of the portrayal of heart disease in the 20 magazines with the highest circulation in Canada. Looking at manifest content, they identified three frames: medical, lifestyle, and social-structural. They found that the medical frame was dominant. It portrayed "supreme optimism," describing "medical interventions . . . as if they occur in highly optimistic contexts and have only positive consequences." Medicine was depicted as good and heroic while the body was characterized as "bad" (2006:42–3). The lifestyle frame encouraged individuals to take responsibility for their own health by adopting a "list" of healthy habits. Yet, as Clarke and Binns also observed, when celebrities with heart disease were discussed, the articles attributed their conditions to external factors, such as the unavoidable stress of their jobs, rather than to individual lifestyle choices. Least common were articles that used the social-structural frame, despite the fact that many studies have shown that income is one of the strongest predictors of health status.

Reflecting current concerns related to aggression involving older adults, Laura Funk and colleagues (2020) explored how Canadian news sources such as the *Globe and Mail* and CBC frame aggression among older adults. They discovered that the vast majority of coverage deals with aggression among older adults who live in institutional settings such as nursing homes. This media coverage reinforces "fear inducing frames of aggression that contribute to stigmas associated with aging and dementia" (p. 4) rather than exploring context and environmental issues that may be related to, for example, under-staffing or lack of privacy. Funk, Herron, Spencer, and Thomas concluded that the media's framing "not only draw[s] on but *further reinforce[s]* ageism, dementiaism, apocalyptic demography [that suggests that having an aging population is detrimental to society] . . . and an atmosphere of nursing home scandal" (emphasis in original) (p. 9).

Researchers also use content analysis to compare how the media characterize different social groups. Kristen Gilchrist (2010) used interpretive content analysis to explore the coverage of missing and murdered Indigenous women compared to missing/murdered white women. Box 8.2 presents an overview of some of her most important findings.

Advertisements

Almost everywhere we go, we see advertisements. We see them so frequently that we tend to take their often-bizarre content for granted or at least accept it as normal. As Shulamit Reinharz (1992:152) commented, "most [North] Americans are accustomed to seeing giant females in various states of undress smiling and caressing

Box 8.2 Interpretive Content Analysis

Kristen Gilchrist (2010) explored the differences in how local print media covered stories of missing/murdered Indigenous and white women. White women received more than three times the coverage of Indigenous women. Gilchrist used "interpretive content analysis" (p. 378) to look more deeply into the coverage of six missing women: three Indigenous and three white. She analyzed headlines, articles, and accompanying photographs.

The qualitative dimensions of Gilchrist's analysis illustrate that the media's coverage of the Indigenous women constructed them as less valuable than white women, primarily through a more detached way of talking about them. The headlines, for example, referred to the Indigenous women in a more impersonal fashion:

> Headlines printed about the Aboriginal women, often referred to them impersonally and rarely by name. For example, "RCMP identifies *woman's* remains" (Pruden 2006, p. A3; emphasis Gilchrist's). . . . Detached descriptions of the Aboriginal women were in opposition to headlines about the White women referring to them by first and last names, and nicknames. Headlines were often also written as heartfelt personal messages from the victims' friends and family to the women, as with "*Ardeth Wood* 'lives in the light of God'" (Harvey 2003, p. B1 [emphasis Gilchrist's]. (2010:380–1)

Gilchrist also analyzed the photos of the missing women. She found that photos of white women were "large, centrally placed, continuing on in series for several pages, and often depicted [them] as young children or alongside family members." The photos of Aboriginal women were "considerably smaller, normally passport sized . . .less visible, not centrally placed, and less intimate" (2010:382). These photos rarely showed the victim's family, and there were no childhood photographs.

Gilchrist concluded that the lack of coverage of missing/murdered Indigenous women constructs their stories as "not dramatic or worthy enough . . . [their] victimization [as] routine or ordinary, and/or irrelevant to (White) readers" (2010:385).

products such as whiskey, foods, and records." Qualitative analyses have the potential to shed light on items that are so familiar that they are almost invisible.

As Reinharz's comment might suggest, advertisements have been a favourite source of data among researchers interested in gender roles and ideals. Ads often depict "cultural ideals to which the media and the marketplace would like us all to aspire . . . [to the] type of body and appearances marketed to . . . and often sought after by teenage girls or boys, or adult women and men" (Warren and Karner 2010:178–9). Erving Goffman (1979 as cited in Holder 2010) did an early analysis of "gender displays" in advertising. He found that, compared to men, women were presented in a diminished capacity, objectified, over-feminized, and portrayed in insular terms. Goffman also noted that when women and men were posed together, the men were portrayed as central, strong, and dominant in comparison to the women.

Jean Kilbourne has made a series of powerful films that analyze images of women in advertising: *Killing Us Softly* (1979), *Still Killing Us Softly* (1987), *Killing Us Softly 3* (2000), and *Killing Us Softly 4* (2010). Through skillful analysis of a wide array of advertisements, Kilbourne identified a number of recurring themes that exploit the female image. She found that many ads are sexist and violent, promote an ideal of beauty that is not achievable for the vast majority of women, reduce women to body parts or otherwise objectify women, and/or make women seem helpless.

Other researchers have looked at how men are represented in advertisements. For example, Toni Calasanti and Neal King (2007) examined the portrayal of masculinity in Internet ads created by companies that promote products claiming to keep one looking and staying young. In particular, they analyzed ads on websites that sell anti-aging products. They concluded that the ads "include revolutionary depictions of old people forestalling or even defeating the physical incursions of age . . . by affirming a masculine heterosexuality that subordinates women and treats youth as the ideal phase of development" (Calasanti and King 2007:367). The researchers also noted that the standard for successful aging that these advertisements provide, similar to those standards presented in ads that promote beauty ideals for women, is unattainable for most men.

Fiction

While fictional representations, by definition, depart from reality, they still reflect certain aspects of our world and our experiences. Thus, as Hammersley and Atkinson (1983:131) suggest, researchers can analyze the "themes, images, [and] metaphors" used in fiction to become aware of and "sensitized to cultural themes pertaining to sex, gender, family, work, success, failure, commitments, health and illness, the law, crime, and social control."

To get a better sense of how researchers can draw meaning from fictional representations, let us look at a study Deborah conducted with Will C. van den Hoonaard in which they analyzed the portrayal of airports in fictional children's picture books and in fictional films for adults. They chose to compare these two media because they represent "some of the most generalized ways to offer anticipatory socialization to large numbers of people" (1991:3).

Children's literature is often didactic, with the aim of educating children about some aspect of the world. Thus, we were not surprised to discover that the five books Deborah and Will examined (all published between 1967 and 1982) focused on preparing children for the "airport experience." The books took three principal approaches to achieving this goal. First, they introduced children to unfamiliar technologies. Almost 42 per cent of the pictures in the texts dealt with repairs and plane maintenance. Second, the books introduced children to the organization of airports. Third, the books introduced children to the laws and control measures that govern people's behaviour in airports, with 12 per cent of images relating to this concern.

Notable was the absence of images depicting children interacting with the airport environment. The images showed children reading and waiting, but there were no images of children playing with airport social organization (perhaps running down the very long hallways, crawling, or climbing on chairs), no instructions for what children should do if they become lost in an airport, and no mention of friends or family members who might greet children after their flight.

What about the portrayal of airports in Hollywood films? Deborah and Will discovered that airport scenes were often used to facilitate major changes in characters' lives, and that, by extension, these scenes functioned to prepare audience members for dealing with major changes in their own lives. The iconic airport scene in *Casablanca* (1942), perhaps the earliest airport scene in a feature-length movie, set the stage for later films. In particular, this scene exhibited the classic elements of what van Gennep (1909/1960) called **rite of passage**, elements that recur in many subsequent airport scenes. The rite of passage includes three stages: (1) separation from one's former status and role; (2) transition (or liminality) when one is sanctioned to be different, to not follow accepted norms; and (3) incorporation, during which one assumes a new identity. These three stages were present in all nine movies that Deborah and Will studied.[4]

When Deborah and Will compared the portrayal of airports in children's books to that in movies, they found that both representations depicted caricatures of airports but that these caricatures were drawn to reflect very different aspects of real airports. While the children's literature idealized the experience, the movies equated airport experience with disruption and change. Both the children's books and the movies offered anticipatory socialization to their intended audience, but the former did so on a literal level (preparing children for their first trip to the airport), while the latter did so on a metaphorical level (preparing adult viewers for dealing with significant life changes).

In a separate study, Deborah analyzed fiction for a somewhat different purpose. She looked at novels and movies to identify common stereotypes and conceptions of widowers. Deborah found that there are generally two characterizations of widowers in these media. The first, more common, is that of the young widower whose wife has died violently, often in an accident or at the hands of a murderer, or "passed away" after struggling with a disease. This young man is often a romantic character. You might think of Matt Damon's character in *We Bought a Zoo* (2011), whose wife died of a brain tumour. The second characterization is that of the lost older man, such as Jack Nicholson's character in *About Schmidt* (2002), whose life falls apart as he retires and becomes widowed almost simultaneously.

Television

Television is a unique medium in that it brings together fictional and non-fictional representations of reality in various ways. In a two-hour period of watching television, a viewer might take in a scripted sitcom about college students, a "reality" show about life as a former rock star, a news program discussing local and global events, and a documentary on climate change, all the while being bombarded with advertisements at regular intervals. If the viewer chooses to "flip" between channels or stream from various providers, they may be exposed to any number of influences in two hours. With this in mind, some researchers have analyzed how television programming, in all its forms, reflects widespread conceptions of social issues.

Diana Rose (2004, 1998), for example, has looked at how mental illness is portrayed on television in the United Kingdom. Rose looked at mental illness as it appeared on prime-time TV, whether in news programs, documentaries, soap operas, dramas, or situation comedies. She found that mental illness is frequently associated with danger and violence. Rose also discovered that "people with mental illness tend to be filmed alone and with close-up or extreme-close-up shots whilst others are filmed medium-close-up to medium-wide and they are often not alone in the shot" (1998:223). Rose further documents a theme of community neglect of the mentally ill, which points to concern with the failure of public policy, a major topic of discussion at the time of her study.

Researchers also analyze entertainment shows on television. Lisa-Jo, Clare Forstie, and Savina Balasubramanian (2015) carried out an **ethnographic content analysis**, which focuses on the "underlying meanings, patterns and processes" of the document under investigation (Altheide 2008:287). They studied exit rituals on three types of reality shows in which contestants are voted off by the audience (e.g., *American Idol*), by the other contestants (e.g., *Survivor*), or by a "choosing individual" (e.g., *The Apprentice*). They analyzed the exit rituals of 117 episodes of six shows in three seasons and coded them to identify themes that characterize what contestants do when they are eliminated from the shows. The departures for each type of show have a distinctive formula. Van den Scott et al.'s work demonstrates that the rituals serve as symbols for death, which is an allegory for loss. Therefore, the contestants do **eulogy work** as a transition from life on the reality show back to life in the real world to frame their symbolic death as a "good death." If you think of a show like *Survivor*, for example, when a contestant is voted off, their torch is immediately extinguished, and the person immediately leaves the show's setting. The individual then makes a statement about their thoughts about having been on the show and being voted off. In shows in which "America" (or Canada) decides who stays and who goes—for example, *American Idol*—there is a montage shown of the contestant's time on the show and then the self-eulogy. The authors argue that contestants' eulogy work "encompasses the conception and framing of self within the show at the moment of symbolic death" (van den Scott et al. 2015:418).

Analyzing Physical Objects

While analysis of physical objects might not be appropriate for all studies, everyday objects can provide the astute researcher with more information than you might think. Deborah first realized how much objects can reveal while she was collecting garbage with an organization that "adopted" a stretch of road near her home. They went out twice a year to pick up items that people had dumped onto the side of the road. The group always spent some time comparing what they found and thinking about what it might tell them about their community. For example, they always picked up many "Tim's cups" along the roadway. Most likely, this indicates the popularity of Tim Hortons among drivers in the community, but it may also suggest, among other possibilities, a correlation between drinking Tim Hortons' coffee and throwing cups out of moving vehicles. Some parts of the road seemed to almost grow beer bottles, suggesting that these locations may be near sites where people come to drink beer in the woods. The most interesting thing Deborah has ever found was an "anger journal" that had likely belonged to a man who had been ordered to keep the journal after he had been charged with abusing his wife— possibly, he threw it on the side of the road in a fit of anger.

Deborah's group never did a systematic analysis of what they found, but they certainly could analyze how many pieces of what kind of garbage they picked up and where they were placed (for example, there tended to be less garbage in front of houses). The group might even start by thinking about what the presence of the "Adopt-a-Highway" program says about the community. Surely, a community would not need such a program if people did not regularly litter or if residents did not care about the litter along the road.

Jeff Ferrell (2006) has done a systematic study of what people have thrown out. He calls his work a "close ethnography of objects lost and found" (2006:4). Ferrell's methods of "data collection" included Dumpster diving, trash picking, and street scavenging. Through his careful sorting, counting, and categorizing of what other people had discarded, he "developed a critical, grounded understanding of contemporary consumption and its relation to collective wastefulness" (2006:6).

Ferrell found two kinds of garbage that tell a great deal about contemporary society. First, he came upon what he calls an "overwhelming, inundating surplus" of things that were "useful, functional, desirable, [and] many times unused and unmarred" (2006:16–17) that indicated the wastefulness and extreme consumerism that are characteristic of our culture. In his analysis, Ferrell provides a wealth of evidence to make the case for the prevalence of overconsumption (see Box 8.3).

Second, he found a type of curbside trash that is the "residue of significant life changes." These include the thrown-out objects that result from events such as divorces and deaths. This sort of garbage includes "the material residue of shared meaning . . . : bronzed baby shoes, diplomas, wedding photos, ticket stubs, [and] old newspaper clippings." Ferrell refers to these items as "material postmortems" (2006:19). This second type of trash indicates our desire to rid ourselves of unhappy reminders of the past after we go through a major change in our life.

While Deborah's group found Tim Hortons cups, Ferrell, who did his study in Texas, found bullets "everywhere [he] scrounge[d]" (2006:59). In all the years that Deborah picked up trash in New Brunswick, she never found a single bullet, and she lives in deer-hunting country. Such factors indicate very different ways of life.

Box 8.3 Meaning in Trash

In *Empire of Scrounge*, Jeff Ferrell (2006) systematically documents many instances of finding perfectly good, often unused merchandise thrown out as though it were useless. Early in the text, he notes the surprising contents of one particular pile of trash, which he found on a street running behind a strip of mansions in a highly affluent neighbourhood:

> Working my way through the bags and boxes, I discovered that they were full of pretty party favors, decorations, gift wrap, used paper plates and paper cups, and expensive baby gifts. Many of the gifts, in fact, were still sealed new in their gift boxes—the absurd aftermath of a baby shower meant mostly for show. (Ferrell 2006:20)

Although Ferrell is probably correct in his interpretation of the "trash" from the baby shower, it is also possible that the expectant mother in this particular case had a miscarriage after the shower and that the mountain of trash is actually evidence of a sudden tragedy. This possibility exposes a limitation of using material objects as data. They are not direct evidence of what has happened and what it has meant.

Innovations in Research

More recently, researchers have developed new ways to study things that already exist. We will look at two new areas. First, visual sociology recognizes the richness in images to contribute to our understanding of social life. Second, and not surprisingly, researchers have used the virtual world, particularly blogs and social media, in their research.

Visual Sociology

Visual sociology entails the use of images as data. With the ubiquity of images in our daily lives—in magazine and newspaper articles, in advertisements, and in videos, to name only a few of the most common sources—it is no wonder that there is an increasing interest among sociologists to incorporate images into their research methods. Yet the approach is not entirely new. In the inaugural issue of the journal *Visual Studies* (1986), Tim Curry notes that the American Sociology Association devoted a session to visual sociology in 1974, and the International Visual Sociology Association (IVSA), which publishes *Visual Studies*, was founded in 1981 (IVSA 2010).

Visual sociologists use images to study a wide range of topics. Beverly Yuen Thompson (2010a), for example, used a combination of fieldwork, interviews, participation, photography, and video recordings to complete her study of heavily tattooed women. She asked, "What is it like to be a heavily tattooed woman?" and "What is it like to be a woman tattoo artist in a field dominated by men?" Over three years, she filmed and interviewed 70 women. The result was the film *Covered: Women and Tattoos* (2010b), which makes a powerful statement about the stigma associated with being a tattooed woman. It also reveals the amount of work that Thompson put into using images in her study; she did not simply take a few photographs and hope that she interpreted them correctly![5]

Mitchell Duneier (1999) used photography in his ethnography of sidewalk magazine and book vendors in Greenwich Village, New York. He recruited Ovie Carter, a professional photojournalist, to take pictures "to illustrate the things [Duneier] was writing about" (1999:12). Duneier noticed things in the photographs he would not have seen otherwise. He included photographs of the vendors and the neighbourhood in which they worked in his book, *Sidewalk*. If you take a look at *Sidewalk*, you will see how the pictures make the study and its participants come alive as they could not have through the written word alone. The visual aspects enriched the ethnography and contributed to its effectiveness.

Visual sociology also contributes to an understanding of **mundane technology**. Lisa-Jo (2016) studied the introduction of permanent walls among Inuit of Arviat, Nunavut. Because they were forced off the land and into a sedentary settlement in the 1960s, there are still people who remember living on the land in igloos and caribou-skin tents, depending on the season. As part of her ethnography, Lisa-Jo asked them to take her on a tour of their walls and discovered they used the walls in ways that made sense to them and increased their sense of Inuit-ness (see Figure 8.1). Because one Inuit value is finding a use for everything, the participants used their walls as tools. First, they used their walls as a safe place to store articles such as mementoes and important documents. Other items might be put on the wall for long-term storage, such as a plastic floral arrangement intended for a participant's grave when she dies. Second, because there is a desire to make use of things rather than simply throw them away, a broken object might be put on the wall for display, where it is not merely out of the way but also has an aesthetic purpose. Items might also be stored on the wall for occasional use, such as Christmas decorations, visible during the rest of the year but only "used" during the Christmas season. Finally, the walls might be used for easy access. There may be hooks for keys or creative storage areas for sunglasses, which are very important because they prevent snow blindness. Lisa-Jo concludes:

> Walls came with no handbook of uses and meanings. The Inuit were able to approach with fresh eyes and to determine a meaning, through use, which—while not entirely unique—consciously reflects their firm practice of and belief in resourcefulness and practicality. The wall becomes a convenient location in a way that would not have occurred to these participants had they been restricted to layered and historical meanings. . . . Wall-as-tool for storage is one of the meanings that [members of this hamlet] have ascribed to the technological artifact . . . a

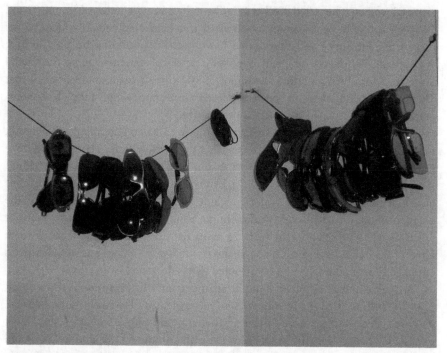

Figure 8.1 Innovative storage for sunglasses in Arviat, Nunavut: A demonstration of Inuit ingenuity and Inuit-ness in the use of walls

Source: van den Scott, L.-J.K. 2016. "Mundane Technology in Non-Western Contexts: Wall-as-Tool," Pp. 33–53 in *Sociology of Home: Belonging, Community, and Place in the Canadian Context*, edited by G. Anderson, J.G. Moore, and L. Suski. Toronto: Canadian Scholars Press.

> use that was mediated through the social: through the performance of Inuit-ness to their ... creative and innovative uses for the new technology. (van den Scott 2016:51)

There are also visual sociologists who focus on studying images in popular culture. This type of research is called **cultural studies**. Researchers who work in cultural studies use items such as magazines, movies, and websites to identify representations of culture. They can analyze images in the media to uncover changing social attitudes. For example, in the past few decades, there are more interracial couples in advertisements; this change indicates the general population's increasingly positive attitude towards interracial relationships. Most often, researchers look for common themes in visual representations to identify cultural ideals—ideals to which we are all supposed to aspire. In a typical study, a researcher might analyze images of women in magazine ads and identify the narrow appearance norms of youth and extreme slenderness that are today's ideals for women. Researchers can also find evidence of cultural ideals by looking at contrasting representations. For example, when Linda Caissie and Deborah were looking through *Zoomer* magazine to gather

US Library of Congress, LC-USF34-046511-D

Figure 8.2 Depression-era couple

data for their study on how the magazine frames the aging process, they noticed a photo of a Depression-era old couple on its website (www.zoomermag.com; see Figure 8.2) that stood in stark contrast to the photos in the magazine. While the magazine photos promoted a young-looking, consumerist ideal for today's baby boomers, the Depression-era photo provided a negative reinforcement of this ideal by showing readers an image to which they would not want to aspire (Caissie and van den Hoonaard 2009).

Internet Research

Given the tremendous growth in the presence of blogs, vlogs, and social media on the Internet, it is not surprising that researchers have begun using them as sources of data. In this section, we'll look at researching in the blogosphere and on Twitter.

Researching in the Blogosphere and Vlogosphere

Nicholas Hookway (2008:92) suggests that blogs "provide a publicly available, low-cost and instantaneous technique for collecting substantial amounts of data" and that the "online mask" (2008:96) provides a level of anonymity that allows bloggers to be candid in their approach and possibly less prone to "impression management." Although bloggers might misrepresent themselves, it may not matter to the researcher: first, because such research often addresses the material of blogs rather than offline reality; and second, because we never really know how truthful participants are in any research. Studying blogs requires a systematic approach and new ways of thinking about the research relationship.

An important challenge to doing such research is the tremendous number of blogs. In 2004, there were around 6 million active blogs, while in 2008 that number had increased to 133 million (Dee and Wagner 2006 and Sifry 2008 as cited in Leggatt-Cook and Chamberlain 2012:964). Many people also maintain YouTube channels or engage in other vlogging venues. Researchers use a variety of creative means to whittle down the number of blogs and vlogs they analyze to a manageable quantity.

Chez Leggatt-Cook and Kerry Chamberlain (2012), for example, studied weight-loss blogs. Because there were so many, the authors had to find ways to limit their research. They chose blogs written by women that "contained an explicit statement that the writer was blogging to support their weight-loss efforts; [and] contained substantive content" (p. 966). Leggatt-Cook and Chamberlain found that blogging served as a "technology for weight loss" and provided a supportive community of others who were also trying to lose weight. This community had the responsibility of making the blogger accountable for how successful they were in achieving their goal.

In another example, Juanne Clarke and Gudrun van Amerom (2007) compared websites of organizations whose purpose is to support people with Asperger's syndrome (AS) with blogs written by people who claim to have AS themselves. They found that the organizations' websites "medicalized and pathologized" AS and discussed those with AS in terms of deficits. In contrast, the bloggers "expressed resistance to these organizations, to medicalization and to what they felt was the public stigma associated with AS. Bloggers spoke of celebrating their differences and of anger at neurotypicals [i.e., those who do not have AS] for stigmatizing them" (Clarke and van Amerom 2007:771).

Rebecca Raby and her colleagues (2018) analyzed how young Canadians make vlogs to address social change. They used their research to challenge the prevailing belief that teenagers are isolated and vulnerable online by reporting on 18 Canadian video creators with YouTube channels who produced social-oriented vlogs between 2009 and 2014. They discovered that most of the vloggers "embraced a fairly narrow form of identity politics [for example, gender and sexuality] rather than more broad-based . . . changes to capitalism, for example" (p. 509). Raby, Caron, Théwissen-LeBlanc, Prioletta, and Mitchell argue that their research demonstrates that there are "young people who are not disengaged" and who connect with a "rich, interactive community" online (p. 509).

Another venue for analysis is online reviews, which have become ubiquitous on the Internet. Matthew S. Johnston et al. (2018) drew on anonymous online reviews written by people who were either working for or had worked at Canadian call centres. They found that online review spaces allowed for "collective discussion and critique" in light of "oppressive [work] conditions" call-centre employees encounter (p. 2). The reviews the authors studied "shed light on the conditions of alienation" as well as "strategies for resistance" that reviewers shared (p. 14).

Researching on Twitter

Researchers have also begun to use Twitter in their research. Mark Norman (2012) followed Twitter during the 2011 CBC broadcast of *Hockey Day in Canada*. He identified three themes that dominated tweets: first, the "discursive construction of hockey" as part of Canadian identity; second, comments on corporate sponsorship by Scotiabank; and third, discussion of commentator Don Cherry.

In his book on how social media have influenced policing, Christopher J. Schneider (2016) explored strategies the Toronto Police Service used to present itself to the public on Twitter. He analyzed more than 100,000 official police tweets posted by police officers. Schneider found that the police used Twitter to promote an image of police officers as "down-to-earth" "average Joes" and to diminish the perception of cops as authoritarian figures (p. 93–4). It accomplished this goal by using sports tweets, by addressing officers by their first names, by including non–work-related tweets, and by including humorous tweets such as those playing up the cop–doughnut stereotype.

Twitter, Instagram, TikTok, and other social media venues provide endless opportunities for research. Keep in mind that no matter what data you interpret, there will be some limitations. If you study a hashtag (#) thread, for example, you will not likely have access to demographic data to spot trends across social location.

Summary

In this chapter, we have surveyed some of the myriad approaches to content analysis. We also discussed the benefits and challenges of using pre-existing data rather than data generated by other more participatory methods. We examined recent innovations in unobtrusive research, including visual sociology and Internet research. As we have seen, researchers often do content analysis with a critical eye.

Key Terms

cultural studies	institutional ethnography (IE)	social disorganization
ethnographic content analysis	latent content	unobtrusive methods
eulogy work	manifest content	visual sociology
frame	mundane technology	
identity foreclosure	rite of passage	

Questions for Critical Thought

1. Keeping in mind Jeff Ferrell's study of trash, think about the kinds of things that you routinely throw out and where you discard them. What conclusions might an "ethnographer of trash" reach about your way of life based on what they would find in your trash?

2. Even though romance novels are considered low-status forms of fiction, many women read them voraciously. How might you design a content analysis of this genre to explore how it presents the perfect relationship, the perfect man, and the perfect courtship? What might such a study tell us about widely held conceptions of "romantic" relationships? Think about the possible frames a romance novel might use to construct a definition of the situation about romance.

3. Do you think it is ethical to read people's discarded letters without getting their permission? Why or why not?

4. What might be some limitations of collecting data online? What might be some advantages?

5. Think about the objects with which you come into contact on a daily basis. How might these objects reveal something to a researcher about you and your life?

Exercises

1. Do an analysis of the student evaluation form at your university. (You should be able to get a copy from the registrar's office.) Make a list of the topics of each question, and think about what the list tells you about how the university wants to represent itself to itself, to its faculty, and to its students. If you were to design your own questionnaire, what items would you include? What do the differences between the official form and yours tell you about divergent ideas about what matters in a university class?

2. Choose a contemporary animated film, and do a manifest and latent content analysis on the characterization of the evil characters. Count the number of evil characters, and note their characteristics (class, "race," gender, age, and ethnicity). Look for hidden messages about evil in the film.[6]

3. Watch five hours of scripted television shows, and analyze how aging and older characters are represented. Consider depictions both in the shows themselves and in the advertisements that run during each show. What does the manifest content tell you about the types of characters represented? What does the latent content tell you about how the audience is meant to perceive the characters?

In-Class Exercise

Look at a copy of each of four different magazines, either in print or online—for example, *Maclean's*, *Chatelaine*, *National Geographic*, and *Men's Health*. Examine the ads, and answer the following questions: To what kind of audience is the magazine addressed? What does the magazine suggest are the interests and the preoccupations of its readers? How does the magazine demonstrate how men and women relate to one another? What messages about "race," ethnicity, or age do the images imply? Are there any striking patterns in the photos? If so, what might these patterns suggest?

Suggested Readings

Jeff Ferrell. 2006. *The Empire of Scrounge: Inside the Urban Underground of Dumpster Diving, Trash Picking, and Street Scavenging.* New York: New York University Press. Jeff Ferrell spent eight months living off what he acquired by going through dumpsters and other sources of discarded goods. This book is his account of the community of those who live off the streets and an "ethnography" of the material objects. His photographs and prose provide an intriguing account that would lead anyone to question contemporary consumer society.

Best, Joel. 2020. "COVID-19 and Numeracy: How about Them Numbers?" *Numeracy* 13 (2). Joel Best spent time analyzing media coverage of COVID-19 and showed that statistics are not always as straightforward as they seem.

van den Scott L.-J.K., C. Forstie, and S. Balasubramanian. 2015. "Shining Stars, Blind Sides, and 'Real' Realities: Exit Rituals, Eulogy Work, and Allegories in Reality Television." *Journal of Contemporary Ethnography* 44(4): 417–49. The authors of this article watched and re-watched the exit rituals from various reality television shows to analyze public, symbolic death and the social processes that accompany it.

Related Websites

YouTube
www.youtube.com
There are several videos on YouTube that provide excellent coverage of how researchers have used unobtrusive methods. In particular, you may want to check out Jeff Ferrell's short video about dumpster diving and clips from *Killing Us Softly 4*, Jean Kilbourne's latest instalment of her analysis of advertising's image of women. You can also view videos of various advertisements and analyze them for yourself.

The Gender Ads Project
www.genderads.com/
Scott A. Lukas, who was teaching a gender class at Lake Tahoe Community College, developed this site. He "wanted to share the powerful (and disturbing) images of advertising that depicted women as less than human." He has continued to develop the website, and it now includes more than 3000 images on a variety of themes, including roles, objects, violence, and others.

Sociological Images
http://thesocietypages.org/socimages
This website, maintained by sociologist Lisa Wade, "is designed to encourage all kinds of people to exercise and develop their sociological imagination by presenting brief sociological discussions of compelling and timely imagery that spans the breadth of sociological inquiry."

Notes

1. This shift has resulted in the explosion of the market for self-help books. See Kaminer (1992) for a critical discussion of the self-help movement.
2. To understand the influence a "frame" can have on a topic, think about news reports you have heard, seen, or read that discuss elderly drivers. You will likely notice that such stories usually have a bio-medical frame. That is, these articles usually focus on the physical decline that comes with aging. The

stories often discuss whether doctors can or cannot determine who should not be allowed to drive, or they focus on the need to require driving tests for "seniors" to ascertain whether or not they are still capable of driving safely. These stories almost never discuss societal issues that may affect older drivers. For example, perhaps in recognition of demographic changes, we should not be designing roads, street signs, and speed limits with young drivers in mind. The absence of these discussions in the news media is largely a result of the biomedical framing of the issue.

3. As you think about these findings, keep in mind that this study was done before 2001. We can guess that, since 9/11, there has likely been a more intense focus on fear as the awareness of terrorism has become more prominent.

4. We studied nine films made between 1942 and 1990. You can see these stages during the airport scenes in a more recent film, *Love Actually* (2003). Towards the end of this film, a widowed stepfather and his young stepson, Sam, who has recently lost his mother, race to the airport so that Sam can say goodbye to a girl in his class. When the two get to the airport, liminality takes over as Sam undertakes a traditional activity in the transition stage in movies: the tunnel run. Sam runs at breakneck speed through the airport and even security to get to the gate before the girl disappears into the plane. Norms mean nothing as Sam manages to see his "love" off. In the end, both father and son are reincorporated as men who have what it takes to take a chance on love.

5. Thompson has created a website for her film (http://coveredthemovie.wordpress.com/) on which she has posted various resources, including excerpts from her film and a short video about the making of *Covered*. In the videos, you can see how effective and meaningful the images of the women are.

6. This exercise is adapted from an assignment developed by Dr Sandra Wachholz, Criminology Department, University of Southern Maine, with appreciation for her generous sharing.

9 Trust the Process: Analyzing Qualitative Data

Learning Objectives

- To become familiar with the process of data analysis
- To understand how to go about coding
- To grasp how to develop and use themes, sensitizing concepts, and generic social processes in your analysis

Introduction

Qualitative research, whether it involves fieldwork, in-depth interviews, or document analysis, yields mountains of data that can intimidate any researcher, novice or experienced. The most basic fear of all qualitative researchers is that they won't find anything in their data. Deborah and Lisa-Jo have this feeling every time they do a study. But there are always things to find, usually more than a single study can address. So it is very important to **trust the process** and to have faith that there are important themes in your data that you will have the insight and skill to find and tie together in meaningful ways. Although data analysis involves what Lofland and Lofland (1995:181) have referred to as "routine activities"—for example, writing up full field notes, transcribing interviews, correcting transcripts, reading and rereading transcripts and notes, and **coding** data—the process is open-ended and creative, with high points of excitement that accompany unexpected insights.

There are different ways to go about analyzing qualitative data, and the choice depends on the researcher's theoretical perspective, professional interests, and research questions. We do our work from a symbolic interactionist perspective, so we tend to highlight how our participants understand their everyday lives and how they go about explaining them to us. When we conduct interviews, we take an active-interview approach and, therefore, pay close attention to how the interaction has played out in the interview. In addition, because Deborah has an ongoing interest in issues of gender, she always keeps an eye out for how gender identity affects a person's understanding of their social world.

Although you may follow an approach that reflects your perspective, never begin with predetermined concepts, hypotheses, or theoretical frameworks. Some novice researchers, overwhelmed by the amount of data they uncover, are tempted to choose a hypothesis and then search for items in their field notes or interviews that support that hypothesis. Resist this impulse. As Maria Mayan (2009:93) points out, if you were to give in to this temptation, you would be importing a deductive approach into your research and would "squash any opportunity for new ideas or notions of the phenomenon" you are studying. Your process may then come to resemble Cinderella's stepsisters' attempts to force their big feet into her tiny glass slipper by cutting off their toes. You do not want to mutilate your data to fit preconceived notions.

Many researchers engage in **reflexivity** as they interpret their data. They recognize that their own experiences and status (their gender, age, class, profession, etc.) affect the way that participants interact with them. For example, as Deborah thought about her interviews with older widowers, she took into account that she, as a middle-aged woman, was the type of person with whom some of the men might be interested in forming a romantic relationship. Thus, Deborah had to accept that some of her participants may have been trying to impress her during the interview process. Lisa-Jo was constantly aware throughout her research that she was a non-Indigenous person doing research with Indigenous people (van den Scott 2018). She constantly reminded herself that her presence had certain meanings for her participants that may not always have been positive.

Angela Wisniewski (2013), a young, slim woman, interviewed middle-aged women who had engaged in weight-loss practices about their experience with losing weight. She found that the women felt, to some extent, that she could not relate to their experiences because she had never been overweight. Wisniewski used this knowledge in her analysis of her data. Many researchers also consider how their own perceptions and experiences influence their interpretation of the data (Dowling 2008).

Although there are a number of software packages on the market to use in qualitative data analysis (for example, NVivo), we will not discuss them in this chapter for two reasons. The first is that they do not do the conceptual work for you. It is essential to learn how to analyze data before turning to a data-management tool for help. Jumping into the software too soon is like using a calculator before you learn to add. If you do not understand the process, you will not have any way of knowing if your analysis makes sense. The second reason is an extension of the first: when you code data using a software package, especially if you are a novice researcher, you may cut off options too early in the process and lose some of the flexibility that is the strength of qualitative research. If you do choose to use one of these programs, remember that you will likely have to either go back to your data to develop new **codes** as you go along or risk compromising your analysis by sticking to decisions you made too early in the coding process. We use a word-processing program when we are analyzing our data and find it works very well.

Unlike data analysis in quantitative research, which begins only after all the data have been collected, analysis goes on throughout the life of a qualitative study. We have already discussed some of the early steps in data analysis (for example, writing up full field notes and transcribing interviews). In addition, we will continue to discuss certain aspects of analysis in Chapter 10 as we discuss the process of writing up your research. In this chapter, we look at processes most central to analysis. First, we consider how memos can help you to keep track of your ideas throughout the research process. We also learn about coding interview transcripts and field notes, using stories and sensitizing concepts to gain a deeper understanding of your participants' perspectives, and identifying and analyzing generic social processes to get at the heart of your material. We then discuss how you can join the broader research conversation and make a real contribution to the field. Finally, we look at two newer approaches, discourse analysis and narrative analysis.

Beginning with Memos

Analysis starts as soon as you begin to collect your data. For this reason, you should keep something with you at all times for jotting down **memos**. You never know when an idea will hit you, and you do not want to lose any valuable insight. Include in your memos anything that might help you to understand your data later: your own preliminary ideas, connections you make while in the field, references to articles or books that may contain useful information, and so on. Also record any pertinent comments others make about your research. They can help you to approach your research topic from a wider perspective. When Deborah was interviewing widowers, for example, many of her friends and colleagues commented that widowers get married too soon after their wives die. These comments led her to investigate how widowers think about re-partnering as an intrinsic part of widowhood.

Once you leave the field, transfer your notes to a computer file. This process will force you to make sense of them and provide you with a back-up copy in case you lose your notebook or device. Make sure to date each memo and note what you were reading, thinking about, or doing at the time you got the idea. Box 9.1 includes sample memos from Deborah's study of older men's experiences as widowers (see van den Hoonaard 2010). Several of the memos contain ideas and questions that occurred to her while she was reading interview transcripts or listening to the recordings of interviews; others are meant to remind her of literature Deborah wanted to keep in mind as she did her analysis.

You will find it useful to read through your memos on a regular basis while you are analyzing and writing up your data. This perusal will remind you of your early ideas as you work. Good memos may help you flesh out concepts or theoretical explanations that will help you understand your findings (Charmaz 2006).

As time goes on, you will want to consult your field notes or interview transcripts and begin the process of coding.

Box 9.1 Sample Memos

26 April 2002

From interview with "DL"

- Thoughts about being a widower—incl. stereotypes
- Participants' tendency to turn topic of interview to their own accomplishments
- Is having a woman something that is just part of being a man?
- Note: he doesn't mention his wife when he talks about his son's dyslexia—she's an invisible presence in his interview

3 May 2002

From interview with "FL"

- Finances—he bought a computer program to figure out finances—vs. women who find a person, usually a male relative or financial advisor, to help them
- Two aspects of parenting—functional (e.g., getting food on the table) and emotional
- Widower identity—does not seem to exist, and some men look for other ways to self-identify to avoid the ambiguity of calling themselves widowers. So, if there's no image, then self-identifying is empty.

8 May 2002

From interview with "GA"

It seems that, for women, not looking for another man is a badge of honour in some ways—she is loyal to a man who was wonderful. For men, it may be that not being interested in other women or not being able to find one may be a weakness—they're too attached to their wives. Hmm.

11 November 2005

Revisit Sarah H. Matthews, *The Social World of Old Women*, maintaining a precarious self-identity. She identifies strategies old women use to distance themselves from the self-identity of old women . . . maybe this would work in identifying strategies men use to maintain a sense of masculinity.

- p. 82: "justifying labels"
- maybe p. 83: attaching new meaning to old activities

Coding Interview Transcripts and Field Notes

Analyzing qualitative data is labour intensive, and it requires time for you to think and let ideas percolate. There are no real shortcuts to interpreting data. Lofland and Lofland (1995:185–6) liken analysis to the solving of a puzzle and explain that finding theoretical propositions in the "chaos of 'mere data'" can be exciting and exhilarating. They exhort us to "go for the high!"

Once you have typed up your interview transcripts or field notes, it is time to read them through. When you are finished reading them, read them again, think about them, and read them again, all the while writing memos. Andrea Doucet (2007:278–84) finds it useful to focus on a different aspect with each pass when she is analyzing her interviews. First, she reads each transcript with attention to the story that her participant is telling and tries to understand "what is going on here." Then she "reads [her]self" into the story and thinks about her own reactions to what the participant said and did in the interview. Her third reading is an "I" reading, during which she focuses on how the person speaks about themselves. This reading sheds light on how the participant sees and presents themselves in the social world. In later readings, she looks at the location of the participant in their social network and in wider social structures.

As you analyze your data, you will be refining your research questions. Remember that because analysis occurs throughout the research process, your research questions will change across the life of your study. Howard S. Becker (1998:121) suggests an approach that involves finding a question in the data: "The data I have here answer a question. What question could I possibly be asking to which what I have written down in my notes [or transcripts] is a reasonable answer?" Similarly, Kathy Charmaz (2001:678) advises that we ask of our data, "What is happening here?" The approach suggested by Becker and by Charmaz reminds us of the quiz show *Jeopardy*: the data provide the answer, and you have to figure out the question.

To determine the questions that your data answer, begin by coding your data. The word *code* may be intimidating, and it may seem as though developing codes is a complex business, but there is no need to over-complicate the process. Codes are simply names for the topics, activities, events, and people that come up in your transcripts or field notes. While the term *coding* is borrowed from quantitative analysis, in which words and ideas are translated into numbers, we do not reduce data to numbers in qualitative research. Coding, in our case, simply means finding terms or phrases to categorize chunks of the data so that we can work with them. When you code, you first identify the themes that appear in your data. Later in the process, you will look for and develop more detailed sub-themes and concepts.

The first step in coding is called **open coding**, a process closely associated with **grounded theory** (Glaser and Strauss 1967; Charmaz 2006). Open coding involves labelling the themes that you find in your transcripts or field notes. At this early stage, do not try to narrow down what you are looking for, and do not limit your codes to what seems relevant to your research questions. Do not decide on your codes in advance, or you may lose the richness of your data and, in fact, misrepresent them. Kathy Charmaz (2006) encourages speed and spontaneity for this initial coding because it can spark creative thinking. Later, you will revise and improve on these initial codes.

While you do not want to narrow your focus too much in advance, you will find that your background knowledge and experience shape the types of information you find. This is natural, and it can lead you to become aware of things that other researchers might not have found, given the same data. For example, if you are familiar with your research topic, you may notice that some theme seems to be missing from your transcripts or field notes. If you have strong reasons to believe that a theme is important even if your participants have not discussed it, reread your notes or transcripts to see if you can find any clues as to what is going on.

Deborah has often gained insight into her participants' experiences by investigating themes that seem to be missing. In her interviews with Iranian Bahá'ís who came to Canada as religious refugees, Deborah noticed that none of the people she interviewed discussed the issue of racism. Yet Deborah knew that at least some of these people must have experienced some racism. Therefore, she **problematized** the issue and looked for clues in the data to explain the absence of racism in the interviews. Deborah found that the participants had described extreme persecution in their country of origin and that their experiences led them to minimize any less severe problems they had in Canada. As a result, they downplayed the racism they encountered in their new surroundings and excused racist behaviour as understandable or characteristic of only a few individuals. Questioning the absence of the theme of racism in the interviews led to a deeper appreciation of the creativity the participants used to find a place for themselves in their new communities.

As you begin your process of coding, try to analyze your data in manageable pieces. If you are working with field notes, you might want to look at your notes for each session and identify a few recurring themes. When looking through transcripts, try to identify a few themes that characterize each interview. Anthropologist Sharon Kaufman (1986) used this method for her classic study, *The Ageless Self.* She explains that the theme of an interview is a topic or issue that comes up over and over again. In Deborah's own research, one widow she interviewed repeatedly brought up the poor relationship she had with her stepchildren. This topic became the theme of her interview. Ginter and Radina (2019: 58) also suggest that "linguistic connectors" such as *since* and *because* that link one event or belief to another can be useful for identifying themes.

At this early stage, you do not have to worry about how everything fits together. Trusting the process means taking one step at a time. Trying to do everything at once would, indeed, be overwhelming. You will likely find that your early codes are "numerous and varied" (Lofland and Lofland 1995) because they identify the issues that your participants brought up. In addition, you may find that individual items, events, or stories fit into several thematic categories. As you accumulate more data, you will also likely realize that you cannot develop all the topics that show up in your notes or transcripts. All of this is fine—the most important themes and questions will become clear as your analysis progresses.

Once you have coded each transcript or set of field notes, your next step is to bring the material together. This requires assembling the data related to each theme in one place. If your transcripts or notes are quite long and your research question is broad, you might find it useful to think of organizing your themes into chapters, as in a book. When Deborah was analyzing her data on women's experiences of widowhood, she grouped sections of her interview transcripts under headings: "What does it mean to be a widow?" "How do widows' relationships with their children change?" "What kinds of new things do widows learn to do?" Next, read over each transcript or set of field notes (again!), make a file for each theme, and copy all the data related to each theme into the appropriate file. You should also note where each chunk of data came from so that you can always place it in its original context.

As you are compiling your data into thematic chapters, continue to develop memos on your ideas for organizing your data, both within each chapter and throughout your written analysis as a whole. Box 9.2 includes Deborah's ideas for a chapter on widows' relationships with men. At this point, you may also decide on a tentative outline or table of contents to use when you are writing up your study (see Chapter 10), but keep in mind that the table of contents is not set in stone. Its purpose is to help you to think about the overall narrative or way that you can explain what you have found.

Once you have finished sorting your data into open codes, you are ready for the next step—**focused coding**. During this phase, go through the material that relates to each broad, open code, and recode for specific aspects of the theme. So, for example, in the widowhood study, after pulling together all the data related to the theme of learning new things, Deborah did focused coding and made separate files for the more specific sub-themes of learning to do new things, in general; learning to live alone; learning to drive/learning to drive alone; and changing self-concepts related to learning to do new things. Then she worked with each file separately.[1]

During this process, you will winnow out less useful codes and focus on a select number of more productive codes (Lofland and Lofland 1995:192). As

Box 9.2 Memo: Ideas for Chapter on Widows' Relationships with Men

- Experiences with men—new ways of relating
- Comments about male guests and gossip ("J," "M," "R," "D")
- For the widows who had a relationship ("D," "C") this was a theme of the interview
- Strategies for male companionship—safe ways to go about it ("A" with ballroom dancing; "D" and "I" at church)
- Men's attitudes
- Wedding-ring issues
- Kids' attitudes about remarriage

you go through the data more closely, you will discover concepts and have ideas that escaped your attention when you were reading to identify your initial codes (Charmaz 2006:50). By staying very close to the data, you can avoid the mistake of "imputing your motives, fears, or unresolved issues to your respondents and . . . data" (Charmaz 2006:53).

As you are coding your data, remember that a primary goal of qualitative research is to understand the participant's situation from their point of view. Because the participant is the expert on their own life, you can understand the data only if you know what the data mean to each participant. Next, we will look at two approaches to understanding your participants' situations in depth: analyzing **stories** and developing **sensitizing concepts**.

Stories in Western Cultures

A story is a refined version of events. Often, when someone tells a story, they have told that story before and have, with each telling, crystallized the meaning that the narrative holds for them. Telling a story is usually purposeful; there is a moral to the story that addresses the issue at hand that the teller wants the listener to understand. Many people adopt a storytelling tone to communicate the story's importance.

Often, you will learn the most about a participant's situation and self-perception by listening to what Kenyon and Randall (1997:46–7) have referred to as "signature stories." These are tales people like to tell about themselves or situations that they like to narrate. Signature stories reveal something about what makes us tick, about turning points in our path, about why our life has turned out the way it has. They also indicate something about our fundamental beliefs, convictions, and habits. You probably have particular stories that you like to tell about yourself, perhaps to create an impression about the type of person you are and to develop a moral self for your listeners. These stories contribute to the process of what sociologists often call "impression management" (see Goffman 1959).

In interpretive research, we can analyze stories to understand how our participants understand their place in the world and how they interpret their own status in relation to others.[2] Consider what the following story tells about the man, a widower, who told it to Deborah:

> If you follow all these money grabbers' wishes. Like I went to [the store]; I knew [my wife] used to have [their] credit card. And she had [their customer-loyalty card]. So I went in one day, probably two months after [her death] to try and transfer her . . . points to my name. No way in hell. No, they wanted a copy of her will to see that I was going to get her stuff. They wanted her death certificate, and they wanted her medical and doctor's certificate. So that kind of ticked me off. I was getting kind of ugly at that point. It was stupid. I knew she was dead . . . well, they

say, "well, maybe you kicked her out and you're trying to take all her stuff." And all this stuff. And I said, "well, does she owe you any money?" They wouldn't tell me that either. So finally, I said to the girl, "well, I hope she does. . . . You're going to have to find her to get it." And I never heard from them after that. (van den Hoonaard 2010:59)

In telling this story, the man has established himself as a heroic individual who is willing to take on big business, the "money grabbers." In contrast, he describes the store's representatives as oppressive and unjust, falsely accusing him, the victim, of kicking his wife out and then attempting to steal from her. Finally, he turns the situation around, suggesting that he has power in the relationship because the store might want something from him in the future.

Now, compare the previous story to the following one, in which one of Deborah's participants, a widow, relates an accomplishment:

Well there's one thing for instance, and it's so simple, like you know when the hydro goes out on the VCR and the clock, you know, it's blinking twelve o'clock, twelve o'clock, I never ever, now this is so simple, I never adjusted that thing, and I just didn't even know how to open this little box there. . . . I left it for about, oh it must have been about a week blinking. Well, I put a book up so I wouldn't see it. [So you wouldn't see it.] Yeah, I put a book up and said I don't know how to do it. So one day I went downstairs and I took my glasses and I said, "I'm going to fix this thing or else it's going to be unplugged." So I sat down and I got the instructions out and I just went step by step and I thought this was a major, oh I did a major job on that. Finally, I got it. And it was just the idea, I had never done it and I had never even looked at the instructions. And a child, of course, could do it. But it was a big achievement there. (van den Hoonaard 2010:59)

Here, the woman telling the story doesn't depict herself as a hero but, rather, as an average person who persevered when faced with a difficult task. The woman's purpose in telling the story was to explain how she had developed a sense of confidence that she had not had before.

Stories in Research with Indigenous Communities

As we noted in Chapter 2, Indigenous cultures have a more collective outlook on what it means to be a human being than Western cultures (Bull 2016). It's not surprising that this focus on the collective or on the community would result in stories' having a purpose different from that of a research participant's telling a story about themselves to tell you what kind of person they are.

Chilisa Bagele (2012:139) explains that Indigenous stories reflect "the values of a society and act as teaching instruments [and are] commentaries on society, family, or social relations." Linda Tuhiwai Smith (2012:145) adds that the point is not that stories "simply tell a story or tell a story simply. [Rather], the story and the story teller both serve to connect the past with the future, one generation with the other, the land with the people and the people with the story."

It is for these reasons that Lina Sunseri (2011) opens her book *Being Again of One Mind: Oneida Women and the Struggle for Decolonization* with the Oneida creation story "One Woman Falling from the Sky" and repeats it later in the book. She notes that the importance of women in the creation story of the Oneida nation allows us to understand the centrality of women, the spiritual connection that the Oneida people have with the land, the importance of kinship relations, and the theme of twinship, which "implies two sides in need of each other in order to bring harmony and balance to all of life, including the nation" (p. 48–50).

Stories help us to interpret concepts, such as power and balance, that have different connotations in Indigenous and Western cultures. For example, power in the Western context often refers to domination and control, while in the Oneida context, it "refers to a strength inside of us . . . that allows us to be self-determining and to act upon our responsibility" (Sunseri 2011:158).

Sunseri also notes that every time someone narrates a story, the context changes and the listener can learn new lessons. When Deborah was conducting her interview research with widows, she happened to interview an Indigenous woman whose daughter had introduced them. During the course of the interview, this woman told Deborah the story of her experience as a young girl. It was required that she stay in school until she was 16, but the school near her reserve only went to Grade 8. Because the priest gave permission for only a few people to go into the nearby city to attend school, this participant had to repeat grade 8 three times. At the time, Deborah didn't really understand why her participant had told her this story, but it is the element of her interview that has stayed with Deborah for more than 20 years. It was not simply a story about an individual; it has helped Deborah understand more about the relationship between Indigenous people and Canada.

Lisa-Jo focused on storytelling as central when doing interviews with Inuit participants, encouraging storytelling whenever possible. These stories illustrated community life and beliefs. For example, one of her participants told Lisa-Jo about her wedding day and how the priest had told her and her now-husband that they should get married in the church. She continued on about how a teacher helped her to get dressed up and provided some things that one "needs" for a wedding. Despite the fact that this story was told with much laughter, it also demonstrated for Lisa-Jo something about how colonial pressures were exerted and how the judgment of the "south" impacted practices in the "north."

Hence, when we are analyzing stories in Indigenous research, we need to think about the purpose our participants have for telling us particular stories. Rather than highlighting personal characteristics, they tell us about a culture and a society's values.

Sensitizing Concepts

Researchers develop sensitizing concepts to help them understand their participants' world views. Herbert Blumer (1954 as cited in van den Hoonaard 1997:29) first articulated the idea of sensitizing concepts as "holding pens"—tools to group similar data together—that we can use to "frame" the activity we are studying. For the most part, as with the codes we discussed above, sensitizing concepts come from the data themselves rather than from ideas we have before we collect those data.

The first step in developing a sensitizing concept is to look for concepts that the participants in the study formulate for themselves. As you are assessing your data, ask yourself these questions: "What is this person talking about?" "Is the idea or process important?" "What does this idea or process mean to this person?" Look for words, phrases, and ideas that your participants use frequently, especially those that are not in common usage outside of the group involved in the study. Don't take any terms for granted. Rather, question how participants use them and what they imply about social life. To get a better understanding of how researchers identify, develop, and use sensitizing concepts in their research, let's look at some examples from real-life studies.

When Deborah was interviewing widows, many of the women repeatedly used two phrases when they talked about their relationships with their friends: "keeping up appearances" and "couples' world." The women used the first phrase to explain that if they wanted to keep their friends, they had to give the impression that they were doing okay. If they seemed too depressed or talked about their husbands all the time, their friends would drop them like "a hot potato." They used the second phrase to capture their feelings of discomfort and exclusion in many social settings due to their status as a single person. One widow emphasized the meaningfulness of the phrase when she told Deborah "it's a couples' world," defined what she meant, and then repeated, "I tell you, it's a couples' world." These two concepts contributed to Deborah's theoretical understanding of the changed status women experience when they become widows.

In her study of Inuit residents in Arviat, Nunavut, Lisa-Jo (2009) identified the concept of "Southern clothes" as central to the experiences of the residents. The only access this town has to the rest of Canada is on four daily flights. Lisa-Jo noted that, at the airport, one can easily determine who is leaving and who is not by the way each person looks. She writes:

> Travellers' hats are off, hair is often styled, shoes have now replaced boots.... It is commonplace for travellers to leave their Arctic parkas behind and to walk, or run, to the plane through the cold. (2009:215)

The locals refer to this attire as "Southern clothes," but Lisa-Jo notes that the concept connotes more than simply a change of style. It refers to "a way of reaffirming and performing identity and differentiating between [Nunavut and the South]" (2009:215).

Consulting the Literature

Some sensitizing concepts are broad and relate to many social contexts. Thus, as you read literature related to your study, you may come across previously identified sensitizing concepts that help you to understand your participants' situation. When this happens, create a memo to record the source of your inspiration. This memo will help you in case you want to go back and consult the literature at a later time, and you will need this information if your idea proves fruitful and you end up using the idea in your final written analysis. (We will discuss writing up your study, an extension of the process of analysis, in Chapter 10.)

One example of a generalizable sensitizing concept is **civil inattention**. Erving Goffman first identified this concept in his influential text *Behavior in Public Places* (1963), in which he analyzed "ordinary human traffic and the patterning of ordinary social contacts" (p. 4). Goffman developed the concept of civil inattention to explain individuals' habit of subtly acknowledging the presence of others but not focusing on them too intently, thus avoiding any feelings of threat or confrontation (1963:84).[3] It has broad application, since most of us use some form of civil inattention every day—while walking down a crowded street, eating at a restaurant, or even attending a class. Thus, the concept Goffman developed might be adapted to various situations; indeed, many researchers have used the concept of civil inattention to gain an understanding of their participants' behaviours. Let us look at some other examples.

Arlie R. Hochschild (1979) was the first researcher to develop the concepts of **emotion work** and **feeling rules**. She described these concepts in her study of flight attendants and the commercialization of emotions, in which she discovered that the attendants work to make themselves feel a certain way (they engage in emotion work) so that they can display the feelings they are required to have while they are working (feeling rules). More recently, Hochschild has explored the emotion work and feeling rules surrounding how surrogate mothers in India deal with carrying a baby they will hand over to parents in other parts of the world—for example, Canada. She found that these surrogates were instructed to think of their wombs as "carriers" and themselves as "prenatal babysitters to detach themselves emotionally from their baby and their clients" (2011:24).

Many other researchers have found Hochschild's sensitizing concepts useful in understanding their own participants. These concepts informed Deborah's understanding of the ways in which widows described their efforts to "keep up appearances" by doing the emotion work to conform to feeling rules of not being too depressed. More recently, Marlene Santin and Benjamin Kelly (2017) brought Hochschild's concept of emotion work into the post-9/11 era by studying how institutional norms that are focused on security rather than on service have empowered flight attendants to have more control over how they perform emotional labour. Lisa-Jo, Clare Forstie, and Savina Balasubramanian (2015) also expanded on Hochschild's concept of emotion work to coin the term "eulogy work," referring to the emotion work those voted off reality television must do in their final moments on the show.

McLuhan, Pawluch, Shaffir, and Haas (2014) and McLuhan (2020) turn the concept of the cloak of competence that we discussed in Chapter 2 on its head to explore the idea of a "cloak of incompetence." They suggest that individuals often purposefully create an impression of diminished competence in a variety of circumstances. When Deborah read their article, she recognized this process of interaction in her interviews with widowers. As Deborah noted in Chapter 6, the widowers behaved in an assertive manner to establish their masculinity during the interviews. In those same interviews, the widowers donned a cloak of incompetence in traditional, feminine tasks, such as housecleaning and cooking, as a "hedge against [the] potential identity loss" (McLuhan et al. 2014:376) of appearing to be too much like a woman. Widowers who knew how to cook provided accounts of cooking masculine food, such as steaks, associated with masculine activities, such as coaching hockey, to "ward off . . . a "competent designation" (McLuhan 2020:133) related to a traditionally feminine activity that might challenge their masculinity (van den Hoonaard 2010). As McLuhan et al. suggest, the generic process of "cloaking behavior" is a "presentational strategy that individuals employ as they seek . . . to position themselves along a competence/incompetence continuum" (p. 380). You can probably think of times when you found it useful to appear less capable of doing something than you really are.

In their influential text *Awareness of Dying* (1965), Glaser and Strauss identified a series of related concepts to capture the continuum of how much dying patients know about their terminal status. These concepts include "closed contexts," when the patient is completely in the dark; "suspicion," when the patient suspects that they are dying but no one else will admit the situation; "mutual pretense," when everyone knows about the impending death but pretends otherwise; and "open context," when everyone involved both knows and admits to knowing that the patient is dying. Today, these concepts are well known and have been adapted to a variety of other situations. Karen March (1995) used them to help her understand and explain the situation of adoptees who were attempting to control stigma associated with their identities of being adopted.

The more reading you do of others' work, the more potential concepts you will have to help you understand your data. Of course, all the concepts you use have to "earn their way into your analysis" (Glaser 1978 as cited in Charmaz 2006). Hence, if a concept does not present itself based on your data, do not include it in your analysis.

As your analysis proceeds, you will continue to re-evaluate your previous findings in light of your new understandings. Eventually, you will have accumulated enough data to identify generic social processes that relate to your study. In the next section, we will discuss how to go from codes, concepts, and themes to results you can use in your final write-up.

Bringing It All Together: From Codes to Generic Social Processes

Once you have coded your data, identified major themes and sub-themes, and located sensitizing concepts, it is time to think about what it all means—to address what Esterberg (2002:166) calls the "'so what' question." You need to think about how your various themes and concepts relate to one another and to make connections among them. One way of doing this is to interpret them in light of social processes.

Identifying generic social processes within your data can help you to describe and explain how things happen and why people do the things they do. To identify such processes, look for commonalities in the ways your participants approach and interpret their situations. Doing background reading on the types of processes other researchers have analyzed in their studies can also inspire you to identify such processes in your own data. While you should never try to force your data to fit with a particular generic social process, being aware of such processes can help you to understand your participants' social world.

The best way to grasp how researchers identify and use generic social processes in their analysis is to look at examples from previous studies. As you read through the examples below, note how some researchers have identified the broader implications of their findings by comparing what they have discovered about their participants to individuals' situations beyond the limits of their study. Such comparisons often present themselves at the end of the analysis process—once the researcher has gained a full understanding of their data.

Antony J. Puddephatt (2003) explored, through participant observation and interviews, interactions within a community of amateur chess players. He observed that the players had common approaches to the generic social process of performing activities. He identified the shared practices of strategic interaction that chess players use and suggested dimensions of that interaction, including how people create an image (image work) by masking their intentions and fears and by keeping their attack plans veiled. He then connected this process to the way hustlers and magicians use deception and image work in their activities.

In her study on the use of alternative therapies, Jacqueline Low (2004) identified a shared approach to the process of problem-solving among her participants. Her participants saw "taking control" and "being subject to self-control" as ways of solving the problem of "achieving wholeness and balance." Low notes that solving the problem by taking control involved wresting control from medical professionals, asking questions, getting second opinions, and finally trusting practitioners enough to hand over control to them. Being subject to self-control involved doing independent research and making lifestyle changes.

When you hand in an essay to your professors, it may seem that the marks they assign are arbitrary. We remember jokes about professors' tossing the essays up a flight of stairs and assigning grades based on which step each essay landed. Scott Grills (2017) took up the challenge of studying the generic social process of assigning relative value to a social object—the university essay. Grills identified three themes in how the faculty he interviewed across disciplines said they graded essays: the evaluation of 1) "the student's ability to work independently, . . . 2) the students' ability to construct a research question, conduct research, . . . and develop an argument, and 3) . . . the student's ability to present thoughts clearly [and] concisely" (p. 73). As with many social objects, such as works of art, the evaluation of student essays is not conducive to objective measures, despite attempts to impose the above seemingly objective standards. As a result, some professors adopt a comparative approach to grading, ranking each essay in comparison to the others in a particular class, while other professors have a more fixed standard. The fixed-standard approach appears more objective and may involve a score sheet or rubric that "awards points for particular outcomes" (p. 78). Grills demonstrates that in marking essays, professors are engaging in the generic social process of "determining the relative worth of social objects" (p. 81).

Daniel and Cheryl Albas, whom we first encountered in Chapter 2, provide an exemplary illustration of how identifying and analyzing concepts and social processes can lead researchers to draw meaningful conclusions in their studies. As you may recall, the Albases have spent many years studying student life in its various aspects. In analyzing students' approach to exams, they identified the concept of magic and then observed how magic fits into the social process of dealing with uncertainty:

> One of the most fascinating yet difficult features of the study to understand was the . . . extent to which students employed magical rituals and charms . . . seemingly irrational and bizarre behaviour, for example, the student who reported that she always studied in the presence of one of her torn toenails . . . because it "brought her good luck." . . . This led us to start collecting, classifying, and evaluating the occurrences our students told us about . . . material items (e.g., lucky sweaters) or behaviour (e.g., ritual formulae or prayer) prescribed for luck or to be avoided (e.g., don't let anyone wish you good luck or don't sit near anyone wearing something pink). . . . We define magic as action directed to the achievement of an outcome with no logical relationship between the action and the outcome itself. (Albas and Albas 2009:109)

Thus far, we can see that the Albases have identified a concept to help them understand the students' behaviours around dealing with the uncertainty of exams.

Once they had made their primary observations, the Albases problematized the concept of magic by thinking about the social context and how the magic they had observed differed from magic in other situations. They then did background research on other settings where people use magic. First, they looked at preliterate societies. In those contexts, the rituals were performed publicly, passed down from one generation to another, and widely shared. Second, the researchers investigated more contemporary groups who use magic, such as actors, soldiers, and athletes. They found that members of these groups share knowledge about their rituals—most actors know to refer to the "Scottish Play" rather than *Macbeth*, and most hockey players are aware of the common superstition associated with shaving during the Stanley Cup playoffs. In these contexts, magic had a more collective orientation. In contrast, the students' rituals were made up by each student, practised at an individual level, and kept secret.

As the Albases' example suggests, reading material related to your study can help you to contextualize your data and uncover the wider implications of your findings. Reading a variety of sociological studies can also help you to find connections between your own findings and the findings of other researchers. When you take the next step of writing up your research, the topic of Chapter 10, you will include such comparisons in your write-up. By relating your findings to those that have come before, you join the research conversation already in progress in the literature and contribute to an increased understanding of social life. As we discussed in our introduction to generic social processes in Chapter 2, this is the "generalizability" of qualitative research.

Innovations in Analysis of Research

Over the past few decades, there has been a great deal of innovation in how qualitative researchers go about interpreting data. This section will familiarize you with two influential approaches: discourse and narrative analysis.

Discourse Analysis

Discourse analysis[4] is an interpretive approach influenced by the writing of Michel Foucault, a French philosopher. Foucault believed that language is not only a tool that describes reality but also a "social practice, a way of doing things" (Wood and Kroger 2000:4). Foucault suggested that discourse—the language we use to describe ourselves and our world—controls the way we define and think about our place and others' places in the world. In short, he suggested that discourse constitutes, rather than reflects, social life. Hence, discourse limits how we think, and Foucault believed that powerful components of society control the way we talk about phenomena and, thereby, define them (Rabinow 1984). These powerful components might be dominant populations within a society or any individual or group with enough sway to influence public discourse. If we think about the concept of the *definition of the situation*, we might say that discourse constructs the possible definitions of the situation and, therefore, has real consequences. It "shapes the ways in which individuals understand and experience their world and their self" (Lafrance 2011:83). It is for this reason that marginalized groups challenge taken-for-granted terms. For example, the label *handicapped* locates problems of mobility in the individual, while adopting a discourse of *disability* locates these problems in societal barriers to full participation. Challenging the dominant discourse can invoke the sociological imagination and transform a personal problem into a social issue (Mills 1959/1976). Discourse analysis often identifies and critiques everyday concepts and demonstrates how they serve the interests of those in power, those at the top of the hierarchy of credibility.

Let us think about how the words people use to describe themselves shape their social reality. In the past, most Canadians referred to and thought of themselves as *subjects* of the British Crown. By defining themselves as such, they established their identities as subservient to England and its monarchy. Later, when Canada began to see itself as a separate country, Canadians called themselves *citizens*. In adopting the discourse of citizenship, they saw themselves as participants in the country's social and political life, and they emphasized their constitutional rights and obligations Now, Canadians often refer to themselves as *taxpayers*. This term encourages people to see their social power in terms of money, and popular discourse focuses on government as accountable to the taxpayers because it uses *their* money. The term notably excludes those who do not make direct financial contributions to the government—for example, children, individuals on social assistance, some older people, and parents who care for their children at home and do not participate in the labour force. Therefore, the government becomes accountable only to those we recognize as paying taxes, even though others contribute to society in important ways.

In recent years, Indigenous peoples have begun to refer to those of European descent as *settlers*. By adopting this term, they are claiming legitimacy as inhabitants of Turtle Island long before Canada existed. An analysis of the national discourse on Canadian identity, then, reveals much about the dominant population that has the power to control the discourse. Such analysis also reveals that not everyone has such power.

Because discourse analysis assumes that terms and metaphors not only reflect what is already there but actually create the social world, the analysis seeks to explain what the discourse is doing and how it is being accomplished. It addresses "how the discourse is structured or organized to perform various functions and achieve . . . consequences" (Wood and Kroger 2000:95). Researchers, therefore, use a more detailed and technical form of transcription than other qualitative researchers that allows them to explore more closely the way participants say things, not just the words they use. Transcription in discourse analysis uses particular symbols to capture pauses, laughter, and overlapping conversation that might contribute to researchers' ability to analyze the functions of the discourse.

Often, prevailing discourses are so deeply rooted in our understanding of our social world that we do not question where they originated or who controls them. Consider the widespread acceptance of biomedical discourse. As the language and terminology of doctors, pharmaceutical companies, and medical specialists have taken hold, biomedical discourse has come to influence more and more of our understanding of ourselves in terms of medical conditions. In 1966, a doctor named Robert Wilson identified menopause, previously accepted as part of the natural aging process, as a "hormone deficiency disease." Since that time, the discourse that surrounds menopause has shaped our conception of women over 50—these women now see themselves and are seen by society as not entirely healthy. By examining the roots of such discourses, researchers can identify who controls the discourse and how their interests affect the way we interpret ourselves and the world around us. Monica Stelzl and her colleagues, whose work we looked at in Chapter 8, similarly identified medical discourse around the definition of social problems. They ask: Who benefits from this discourse, and how does it "interact with power and inequality" (2018:151)?

Gül Çalişkan and Kayla Preston (2017) have looked at how colonial thinking has permeated Western discourse and is reflected in Trumpism. Such thinking encourages belief in the superiority of the "West over the Rest" (p. 2). These researchers conducted a critical discourse analysis of seven speeches Donald Trump delivered between 2015 and 2017 when he was running for and elected president of the United States. Çalişkan and Preston demonstrate how Trump's speeches make use of colonial discourse to construct and dehumanize those he considers the Other. They argue that the powerful use discourse to consciously manipulate reality through the repetition of "'false truths' . . . until they become the only definition of truth that the masses know" (p. 12). In addition, Angela Cora Garcia (2019) looked at how the speeches of President Trump use discourse, such as "illegal alien killers" to refer to undocumented people to "convey the impression of otherness or . . . dehumanize people in this group" (p. 577).

Since 2000, researchers have been studying the impact of discourses of risk on various components of society. Let us look at studies that deal with policing (Sanders and Hannem 2012), how security guards in hospitals justify being violent as part of their jobs (Johnston and Kilty 2016), and how discourses around raising children have changed in *Chatelaine* magazine to construct mothering as risky (Clarke 2014).

Carrie Sanders and Stacey Hannem (2012) studied how discourse constructs information technology (IT) used in policing as "absent of social bias" and able to predict risks based on past "'dangerous' or 'troublesome behaviour'" (p. 391). They found that IT has changed policing and "legitimates 'control' of persons perceived as risky" (p. 401). As a result, those who live and work in particular neighbourhoods become "marked as 'risky'" (p. 407) by definition.

Matthew Johnston and Jennifer Kilty (2016) studied how the discourse that constructed psychotic patients as "always-already risky and potentially dangerous" (p. 184) led to security guards' interpreting their own, often violent, actions as "heroic and proactive" (p. 186). The discourse that focuses on risk allowed the guards to minimize their accountability for patients' suffering.

Juanne Clarke (2014) compared discourses of advice to mothers in *Chatelaine* magazine in two periods: between 1928 and 1940 and between 1990 and 2012. In the early period, scientific experts advised mothers to have a "distant, objective and scientific attitude" (p. 257) towards their children. In the 1990s, mothers were to "focus closely, compassionately and empathetically on their . . . individual children" (p. 259). Between 2000 and 2010, many stories dealt with psychiatric pathology and mental illness. Clarke observes that the "risk society" now constructs mothering as involving "risks to both physical and emotional/mental health" (p. 263) of children.[5]

Will C. van den Hoonaard (2011:190–8) carried out a discourse analysis of letters that research ethics boards sent to researchers in response to their applications. He analyzed how the discourse of those letters "carried authority" and presented "a semblance of appealing to higher ethical principles" than those held by researchers. He concluded that the use of the passive voice and "words of insistence (such as 'please clarify')" served a number of functions. It was a form of "institutional display" that "demonstrated both the diligence of the ethics committees" and their authority.

Michelle N. Lafrance (2009) has done a feminist discourse analysis of the experience of women who have been depressed. She identified discourses that construct men as dominant and women as subservient. She also considered the dominant biomedical discourse of depression as a medical condition. Her participants strove to meet a "good-woman ideal" that was impossible to achieve, while the "dominant understanding of depression as a biomedical problem" hid women's oppression and made them feel as if their suffering was "not real" (2009:174). She concludes:

> [W]omen who are depressed face pervasive delegitimation and silencing forged by both discourses of femininity and biomedicine. The interlocking discourses were similarly implicated in the silencing of a host of health problems that are particularly common among women. . . . Thus, the effect of this interlocking set of discourses is to marginalize and silence women's pain. This silencing maintains the status quo and the hegemony of both patriarchy and its bedfellow—biomedicine. (Lafrance 2009:174–5)

Lafrance's research is an excellent example of discourse analysis. She demonstrates how language has shaped women's experience with and understanding of depression.

Narrative Analysis

Narrative analysis has become a popular approach in a variety of fields, and it takes many forms. In all cases, researchers who use narrative analysis recognize the centrality of stories in the way people understand and talk about their lives. Sociologists focus on the stories people tell, the ways in which tellers structure their stories, the identity of the audience, and the social context or narrative environment within which stories develop (Gubrium and Holstein 2009). In narrative analysis, the stories themselves are the object of research (Riessman 2001). Some scholars even suggest that, in essence, "people are stories" (Kenyon and Randall 1999). Also, as David R. Maines (1993) has pointed out, narratives can constitute social acts.[6]

Stories can be particularly powerful when they extend beyond the individual to reinforce a group's identity or values. Hence, towns, countries, and ethnic or religious groups often have prototypical stories that they tell and retell, as we have seen with the Oneidas' creation story.

Researchers can also combine individuals' narratives to build a "collective story," to "narrativize the experience of a social category" (Richardson 1990:24–5). If they do a good job of building the collective story, individuals who are members of the category will respond with "That's my story. I am not alone" (Richardson 1990:25). As well, collective stories illuminate "the intersection of biography, history, and society" (Riessman 2001:697).

Gay Becker (1997) developed a collective story out of the narratives of people who had experienced sudden disruptions in their lives. She created this story by bringing together personal narratives on such topics as infertility, mid-life disruption, stroke, late-life transitions, and the experiences of ethnic minorities. Becker argues that narratives help people to make sense of disruptions caused by illness or personal misfortune because people use narratives to shape their experience and to create continuity. She also suggests that this collective story has reverberations beyond the focus of her study into the wider culture of America because the attempt to create continuity is an important value in American culture.

Deborah tried her hand at narrative analysis to interpret the stories widows told about their husbands' deaths (see van den Hoonaard 1999). Deborah looked at how the women structured the stories, the content of the stories, and the context in which the women developed their stories. Three themes, or stages, were common to all the stories: (1) learning that the husband was dying, (2) taking care of the husband, and (3) meeting the husband's death. Box 9.3 includes quotations to illustrate each of these themes. Notice how the first-person narration provides force to the story and how the story includes plots, characters, and time. Deborah concluded that these stories served as a bridge that eased the women's transition from the status of wife to that of widow, from a higher to a lower status.

Jaber F. Gubrium and James H. Holstein (2009) remind us that narratives always occur within a social context. They argue that analyzing a transcribed narrative (for example, a story taken from an interview) without being aware of the environment or interactional context in which the story was told can provide only a partial understanding. Particular circumstances, or narrative environments, influence whether or not a story will emerge and the shape it will take. An example of a narrative environment is an Alcoholics Anonymous (AA) group meeting. Norman K. Denzin, in *The Alcoholic Self* (1987), demonstrated how the AA environment shaped the stories that members told about themselves: at meetings, members constructed their stories so that they told the story of AA in the process. Similarly, Jaber F. Gubrium (1986), in his study of Alzheimer's support groups, found that different groups valued different kinds of stories about caregiving and the stories members told during the meetings reflected the values of each group.

Box 9.3 Narrative Analysis: Stories and Themes

||||||||||||||||||||||||||||||||||||||||||||||||||||||||||||||||||||||||||||||||||||||||||||||||||||||||||||||||||||||||||||||||||||||||||||||||||||||||

Theme One: Learning That Their Husbands Were Dying

So I said, when he came out to the car. I said, "What did they say?" He said, "Oh, we'll talk about it when we get home." . . . So we went home . . . and he said, "I have cancer." Like that, I felt. I felt like, you know, I can't move.

Theme Two: Taking Care of Their Husbands

We realized our time was short. So we made the best of it. . . . We did some trips and enjoyed ourselves. And probably had the most serene and loving kind of relationship . . . it was a time given to us especially.

Theme Three: Meeting Their Husbands' Deaths

A very peaceful death for him . . . he wasn't aware of anything. . . . We had gone to bed later on a Friday night . . . we were laying [sic] there, and he had his arm under my pillow and his other arm around me. . . . And about five minutes before he had said, "I love you so much." And then he said, "I've got to move." And I said, "Have I got your arm pinched?" . . . And he said, "No, I'm dizzy." And that was it.

Source: Quotations from D.K. van den Hoonaard, 1999.

As Mitchell Duneier (1999) notes, in a research setting, the social force of the narrative environment is often greater than the influence of the researcher. Duneier calls this the "Becker principle," after Howard S. Becker, who taught that social situations "practically require people to do or say certain things [or tell certain stories in particular ways] because there are other things going on that . . . are more influential in [their day] than a researcher" (Duneier 1999:338). Thus, while we must always be aware of the influence of our presence as researchers, we can reasonably assume that participants will generally say and do what seems appropriate in the setting despite our presence.

Summary

In this chapter, we have looked at how to transform mountains of data into research findings. We discovered that qualitative data analysis is an ongoing, labour-intensive process, but the mantra of "trust the process" encourages you to have faith that, with enough effort, you will find valuable connections among your data. We learned that coding can help you to identify these connections and that memos can help you to keep track of your insights and ideas. We saw how stories and sensitizing concepts can assist you in understanding your participants' situations from their points of view, and we examined the difference between the role of stories in Indigenous and Western cultures. We also encountered illustrations of how researchers have used concepts and generic social processes in their analyses. Finally, we looked at discourse and narrative analysis. At this point, it is time to start writing up your research. As you will learn in Chapter 10, writing is an extension of the process of analysis because you continue to gain further insights and generate more ideas about your data while you write.

Key Terms

civil inattention	focused coding	reflexivity
codes	grounded theory	sensitizing concepts
coding	memos	stories
discourse analysis	narrative analysis	trust the process
emotion work	open coding	
feeling rules	problematize	

Questions for Critical Thought

1. Some researchers suggest that you should show your interpretation of your data to your participants. To what extent should the researcher privilege their own analysis over the individual research participants' analysis?

2. Are there feeling rules that apply to how you should react when receiving your grade on a final exam? What are those feeling rules? Do you find yourself doing emotion work to conform to these feeling rules?

3. How do Indigenous stories differ from those told by individuals in Western cultures? Should you use particular methods for interpreting them differently?

4. Consider the terms *mother* and *father*. How might the collective meaning we give these terms in our discourse influence practices in our society?

5. How might open coding affect later analysis? Why is it important, then, to spend a good deal of time with your data?

Exercises

1. Think about a social group that you are interested in studying and of which you are not a member. Based on your experiences with members of this group, develop a sensitizing concept that could help you to understand their social world from their perspective.

2. Think about a group you belong to, and write a list of words or ideas that a researcher could use as sensitizing concepts in a study of the group. Did you find this task easier than the one given in the previous exercise? If so, why do you think this was the case?

3. Do some open coding of an interview transcript or a set of field notes. Write down, in memo form, any ideas you had while doing the coding that might help you to understand your data. See if you can identify the particular discourses the research participant uses. What do these discourses tell you about what kind of person the participant thinks they are?

In-Class Exercise

Do you ever use the kind of "magic" that the Albases described as a "private ritual"? Make a list of social settings you might investigate to find different interpretations of the concept of magic.

Suggested Readings

Kathy Charmaz. 2013. *Constructing Grounded Theory*. 2nd ed. Thousand Oaks, CA: Sage. Charmaz was one of the foremost contemporary writers on the use of grounded theory. The concrete suggestions and examples she includes in this text are invaluable for thinking about data analysis whether you use grounded theory or not.

Will C. van den Hoonaard. 1997. *Working with Sensitizing Concepts: Analytical Field Research*. Thousand Oaks, CA: Sage. This book, which belongs to Sage's research methods series, provides practical advice on how to identify and work with sensitizing concepts.

Susan Strega and Leslie Brown, eds. 2015. *Research as Resistance: Revisiting Critical, Indigenous, and Anti-Oppressive Approaches*. 2nd ed. Toronto: Canadian Scholars Press. This edited volume includes challenging chapters that address how to approach and, therefore, analyze research with Indigenous and other marginalized groups. Its chapters provide invaluable advice on how to become an anti-oppressive researcher.

Lindsay C. Sheppard, R. Raby, W. Lehmann, and R. Estabrook. 2019. "Grill Guys & Drive-Thru Girls: Discourses of Gender in Young People's Part-Time Work." *Journal of Childhood Studies* 44(3):156–69. Lindsay C. Sheppard and her colleagues explore how calling themselves "go-getters" influences young teenage girls' views of themselves and their likelihood to work at an early age.

L.T. Smith. 2012. *Decolonizing Methodologies: Research and Indigenous Peoples*. London: Zed Books.

Related Website

Qualitative Research in Information Systems, Association for Information Systems
www.qual.auckland.ac.nz
This website includes an overview of various methods of collecting and analyzing qualitative data. It provides a useful discussion of varied philosophical approaches to analyzing qualitative data as well as links to other websites and publications.

Notes

1. Box 9.2 illustrates a memo Deborah wrote while doing focused coding.
2. Those who do narrative analysis focus on the structure of the story as much as its content. For our purposes here, we will focus on the content of the story to provide material for analysis.
3. Often, people use civil inattention to avoid embarrassing someone else. Will C. van den Hoonaard (2010, personal communication) notes a good example of this use of civil inattention that comes from a trip he took to Oslo, Norway. He reports that he was reading his morning newspaper in a restaurant when the paper suddenly caught fire! He dropped the newspaper onto the table and banged on it to put out the flames. His silverware was bouncing around and making a great deal of noise. When he looked up, he saw that all the other people in the restaurant were "looking into their cups as if they'd never seen coffee before." Through their civil inattention, the people were preserving his dignity and avoiding his and their own embarrassment.
4. This section focuses on the Foucauldian approach to discourse analysis that is most often used by sociologists. Some researchers use conversation analysis, which has a more micro-analytic focus and which some argue has a more quantitative approach (Wood and Kroger 2000).
5. There is a long history of experts telling mothers how to raise their children. *For Her Own Good: 150 Years of Experts' Advice to Women* (Ehrenreich and English 1989) provides a fascinating chronicle of the types of advice experts who are almost always men have given to women.
6. Maines (2001) illustrated this point when he analyzed data from his research on diabetes self-help groups using a narrative approach and discovered that the narratives functioned to establish group boundaries and hierarchy within the groups.

10 Writing Up Qualitative Research

Learning Objectives

- To discover and trust the process of writing
- To become familiar with the parts of a qualitative research report
- To understand the need to start writing early and to write several drafts
- To develop an engaging style of writing

Introduction

In Chapter 9, we talked about learning to trust the process of data analysis. Your analysis continues as you write up the results of your research. As you write, you will gain further insights and create more ideas about your data. Once again, you may be questioning your ability to bring together your data in a meaningful way. We urge you to trust the process—this time, the process of writing.

Writing a report requires you to stay close to your data while learning to connect with what others have written. Even if this is your first study, you are joining the research conversation when you write it up and share it. This chapter offers advice that will help you to create a worthwhile contribution to this conversation. You will learn how to develop the various parts of your report. You will also encounter tips on how to engage your reader and keep your message clear. And you will discover special considerations for reporting on Indigenous research and innovative ways of presenting that research.

The writing process is creative and exciting, but it can also be frustrating if you do not know where to begin. Therefore, let us first turn to ideas about how to get started.

Getting Started

Many of us find it difficult to start writing. We might sit and stare at the computer screen or a blank piece of paper for a very long time, trying to find just the right opening sentence. Howard S. Becker (1986:43–67) suggests that many people have a great deal of trouble writing because they believe there is "One Right Way" to construct a report. Hence, they believe that there is only one way to get the writing process started, and they spend an inordinate amount of time looking for the perfect opening sentence. This sort of thinking can make starting very difficult.

To overcome such difficulties, begin by recognizing that there are many ways to write a good report. With practice, you will discover the method that works best for you. When Deborah was a student, she was taught that before she started writing, she should do all her research, make a good outline, and only then, only when she knew exactly what she was going to say and in what order, start writing. Since then, Deborah has discovered that those directions do not work for her. Instead, she finds it helpful to start writing early. Deborah likes to get her thoughts down on paper so that she can reflect on them and adapt them as her research project progresses. Lisa-Jo finds that writing is part of her analytic process, and she often discovers new insights as she writes.

Begin Early

Many researchers have identified the benefits of putting their thoughts into writing early in the research process. Becker (1986) recommends writing a first draft *before* you have all your data, while Harry F. Wolcott (1995) suggests starting to write even before you begin your research. Wolcott calls this early writing **prewriting** and points out that such writing can help you to identify what you already know, what you only *think* you know, and your own biases. You might discover at this stage that your study is secretly "intended only to validate a personally held position," in which case you might as well write a polemical piece and skip the research (Wolcott 1995:201).[1]

Beginning to write at an early stage can also help you to avoid the all-too-common situation of having to rush through your final draft because you have run out of time. Inevitably, if you take such a hurried approach, you will end up with a poorly written report. Good writing, like good analysis, takes a lot of time and effort, but the work you put into it always pays off in the end.

Make Mental Preparations

Many books on writing note that you should find a way to mentally prepare yourself for the process of writing. Often, this involves separating yourself from distractions to focus on the task at hand. Thus, many writers like to find a quiet place, such as a library, where they can be alone with their thoughts. At the same time, every writer has different needs. For instance, Deborah has a colleague who prefers to write in his local coffee shop. The ambient noise of this public space helps him to concentrate, and, in fact, he has written a book about it (Randall 2015). As with all aspects of the writing process, you should find the conditions that best facilitate your own ability to write.

You may also find that certain rituals help you to stay focused on your writing. As we discussed in Chapter 9, Albas and Albas (2009) have found that many students develop magic rituals to help them with their studies. Becker (1986) has observed that academic writers often use magic to facilitate their writing. After talking with his graduate students, he noted that many had "peculiar habits" associated with writing—for example, one woman felt that she "could only write on yellow, ruled, legal-sized pads using a green felt-tip pen" (1986:2–4). Similarly, Dawne A. Clarke (2010:103) has found that university professors use rituals to help them write. One of her research participants can write only when they are wearing pyjamas, while another can write only in a rented motel room with country music playing in the background, and yet another can write only when using one special pen. Clarke explains that there is a "mystique around writing" that leads us to control the parts of the process we can with these superstitious practices. If you have a ritual that helps you to mentally prepare for the task of writing, by all means use it.

Focus on Your Reader

You can also mentally prepare yourself for the writing process by identifying your reader's expectations. As a student, your primary reader is often your professor, and you may naturally feel anxious about submitting a report to someone with such authority. This anxiety can be particularly intense if you do not know your professor very well or if your professor has a reputation, deserved or not, for being a hard marker. Talking to your professor in person may lessen your fear because it will help you to get to know your intended reader and what they expect.

You should always follow the guidelines your professor gives you about format and style. At first, you may object that the prescribed format is too artificial and restrictive, but this is one area of preparation in which you should not simply go with whatever works best for you. Think of your professor's requirements as the rules of a sport: as a player of the sport, you agree to abide by the rules. Hockey players do not argue with their coaches or officials that the offside rule in hockey should not apply to them because they do not like it; they simply follow the rule as much as they can and pay the price when they are caught offside.[2] Just as different sports have different rules, different professors have different formats that they will require you to use. When you follow the format that your professor asks for, they will have a better first impression of your report. Knowing this and understanding what your professor expects is a surefire way to reduce your anxiety about writing. Also, being able to adapt to different formats will, in the end, make you a more flexible and versatile writer.

Envisioning your intended reader can also help you to ease into the writing process. Remember that your reader is a real person and that you want to keep their attention. We will talk later in the chapter about certain stylistic choices you can make to engage your reader, but for now you should simply remember that making a good impression matters. Remember that your report is only one among many that your professor will be reading, so make sure that it will grab your professor's attention and provide an enjoyable read.

May Chazan (2015:3) tells a moving story of how she thought about her audience in her book, *The Grandmother Movement: Solidarity and Survival in the Time of AIDS*. She studied the Grandmothers to Grandmothers Campaign that brought Canadian grandmothers together with Africa's grandmothers who had lost children to AIDS and were raising their grandchildren. The preamble begins with the intriguing "'Tell me, May,' S'fiso asked me one day . . . with a teasing grin on his face, 'will I make it into your book?'" Chazan explains that she was confused because he certainly was not one of the *gogos*, the isiZulu word for *grandmothers*. S'fiso then asked, "Will I at least be able to understand it?" S'fiso died before Chazan would have a chance to see him again, but his question led her to write a book that he would have been able to understand.

Writing Your Report

Published work usually reads as though it were written in a single attempt and in a linear fashion—as though the author started with the first sentence of the introduction and then simply continued writing until they got to the end. Any honest author will tell you that this is not the case. Most often, writers go through many drafts before coming up with the final version. If you were to look through the files on Lisa-Jo's and Deborah's computers, you would see three or more files for each chapter of any books they have written—each file reflects at least one draft of the chapter. In addition, most experienced writers will tell you that you should write the introduction to your work last. In fact, Deborah wrote Chapter 1 of this textbook after she finished writing all the other chapters. This way, she was aware of the content before she wrote the introductory material. While Deborah began the writing process by developing a table of contents and a brief description of each chapter, the creative process of writing shaped the chapters in ways she could not have anticipated.

The next sections of this chapter give advice on how to write the different sections of your report. We have covered the sections in the order in which we suggest you write them—findings, literature review, methods section, conclusion, then introduction—but you may find a slightly different order that works for you. Later in the chapter, we will discuss the order in which they should appear in your final report.

The Findings: Working with Your Data

Many qualitative researchers begin their first draft by organizing their findings, in whatever state they are in, into a preliminary order. This usually involves piecing together a rough list of themes or a tentative table of contents. As you write about the various themes, continue to think about how they hang together; you will likely revise your list as you proceed. Luckily, you can move what you write as many times as necessary until everything makes sense.

Once you have a general conception of how everything might fit together, focus on the theme in your research that is most interesting to you (Lofland and Lofland 1995:205; Charmaz 2006:156). Then, pull together all the material you have for that particular theme. If you have followed the advice on analyzing your data given in Chapter 9, you will have already started a file with data that pertain to this theme. If you have not already done so, read the interview segments and/or field notes through several times, and then start to fine-tune the sub-themes by bringing together all the quotes or excerpts you have that relate to each sub-theme.

Next, try writing a paragraph about the theme. The paragraph does not have to be well organized or have a good beginning or end at this early stage. As Kristen Esterberg (2002:202) notes, you do not have to know exactly what you want to say before you begin; you will "discover it as you go along." Esterberg suggests that if you are stuck, you can always start with a phrase such as "This section is about . . ." and go from there (2002:202). Once you have written a paragraph or two, you can start working with your data and shaping the section you have started writing. You will find that the writing process will help you to see clearer connections in your data and to discover new categories or ones that you have overlooked. When this happens, go back to the data. As Kathy Charmaz (2006:154) notes, "learning to trust in the writing process . . . is like learning to trust the . . . analytic process: our writing, like our analysis, is emergent."

Deborah uses this approach in her own writing. For example, when she was getting ready to write the chapter of *The Widowed Self* (2001) that discusses the theme of widows' learning to do new things, Deborah made separate files for each of the following sub-themes:

- Learning to do new things, in general
- Learning to live alone
- Learning to drive and learning to drive alone
- Changing self-concepts related to learning to do new things

Then Deborah worked with each sub-theme separately. Box 10.1 includes her notes on learning to drive, and she developed her outline for the section on driving based on these notes. Once Deborah had the outline, she started writing and chose quotations from the interviews that illustrated her points. As she went along, Deborah honed the sub-topics even more. Occasionally, she went back to the data when a new idea emerged in the process of writing.

As you might expect, it is very important to choose strong, representative quotations or excerpts to include in your write-up. Next, we will examine how to select the best quotations from your notes and how to use these quotations to the greatest effect.

Box 10.1 Notes on Widows and Driving

Comfortable Driving	Limited	No Driving	Bought Car
"D," "R," "G,"* "S," "TH,"* "C," "RC,"* "MT," "F,"* "A," "I," "J"	• "B": challenge of finding her way around; went to Toronto • "J": only drives in town • "E": learned to drive since husband's death • "JS": learned to drive when husband was sick • "I"*: does not drive long distances	• "K": used to drive • "L": daughter discourages her from driving; used to drive before marriage • "J": eyes bad; used to drive • "E": used to drive until husband teased her (at 21 yrs)	• "S": went with husband • "BH": ignored at first • "A": story about gauge light • "I": ignored at first, called dealer whom she knew

*Commented about being fortunate to know how to drive or that others should learn how to drive

Note: Deborah used initials in place of names to protect the anonymity of the women who participated in the study. In her final write-up, she used pseudonyms to represent each participant.

Including Excerpts

Choosing excerpts from interview transcripts and field notes can be one of the most fun parts of writing up qualitative research. It gives you a chance to go back through your notes and reconnect with your participants—this time from a more informed perspective. Focus on selecting excerpts that will illustrate a point you want to make and that will draw the reader into your study. As Sally Thorne (2008:185) notes, "the best examples will typically be those that not only show the point you are making but also do so in some utterly human and interesting manner." In addition, ensure that the excerpts you use are characteristic of your data. You can highlight an unusual point of view, but you must note that that particular excerpt is not typical of your data in general.

When using quotations, try to keep them short and to the point. Laurel Richardson has observed that "readers are more likely to read short, eye-catching quotations" than long ones (1990:41). You may find it helpful to smooth out the quotation to make it more direct, but be careful not to alter the speaker's meaning. While starts and stops are common in spoken conversations, a long excerpt that starts, stops, and changes direction can be difficult to follow in written form, where there are no verbal inflections to enhance the meaning. When you do adjust a quotation, use an ellipsis (. . .) to indicate where you have removed words, and place square brackets ([ ]) around any words or comments you have inserted that are not part of the original quotation.

Using your research participants' words gives power and emotional depth to your report. It also helps the reader to understand the participant's perspective. Take a look at the first quotation Deborah used in *The Widowed Self* (you may recognize this quotation from our discussion of in-depth interviewing in Chapter 6):

> What was it like to lose him? I suppose first of all, you have to say what it was like to have him because that would mean that you have . . . he was a very supportive person. He was quite romantic, in a way. We met in a romantic manner . . . during the war in London. We did our courting during the Blitz, so he actually saved my life once in the Blitz at some risk to himself. And then he was overseas, too. (van den Hoonaard 2001:8)

In using this quotation, Deborah wanted to show that the participants understood their situations as widows not only in terms of what had happened since their husbands died but also in terms of their experiences with being married. She also wanted to move the reader. By carefully choosing an informative and "utterly human" quotation, she accomplished both of her purposes.[3]

You can also use quotations to illustrate similarities and differences among your participants. Several short quotations in a row can be a useful rhetorical device to emphasize similarities. For example, when Deborah was writing *By Himself*, her study of widowers' experiences, she wanted to illustrate how consistently the widowers she interviewed described their need to avoid spending too much of the day in their houses "sitting around." For them, not leaving the house during the day symbolized giving up on life. Deborah used several brief quotes, one after another, with the phrase "sitting around" highlighted in italics to emphasize the point:

> I'm not just *sitting around* the house moping.
> It's better to be busy than *sitting around* doing nothing, *sitting around* and thinking.
> Now I don't want to *sit around* . . . what am I going to do with myself?
> I didn't just want to *sit home*.
> Just come in here and *sit down* or lay down on the couch and give up. [emphasis added] (van den Hoonaard 2010:127)

You may have noticed that "sitting around" sounds like—and is—a sensitizing concept (see Chapter 9). Including sensitizing concepts in your report brings in theoretical observations. Kathy Charmaz (2006:173) points out that your theory is more accessible when you weave it into the narrative.

An effective way to illustrate differences within the group you are studying is to present two or more quotations in close proximity to one another and then conduct a compare-and-contrast analysis on the quotations. For example, in *By Himself*, Deborah wanted to explain that widowers in Atlantic Canada and widowers in Florida have different comfort levels with women's assertiveness in pursuing a romantic relationship. To illustrate this point, she included quotations that demonstrate that the different cultural contexts led to different interpretations of similar actions. The men in Atlantic Canada were put off and intimidated if women seemed to take the initiative:

> I've really learned that widows are lonely and they're really looking for a man . . . if you said the wrong thing. If you've said anything at all, it might make them think that . . . you're maybe interested in them. And that, uh, you'd better watch out. (van den Hoonaard 2010:95)

A contrasting quotation from an interview with a Florida widower who was not uncomfortable that the woman who became his girlfriend had been assertive in establishing their relationship makes the point:

> After, she decided that she liked me. . . . She came over a lot more than I realized.
> I didn't mean to make a regular routine of it. I just asked her out once; and before
> I knew it, here she's coming in like she's my girlfriend . . . she pushed herself into
> it. (van den Hoonaard 2010:98)

These quotations illustrate how different definitions of the situation affected widowers' interpretations of women's similar behaviour.

The way you introduce and comment on quotations is as important as your choice of the quotations themselves. As the writer, it is your job to tell your readers what you want them to see in the excerpts so that you and they share the same interpretation (Stoddart 1991:246). If you simply drop the quotation into your report without explaining why it is there, you are asking your readers to do too much work, to read your mind. Box 10.2 provides a good example of how to frame your excerpt with your own commentary. The example starts with an orienting paragraph that explains what the quotation is about, follows with an indented quotation, and ends with Deborah's analytic commentary. Notice that she has not asked the reader to do the work of interpreting the text.

As you go through your notes to find useful quotations, you should assign **pseudonyms** to your participants. Pseudonyms allow you to maintain confidentiality while humanizing the participants. Some researchers ask the people they interview to choose their own pseudonyms. By contrast, Clarke (2010) chose names from the television show *Coronation Street*. Lisa-Jo uses Christian names for her Inuit participants because they predominantly use Christian names when dealing with outsiders. She also would not feel right making up fake-sounding Inuktitut names. She cannot use real names because there are a limited number, and she would inevitably be using the name of someone in the community. In small communities or groups with few members, you may want to use **discontinuous identities** (Khyatt 1992). This practice involves using more than one pseudonym for individual participants to enhance their anonymity. For example, Lynne Gouliquer

Box 10.2 Excerpt and Commentary

For men, becoming widowed is definitely *not* an "expectable event" (Martin-Matthews 1991). In fact, when I asked participants if there was anything that surprised them about their experience with being widowed, seven explicitly answered that simply the fact of being widowed was the most surprising aspect. One man made the following observation:

> No [surprises] . . . Because I *never* thought about it. . . . You know, my wife, it was a standing thing that I was going to die a long, long time before her. . . . It *never* entered my head, or I *never* even thought about what I was going to have to do when I was alone. No plans, I *never* dreamed that . . . I *never* even thought about what it would be like. . . . That wasn't a part of what was supposed to happen. [emphasis added]

. . . Even the men whose wives were ill for some time before they died had still believed that, somehow, they would die first. The repetition of the word *never* in the quotation above underlines the complete lack of anticipation of becoming a widower for this man. [He] and other widowers had not imagined in their wildest dreams that they might find themselves in this position. This unexpectedness contributes in important ways to many men's uncertainty about how to relate to themselves as widowers.

Source: Deborah K. van den Hoonaard, 2010, p. 22.

(2000) and Carmen Poulin (2001) have used this practice to protect the identity of lesbians in the Canadian military.

Once you have written up your findings, or have at least begun your discussion of your themes, it is time to turn your attention to planning and writing the rest of your report. At this point, we usually turn to the literature review, but you may choose to work on your methods section.

The Literature Review: Connecting to the Literature

As we discussed in Chapter 3, literature reviews serve a different purpose in qualitative studies than they do in quantitative research. Rather than reading to develop hypotheses, the qualitative researcher reads to situate their particular study in relation to the research that others have done. Thus, when you are writing your own literature review, you should demonstrate that you are familiar with what others have said and that your work allows you to have a conversation with other researchers. You should use the literature review to establish the rationale for your study (Kamali 1991; Stoddart 1991).

Connecting to the literature will help you to discover the broader implications of your findings. In many cases, your findings will connect to previous research in unexpected ways. Yet you can only make these connections if you are familiar with a range of past studies. Thus, you should try to read as broadly as possible. Becoming familiar with other researchers' work will also help you to discuss your own work in terms that are familiar to other sociologists. In turn, these established terms will give you a foundation on which you can build your own analysis. Remember, your job is not to reinvent the wheel.

In our own research, we have found that our extensive reading has led us to make unexpected connections. For example, when Deborah was thinking about how her participants acquire the identity of a widow, she noticed that they talked of an awareness that came suddenly like "a punch in the stomach." Their way of talking reminded Deborah of how Kathy Charmaz (1991) described the *identifying moment* that chronically ill people experience. Thus, in her literature review, Deborah referred to Charmaz's study to help her make sense of her own findings. Similarly, when Lisa-Jo and her co-authors (2015) were developing the concept of "eulogy work," they also thought of Arlie R. Hochschild's (1979) discussion of the *emotion work* that airline stewardesses do to ensure that they present the feelings that they are expected to display. In both examples, reading studies on topics that did not at first appear related to our own led us to make significant connections to the literature and join the research conversation already in progress.

When you are writing your literature review, be careful to avoid two common problems that many students have. The first is relying too heavily on external sources. The second is summarizing rather than integrating what you have read. Let us look at ways to avoid these problems.

Avoiding Common "Lit Review" Traps

When we were students, one of the biggest problems we had in dealing with our sources was that the authors we were reading all wrote so much better than we did. We found ourselves quoting them far too often. The result was a report that contained a bunch of quotations strung together with very little of our own input. We might as well have photocopied everything we read and handed it in to our professors. You may have the same difficulty. After all, the articles and books you have read were far from first drafts, and their authors are often experts in the field. How can you escape the temptation to rely too heavily on your sources?

First, as Kirby, Greaves, and Reid (2006:247) suggest, you should have a "firm grasp of your data analysis" before turning to the literature. They comment that if you go to the literature too soon, the sheer authority of the printed page may overwhelm your own analysis. In that case, you may feel that you have a glass-slipper problem that is similar to the one you get when you try to make your data fit with a pre-existing hypothesis or theoretical framework (see Chapter 9).

Second, you should write a rough draft of your literature review without consulting the literature itself. Deborah used to write the literature section of her reports in a completely different room from where she had her notes and articles. It was the only way she could avoid the temptation to rely too heavily on quotations. Lisa-Jo creates one index card with the main argument paraphrased per article or book and only refers to that, rather than her notes, when she writes her literature review. As much as possible, try to use your own words to express what others have written. Phyllis Creme and Mary Lea (2008:121) provide "linking words" that you can use to begin your summary: for example, you might say that the author "discusses," "points out that," "illustrates," "claims that."

Organizing the literature review also challenges many students. You may be tempted to describe each item you have read separately, one after the other. This approach reminds us of listening to a small child tell us about a movie they have seen. Rather than highlighting the most important points in the plot, the child will start with what happened in the first scene and talk for hours without drawing any connections among the various parts of the movie. We have usually stopped listening after a few minutes and have no idea what we have heard by the end. As Kristen Esterberg (2002:211) points out, discussing each study on its own, without pointing out how it relates to other studies and to your own findings, will bore you as you write it and bore your readers as they read it.

The best way to avoid this trap is to organize the literature by theme. This approach forces you to think about and discuss how the studies relate to one another and to your own work. It will also help you to maintain your reader's interest by drawing connections rather than asking them to do the work of interpreting how everything fits together. In addition, forcing yourself to synthesize what you have read demonstrates that you have understood it and are able to make sense of it. Your literature review tells your professor that you are familiar with and comprehend what other researchers have said about your topic and theoretical approach.

The Methods Section: Describing What You Did

The methods section of your report may be the easiest part to write because, for the most part, all you have to do is describe what you have done. You can write it at any point. We often work on the methods section when we are waiting for inspiration on another part of our reports.

The methods section of your report accomplishes three things. First, it situates your research in a particular research tradition and gives credibility to your findings. Second, it tells the reader how you carried out your research. Third, it orients the reader to the setting and the participants involved.

To situate your research in a particular tradition, you should draw parallels between the approach you used and what other qualitative researchers have done before you. Qualitative methods are highly adaptable, creative, and flexible, but they also involve the use of "sanctioned procedures" (Stoddart 1991:245). In most cases, therefore, you can draw on the body of literature to support and explain the strengths of the methods you used in your study. In addition, you can add credibility to your study by clearly describing how you collected and worked with your data. The professionalism you show in this section will reassure the reader that your approach was systematic, that your analysis was sound, and that your findings are not simply based on anecdotal evidence.

As you discuss the way you conducted your research, ask yourself "What happened?" and organize your response in a chronological order. Describe how you planned your study, carried out your research, and analyzed your data. Also note any unanticipated events you encountered and how you dealt with any setbacks. For example, when Deborah was writing her methods section for her study on widows, she noted that a gatekeeper did not allow her to observe a support group, and she explained what she did to compensate.

There are many ways that you can use the methods section to orient the reader to the study's setting and the research participants. If you have done fieldwork, provide a brief description of your setting. If you conducted interviews, explain how you decided whom to interview, describe how you recruited your participants, and include your impressions of the participants. You may also want to include some demographic information. To orient the readers of her work in Arviat, Nunavut, Lisa-Jo not only describes the community but also highlights how inaccessible and remote Arviat is, since that impacts daily life and may be difficult for those who have not lived in remote locales to envision.

The Conclusion: Summing It All Up

In your conclusion, you will sum up what you have written and explore the implications of your study. A brief summary will give your report a finished quality: This is what I said I was going to do, this is what I have done, and this is its significance. When the reader has finished reading the last sentence, they should have the feeling that the report has an end, that it does not simply fade off into space.

When you are writing your conclusion, imagine that you have to answer the "So what?" question: "Okay, I have done all this research, and I have identified these themes, but so what? Why does it all matter?" You can begin by explaining how your research relates to existing literature. If appropriate, you can identify points of agreement or disagreement. Differences do not necessarily mean that you are right and other researchers are wrong or vice versa. The conclusion or discussion of your report provides a place for you to discuss what may have contributed to these seeming discrepancies.

You can also identify the limitations of your study and acknowledge its shortcomings in your conclusion (Kirby et al. 2006:248). Discussing these limitations gives you the opportunity to suggest further areas of research that might fill in the gaps in your own study. You might also mention interesting themes in your data that were beyond the scope of your report but could inform a future study.

Your conclusion should not be very long, and it should not present any new data. If you are tempted to include new data, go back and find a better place to put them. If you cannot find an appropriate place, leave them out.

Once you have finished writing your conclusion, it is finally time to write your introduction.

The Introduction: Creating a First Impression

The introduction provides the first and most lasting impression of your report. It should, therefore, draw the reader in and orient them to your study. Mitchell and Charmaz (1996:151) explain that the first paragraph should "pull us into the story and convince us to continue" because it "invites, entices, and involves the reader to stay with the story." The best introductions start with an attention-getting opening (Emerson, Fretz, and Shaw 1995:198). Recognizing the importance of the opening sentence, Marjorie DeVault (1999:187) explains that she puts a lot of thought into devising a sentence that "feels genuine and bold . . . that will open space, and claim attention for [her] voice." Box 10.3 includes exemplars of opening sentences that make the reader want to continue. When we read opening lines like the ones in this box, we figure we are in for a great read.

Box 10.3 Opening Sentences That Draw the Reader In

A midnight run shatters the night air. Thirty Harley-Davidson motorcycles stretch out for a quarter-mile, thundering down the highway.

—Daniel R. Wolf, *The Rebels: A Brotherhood of Outlaw Bikers* (1991)

Cheering students filled River High's gymnasium. Packed tightly into the bleachers, they sang, hollered, and danced to loud hip-hop music. Over their heads hung banners celebrating fifty years of River High's sports victories. The yearly assembly in which the student body voted for the most popular senior boy in the school to be crowned Mr. Cougar was under way, featuring six candidates performing a series of skits to earn student votes.

—C.J. Pascoe, *Dude, You're a Fag: Masculinity and Sexuality in High School* (2012)

I got my first job working in a toy store when I was forty-one years old.

—Christine L. Williams, *Inside Toyland: Working, Shopping, and Social Inequality* (2006)

The warehouses on the street had been closed for hours. Taxis thumped down the pothole-plagued city block. Rap music blasted from a nearby nightclub. I locked my Club onto the steering wheel of my car, double-checked the parking sign, and headed down the street. The pavement glittered under my boots, embedded glass reflecting the reassuring lamplight in this downtown district. Halfway down the block, I stopped at a brick wall. I parted the dirty clear plastic vertical blinds that obscured the threshold, and walked inside. A tall, thin disheveled man was perched on a stool just inside the unlabeled doorway. He nodded at me as I entered.

—Staci Newmahr, *Playing on the Edge: Sadomasochism, Risk, and Intimacy* (2011)

Once you have grabbed the reader's attention, identify the question or topic your report addresses and your rationale for studying and writing about it. Your rationale may include evidence that the topic is important or that researchers have not studied it in the past. You can also simply give the reason that your particular setting or group of people intrigued you in the first place. Include a brief description of the data and the theoretical approach you took while conducting your study.

In the final part of your introduction, provide an overview of the report, a road map that will help the reader to follow your argument as it develops. For some reason, many students resist including this road map in their reports. It could be that they have not followed the dictum to write the introduction last and cannot map something that does not yet exist. Howard S. Becker (1986:51–3) suggests that perhaps writers think they need to "reveal items of evidence one at a time, like clues in a detective story" and then come up with the denouement at the end. His suggestion is to put the last "triumphant paragraph" first so that readers know where the report is going and can connect each part to the overall argument as they are reading. We love a mystery but not in the form of a research report. We want to know where we are going, and your professors do, too.

As we have seen, your introduction should pull in your reader. But to maintain your reader's interest, your writing must be clear and engaging. In the next section, we will discuss some techniques that you can use to make your writing more readable.

Attending to Matters of Style

As with any other skill, the more you practise writing, the better your writing will become. You will find that taking the time to edit and rewrite your work will help you to develop your writing skills. In addition, reading others' work—novels, short stories, articles, book-length ethnographies—will help you to discover your own voice, build a rich vocabulary, and become accustomed to the conventions of punctuation, grammar, and usage. In the next sections, you will find some concrete advice on how to improve your writing. First, we examine using simple language. Then, we discuss using the active voice and the first person in your writing.

Simple Writing

Many students find themselves seduced by the idea of using academic language and **jargon** to display their intelligence. Deborah can recall one student who used so many obscure words that she felt as though they were giving her a vocabulary test. This student so deeply resented Deborah's advice to write simply and clearly that they dropped the class! Nonetheless, every modern guide to practical writing stresses the importance of writing simple prose. Let us think about what this means.

The best way to simplify your writing is to avoid the "jargon trap" (Van Manaan 1988:28) or to do what Becker calls "writing in a classy way" (1986:31). Relying on unnecessary jargon is a way to "strike a pose" (Van Manaan 1988), to "sound like [and] maybe even be" a certain kind of person (Becker 1986:31). There is an elitism hidden in this kind of writing that makes it inaccessible to anyone who is not familiar with the jargon. You gain nothing if your writing is accessible only to your little club. The best way to avoid the jargon trap is to use a conversational tone and avoid "being overly flippant, judgmental, arrogant, emotional, or self-absorbed" (Thorne 2008:183). Write your report in such a way that someone who knows very little about your topic could understand what you have written.

In addition to avoiding jargon, you can keep your writing simple by composing relatively short sentences. If you find yourself getting lost in long, convoluted sentences, you can bet your readers will also be lost. It is easy enough to turn a complex sentence into two or more shorter sentences. Writing in the active voice and in the first person will also make your writing clear and inviting.

The Active Voice and the First-Person Perspective

Almost every text on writing urges us to use the **active voice** rather than the **passive voice** as much as possible when we write. Why? First, as Howard S. Becker (1986:79) notes, using the active voice "almost always forces you to name the person who did whatever was done." Why is this important? Consider the following sentence, which is written in the passive voice:

The interview was conducted.

What is wrong with this sentence? It doesn't reveal *who* conducted the interview. Was it the lead researcher? A research assistant? Another participant? *Omitting the doer in this case could affect the way your reader interprets the situation.* Of course, we could include the doer of the action while maintaining the passive voice, but such a construction would sound awkward and unnatural:

The interview was conducted by the researcher.

Now, compare this sentence to the following sentence, which conveys the same information but is written in the active voice:

The researcher conducted the interview.

This sentence is more fluid and interesting.

Another common problem in student writing is avoiding the first-person perspective in formal reports. Many students believe that first-person pronouns establish a tone that is too informal for academic work. In contrast, they see writing in the third person as a way to make their work more detached and, therefore, more scientific. Yet, is a sense of detachment necessary in a research study? Certainly not in a qualitative study in which the researcher is often in direct contact with their participants. Compare the effects of the following two sentences:

> Third-person: The researcher noticed that the participants hesitated when she asked them about their experiences with gambling.
> First-person: I noticed that the participants hesitated when I asked them about their experiences with gambling.

The first sentence is factual, but it is dry. The second sentence is just as factual, but the writer's role is clear and the sentence is more active and engaging.

So you can see the benefits of writing in the active voice and using the first person. Yet we offer one warning: when you write in the first person, do not allow your voice to become so prominent that the story of your research becomes about you rather than the setting or the participants. If your report becomes an "egocentric revelation" of your research process, you have strayed into what Van Manaan (1988) calls a "confessional tale."

After you have written your drafts of each section, you will begin to put the finishing touches on your report.

Cleaning It All Up

Regardless of the order in which you wrote the sections of your report, your professor will expect you to use a fairly standard order in your final submission: introduction, literature review, methods, findings, and conclusion (sometimes called a discussion). Almost always, you will attach a cover page to the front of your report, and your bibliography or references section will go at the end.

When you are polishing your final report, you want to make sure that all the parts are cohesive, that the report hangs together as a "whole rather than a series of disconnected bits" (Creme and Lea 2008:158). As you move from one section to the next, use bridging sentences to help your reader follow the transition. You also add cohesion to your report by using consistent formatting. Make sure that you use a single font for your running text and that you use the same style for all headings.

As you edit your report, look for typographical errors, grammatical mistakes, awkward wording, and missing citations. When we are looking for such errors, we usually print a copy of our report so that we can see what the final version will look like on paper. Then, we carefully go through it—word by word, sentence by sentence, and paragraph by paragraph. We look closely at our punctuation and make sure that the subjects and verbs of our sentences agree, that the verb tenses are consistent, and that we have caught and corrected all our typos. We find that reading our paper aloud helps us to find typos and other errors. Never rely on your word-processing program's spelling and grammar checker to do the job. It will often miss typos such as *form* instead of *from*. As professors, we find that when students do not use proper grammar and spelling, we cannot always decipher what they are trying to say.

At this stage, you also want to look for extraneous words and meaningless expressions that can complicate your writing. Howard S. Becker (1986:80) uses a "simple test" to look for unnecessary words: "I check each word and phrase to see what happens if I remove it. If the meaning does not change, I take it out." Also look for vague expressions and words that allow you to avoid making a definite statement or claim. For example, in the Maritimes, rather than saying that it is hot outside, we might say that it is not overly cold. This roundabout way of communicating works well in informal contexts, but it will only obscure your meaning in a formal report. Some particularly vague words include *somewhat, relatively,* and *basically.* You never lose the meaning of your writing when you remove these words. In fact, you make the meaning clearer.

You should also remove any unnecessary repetition. While you were writing your report, you may have inadvertently made the same point twice, and now is the time to correct this mistake. Unnecessary repetition will not only make you look like a careless writer, it will also bore your reader. In addition, look for expressions that you use too often because they can make your report feel repetitious. For example, a while ago Deborah noticed that she was using the word *hence* too often in her writing; now, when she edits, she makes sure to delete *hence* if it appears frequently.

Finally, when you think you are just about finished, show your report to a friend who is willing to read it. Ask them to tell you if something is not clear or does not make sense, if the organization is not logical, if there is unnecessary repetition, or if there are any mistakes in referencing. Remember that your bibliography or references section should include only sources that you have mentioned in your text.

A Word about Plagiarism

So far, we have not said anything about **plagiarism**, although your professors worry about it a great deal. Simply stated, plagiarism is taking someone else's ideas and passing them off as your own, even if you do so inadvertently. Many professors have noted that plagiarism has become more common in recent years. Some have posited that the ease of cutting and pasting content from the Internet and other electronic sources has made it difficult for many students to grasp the idea of giving credit where credit is due. Plagiarism has become such a widespread issue that most universities have developed elaborate materials to help students avoid committing plagiarism. Some universities even subscribe to online sites that screen students' papers for plagiarism. Penalties typically range from a failing grade on an assignment to a failing grade in the entire class.

So, how do you avoid committing such a crime? In short, you must reference any source that you quote word for word or that you paraphrase. You can easily avoid committing plagiarism by citing your sources as you write and keeping the file for your bibliography or references section up to date.

Presenting Research with Indigenous Communities

As we have seen throughout this book, there are particular considerations for reporting on research with Indigenous communities. In this section, we look at what to take into account. When planning how to disseminate Indigenous research, it is worthwhile to keep in mind Adam Gaudry's (2015:248) list of four principles for conducting Indigenous research:

1. Research is grounded in, respects, and validates Indigenous world views.
2. Research output is intended for use by Indigenous communities.
3. Researchers are responsible to Indigenous communities for the decisions they make, and communities are the final judges of the validity and effectiveness of research projects.
4. Research is action oriented and inspires direct action in Indigenous communities.

These principles underline the importance of researchers' relationship with Indigenous communities. Therefore, researchers are particularly conscientious about presenting the data and analysis in an accessible way, often with the advice of the community, particularly elders.

Lina Sunseri (2011:99) notes that she was committed to giving "respectful space" to the words of the women who participated in her research. Therefore, she not only included their voices throughout *Being of One Mind: Oneida Women and the Struggle for Decolonization*, but she also asked them how they "wanted the book organized and how they wished to have their voices integrated therein." She notes that the approach she took in the book was chosen by her participants.

Heather Castleden (2007) provides a particularly moving account of the impact of being action oriented and working in partnership with an Indigenous community. Her research involved photovoice, and she and the community held regular potluck dinners that reported on the progress of the research and created a sense of community ownership (Castleden, Garvin, and Huu-ay-aht First Nation 2008). Before Castleden published her research, the Huu-ay-aht Council and Advisory Committee reviewed her findings and shared ownership. In the 2008 article "Modifying Photovoice for Community-Based Participatory Indigenous Research," the Huu-ay-aht First Nation appears as a co-author.

Innovations in Presenting Research

In recent years, researchers have experimented with new ways to report on their research. Some, to protect their participants' anonymity, have fictionalized their research, while others have used poetry to communicate their findings. If you look through the journal *Qualitative Inquiry*, you will see the variety of ways researchers report on their work. In this section, we will look at two forms, autoethnography and ethnodrama, but ways of presenting research are limited only by one's imagination.

Autoethnography

Researchers sometimes use narratives to tell their own story in a practice known as **autoethnography**. Although we are discussing autoethnography in the chapter on writing up qualitative research, it is a qualitative method in its own right. In autoethnography, the researcher includes their biography as a part of what they are studying and includes it in the write-up of the research. According to Carolyn S. Ellis (2008), a prolific author of autoethnographic works, autoethnography involves the researcher's shifting back and forth between the social and cultural and their inner experience. Autoethnographies often appear in the form of personal narratives, which can transport the reader into the author's experiences. Ellis's 1993 article about her brother's death in an airline crash is riveting; it provides a window into this devastating experience. Ellis argues that telling her story in the first person connects her "lived experience" to the sociology of emotions and avoids the ordinary approach of sociologists that assumes that "WE study THEM" (1993:724), as though researchers somehow escape the social processes they study. In contrast, the autoethnographer is at the centre of the story they are telling.

One of the important decisions that the autoethnographer makes is the extent to which their analysis goes beyond their own experience and brings in a sociological analysis. It is for this reason that Wall (2008) identifies autoethnography as one of the "most challenging" of qualitative approaches. Amani Hamadan (2012) suggests that autoethnography involves one's trying to "narrate one's own voice . . . coming from one's own soul" (p. 600), but we must also attend to Wall's question as to whether our work is about "our own musings or is it ethnography?" (2016:5). As sociologists, we suggest that researchers who are working in the area of autoethnography need to not only provide a well-written, evocative account of their experience but also analyze their experience for what we learn about culture. As Hine (2020:31) points out, a good autoethnography includes both an "evocative account" and what that experience tells us about the social context.

As with the process of finding a research topic that we discussed in Chapter 3, researchers often get the idea for a particular autoethnography when they experience an epiphany or a situation that Carolyn Ellis describes as "knock[ing] me for a loop" (Adams, Jones, and Ellis 2015:39). When a researcher writes up their autoethnography, their narrative takes centre stage, and they connect it to their social context to avoid its "devolv[ing] into self-absorption" (Anderson 2006: 385).

JoAnn Franklin Klinker and Reese H. Todd (2007) carried out a joint autoethnography to study their individual experiences of "an emerging social phenomenon, middle-aged women leaving comfortable lives to explore new horizons."

Both women started careers as university professors and "accepted the challenges of commuter marriages" in mid-life (2007:166). In a process they eloquently describe as conducting "interviews with our memories [that] reconstructed our past selves," each researcher wrote about her past and how it led to her decision to become a professor (2007:169). Klinker and Todd, citing Holt (2003), observed that autoethnography involves "highly personalized writing" in which "authors draw on their own experiences to extend understanding of a particular discipline or culture" (2007:169). The authors connect their own experiences to the sexism and ageism that women, in general, face in contemporary culture. They found that cultural influences had had more impact on their personal experiences than they had originally thought.

Autoethnography has led to much creativity among its practitioners. Researchers have used a variety of unusual formats, including poetry and drama, to tell their stories. Laurel Richardson (2007), for example, published an autoethnographic book that comprises the journal entries in which she recorded her experiences during the last 10 months of a close friend's life:

> Last Writes: A Daybook for a Dying Friend tells two interlocking stories. The first
> . . . is a friendship story in which I tell of the last ten months of my best friend's
> life and our thirty-five-year complex and sometimes difficult friendship, a deep
> friendship between two women. The second story is the story of the writing.
> (2007:9)

In taking this dualistic approach, Richardson acknowledges the importance of both her experience and her process of interpreting that experience.

Julie Bull (2019) provides an exemplary autoethnography, "Relational and Reflexive Research: Peoples, Policies, and Priorities at Play in Ethically Approving Research with Indigenous Peoples." Bull, who identifies as Southern Inuk, points out that in Indigenous epistemologies, it is impossible to separate out the individual from society or nature. Her approach, therefore, inevitably involves an autoethnographic component as she connects it to the wider social and natural contexts. She argues that "we cannot artificially separate different parts of ourselves and world from the research we are doing or creating" (p. 41). As you can see from the title of her work, Julie Bull loves alliteration. Her work is replete with strong personal experience, social analysis, and poetry (see Suggested Websites for link). Her work demonstrates the potential of combining academic approaches with autoethnography and the arts.

Ethnodrama

It is not only autoethnographers who have experimented with new ways of communicating their findings. Some ethnographers develop their research into **ethnodramas**, or performance ethnography. They choose this medium "to create the most credible, vivid, and persuasive portrait of the participants' culture and lived experiences" (Saldaña 2008:283). Performance ethnography is particularly effective when the researcher is looking to disseminate information to a specific audience or to the general public in an emotion-generating manner.

Pia C. Kontos and Gary Naglie (2006) developed an ethnodrama to bring life to their study of personhood in Alzheimer's disease. Their findings, generated from fieldwork, challenge the assumption that those with cognitive impairment have no sense of self. They argue that their ethnodrama "opens a space" for people who care for others to see the "humanity of persons with dementia" and thereby facilitate more "humanistic approaches" to care practice (2006:302). This mode of communication makes their research accessible to a broad spectrum of people, and the audience's emotional engagement may overcome resistance to new ways of thinking.

Other forms of dramatic presentation have also been quite successful, such as poetry slams, plays, and dramatized vignettes. Lynne Gouliquer and colleagues (2018) published their study of the experience of lesbians in the Canadian military as a short story. They interviewed individuals across Canada and, in their abstract, note that their participants had been targeted by the incorrect belief that LGBTQ soldiers were a threat to national security. Gouliquer, Poulin, and Moore note that "personal details have changed . . . but it is their voices that tell the story" (p. 323). Adapting their findings into a short story not only protected the anonymity of their participants but also is also a powerful way to emotionally communicate the negative impact of past Canadian policies on these soldiers.

Summary

We have looked at how to go about writing up your research report. You are encouraged to start early, to have fun choosing the best excerpts to include in your work, and to write more than one draft. We have also looked at special considerations for reporting on Indigenous research and innovative ways to present research. As you write your first research report, you may find it useful to consult the checklist located in Appendix C of this text. As you will discover, the more you write, the more you will develop your skills as a writer. Go forth and write!

Key Terms

active voice	ethnodrama	plagiarism
autoethnography	jargon	prewriting
discontinuous identities	passive voice	pseudonyms

Questions for Critical Thought

1. What are the barriers you face when you are getting ready to write an academic paper? What are some ways you can overcome those barriers?

2. Do you use any "magic rituals" to help you get started writing? Do they work for you?

3. Think about the best assignment you have ever written. What did you do that contributed to its quality?

4. In Chapter 4, we talked about the importance of presenting a balanced view of findings in writing up your research report. How does a balanced view preserve the dignity of your reader?

5. What alternative forms of presentation might you use to present findings to the general public?

Exercises

1. Without summarizing the plot, write a paragraph describing the theme of a movie you recently watched.

2. Look through an interview transcript or a set of field notes, and identify the best excerpts. What made you choose those excerpts?

3. Choose a journal article that discusses a qualitative research project and that you find well written and informative. Write a short analysis of the article, paying close attention to the ways the author addresses the presumed readership, uses excerpts as evidence, connects to the literature, and discusses the methods they used to conduct the research. What changes would you make to improve the article's argument?[4]

In-Class Exercise

Without looking at your data, write a paragraph that summarizes your research findings. If you have not yet conducted your own study, write a paragraph that summarizes what you learned in your last lecture class without looking at your notes.

Suggested Readings

Howard S. Becker. 1986. *Writing for Social Scientists*. Chicago: University of Chicago Press. This book not only offers practical advice but also includes sociological discussions about why writing is challenging for all of us. Becker is well known as a clear and engaging writer, and this book is a pleasure to read.

Christopher J. Schneider. 2018. "Disseminating Qualitative Research in Media." Pp. 365–72 in *The Craft of Qualitative Research*, edited by Steven W. Kleinknecht, Lisa-Jo K. van den Scott, and Carrie B. Sanders. Toronto: Canadian Scholars Press.

P.C. Kontos and G. Naglie. 2006. "Expressions of Personhood in Alzheimer's: Moving from Ethnographic Text to Performing Ethnography." *Qualitative Research* 6(3): 301–17. You have to read this article to get a sense of how moving an ethnodrama can be. Even if you do not have the slightest interest in Alzheimer's disease, you will see the power of performance ethnography. The article includes an excellent description of the transformation of data into drama.

Related Websites

HyperGrammar, The Writing Centre, University of Ottawa
www.writingcentre.uottawa.ca/hypergrammar
This website explains the rules of grammar in clear language. You can use it for easy reference when you are not sure if your grammar is correct. It contains sections on a variety of elements, including parts of speech; punctuation; and how to build phrases, clauses, sentences, and paragraphs.

How Not to Plagiarize, Writing Advice, University of Toronto
www.writing.utoronto.ca/advice/using-sources/how-not-to-plagiarize
This website contains concrete and useful advice to help you avoid inadvertently plagiarizing someone else's work.

Julie Bull Digital Story, November 2017
www.youtube.com/watch?v=BXbVq5v6UaA
This powerful spoken-word performance includes poetry and images. It is an exemplar of how one can use the arts to communicate excellent analytical, autoethnographic work from an Indigenous perspective.

Notes

1. You will recall that earlier, in Chapter 3, we suggested that it is a good idea to start your project from where you are but that the project should not end there. Wolcott is making the same point. If you find that you feel so strongly about a topic or research question that data are unlikely to change your opinion, the topic is not for you. Early writing may help you to discover this situation.
2. This analogy was inspired by a conversation with a colleague, Christine Cornell, some years ago.
3. When Deborah was interviewed on CBC Radio about *The Widowed Self*, the interviewer told her that she had cried through the first chapter.
4. This exercise is loosely based on Richardson (1994:525).

Appendix A
A Guide to Student Presentations

When it comes time for you to do a presentation, you may be nervous, but that is a normal feeling. Remember that your professor, fellow students, or conference attendees want to enjoy your presentation. This is true even if your professor puts on a show of tough love. In addition, nobody wants to sit through a disjointed and poorly presented talk, so for this reason, too, they want you to succeed. Approach your presentations with the knowledge that you are supported and people are rooting for you.

First, you must put together a presentation worth rooting for. When you sit down to begin preparing, it can be helpful to create an outline, or a flow chart, of ideas and main points you want to present. This way, you can see which ideas flow into the next. This step can be as simple as jotting key words down. The success of your presentation depends on its clarity and organization. Take some time to look at your outline. Does its organization make sense? Rearrange the ideas until you are happy with their order. As you continue to prepare your presentation, you might find that you want to change the order of topics.

Once you have the outline nailed down, it is time to start fleshing it out. Now you must ask yourself what your main argument is. What is the thread that ties your presentation together? What is the one main thing you are trying to get across? Keep in mind that in a short presentation, you can only really argue one main idea. Do not try to fit too much into your talk. This is a perpetual balancing act that we all face: breadth versus depth. Once you have your main idea, review your outline, and decide if there are any points you can get rid of or any you would like to add. Get rid of any clutter.

Now it is time to frame your presentation. This happens in your introduction. The first things you say will determine how the rest of your presentation is understood. Start out with your main argument. The audience will want you to state clearly what it is they should pay attention to throughout your presentation. The main argument acts as a touchstone throughout the talk. Everything should relate back to this argument.

You will also need to tell the audience what the organization of the talk will be. What will you bring up to support your main argument? In what order? This does two things. It allows the audience to be brought along with you, but it also allows them to feel confident that you have things under control. You need to show them that they are in good hands by reassuring them, with an organizational structure, that you know where you are going in your talk and what you are doing.

There are some standard topics you will need to cover, particularly when talking about primary data you have collected. After your introduction, people will expect you to let them know to what literature you are connecting your data and analysis. One common mistake is to make this section too long and detailed. The interesting part is the data, so you do not want to use up too much of your time summarizing the literature. Try to be clear and concise when you talk about the literature. Identify if you are filling a gap, extending a theory (and whose), or taking a stand against or for a perspective. Once you have provided enough information that your audience can place your work in the literature, move on to your methods.

This is another area that students commonly make too long. It is tempting to do so because it is a chance to show how much work you have done, but that will come through in your data and analysis. Keep it simple. Let the audience know what you did and how but with clear and concise language. How many people did you interview? What kind of comics did you analyze? Where did you conduct your ethnography? Imagine the audience asking you what you did, and then briefly tell them so that they are aware of how and where you collected your data. You should also briefly include a few words about what you did with that data. Did you read for themes? With just a few sentences, you should be able to summarize this information so that you can quickly move on to the most interesting part of the talk: your data and analysis.

You can now refer back to the outline you made. Create a section for each item on your outline. Remember that your main argument is the touchstone, so make it clear how each section of your talk relates back to your main argument. Is each section, for example, a sub-theme of a larger theme? If you are using slides, you should plan for one slide per section. Work your way through each section, rereading your presentation for clarity, good organization, and good English.

If you are presenting data, you will need to strike a balance between your analysis and examples from your data. A good rule of thumb is to first introduce with a sentence or two this section of your analysis, which may include stating a sub-theme. Then select an example or two representative of your data. Try not to get carried away. One or two examples for each element of your analysis should suffice. After reading those examples, be sure to provide your audience with an analysis because they will not necessarily know why those quotes are relevant. State clearly how those quotes relate to your argument.

Congratulations, you are almost at the end of your presentation! The last thing you need is a conclusion. Be sure not to present any new data or information during your conclusion. A strong conclusion does not need to be long but rather clear and concise. State clearly your main argument and how you demonstrated that main argument.

When you're finished, say thank you. That helps to signal to the audience that you are done and helps them jump into action. If there is a question period after your presentation, the few seconds while you wait for a question can seem like hours. Hang in there! The audience needs a moment or two to pull their thoughts together and to frame their questions. Wait them out with a pleasant expression on your face, and the questions will come soon enough.

A typical structure for a presentation:

- Introduction
- Literature
- Methods
- Data
- Conclusion

How to prepare a strong presentation:

- As you work on your presentation, be sure to follow any instruction your professor has provided, either in class or on the syllabus. It is often a good idea to reread your syllabus to ensure that you know what your professor expects.
- Make an outline or flow chart of your ideas/main points. Decide on your main argument or main point. At this point, it is helpful to revisit your outline and decide which points to keep, omit, or add.
- Create an introduction that presents your main argument and lays out the organization of your talk.
- Briefly mention the literature you engage with and your methods, if applicable.
- Present each consecutive point clearly, omitting extraneous information. Your presentation should be clutter-free. Use examples as necessary.
- Summarize by reiterating your main argument and how you have demonstrated this argument.
- Clarity and good organization are the name of the game!

How to deliver a strong presentation:

- Speak slowly and clearly. If you are naturally a fast speaker, speak at half the speed you think you should be speaking.
- Maintain a professional demeanour. This includes dressing appropriately and using professional language. Professional language does not have to be riddled with jargon but should omit slang.
- Time your talk in advance so that you know if you fit into the allotted time.
- If you are using slides, under no circumstances should you turn your back on your audience to read your own slides. Be sure to print out a copy of your slides so that you can have them in front of you. This will help you to stay facing the audience and provide a backup should your technology fail.

To PowerPoint or not to PowerPoint

Too often, students (and even faculty) default to PowerPoint presentations. You should make a conscious decision about (a) whether PowerPoint or other visuals are right for this presentation and (b) if so, what kind of information to put on the slides.

First, when deciding whether or not to use PowerPoint, think about how much time you have. If you are giving a three-minute class presentation, setting up a PowerPoint element before you begin will eat into your time and may be more frustrating than useful. If, however, your data includes photographs and you have a longer period of time to set up your technology, PowerPoint will help to draw your audience in. Before you begin, sit down and make a list of the pros and cons of using PowerPoint for this particular presentation. Lisa-Jo uses a lot of photography in her work, so she tends to put together a collection of photographs for her presentations. Deborah almost never uses PowerPoint. It's not unusual for members of the audience to thank her for the novelty of presenting without it.

Second, think back to a presentation you have attended in which the slides seemed to go on and on. You want to avoid this. Typically, your first slide would be a title page, and your second slide, which you would have up during your introduction, would have an outline of your talk and perhaps your main argument. After that, you should strive for no more than one slide per section of your talk. Lisa-Jo prefers to use slides for data rather than summarizing what others have said, but your approach will depend on the guidelines your professor has given you and whether or not you are presenting original data.

The key to a successful PowerPoint presentation is (1) to not go overboard with your slides, (2) to use them to support a clear organization or framework rather than depend on them to create organization, and (3) to be sure that the text on your slides is big enough to read. Eliminate all unnecessary text from your slides. If you have a long quote to share, excerpt the most relevant parts of that quote for the slide. You can still read out loud the whole quote if that is appropriate. Do not fall into the trap of putting so much text on a slide that the audience cannot read it and/or reads it instead of listening to your presentation. Whatever you do, do not give your presentation with your back to the room, looking at your slides, and do not simply read your slides to the audience. If you are presenting online, even though your own image might be small if you have slides, be sure to look up into the camera and maintain an open and connected face for your audience. Do a trial run with the program that you will be using to minimize unforeseen technical problems.

Dealing with Fear

We all feel nervous before we present to varying degrees. This is a normal part of presenting and should not necessarily be taken as a negative. That nervous energy can fuel an excellent presentation. Lisa-Jo is always amazed at how her most anxious students usually give the strongest presentations. Unfortunately, the only way to get less nervous about presenting is to do it often. The more you present, the easier it gets. If you suddenly feel lost while you are presenting, it helps to focus on the texture of the paper in your hand. You can even pause, take a breath, and remind yourself of where you are in your presentation.

As you present, you should try to look up at your audience as much as possible. Many recommend using only index cards with key words to prevent your reading your whole presentation in a monotone. If you are extremely nervous, you are more likely to not take your eyes off the page. Learning to present takes practice, however. You may need to print your whole presentation, word for word, and to cling to the paper in your first presentation. That is okay. The key is to make progress. For your next presentation, you can look up more. Then progress to cue cards. Ultimately, keep pushing yourself out of your comfort zone to become more and more comfortable presenting. Eventually, you will find what works best for you. Lisa-Jo likes to have her talks printed, but then she highlights the key points. When she presents, she reads the highlighted parts but is able to look up and engage with the audience between those few highlighted words or phrases. Lisa-Jo's heart goes out to her students who are struggling to find the courage to give presentations. You can read her open letter to students here: https://www.mindyourmind.ca/expression/blog/memorial-u-professors-letter-students-your-ideas-are-important-our-society.

Do

- Breathe
- Follow your professor's instructions
- Take your time
- Dress professionally

Don't

- Use too much jargon
- "Um" and "ah" too much
- Turn your back on your audience to read your slides

Appendix B
Sample Field Notes

I wrote these field notes at the end of a three-month trip to South Florida in 2002. The wetlands are part of a water reclamation project. They include a half-mile boardwalk loop, islands, trees, and many different kinds of birds. Alligators are always an attraction and a topic of conversation. In the notes, I have given people whom I recognized nicknames to keep them straight. I can, thus, follow them through all of my field notes. At the time of day I recorded these notes, around sunrise, I observed two types of people: birders and joggers. I already knew, when I wrote these notes, that the two groups do not always get along. The birders put their cameras and tripods "in the way" of joggers, and the joggers make enough noise to startle the birds. I, like many of the joggers, walked around the loop several times each morning, but I also slowed down for the birders. Hence, I had a friendly relationship with members of both groups.

Wetlands, South Florida

14 March 2002, 7:00 a.m.

Well, this morning the woman who's been coming for three years said to me, "I see you're becoming a regular." She didn't stop moving, so I couldn't tell her that I would be leaving soon. The second time I saw her she told me that there was a "huge gator at 8." Remember the numbers on the fence? Anyway, by the time I got to 8, the gator was gone.

The big excitement is the great blue heron. She's drawing 3–5 tripod people each day … two new people come every day. Today there was another young woman with a tripod—she mentioned to someone that she "does this" for a living. She also tried to look, by invitation, in another man's camera, but the eyepiece was too high. While I was there, we got to see the mother feed her two babies. For the first time, a man lent me a pair of binoculars (unasked) and a woman I see all the time told me I should look through a scope set up on a tripod that was aimed beautifully to see the babies. Everybody there seemed to be very cheerful and enjoying the event. There were, of course, walkers who did not slow down at all to join the party.

Also the black woman—always there—said hello as always. This then combines with what's going on with the birders. At one point when we crossed paths where the birders are taking pictures of the great blue heron and her babies (two)—she said to me, that the babies were born and she did not know how many there are. She was visibly excited by this. Then she asked one of the birders and he said two and she said that next time she would bring her binoculars. Also, I heard one tripod man complain to another about the joggers—I didn't see anyone jogging.

Saw a young woman (!) with a tripod—but so different. She was very young—20s I'd say—and she was wearing a Nike T-shirt and no shoes—really bare feet. When she was set up near the great blue heron, she looked towards me as I passed, but I was invisible to her; her face was completely impassive.

Wetlands, South Florida

16 March 2002, 6:50 a.m.

I discovered today that the weekend begins on Friday—I arrived at 6:50—10 minutes earlier than usual. The parking lot was already packed. There were several people there walking whom I didn't know but who seemed to be quite familiar with the place. The woman who's been walking for three years was alone at first but then joined another woman and even changed direction.

The young Nike woman with bare feet was back—this time with shoes. Also another young woman with a tripod. When they saw each other they hugged and one asked the other where have you been. Then Nike woman and tripod man introduced themselves. Turns out that they have been corresponding via email. I also heard one man tell another (both tripods) that people have heard of him.

I think if I were staying, I'd get a pair of binoculars and start hanging out with the birders a little. Right now my whole view of the place is based on my experience as a walker.

The weather is quite warm now—in the 70s and humid when I get there—really almost too warm for a brisk walk. No alligators today.

I did see a few more single women today—almost all with Walkmans—actually almost everyone who walks alone is wearing a Walkman.

I've been seeing a new bird the last few days. First I thought it was the moorhen with the red beak but it seemed to have green and purple feathers. I thought it might be some mating plumage or something, because I heard someone point out that some birds' colourful wings were a mating thing. Anyway, as I was leaving I noticed on that bulletin board right at the start of the walk—the one with the pamphlets on it—that someone had stapled a page from one of those calendars like the trivia calendar we used to get, but this was from the National Audubon Society and it was describing this new bird, which is a purple something.

As I left I noticed licence plates from FL, NJ, and VT. The friendly security guard was there but stayed in his car. I noticed a security camera in the parking lot yesterday.

Appendix C
Checklist for Writing Research Reports

☐ I have devised a title that accurately reflects the contents of my report.

☐ I have included a clear overview of my report in the introduction.

☐ I have kept my topic in view throughout my report (there are no paragraphs that are not directly related to my topic).

☐ I have used bridging terms and phrases to link all my ideas in a smooth and flowing fashion.

☐ I have organized the content of each section in a clear and logical manner.

☐ I have grammatically integrated all quotations into my own writing.

☐ I have written a final paragraph that is conclusive without being repetitive.

☐ I have used the active voice whenever possible.

☐ I have properly cited my sources and included all cited works in a references section at the end of my report.

☐ I have not left an extra space between paragraphs.

☐ I have used an appropriate font size (generally, 12 points for running text).

☐ I have used standard margins (generally, between 1 and 1.25 inches or between 2.5 and 3 centimetres).

☐ I have numbered the pages using the automatic function within the word-processing program.

☐ I have carefully proofread my work to ensure that there are no errors in spelling, punctuation, or grammar.

Glossary

action research See **participatory action research**.

active interview An approach to conducting an interview in which the researcher analyzes not only *what* is said but *how* it is said. It focuses on the interactive process as a source of data that the researcher can analyze to understand the social world of participants.

active voice A style of writing in which the subject of the sentence is the *doer* of the action.

autoethnography An approach to qualitative research in which the researcher analyzes their own experiences.

bargain In relation to accessing a setting for field research, a bargain is an agreement a researcher makes with a gatekeeper in exchange for permission to access a social setting. It often entails a promise of confidentiality.

breaching experiment An experiment using the ethnomethodological perspective in which the researcher breaks one of the unspoken laws of interaction.

career The stages a social group passes through. In focus-group research, there may be a common series of stages that the groups go through in their discussion.

causal knowledge Assumes the world is made up of causes and effects that are external to the individual, observable, and measurable.

Chicago School of Sociology A group that, beginning in the early 20th century, produced the first qualitative studies that relied on an ethnographic style of fieldwork.

civil inattention The wilful lack of attention strangers pay to one another in a social setting, often with the motive of remaining inconspicuous, maintaining civility, and/or avoiding embarrassment.

closed-ended (or forced-choice) question A question that limits the possible responses to options provided by the researcher. Closed-ended questions are characteristic of quantitative surveys.

codes Names for the topics, activities, events, and people that come up in an interview transcript or field notes.

coding Systematically going through data, finding terms or phrases to categorize chunks of data, and organizing the data into a form the researcher can work with.

community-based research A collaborative approach to research that includes community members in the design, implementation, and analysis of a study. The researcher shares control of the study with the community group involved.

complete observer A field researcher's role in which they do not interact with the participants in a social setting and might not inform them that they are doing a study.

complete participant A field researcher's role in which they attempt to become a full-fledged member of the group they are studying, concealing their intent from the group.

cultural studies The study of popular culture and its representations. Often, researchers who engage in cultural studies analyze images in the media to identify cultural ideals.

cyber-ethnography See **virtual ethnography**.

deductive reasoning A process of reasoning in which a researcher (1) puts forth a theory, (2) develops hypotheses based on the theory, (3) collects data based on the hypotheses, and (4) performs an analysis that tests the hypotheses.

definition of the situation A basic concept of symbolic interactionism that states that, in any given situation, individuals' behaviour is influenced more by their understanding of the situation than by any objective aspects of the situation itself. Social groups or cultures often share definitions of the situation.

discontinuous identities Using more than one pseudonym to refer to each research participant when writing a research report to preserve participants' anonymity, such as when a study takes place in a rural setting or when there are few members of the group involved in the study.

discourse analysis An interpretive approach to research, influenced by the writing of Michel Foucault, that sees language as a social practice and therefore constitutive of social life.

double-barrelled question A question that includes two or more sub-questions.

emergent design A characteristic of qualitative research. Research strategies change during the course of the research as the researcher becomes familiar with the research setting or social group.

emotion work The effort expended to try to have feelings that are appropriate in a particular situation (Hochschild 1979).

ethics code A code that defines the character of a system (for example, a professional research system) in which morals—an individual's sense of what is "right" or "proper" in relation to their personal character—are applied.

ethnocentrism The tendency to believe that one's own ethnic group or society is superior to others and, therefore, to use this group as the standard when evaluating other groups.

ethnodramas Plays written by ethnographers that illustrate their research findings.

ethnographic content analysis An unobtrusive method that entails analyzing documents (including photographs, television shows, and print media, among others) for their underlying meanings.

ethnography In-depth study of a group, culture, or society that usually entails fieldwork.

ethnomethodology An approach in which researchers study people to discover how unwritten or invisible rules allow them to go about everyday life. See also **breaching experiment**.

eulogy work The conception and framing of self within a reality television show at the moment of symbolic death, at a contestant's exit, or, more specifically, at the moment of transition and loss.

feeling rules Guidelines that direct how we want to try to feel in a particular situation. First developed by Arlie Hochschild in relation to flight attendants, the concept is used by sociologists to describe many situations.

field notes The detailed records of what researchers see, hear, feel, and do during an observational study.

focus groups A form of in-depth interviewing that uses moderated group discussions as a means of data collection. It uses the discussion and interaction among participants as data.

focused coding A process in which the researcher further refines the codes used in the first stage of coding, open coding.

frame An approach to a topic or issue in which certain aspects are emphasized while other aspects are subjugated. When used in the mass media, frames have the power to influence public perceptions of an issue.

gatekeepers Individuals who have the power to deny or grant the researcher access to a social setting, often, but not always, in an official capacity.

generic social processes Aspects of interaction that transcend individual situations (for example, acquiring perspectives, achieving identity, doing activity, developing relationships, experiencing emotionality, and achieving linguistic fluency).

grounded theory A research approach that begins with collecting data about a particular phenomenon and constructs a theory to explain the phenomenon that is grounded in the data.

hierarchy of credibility The common situation in which those in superordinate positions and "experts" are seen as more credible than those in subordinate or marginal social positions.

ideal types Max Weber's term for abstract concepts that refer to phenomena in general but are not meant to capture the attributes of any particular case.

identity foreclosure In relation to a widow's sense of identity, the process through which a widow loses her sense of identity after her husband dies, even when she attempts to hang on to her identity as a wife. Identity foreclosure takes place on three levels: the subjective level, the interpersonal level, and the institutional level (van den Hoonaard 1997).

Indigenous resurgence Paradigm that includes Indigenous peoples' rootedness in the land, accountability to the community, and transformation through awakening to the impact of colonization and through knowledge that is transformational (Alfred 2015).

impression management Developed by Erving Goffman (1959), this concept explains how people work to control the impression of themselves that they communicate to others through demeanour, expression, dress, and so on.

incorporation The process through which members of a research setting define the researcher's role or social place in the setting.

in-depth interview A directed conversation in which an interviewer encourages a participant or participants to describe their social world in their own terms.

indicators Concrete measures that researchers develop to study abstract concepts.

Indigenous methodologies Ways of carrying out research with Indigenous peoples and communities that take into account the legitimacy of Indigenous knowledge systems, receptivity and relationship between researchers and participants, reciprocity with the community, and stories as a legitimate way of sharing knowledge (Kovach 2015:53).

institutional ethnography (IE) A research method developed by Dorothy Smith (1987) that emphasizes the importance of social, particularly institutional, factors in influencing individuals' daily experiences. A major component of IE is a recognition that texts, or documents, can "produce and sustain standardized practices" and, through them, "relations of ruling."

interactionists See **symbolic interactionism**.

interview guide A list of questions and/or topics that a qualitative interviewer plans to include in an interview. In the interview, the interviewer may rearrange the order of the questions, decide not to ask certain questions, and ask additional questions as probes or follow-up questions.

jargon Technical or specialized terminology used by a specific group. Some writers use jargon in an attempt to sound more intellectual or to limit understanding to a particular group of readers, but you should avoid using jargon when you are writing an academic report.

jottings Phrases, quotes, keywords, and other short notes that researchers write down in the field and use to develop full field notes.

latent content Subtle or implicit meanings that require interpretation. Qualitative researchers focus on latent content when they do content analysis.

looking-glass self The idea that we see ourselves as we believe others see us.

manifest content Obvious, surface-level meanings that are immediately evident.

memos Records of ideas or concepts that researchers get while conducting their studies.

mixed-methods research A recent approach that combines qualitative methods with quantitative methods. Some argue that this approach can result in research findings that are more complete than could be arrived at by either method on its own.

moderator The individual who facilitates focus groups. This person guides the group with as little intervention as possible while maintaining the group's focus.

moral entrepreneurs Individuals or groups who campaign to establish certain social behaviours as deviant or normative.

mundane technology Forms of technology that are so ubiquitous that they are often overlooked because of their banality. They still have deep consequences and complex meanings in our everyday lives, however.

narrative analysis An approach to qualitative research that recognizes the centrality of stories in the way people understand and talk about their own lives. It often focuses on the structure of a story as much as on its content.

observer as participant A role in which a field researcher makes their presence known to participants but interacts with the group in only limited ways.

open coding A process in which the researcher identifies and labels the major themes in transcripts or field notes.

open-ended question An interview question that allows the participant to supply their own answer and to elaborate on that answer. Open-ended questions are characteristic of qualitative interviews.

operationalize To put a theory into operation by developing hypotheses that are based on the theory.

participant as observer A role in which a field researcher makes their presence known to participants and participates in at least some of the group's activities.

participants See **research participants**.

participatory action research (PAR) A form of community-based research that often aims to identify the needs and priorities of the group and translate findings into a form that can influence social policy or effect interventions to improve the situation of the group.

passive voice A style of writing in which the subject of the sentence is the *recipient* of the action.

photo elicitation The use of photographs in interviews to facilitate discussion. Sometimes researchers take the photographs themselves, and sometimes they ask research participants to take the photos.

plagiarism The act of taking someone else's ideas and passing them off as your own. Citing sources as you write up your paper will help you to avoid plagiarism.

positivism The belief that we can use the methods of science to uncover the "laws" of human behaviour. It implies the ability to predict and, therefore, control human behaviour.

prescriptive Those approaches that dictate right or wrong behaviour. Qualitative research is analytical and descriptive rather than prescriptive.

presentism The belief that we can use today's standards to evaluate older texts and social phenomena.

prewriting The early writing that researchers do before they have begun to collect data. Prewriting helps researchers to realize what they already know or think they know.

primary group A group of people with whom an individual has close and long-lasting relationships. Members of a primary group usually include parents, siblings, and close friends.

probes In in-depth interviews, probes are follow-up questions that ask the participant to elaborate on, explain, or provide a story about what they have said.

problematize Questioning commonly held assumptions and looking for underlying meanings.

pseudonyms Names that researchers use in written reports to refer to individual research participants to ensure participants' anonymity.

random sampling A method of selecting individuals to take part in a study in which every member of the target group has an equal chance of being chosen to participate.

realist perspective A view that assumes that reality is out there waiting to be discovered rather than socially constructed.

reflexivity The process through which qualitative researchers examine and explain

how they have influenced a research project through their social status, situation (gender, age, etc.), and the experiences they bring to the project.

research ethics board (REB) A body that assesses the ethical implications of research studies and has the power to approve or reject a research proposal. All Canadian researchers who conduct research involving humans must submit their plans to a research ethics board for approval before carrying out their study.

research participants People who voluntarily take part in a research project, either by allowing the researcher to interview them or by welcoming the researcher into their social setting.

rite of passage A process of going from one social status to another that includes three stages: separation from a former status and role, transition between the former status and the new status, and incorporation into the new status.

salvage ethnography Early Canadian anthropology's practice of collecting documents, photographs, and artifacts of First Nations and "folk" cultures of Quebec to preserve them in the mistaken belief that these cultures would soon die out.

sensitizing concepts Sociological concepts based on expressions used by research participants that allow the researcher to understand the empirical world of the research participants.

serendipity In general, a lucky coincidence. Researchers often experience an unexpected, spontaneous moment of inspiration that leads them to discover a social setting, research area, or theoretical insight while not actively looking for one.

snowball sampling A method of selecting individuals to take part in a study in which the researcher identifies initial participants and then asks them to introduce the researcher to others who fit the sample criteria.

social disorganization A concept developed by Thomas and Znaniecki (1918) to describe how rapid social change can lead to the loss of norms and values within an established culture.

sociological imagination The capacity to connect the patterns of individuals with those of society. It distinguishes between private troubles and public issues and is used to understand the connection between biography and history. C.W. Mills (1959) called it the "promise of sociology."

spatial fusion Spatial fusion occurs when two or more spaces, physically distant from one another, become symbolically connected and conceived of as components of the same place.

sponsors Individuals who provide access to certain settings and populations in informal ways. They are often central members of their group and lend legitimacy to the researcher by vouching for them.

standardized interviews Thoroughly scripted interviews that aim to collect quantitative data by asking interviewees to choose from a list of predetermined responses. They are most useful when the researcher wants to collect simple, straightforward answers.

stories Narratives that participants use to make a point or to explain their opinion or action.

symbolic interactionism A theoretical perspective that assumes that research participants understand their everyday lives and that seeks to discover how meanings are shared and created through social interaction.

talking circles A practice that originated among the Woodland Tribes in the midwest as a parliamentary procedure. They have a sacred meaning for many Indigenous communities (Lavallé 2009) and involve passing around a small object with each person's having the option to speak or to pass it on. Some Indigenous researchers recommend talking circles rather than focus groups for Indigenous research.

theoretical saturation A stage that occurs when the researcher is no longer learning anything new in collecting data. At this point, the researcher stops collecting data.

tiny publics Small associations of individuals that, as sources of integration, can be "the cornerstone of social order" though which "societal life is shaped" (Fine 2012: 2-3).

trust the process A phrase researchers use to remind themselves to have faith that there are important themes in their data and that they will have the insight and skill to find these themes.

two-eyed seeing Research approach that involves both Indigenous and Western ways of knowing equally for the benefit of all.

unobtrusive methods Research methods that do not involve interaction between the researcher and the participants; the researcher amasses data by collecting and analyzing materials that already exist.

validity The extent to which the research means what the researcher thinks it means. This standard is most useful in evaluating quantitative research.

verstehen German for "sympathetic understanding." Max Weber (1949) used the word to indicate that researchers should strive to see the world from their research participants' perspective.

virtual ethnography In-depth study of an online group or culture in which researchers use online communities as research settings.

visual sociology A research approach in which the researcher uses images as data.

vocabulary of motives The ways in which people describe and explain their reasons for doing things. These "vocabularies" are always tied to a particular social context; as such, they are subject to change and interpretation as one's social circumstances change.

References

Chapter 1

Glassner, B. and R. Hertz, eds. 1999. *Qualitative Sociology as Everyday Life*. Thousand Oaks, CA: Sage.

Kyriakides, C., A. McLuhan, K. Anderson, and L. Bajjali. 2018a. "Status Eligibility to Exist and Authority to Act in Refugee-Host Relations." *Social Forces* 98(1):279–302.

Kyriakides, C., L. Bajjali, A. McLuhan, and K. Anderson. 2018b. "Beyond Refugee: Contested Orientalism and Persons of Self-Rescue." *Canadian Ethnic Studies* 50(2):59–78.

Reinharz, S. 1999. "Enough Already! The Pervasiveness of Warnings in Everyday Life." Pp. 31–40 in *Qualitative Sociology as Everyday Life*, edited by B. Glassner and R. Hertz. Thousand Oaks, CA: Sage.

van den Hoonaard, D.K. 2003. "Expectations and Experiences of Widowhood." Pp. 182–200 in *Ways of Aging*, edited by J.F. Gubrim and J.A. Holstein. Malden, MA: Blackwell Publishing.

van den Scott, Lisa-Jo K., Clare Forstie, and Savina Balasubramanian. 2015. "Shining Stars, Blindsides, and 'Real' Realities: Exit Rituals, Eulogy Work, and Allegories in Reality Television." *Journal of Contemporary Ethnography* 44(4):417–449.

van den Scott, Lisa-Jo K. and Emma Martin. Forthcoming. "Women Leaving and Losing in Politics: Eulogy Work on a Public Stage." In *Extreme Identities and Transitions out of Extraordinary Roles*, edited by S. Scott and J. Hardie-Bick. London: Palgrave.

West, C. 1999. "Not Even a Day in the Life." Pp. 3–12 in *Qualitative Sociology as Everyday Life*, edited by B. Glassner and R. Hertz. Thousand Oaks, CA: Sage.

Chapter 2

Albas, D. and C. Albas. 1984. *Student Life and Exams: Stresses and Coping Strategies*. Dubuque, IA: Kendall Hunt.

Albas, D. and C. Albas. 1988. "Aces and Bombers: The Post-Exam Impression Management Strategies of Students." *Symbolic Interaction* 11(2):289–302.

Alfred, T. 2015. "A Talk by Taiaiake Alfred: Research as Indigenous Resurgence." *Carlton,* SPPA. (https://www.youtube.com/watch?v=myIUkzbiG_o).

Austin, A. 2016. "'There I Am': A Grounded Theory Study of Young Adults Navigating a Transgender or Gender Nonconforming Identity within a Context of Oppression and Invisibility." *Sex Roles* 75:215–30.

Bartlett, C., M. Marshall, and A. Marshall, 2012. "Two-Eyed Seeing and Other Lessons Learned within a Co-learning Journey of Bringing Together Indigenous and Mainstream Knowledges and Ways of Knowing." *Journal of Environmental Studies and Sciences* 2:331–41.

Becker, H.S. 1963. *Outsiders: Studies in the Sociology of Deviance*. Glencoe, IL: Free Press.

Becker, H.S. 1993. "How I Learned What a Crock Was." *Journal of Contemporary Ethnography* 22(1):28–35.

Becker, H.S. 1996. "The Epistemology of Qualitative Research." Pp. 53–71 in *Ethnography and Human Development: Context and Meaning in Social Inquiry*, edited by R. Jessor, A. Colby, and R.A. Schweder. Chicago: University of Chicago Press.

Becker, H.S. 1998. *Tricks of the Trade: How to Think about Your Research While You're Doing It*. Chicago: University of Chicago Press.

Becker, H.S., B. Geer, E.C. Hughes, and A.L. Strauss. 1961/2009. *Boys in White: Student Culture in Medical School*. Chicago: University of Chicago Press

Briggs, J.L. 1970. *Never in Anger*. Cambridge, MA: Harvard University Press.

Briggs, J.L. 2000. "Emotions Have Many Faces: Inuit Lessons." *Anthropologica* xlii:157–64.

Bull, J. 2016. "A Two-Eyed Seeing Approach to Research Ethics Review: An Indigenous Perspective." Pp. 167–86 in *The Ethics Rupture: Exploring Alternatives to Formal Research Ethics Review*, edited by W.C. Van den Hoonaard and A. Hamilton. Toronto: University of Toronto Press.

Bull, J. 2019. "Relational and Reflective Research: People, Policies, and Priorities at Play in Ethically Approving Research with Indigenous Peoples." PhD dissertation. University of New Brunswick, Fredericton, NB.

Cannell, C.F., G. Fisher, and K.H. Marquis. 1968. *The Influence of Interviewer and Respondent*

Psychological and Behavioural Variables on the Reporting in Household Interviews. Washington: Government Printing Office.

Christ, T.W. 2007. "A Recursive Approach to Mixed Methods Research in a Longitudinal Study of Postsecondary Education Disability Support Services." *Journal of Mixed Methods Research* 1(3):226–41.

Cooley, C.H. 1902. *Human Nature and the Social Order.* New York: Scribner's and Sons.

Creswell, J.W. and V.L. Plano Clark. 2007. *Designing and Conducting Mixed Methods Research.* Thousand Oaks, CA: Sage.

Durkheim, E. 1897/1951. *Suicide.* Glencoe, IL: Free Press.

Erasmus, G. and R. Dussault. 1996. *Report of the Royal Commission on Aboriginal Peoples.* Ottawa: Royal Commission on Aboriginal Peoples.

Evans, M., R. Hole, L.D. Berg, P. Hutchinson, and D. Soobraj. 2009. "Common Insights, Differing Methodologies: Toward a Fusion of Indigenous Methodologies, Participatory Action Research, and White Studies in an Urban Aboriginal Research Agenda." *Qualitative Inquiry* 15(5):893–910.

Garfinkel, H. 1967. *Studies in Ethno-methodology.* Englewood Cliffs, NJ: Prentice Hall.

Giddings, L.S. 2006. "Mixed-Methods Research: Positivism in Drag?" *Journal of Research in Nursing* 11(3):195–203.

Haas, J. and W. Shaffir. 1987/2009. *Becoming Doctors: The Adoption of a Cloak of Competence.* Greenwich, CT: JAI Press.

Haas, J. and W. Shaffir. 1994. "The Development of a Professional Self in Medical Students." Pp. 188–202 in *Doing Everyday Life: Ethnography as Human Lived Experience,* edited by M.L. Deitz, R. Prus, and W. Shaffir. Mississauga, ON: Copp Clark Longman.

Hughes, E.C. 1971/1984. *The Sociological Eye.* New Brunswick, NJ: Transaction.

Jones, T.L., M.G. Flaherty, and B.A. Rubin. 2019. "Crystal Balls and Calendars: A Structural Analysis of Projected Futures." *Time & Society* 28(1):153–74.

Kovach, M. 2015. "Emerging from the Margins: Indigenous Methodologies." Pp. 43–64 in *Research as Resistance: Revisiting Critical Indigenous and Anti-Oppressive Approaches,* 2nd ed., edited by S. Strega and L. Brown. Toronto: Canadian Scholars Press.

Kovach, M. 2017. "Considering the Landscape of Indigenous Research." *Social Sciences Laboratories* (SSRL). (https://www.youtube.com/watch?v=hjxofHBqYOQ).

Kuhn, T. 1962/1970. *The Structure of Scientific Revolutions.* 2nd ed. Chicago: University of Chicago Press.

Landry, D. 2013. "Are We Human? Edgework in Defiance of the Mundane and Measurable." *Critical Criminology* 21(1):1–14.

McIntosh, P. 1988. *White Privilege and Male Privilege: A Personal Account of Coming to See Correspondences through Work in Women's Studies.* Wellesley, MA: Wellesley College, Center for Research on Women.

Parmelee, J.H., S.C. Perkins, and J.J. Sayre. 2007. "'What about People Our Age?' Applying Qualitative and Quantitative Methods to Uncover How Political Ads Alienate College Students." *Journal of Mixed Methods Research* 1(2):183–99.

Prus, R. 2005. "Studying Human Knowing and Acting: The Interactional Quest for Authenticity." Pp. 7–23 in *Doing Ethnography: Studying Everyday Life,* edited by D. Pawluch, W. Shaffir, and C. Miall. Toronto: Canadian Scholars Press.

Rubin, H.J. and I.S. Rubin. 1995. *Qualitative Interviewing: The Art of Hearing Data.* Thousand Oaks, CA: Sage.

Shaffir, W., M.L. Dietz, and R. Stebbins. 1994. "Field Research as Social Experience: Learning to Do Ethnography." Pp. 30–54 in *Doing Everyday Life: Ethnography as Human Lived Experience,* edited by M.L. Dietz, R. Prus, and W. Shaffir. Mississauga, ON: Copp Clark Longman.

Small, M.L. 2011. "How to Conduct Mixed-Methods Study: Recent Trends in a Rapidly Growing Literature." *Annual Review of Sociology* 37:57–86.

Smith, L.T. 2012. *Decolonizing Methodologies: Research and Indigenous Peoples.* London: Zed Books.

Tannen, D. 2020. "How the Pandemic Has Changed the Way We Greet Each Other." *Washington Post,* 21 June. (https://www.washingtonpost.com/opinions/2020/06/21/how-pandemic-has-changed-way-we-greet-each-other).

Thomas, W.I. 1937. *Primitive Behavior.* New York: McGraw-Hill.

Truth and Reconciliation Commission of Canada. 2015. *Reconciliation: The Final Report of The Truth and Reconciliation Commission of Canada.* Montreal and Kingston: McGill-Queen's University Press.

van den Hoonaard, D.K. 1994. "Paradise Lost: Widowhood in a Florida Retirement Community." *Journal of Aging Studies* 8(2):121–32.

van den Hoonaard, D.K. 1997. "Identity Foreclosure: Women's Experiences of Widowhood as Expressed in Autobiographical Accounts." *Ageing and Society* 17:533–51.

van den Hoonaard, D.K. 2001. *The Widowed Self: The Older Woman's Journey through Widowhood*. Waterloo, ON: Wilfrid Laurier University Press.

van den Hoonaard, D.K. 2002. "Life on the Margins of a Florida Retirement Community." *Research on Aging* (Special Issue on Retirement Communities) 24(1):50–66.

van den Hoonaard, D.K. 2019. "Learning to Be Old: How Qualitative Research Contributes to Our Understanding of Ageism." *International Journal of Qualitative Methods* 17:1–8.

van den Hoonaard, Will C. 2009. *Personal communication*.

van den Scott, Lisa-Jo K. 2009. "Cancelled, Aborted, Late, Mechanical: The Vagaries of Air Travel in Arviat, Nunavut, Canada." Pp. 211–26 in *The Cultures of Alternative Mobilities: Routes Less Travelled*. Edited by Phillip Vannini, Surrey: Ashgate.

van den Scott, Lisa-Jo K. 2016. "Mundane Technology in non-Western Contexts: Wall-as-Tool." Pp. 33–53 in *Sociology of Home: Belonging, Community and Place in the Canadian Context*. Edited by Laura Suski, Joey Moore, and Gillian Anderson. Toronto Canadian Scholars Press International.

van den Scott, Lisa-Jo K., Clare Forstie, and Savina Balasubramanian. 2015. "Shining Stars, Blindsides, and 'Real' Realities: Exit Rituals, Eulogy Work, and Allegories in Reality Television." *Journal of Contemporary Ethnography* 44(4):417–449.

Walker, C. and J. Baxter. 2019. "Method Sequence and Dominance in Mixed Methods Research: A Case Study of the Social Acceptance of Wind Energy Literature." *International Journal of Qualitative Methods*. (https://doi.org/10.1177/1609406919834379).

Weber, M. 1949. *The Methodology of the Social Sciences*. Translated by E.A. Shils and H.A. Finch. Glencoe, IL: Free Press.

Chapter 3

Adler, P.A. and P. Adler. 1998. *Peer Power: Preadolescent Culture and Identity*. New Brunswick, NJ: Rutgers University Press.

Adler, P.A. and P. Adler. 2009. "Using a Gestalt Perspective to Analyze Children's Worlds." Pp. 225–37 in *Ethnographies Revisited: Constructing Theory in the Field*, edited by A.J. Puddephatt, W. Shaffir, and S.W. Kleinknecht. New York: Routledge.

Adler, P.A. and P. Adler. 2011. *The Tender Cut: Inside the Hidden World of Self-Injury*. New York: New York University Press.

Albas, D. and C. Albas. 2009. "Behind the Conceptual Scene of Student Life and Exams." Pp. 105–20 in *Ethnographies Revisited: Constructing Theory in the Field*, edited by A.J. Puddephatt, W. Shaffir, and S.W. Kleinknecht. New York: Routledge.

Assembly of First Nations. 2009. "Ethics in First Nations Research. Assembly of First Nations, Environmental Stewards Unit." (www.afn.ca/uploads/files/rp-research_ethics_final.pdf).

Atkinson, M. 2003. *Tattooed: The Sociogenesis of a Body Art*. Toronto: University of Toronto Press. (http://site.ebrary.com/lib/unblib/Doc?id=01218915&pp=9-10).

Bastida, E.M., T.S. Tseng, C. McKeever, and L. Jack Jr. 2010. "Ethics and Community-Based Participatory Research: Perspectives from the Field." *Health Promotion Practice* 11(1):16–20.

Becker, H.S. 1967. "Whose Side Are We On?" *Social Problems* 14(3):239–47.

Bella, L. 1992. *The Christmas Imperative: Leisure, Family and Women's Work*. Halifax: Fernwood Publishing.

Benjamin-Thomas, T.E., A.M. Corrado, C. McGrath, D. Laliberte Rudman, and C. Hand. 2018. "Working towards the Promise of Participatory Action Research: Learning from Ageing Research Examples." *International Journal of Qualitative Methods* 17:1–13.

Berg, B.L. 2009. *Qualitative Research Methods for the Social Sciences*. 7th ed. Boston: Allyn and Bacon.

Bull, J. 2019. "Relational and Reflective Research: People, Policies, and Priorities at Play in Ethically Approving Research with Indigenous Peoples." PhD dissertation, University of New Brunswick, Fredericton, NB.

Chambers, L.A. 2018. "Because She Cares: Re-membering, Re-finding, and Poetically Retelling Narratives of HIV Caring Work with, for, and by African Women Living with HIV." PhD dissertation, McMaster University, Hamilton, ON.

Charmaz, K. 1991. *Good Days, Bad Days: The Self in Chronic Illness and Time*. New Brunswick, NJ: Rutgers University Press.

Charmaz, K. 2009. "Recollecting Good and Bad Days." Pp. 48–62 in *Ethnographies Revisited: Constructing Theory in the Field*, edited by A.J. Puddephatt, W. Shaffir, and S.W. Kleinknecht. New York: Routledge.

Davidman, L. 1991. *Tradition in a Rootless World: Women Turn to Orthodox Judaism*. Berkeley: University of California Press.

Davidman, L. 1999. "The Personal, the Sociological, and the Intersection of the Two." Pp. 79–88 in *Qualitative Sociology as Everyday Life*, edited by B. Glassner and R. Hertz. Thousand Oaks, CA: Sage.

Denzin, N.K. 2009. "Researching Alcoholics and Alcoholism in American Society." Pp. 152–68 in *Ethnographies Revisited: Constructing Theory in the Field*, edited by A.J. Puddephatt, W. Shaffir, and S.W. Kleinknecht. New York: Routledge.

Diamond, T. 1992. *Making Gray Gold: Narratives of Nursing Home Care*. Chicago: University of Chicago Press.

Dickson, G. 2000. "Aboriginal Grandmothers' Experience with Health Promotion and Participatory Action Research." *Qualitative Health Research* 10(2):188–213.

Dohaney, M.T. 1989. *When Things Get Back to Normal*. Porters Lake, NS: Pottersfield Press.

Doucet, A. 2007. *Do Men Mother? Fathering, Care, and Domestic Responsibility*. Toronto: University of Toronto Press.

Drenton, J., L. Gurrieri, and M. Tyler. 2018. "Sexualized Labor in Digital Culture: Instagram, Influencers, Porn Chic, and the Monetization of Attention." *Gender, Work, and Organization* 27(1):41–66.

Dunn, J.L. 2009. "The Path Taken: Opportunity, Flexibility, and Reflexivity in the Field." Pp. 277–88 in *Ethnographies Revisited: Constructing Theory in the Field*, edited by A.J. Puddephatt, W. Shaffir, and S.W. Kleinknecht. New York: Routledge.

Ebaugh, H.R. 1988. *Becoming an Ex: The Process of Role Exit*. Chicago: University of Chicago Press.

Esterberg, K. 2002. *Qualitative Methods in Social Research*. Boston: McGraw-Hill.

Fals-Borda, O. 1987. "The Application of Participatory Action Research in Latin America." *International Sociology* 2(4):329–47.

Ferris, K.O. 2004. "Seeing and Being Seen: The Moral Order of Celebrity Sightings." *Journal of Contemporary Ethnography* 33(3):236–64.

Furedi, F. 2010. "Celebrity Culture." *Society* 47(6):473–7.

Furman, F.K. 1997. *Facing the Mirror: Older Women and Beauty Shop Culture*. New York: Routledge.

Gubrium, J.F. 2009. "How Murray Manor Became an Ethnography." Pp. 121–34 in *Ethnographies Revisited: Constructing Theory in the Field*, edited by A.J. Puddephatt, W. Shaffir, and S.W. Kleinknecht. New York: Routledge.

Harman, Lesley D. 1989. *When a Hostel Becomes a Home: Experiences of Women*. Toronto: Garamond Press.

Heilman, S. 2009. "The Ethnography behind Defenders of the Faith." Pp. 197–211 in *Ethnographies Revisited: Constructing Theory in the Field*, edited by A.J. Puddephatt, W. Shaffir, and S.W. Kleinknecht. New York: Routledge.

Husting, G. 2015. "The Flayed and Exquisite Self of Travelers: Managing Face and Emotions in Strange Places." *Symbolic Interaction* 38(2):213–34.

Jamal, A. 2015. "Engaging Men for Gender Justice: Overcoming Barriers to Girls' Education in the Pashtun Tribes of Pakistan." *International Journal of Social Welfare* 24:273–86.

Jordan, S. 2008. "Participatory Action Research." Pp. 601–3 in *The Sage Encyclopedia of Qualitative Research Methods*, edited by L. Given. Los Angeles: Sage.

Kovach, M. 2015. "Emerging from the Margins: Indigenous Methodologies." Pp. 43–64 in *Research as Resistance: Revisiting Critical Indigenous and Anti-Oppressive Approaches*, 2nd ed., edited by S. Strega and L. Brown. Toronto: Canadian Scholars Press.

Lavallé, L.F. 2009. "Practical Applications of an Indigenous Research Framework and Two Qualitative Sharing Circles and Anishnaabe Symbol-Based Reflection." *International Journal of Qualitative Methods* 8(1):21–40.

Litosseliti, L. 2003. *Using Focus Groups in Research*. London: Continuum.

Lofland, J., and L.H. Lofland. 1995. *Analyzing Social Settings: A Guide to Qualitative Observation and Analysis*. Belmont, CA: Wadsworth Publishing Company.

Loseke, D.R. 2009. "Solving the Mysteries of Shelter Work for Battered Women." Pp. 263–76 in *Ethnographies Revisited: Constructing Theory in the Field*, edited by A.J. Puddephatt, W. Shaffir, and S.W. Kleinknecht. New York: Routledge.

Low, J. 2020. "Stigma Management as Celebration: Disability, Difference, and the Marketing of Diversity." *Visual Studies*, doi: 10.1080/1472586X.2020.1763194.

Luxton, M. 1980. *More than a Labour of Love: Three Generations of Women's Work in the Home*. Toronto: Women's Press.

Malacrida, C. 2015. *A Special Hell: Institutional Life in Alberta's Eugenic Years*. Toronto: University of Toronto Press.

Malacrida, C. 1998. *Mourning the Dreams: How Parents Create Meaning from Miscarriage, Stillbirth and Early Infant Death*. Edmonton: Qual Institute Press.

Mandell, D. 2002. *Deadbeat Dads: Subjectivity and Social Construction*. Toronto: University of Toronto Press. (http://site.ebrary.com/lib/unblib/Doc?id=10219353&ppg=14).

Maxwell, J.A. 2005. *Qualitative Research Design: An Interactive Approach*. 2nd ed. Thousand Oaks, CA: Sage.

McIntyre, A. 2008. *Participatory Action Research*. Los Angeles: Sage.

Milkman, R., P. Lewis, and S. Luce. 2013. "The Genie's out of the Bottle: Insiders' Perspectives in Occupy Wall Street." *Sociological Quarterly* 54:194–8.

Mills, C.W. 1959/1976. *The Sociological Imagination*. New York: Oxford University Press.

Mishna, F., K.J. Schwan, A. Birze, V.W. Melissa, A. Lacombe-Duncan, L. McInroy, and S. Attar-Schwartz. 2020. "Gendered and Sexualized Bullying and Cyber Bullying." *Youth and Society* 52(3):403–26.

Morgan, D.L. 1997. *The Focus Group Guidebook*. Thousand Oaks, CA: Sage.

Pawluch, D. 2009. "Conceptualizing a Profession in Process: The New Pediatrics Revisited." Pp. 318–30 in *Ethnographies Revisited: Constructing Theory in the Field*, edited by A. J. Puddephatt, W. Shaffir, and S.W. Kleinknecht. New York: Routledge.

Prus, R. 1987. "Generic Social Processes: Maximizing Conceptual Development in Ethnographic Research." *Journal of Contemporary Ethnography* 16(3):250–93. (http://jce.sagepub.com/cgi/content/refs/15/3/250).

Sanders, C. 1989. *Customizing the Body: The Art and Culture of Tattooing*. Philadelphia: Temple University Press.

Sanders, C. and D.A. Vail. 2008. *Customizing the Body: The Art and Culture of Tattooing*. Revised and expanded edition. Philadelphia: Temple University Press.

Smith, L.T. 2012. *Decolonizing Methodologies: Research and Indigenous Peoples*. London: Zed Books.

Stebbins, R.A. 2008. "Serendipity." Pp. 814–15 in *The Sage Encyclopedia of Qualitative Research Methods*, edited by L. Given. Los Angeles: Sage.

Strega, S. and L. Brown. 2015. "From Resistance to Resurgence." Pp. 1–16 in *Research as Resistance: Revisiting Critical Indigenous and Anti-Oppressive Approaches*, edited by S. Strega and L. Brown. Toronto: Canadian Scholars Press.

Thurairajah, K. 2018. "The Person behind the Researcher: Reflexivity and the Qualitative Research Process." Pp 10–16 in *The Craft of Qualitative Research: A Handbook*, edited by Stephen W. Kleinknecht, Lisa-Jo K. van den Scott, and Carrie B. Sanders. Toronto: Canadian Scholars Press.

van den Hoonaard, D.K. 1992. "The Aging of a Florida Retirement Community." PhD dissertation, Department of Sociology and Anthropology, Loyola University of Chicago, Chicago.

van den Hoonaard, D.K. 1994. "Paradise Lost: Widowhood in a Florida Retirement Community." *Journal of Aging Studies* 8(2):121–32.

van den Hoonaard, D.K. 2001. *The Widowed Self: The Older Woman's Journey through Widowhood*. Waterloo, ON: Wilfrid Laurier University Press.

van den Hoonaard, D.K. 2010. *By Himself: The Older Man's Experience of Widowhood*. Toronto: University of Toronto Press.

van den Scott, Lisa-Jo K. 2018. "Role Transitions in the Field and Reflexivity: From Friend to Researcher." *Studies in Qualitative Methodology* (Special Issue: Emotion and the Researcher: Sites, Subjectivities and Relationships) 16:19–32.

Wilson-Forsberg, S. 2012. *Getting Used to the Quiet: Immigrant Adolescents' Journey to Belonging in New Brunswick, Canada*. Montreal and Kingston: McGill-Queen's University Press.

Wolf, D.R. 1991. *The Rebels: A Brotherhood of Outlaw Bikers*. Toronto: University of Toronto Press.

Chapter 4

Albas, D. and C. Albas. 2009. "Behind the Conceptual Scene of Student Life and Exams." Pp. 105–20 in *Ethnographies Revisited: Constructing Theory in the Field*, edited by A.J. Puddephatt, W. Shaffir, and S.W. Kleinknecht. New York: Routledge.

Baba, L. 2013. *Cultural Safety in First Nations, Inuit and Métis Public Health: Environmental Scan of Cultural Competency and Safety in Education, Training and Health Services*. Prince George, BC: National Collaborating Centre for Aboriginal Health.

Becker, H.S. 1996. "The Epistemology of Qualitative Research." Pp. 53–71 in *Ethnography and Human Development: Context and Meaning in Social Inquiry*, edited by R. Jessor, A. Colby, and R.A. Schweder. Chicago: University of Chicago Press.

Brunger, F. and J.R. Bull. 2011. "Whose Agenda Is It? Regulating Health Research Ethics in Labrador." *Études/Inuit/Studies* 35(1–2):127–42.

Brunger, F., J.R. Bull, and D. Wall. 2014. "The NunatuKavut Model of Research Oversight: Innovation through Collaboration." Pp. 51–9 in *Toolbox of Principles for Research in Indigenous Contexts: Ethics, Respect, Equity, Reciprocity, Cooperation and Culture*, edited by N. Gros-Louis McHugh, K. Gentelet, and S. Basile. Centre de recherche en droit public, Université du Québec in Abitibi-Témiscamingue.

Brunger, F., R. Schiff, J.R. Bull, and M. Morton-Ninomiya. 2014. "Animating the Concept of Ethical Space: The Labrador Aboriginal Health Research Committee Ethics Workshop." *International Journal of Indigenous Health* 10(1):3–15.

Bryant, C.D. 1999. "Gratuitous Sex in Field Research: 'Carnal Lagniappe' or 'Inappropriate Behavior.'" *Deviant Behavior: An Interdisciplinary Journal* 20:325–9.

Bull, J. 2010. "Research with Aboriginal Peoples: Authentic Relationships as a Precursor to Ethical Research." *The Journal of Empirical Research on Human Research Ethics (JERHRE)* 5(4):13–22.

Bull, J. 2016. "A Two-Eyed Seeing Approach to Research Ethics Review: An Indigenous Perspective." Pp. 167–86 in *The Ethics Rupture: Exploring Alternatives to Formal Research Ethics Review*, edited by W.C. van den Hoonaard and A. Hamilton. Toronto: University of Toronto Press.

CIHR, NSERC, and SSHRC (Canadian Institutes of Health Research, Natural Sciences and Engineering Research Council of Canada,

and Social Sciences and Humanities Research Council of Canada). 1998. *Tri-Council Policy Statement: Ethical Conduct for Research Involving Humans*. Ottawa: CIHR, NSERC, and SSHRC.

CIHR, NSERC, and SSHRC. 2010. *Tri-Council Policy Statement: Ethical Conduct for Research Involving Humans*. Ottawa: CIHR, NSERC, and SSHRC.

Conn, P.J. 1971. "Roderick Hudson: The Role of the Observer." *Nineteenth-Century Fiction* 26(1):65–82.

Diamond, T. 1992. *Making Gray Gold: Narratives of Nursing Home Care*. Chicago: University of Chicago Press.

Ermine, W. 2007. "The Ethical Space of Engagement." *Indigenous Law Journal* 6(1):193–203.

Festinger, L., H.W. Riecken, and S. Schachter. 1956. *When Prophecy Fails*. New York: Harper and Row.

Gans, H. 1967. *The Levittowners: Ways of Life and Politics in a New Suburban Community*. New York: Random House.

Hochschild, A. R. 1989. *The Second Shift: Working Parents and the Revolution at Home*. New York: Avon.

Hochschild, A.R. 1997. *The Time Bind: When Work Becomes Home and Home Becomes Work*. New York: Henry Holt.

Humphreys, L. 1970. *Tearoom Trade: Impersonal Sex in Public Places*. Chicago: Aldine Publishing.

Institutional Review Blog. 2009. "After Human Terrain, Will AAA Debate IRBS?" (www .institutionalreviewblog.com/2009/12/after-human-terrain-will-aaa-debate.html).

Kenney, J.S. 2016. *Brought to Light: Contemporary Freemasonry, Meaning, and Society*. Waterloo, ON: Wilfrid Laurier University Press.

Kitchin, H. 2002. "The Tri-Council on Cyberspace: Insights, Oversights, and Extrapolations." Pp. 160–74 in *Walking the Tightrope: Ethical Issues for Qualitative Researchers*, edited by W.C. van den Hoonaard. Toronto: University of Toronto Press.

Least Heat-Moon, William. 1991. *PrairyErth (A Deep Map): An Epic History of the Tallgrass Prairie Country*. Boston: Houghton Mifflin.

Leyton, E. 1978. "The Bureaucratization of Anguish: The Workmen's Compensation Board in Industrial Disaster." Pp. 71–134 in *Bureaucracy and World View: Studies in*

the Logic of Official Interpretation,
edited by D. Handelman and E. Leyton. St
John's: Institute of Social and Economic
Research, Memorial University of
Newfoundland.

Smith, V. 2002. "Ethnographies of Work and
the Work of Ethnographers." Pp 220–33
in Handbook of Ethnography, edited by P.
Atkinson, A. Coffey, S. Delamont, J. Lofland,
and L. Lofland. London: Sage.

van den Hoonaard, W.C. 1987. "Guy D.
Wright, Sons and Seals." Anthropologica
29(2):214–16.

van den Hoonaard, W.C. 2003. "Is
Anonymity an Artifact in Ethnographic
Research?" Journal of Academic Ethics
1(2):141–51.

Weinberg, M. 2002. "Biting the Hand That
Feeds You and Other Feminist Dilemmas
in Fieldwork." Pp. 79–94 in Walking the
Tightrope: Ethical Issues for Qualitative
Researchers, edited by W.C. van den
Hoonaard. Toronto: University of Toronto
Press.

Wolf, D.R. 1991. The Rebels: A Brotherhood
of Outlaw Bikers. Toronto: University of
Toronto Press.

Wright, G. 1984. Sons and Seals: A Voyage to
the Ice. St John's: Institute of Social and
Economic Research, Memorial University of
Newfoundland.

Chapter 5

Adler, P.A. and P. Adler. 1987. Membership Roles
in the Field. Thousand Oaks, CA: Sage.

Allen, R. 1971. The Social Passion. Toronto:
University of Toronto Press.

Ames, H.B. 1897/1972. The City below the Hill.
Toronto: University of Toronto Press.

Anderson, N. 1923. The Hobo. Chicago:
University of Chicago Press.

Assembly of First Nations. 2009. "Ethics in
First Nations Research." Assembly of First
Nations, Environmental Stewards Unit.
(www.afn.ca/uploads/files/rp-research_
ethics_final.pdf).

Atkinson, M. 2003. Tattooed: The Sociogenesis of
a Body Art. Toronto: University of Toronto
Press. (http://site.ebrary.com/lib/unblib/
Doc?id=01218915&pp=9-10).

Battiste, M., ed. 2000. Reclaiming Indigenous
Voices and Vision. Vancouver: University of
British Columbia Press.

Baym, N.K. 2000. Tune In, Log On: Soaps,
Fandom, and Online Community. Thousand
Oaks, CA: Sage.

Becker, H.S. 1963. Outsiders: Studies in the
Sociology of Deviance. Glencoe, IL: Free
Press.

Becker, H.S. and B. Geer. 1957. "Participant
Observation and Interviewing: A
Comparison." Human Organization
16(3):28–32.

Becker, H.S., B. Geer, and E.C. Hughes. 1968.
Making the Grade. New York: John Wiley.

Becker, H.S., B. Geer, E.C. Hughes, and A.L.
Strauss. 1961/2009. Boys in White: Student
Culture in Medical School. Chicago:
University of Chicago Press.

Berg, B.L. 2009. Qualitative Research Methods
for the Social Sciences. 7th ed. Boston: Allyn
and Bacon.

Booth, C. 1902–1903. Life and Labour of
the People in London. 17 vols. London:
Macmillan.

Bull, J. 2019. "Relational and Reflective Research:
People, Policies, and Priorities at Play
in Ethically Approving Research with
Indigenous Peoples." PhD dissertation.
University of New Brunswick, Fredericton,
NB.

Burnet, J. 1951. Next-Year Country. Toronto:
University of Toronto Press.

Camara, F. and R. Helmes-Hayes. 2003. Tracing
the Historical Developments of Symbolic
Interactionism in Canada. Paper presented
to the Twentieth Qualitative Analysis
Conference, Carleton University, Ottawa.

Chapoulie, J.-M. 1987. "Everett C. Hughes and
the Development of Fieldwork in Sociology."
Urban Life 15:259–98.

Chapoulie, J.-M. 1996. "Everett Hughes and
the Chicago Tradition." Sociological Theory
14:3–29.

Cooper, A. 2015. "Time Seizures and the Self:
Institutional Temporalities and Self-
Preservation among Homeless Women."
Culture, Medicine, and Psychiatry
39(1):162–85.

Cressey, P.G. 1932. The Taxi-Dance Hall.
Chicago: University of Chicago Press.

Darnell, R. 1997. "Changing Patterns of
Ethnography in Canadian Anthropology:
A Comparison of Themes." The Canadian
Review of Sociology and Anthropology
34(3):269–96.

Dawson, C.A. and W.E. Gettys. 1929, 1935/1948.
An Introduction to Sociology. New York:
Ronald.

Emerson, R.M., R.I. Fretz, and L.L. Shaw. 1995.
Writing Ethnographic Fieldnotes. Chicago:
University of Chicago Press.

Erasmus, G. and R. Dussault. 1996. *Report of the Royal Commission on Aboriginal Peoples.* Ottawa: Royal Commission on Aboriginal Peoples.

Esterberg, K. 2002. *Qualitative Methods in Social Research.* Boston: McGraw-Hill.

Etoroma, E. 2020. "Journeying into Academia via Immersion into Qualitative Research: Professor Shaffir as a Master Guide." *Qualitative Sociology Review* 16(2):52–60.

Falardeau, J.-C., ed. 1953. *Essais sur le Québec contemporain.* Quebec: Les Presses Universitaires Laval.

Faris, R.E. 1967. *Chicago Sociology: 1920–1932.* Chicago: University of Chicago Press.

Fine, G.A. 1996. *Kitchens: The Culture of Restaurant Work.* Berkeley: University of California Press.

Fine, G.A. 2012. *Tiny Publics: A Theory of Group Action and Culture.* New York: Russell Sage Foundation.

Fine, G.A. 2019. "Relational Distance and Epistemic Generosity: The Power of Detachment in Skeptical Ethnography." *Sociological Methods and Research* 48(4):828–49.

Firestone, M.M. 1967. *Brothers and Rivals: Patrilocality in Savage Cove.* St John's: Institute of Social and Economic Research.

Furman, F.K. 1997. *Facing the Mirror: Older Women and Beauty Shop Culture.* New York: Routledge.

Gans, H. 1967. *The Levittowners: Ways of Life and Politics in a New Suburban Community.* New York: Random House.

Gaudry, A. 2015. "Researching the Resurgence: Insurgent Research and Community-Engaged Methodologies in 21st-Century Academic Inquiry." Pp. 243–65 in *Research as Resistance: Revisiting Critical Indigenous and Anti-oppressive Approaches*, 2nd ed., edited by S. Strega and L. Brown. Toronto: Canadian Scholars Press.

Gauldrée-Boileau, C.-H.-P. 1875/1968. "Paysan de Saint-Irenée." In *Paysans et ouvriers québécois d'autrefois*, by R. Savard. Quebec: Les Presses de l'Université Laval.

Gérin, L. 1898/1968. "L'Habitant de Saint-Justin." Pp. 49–128 in *Léon Gérin et l'habitant de Saint-Justin* by J.C. Falardeau. Montreal: Les Presses de l'Université de Montréal.

Goffman, E. 1961. *Asylums.* Garden City, NY: Anchor Books.

Goffman, E. 1974/2004. "On Fieldwork," transcribed and edited by L.H. Lofland. Pp. 147–53 in *Qualitative Research Methods*, edited by D. Weinberg. Malden, MA: Blackwell.

Gold, R.L. 1958. "Roles in Sociological Field Observations." *Social Forces* 36:217–33.

Grahame, P.R. 2018. "Looking at Whales: Narration and the Organization of Visual Experience." *Journal of Contemporary Ethnography* 47(6):782–806.

Grills, S. 2020. "The Virtue of Patience." *Qualitative Sociology Review* 16(2):28–39.

Haenfler, R. 2006. *Straight Edge: Clean-Living Youth, Hardcore Punk, and Social Change.* New Brunswick, NJ: Rutgers University Press.

Hammersley, M. and P. Atkinson. 1983. *Ethnography: Principles in Practice.* London: Tavistock Publications.

Harman, Lesley D. 1989. *When a Hostel Becomes a Home: Experiences of Women.* Toronto: Garamond Press.

Harrison, J. 2009. "Canadian Anthropology." *Encyclopedia of Social and Cultural Anthropology.* Retrieved 23 April 2013. (www.credoreference.com/entry/routencsca/canadiananthropology).

Hay, G. 2010. "Biography of John Howard." Kingston, ON: The John Howard Society. (www.johnhoward.ca/bio.htm).

Heilman, S. 2009. "The Ethnography behind Defenders of the Faith." Pp. 197–211 in *Ethnographies Revisited: Constructing Theory in the Field*, edited by A.J. Puddephatt, W. Shaffir, and S.W. Kleinknecht. New York: Routledge.

Helmes-Hayes, R. 1994. "C.A. Dawson and W.E. Gettys' An Introduction to Sociology (1929): Canadian Sociology's First Textbook." *Canadian Journal of Sociology* 19(4):461–97.

Helmes-Hayes, R. 2010. "Studying 'Going Concerns': Everett C. Hughes on Method." *Sociologica* 2:1–26.

Helmes-Hayes, R. and M. Santoro. 2010. "Introduction," in "The Marginal Master: Return to Everett C. Hughes." *Sociologica* 2.

Hine, C.M. 2008. "Virtual Ethnography." Pp. 921–4 in *The Sage Encyclopedia of Qualitative Research Methods*, edited by L. Given. Los Angeles: Sage.

Hughes, E.C. 1943. *French Canada in Transition.* Chicago: University of Chicago Press.

Hughes, E.C. 1960/2002. "The Place of Field Work in Social Science." Pp. 139–47 in *Qualitative Research Methods*, edited by D. Weinberg. Malden, MA: Blackwell.

Hughes, E.C. 1972. *Rencontre de deux mondes: la crise d'industrialisation du Canada français*. Montreal: Editions du Boréal express.

Hughes, E.C., B. Junker, R. Gold, and D. Kittel, eds. 1952. *Cases in Fieldwork*. Chicago: University of Chicago Press.

ISER (Institute for Social and Economic Research). 2010. "About Us." (www.mun.ca/iser/about).

Jean, B. 2006. "The Study of Rural Communities in Quebec: From 'Folk Society' Monographic Approach to the Recent Revival of Community as Place-Based Rural Development. *Journal of Rural and Community Development 1*: 56–68.

Junker, B. 1960. *Fieldwork*. Chicago: University of Chicago Press.

Kleinman, S. 2020. "The Gift of Vocation: Learning, Writing, and Teaching Sociology." *Qualitative Sociology Review 16*(2):40–50.

Lateiner, D. 2004. "Introduction." In *Herodotus, the Histories*. Translated by G.C. Macaulay. New York: Barnes and Noble Classics.

Lavallé, L.F. 2009. "Practical Applications of an Indigenous Research Framework and Two Qualitative Sharing Circles and Anishnaabe Symbol-Based Reflection." *International Journal of Qualitative Methods 8*(1):21–40.

Leuenberger, C. 2015. "Knowledge-Making and Its Politics in Conflict Regions: Doing Research in Israel/Palestine." *Studies in Symbolic Interaction 44*:12–41.

Li, J., D. Moore, and S. Smythe. 2017. "Voices from the 'Heart': Understanding a Community-Engaged Festival in Vancouver's Downtown Eastside." *Journal of Contemporary Ethnography*. In Press. doi:10.1177/0891241617696808.

Liebow, E. 1967. *Talley's Corner*. Boston: Little, Brown.

Liebow, E. 1993. *Tell Them Who I Am: The Lives of Homeless Women*. New York: Free Press.

Lofland, J. and L.H. Lofland. 1995. *Analyzing Social Settings: A Guide to Qualitative Observation and Analysis*. Belmont, CA: Wadsworth Publishing.

Low, J. 2020. "The Hughesian Legacy: William Shaffir—A Principal Interpreter of the Chicago School Diaspora in Canada." *Qualitative Sociology Review 16*(2):14–26.

Malacrida, C. 1998. *Mourning the Dreams: How Parents Create Meaning from Miscarriage, Stillbirth and Early Infant Death*. Edmonton: Qual Institute Press.

March, K. 1995. *The Stranger Who Bore Me: Adoptee-Birth Mother Relationships*. Toronto: University of Toronto Press.

Marshall, C. and G.B. Rossman. 2006. *Designing Qualitative Research*. 4th ed. Thousand Oaks, CA: Sage.

McLuhan, A. 2020. "Feigning Incompetence in the Field." *Qualitative Sociology Review 16*(2):62–74.

Milne, E. and R. Helmes-Hayes. 2010. "The Rise [and Fall?] of McMaster University as the Centre of Symbolic Interactionism in Canada, 1967–2010." Presented at the annual meeting of the Society for the Study of Symbolic Interactionism, Atlanta, GA.

Miner, H. 1930. *Saint-Denis: A French Canadian Parish*. Chicago: University of Chicago Press.

Newmahr, S. 2011. *Playing on the Edge: Sadomasochism, Risk, and Intimacy*. Bloomington, IN: Indiana University Press.

Nurse, A. 2006. "Marius Barbeau and the Methodology of Salvage Ethnography in Canada, 1911–1951." Pp. 52–64 in *Historicizing Canadian Anthropology*, edited by J. Harrison and R. Darnell. Vancouver: University of British Columbia Press.

Pascoe, C.J. 2012. *Dude, You're a Fag: Masculinity and Sexuality in High School*. Berkeley: University of California Press.

Philbrook, T. 1966. *Fisherman, Logger, Merchant, Miner: Social Change and Industrialism in Three Newfoundland Communities*. St John's: Institute of Social and Economic Research, Memorial University of Newfoundland.

Prus, R. 1993. "The Ethnographic Research Tradition: Studying Human Lived Experience." Paper presented to Symbolic Interaction and Ethnographic Research, Waterloo, ON, 19–22 May.

Riesman, D. 1983. "The Legacy of Everett Hughes." *Contemporary Sociology 12*(5):477–81.

Riesman, D. and H.S. Becker. 1984. "Introduction to the Transaction Edition." Pp. v–xiv in *The Sociological Eye*, by E.C. Hughes. New Brunswick, NJ: Transaction.

Ross, A.D. 1952. "Organized Philanthropy in an Urban Community." *Canadian Journal of Economics and Political Science 18*(4):474–86.

Ross, A.D. 1953. "The Social Control of Philanthropy." *American Journal of Sociology 58*(5):451–60.

Ross, A.D. 1954. "Philanthropic Activity and the Business Career." *Social Forces 32*:274–80.

Rossman, G.B. and S.F. Rallis. 1998. *Learning in the Field: An Introduction to Qualitative Research*. Thousand Oaks, CA: Sage.

Sanders, C.B. and S. Henderson 2013. "Police 'Empires' and Information Technologies: Uncovering Material and Organisational Barriers to Information Sharing in Canadian Police Services." *Policing and Society* 23(2):243–60.

Schatzman, L. and A. Strauss. 1972. *Field Research Strategies for a Natural Sociology*. Englewood Cliffs: NJ: Prentice Hall.

Scheibling, C. 2019a. "The Culture of Fatherhood 2.0: Exploring the 'Tiny Public' of Dad Bloggers in North America." *Feminist Media Studies* 20(6):813–30.

Scheibling, C. 2019b. "Doing Fatherhood Online: Men's Parental Identities, Experiences, and Ideologies on Social Media." *Symbolic Interaction* 43(3):472–92.

Schwartz, H. and J. Jacobs. 1979. *Qualitative Sociology: A Method to the Madness*. New York: The Free Press.

Shaffir, W. 2009. "On Piecing the Puzzle: Researching Hassidic Jews." Pp. 212–24 in *Ethnographies Revisited: Constructing Theory in the Field*, edited by A.J. Puddephatt, W. Shaffir, and S.W. Kleinknecht. New York: Routledge.

Shaffir, W., M.L. Dietz, and R. Stebbins. 1994. "Field Research as Social Experience: Learning to Do Ethnography." Pp. 30–54 in *Doing Everyday Life: Ethnography as Human Lived Experience*, edited by M.L. Dietz, R. Prus, and W. Shaffir. Toronto: Copp Clark Longman.

Shaffir, W., R.A. Stebbins, and A. Turowetz. 1980. *Fieldwork Experience: Qualitative Approaches to Social Research*. New York: St Martin's Press.

Shaw, C. 1930. *The Jack-Roller: A Delinquent Boy's Own Story*. Chicago: University of Chicago.

Ślezak, Izabella. n.d. Social Construction of Sex Work: Ethnography of Escort Agencies in Poland.

Smith, J.M. 2017. "Can the Secular Be the Object of Belief and Belonging? The Sunday Assembly." *Qualitative Sociology* 40:83–109.

Smith, L.T. 2012. *Decolonizing Methodologies: Research and Indigenous Peoples*. London: Zed Books.

Sudnow, D. 1967. *Passing On: The Social Organization of Dying*. Englewood Cliffs, NJ: Prentice Hall.

Tang, S.Y., A.J. Brown, B. Mussell, V.L. Smye, and P. Rodney. 2015. "'Underclassism' and Access to Healthcare in Urban Centres." *Sociology of Health and Illness* 37(5):698–714.

Truth and Reconciliation Commission of Canada. 2015. *Reconciliation: The Final Report of the Truth and Reconciliation Commission of Canada*. Montreal and Kingston: McGill-Queen's University Press.

van den Scott, Lisa-Jo K. 2018. "Role Transitions in the Field and Reflexivity: From Friend to Researcher." *Studies in Qualitative Methodology* (Special Issue: Emotion and the Researcher: Sites, Subjectivities and Relationships) 16:19–32.

Wadel, C. 1969. *Marginal Adaptations and Modernization in Newfoundland: A Study of Strategies and Implications of Resettlement and Redevelopment of Outport Fishing Communities*. St John's: Institute of Social and Economic Research, Memorial University of Newfoundland.

Warren, C.A.B. and T.X. Karner. 2010. *Discovering Qualitative Methods: Field Research, Interviews, and Analysis*. 2nd ed. New York: Oxford University Press.

Waterfield, R., trans. 1998. *Herodotus, the Histories*. Oxford: Oxford University Press.

Whitehead, K. 2010. "'Hunger Hurts but Starving Works': A Case Study of Gendered Practices in the Online Pro-eating Disorder Community." *Canadian Journal of Sociology* 35(4):595–626.

Whyte, W.F. 1955. *Street Corner Society*. Chicago: University of Chicago Press.

Wilcox-Magill, D. 1983. "Paradigms and Social Science in English Canada." Pp. 1–34 in *Introduction to Sociology*, edited by J. Paul Grayson. Toronto: Gage.

Wolf, D.R. 1991. *The Rebels: A Brotherhood of Outlaw Bikers*. Toronto: University of Toronto Press.

Chapter 6

Agocs, T., D. Langan, and C.B. Sanders. 2015. "Police Mothers at Home: Police Work and Danger-Protection Parenting Practices." *Gender & Society* 29(2):265–89.

Ayres, L. 2008. "Semi-Structured Interview." Pp. 810–11 in *The Sage Encyclopedia of Qualitative Research Methods*, edited by L. Given. Los Angeles: Sage.

Bagele, C. 2012. *Indigenous Research Methodologies*. Los Angeles: Sage.

Bampton, R. and C.J. Cowton. 2002. "The E-Interview." Forum Qualitative Sozialforschung/Forum. *Qualitative Social Research* 3(2) (May).

Benney, M. and E. C. Hughes. 1956. "Of Sociology and the Interview: Editorial Preface." *The American Journal of Sociology* LXII (2): 137–42.

Bouma, G.D., R. Ling, and L. Wilkinson. 2009. *The Research Process: Canadian Edition.* Don Mills, ON: Oxford University Press.

Brody, E. 2010. "On Being Very, Very Old: An Insider's Perspective." *The Gerontologist* 50(1):2–10.

Burns, E. 2010. "Developing Email Interview Practices in Qualitative Research." *Sociological Research Online* 15(4):8.

Caissie, L. 2006. "The Raging Grannies: Understanding the Role of Activism in the Lives of Older Women." PhD dissertation, University of Waterloo, Waterloo, ON. Retrieved from Dissertations & Theses: Full Text (Publication No. AAT NR23509).

Castleden, H.E. 2007. "As Sacred as Cedar and Salmon: A Collaborative Study with Huu-ay-aht First Nation, British Columbia in Understanding the Meaning of 'Resources' from an Indigenous World View." PhD dissertation, Department of Earth and Atmospheric Sciences, University of Alberta, Edmonton, AB.

Castleden, H., T. Garvin, and Huu-ay-aht First Nation 2008. "Modifying Photovoice for Community-Based Participatory Indigenous Research." *Social Science & Medicine* 66:1393–405.

Charmaz, K. 1991. "Translating Graduate Qualitative Methods into Undergraduate Teaching: Intensive Interviewing as a Case Example." *Teaching Sociology* 19:384–95.

Clark-Ibáñez, M. 2004. "Framing the Social World with Photo-Elicitation Interviews." *American Behavioral Scientist* 47(1) 2:1507–27.

Davidson, K. 1999. "Gender, Age and Widowhood: How Older Widows and Widowers Differently Realign Their Lives." PhD thesis, Department of Sociology, University of Surrey, Guildford, Surrey, UK.

DeVault, M. 1999. *Liberating Method: Feminism and Social Research.* Philadelphia: Temple University Press.

Esterberg, K. 2002. *Qualitative Methods in Social Research.* Boston: McGraw-Hill.

Firmin, M.W. 2008. "Unstructured Interview." P. 907 in *The Sage Encyclopedia of Qualitative Research Methods*, edited by L. Given. Los Angeles: Sage.

Fontana, A. and A.H. Prokos. 2007. *The Interview: From Formal to Postmodern.* Walnut Creek, CA: Left Coast Press.

Gibson, L. 2010. "Using Email Interviews." (www.socialsciences.manchester.ac.uk/realities/resources/toolkits/email-interviews/09-toolkit-emailinterviews.pdf).

Gouliquer, L., C. Poulin, and J. McWilliams. 2020. "Othering of Full-Time and Volunteer Women Firefighters in the Canadian Fire Services." *Qualitative Sociology Review* 16(3):48–69.

Gubrium, J.F. and J.A. Holstein. 2001. "From Individual Interview to Interview Society." Pp. 3–32 in *Handbook of Interview Research: Context and Method*, edited by J.F. Gubrium and J.A. Holstein. Thousand Oaks, CA: Sage.

Hammersley, M. and P. Atkinson. 1983. *Ethnography: Principles in Practice.* London: Tavistock Publications.

Hodgson, S. 2004. "Cutting in Silence: A Sociological Construction of Self-Injury." *Sociological Inquiry* 74(2):162–79.

Holstein, J.A. and J.F. Gubrium. 1995. *The Active Interview.* Thousand Oaks, CA: Sage.

Ispa-Landa, S. and S. Thomas. 2019. "Race, Gender, and Emotion Work among School Principals." *Gender & Society* 33(3): 387–409.

Keegan, S. 2008. "Photographs in Qualitative Research." Pp. 619–22 in *The Sage Encyclopedia of Qualitative Research Methods*, edited by L. Given. Los Angeles: Sage.

Kovach, M. 2015. "Emerging from the Margins: Indigenous Methodologies." Pp. 43–64 in *Research as Resistance: Revisiting Critical Indigenous and Anti-Oppressive Approaches*, 2nd ed., edited by S. Strega and L. Brown. Toronto: Canadian Scholars Press.

Mamali, E. and L. Stevens. 2020. When Same-Sex Couples Say 'I Do': Display Work and the (Re)production of the Wedding Rite." *Sociology* 1–17. doi:10.1177/0038038520922523.

Marshall, C. and G.B. Rossman. 2006. *Designing Qualitative Research.* 4th ed. Thousand Oaks, CA: Sage.

Mason, J. 2002. *Qualitative Researching.* 2nd ed. Thousand Oaks, CA: Sage.

Meho, L.I. 2006. "E-mail Interviewing in Qualitative Research: A Methodological Discussion." *Journal of the American Society for Information Science and Technology* 57(10):1284–95.

Mishler, E.G. 1986. *Research Interviewing, Context and Narrative.* Cambridge, MA: Harvard University Press.

Oakley, A. 1981. "Interviewing Women: A Contradiction in Terms." Pp. 30–61 in *Doing Feminist Research*, edited by H. Roberts. London: Routledge and Kegan Paul.

Oakley, A. 2016. "Interviewing Women Again: Power, Time, and the Gift." *Sociology* 50(1):195–213.

Oliffe, J.L. and J.L. Bottorff. 2009. "Further Than the Eye Can See? Photo Elicitation and Research with Men." *Qualitative Health Research* 17(6):850–8.

Pinsky, D. 2015. "The Sustained Snapshot: Incidental Ethnographic Encounters in Qualitative Interview Studies." *Qualitative Research* 15(3):281–95.

Potts, K.L. and L. Brown. 2015. "Becoming an Anti-Oppressive Researcher." Pp. 17–41 in *Research as Resistance: Revisiting Critical Indigenous and Anti-Oppressive Approaches*, edited by S. Strega and L. Brown. Toronto: Canadian Scholars Press.

Reinharz, S. 1992. *Feminist Methods in Social Research*. New York: Oxford University Press.

Ross, T. and R. Buluing. 2019. "Access Work: Experiences of Parking at School for Families Living with Childhood Disability." *Transportation Research Part A* 130:289–99.

Rubin, H.J. and I.S. Rubin. 1995. *Qualitative Interviewing: The Art of Hearing Data*. Thousand Oaks, CA: Sage.

Schwalbe, M. L. and M. Wolkomir. 2001. "Interviewing Men." Pp. 203–19 in *Handbook of Interview Research*, edited by J.F. Gubrium and J.A. Holstein. Thousand Oaks, CA: Sage.

Schwartz, H. and J. Jacobs. 1979. *Qualitative Sociology: A Method to the Madness*. New York: The Free Press.

Silverman, D. 1993. *Interpreting Qualitative Data: Methods for Analyzing Talk, Text, and Interaction*. London: Sage.

Silverman, D. 1997. "Towards an Aesthetics of Research." Pp. 239–53 in *Qualitative Research: Theory, Method, and Practice*, edited by D. Silverman. London: Sage.

Smith, L.T. 2012. *Decolonizing Methodologies: Research and Indigenous Peoples*. London: Zed Books.

Strega, S. and L. Brown. 2015. "From Resistance to Resurgence." Pp. 1–16 in *Research as Resistance: Revisiting Critical Indigenous and Anti-Oppressive Approaches*, edited by S. Strega and L. Brown. Toronto: Canadian Scholars Press.

van den Hoonaard, D.K. 2001. *The Widowed Self: The Older Woman's Journey through Widowhood*. Waterloo, ON: Wilfrid Laurier University Press.

van den Hoonaard, D.K. 2005. "'Am I Doing It Right?': Older Widows as Interview Participants in Qualitative Research." *Journal of Aging Studies* 19(3):393–406.

van den Hoonaard, D.K. 2009. "Widowers' Strategies of Self-Representation during Research Interviews: A Sociological Analysis." *Ageing & Society* 29(2):257–76.

van den Hoonaard, Will C. 2000. "Getting There without Aiming at It: Women's Experiences in Becoming Cartographers." *Cartographica* 37(3):47–60.

van den Hoonaard, Will C. 2013. *Map Worlds: A History of Women in Cartography*. Waterloo, ON: Wilfrid Laurier University Press.

van den Scott, L.-J. 2009. "Cancelled, Aborted, Late, Mechanical: The Vagaries of Air Travel in Nunavut, Canada." Pp. 211–26 in *The Cultures of Alternative Mobilities: Routes Less Travelled*, edited by P. Vannini. Surrey, U.K.: Ashgate.

van den Scott, L.-J.K. 2016. "Mundane Technology in Non-Western Contexts: Wall-as-Tool." Pp. 33–53 in *Sociology of Home: Belonging, Community, and Place in the Canadian Context*, edited by G. Anderson, J.G. Moore, and L Suski. Toronto: Canadian Scholars Press.

Warren, C.A.B. and T.X. Karner. 2010. *Discovering Qualitative Methods: Field Research, Interviews, and Analysis*. 2nd ed. New York: Oxford University Press.

Wolcott, H.F. 1995. *The Art of Fieldwork*. Walnut Creek, CA: AltaMira Press.

Chapter 7

Adorjan, M. and R. Ricciardelli. 2019. "A New Privacy Paradox? Youth Agentic Practices of Privacy Management Despite 'Nothing to Hide' Online." *Canadian Review of Sociology* 56(1):8–29.

Aries, E. 1996. *Men and Women in Interaction: Reconsidering the Differences*. New York: Oxford.

Bagele, C. 2012. *Indigenous Research Methodologies*. Los Angeles: Sage.

Crossley, M.L. 2002 "'Could You Please Pass One of Those Health Leaflets Along?' Exploring Health, Morality and Resistance through Focus Groups." *Social Science and Medicine* 55(8):1471–83.

Goffman, E. 1959. *The Presentation of Self in Everyday Life*. New York: Anchor Books.

Goodman, A., K. Flemming, N. Markwick, T. Morrison, L. Lagimodriere, T. Kerr, and Western Aboriginal Harm Reduction Society. 2017. 'They Treated Me Like Crap and I Knew It Was Because I Was Native': The Healthcare Experiences of Aboriginal Peoples Living in Vancouver's Inner City." *Social Science and Medicine 178*:87–94.

Goodman, A., R. Morgan, R. Kuehlke, S. Kastor, and K. Flemming. 2018. "'We've Been Researched to Death': Exploring the Research Experiences of Urban Indigenous Peoples in Vancouver Canada." *The International Indigenous Policy Journal 9*(2): Article 3. doi:10.18584/iipj.2018.9.2.3.

Hall, R. 2016. "Caring Labours as Decolonizing Resistance." *Studies in Social Justice 10*(2):220–37.

Holbrook, B. and P. Jackson. 1996. "Shopping Around: Focus Group Research in North London." *Area 28*(2):136–42.

Hollander, J. A. 1997. *The Construction of Gender through Talk about Violence.* PhD dissertation, Seattle: University of Washington.

Hollander, J.A. 2004. "The Social Context of Focus Groups." *Journal of Contemporary Ethnography 33*(5):602–37.

Holstein, J.A. and J.F. Gubrium. 1995. *The Active Interview.* Thousand Oaks, CA: Sage.

Hydén, L.-C. and P.H. Bülow. 2003. "Who's Talking: Drawing Conclusions from Focus Groups—Some Methodological Considerations." *International Journal of Social Research Methodology 6*(4):305–21. doi:10.1080/13645570210124865.

Kidd, P.S. and M.B. Parshall. 2000. "Getting the Focus and the Group: Enhancing Analytical Rigor in Focus Group Research." *Qualitative Health Research 10*(3):293–308.

Kim, W. 2009. "Drinking Culture of Elderly Korean Immigrants in Canada: A Focus Group Study." *Journal of Cross-Cultural Gerontology 24*:339–53.

Kitzenger, J. 1994. "The Methodology of Focus Groups: The Importance of Interaction be-tween Research Participants." *Sociology of Health and Illness 16*(1):103–21.

Lavallé, L.F. 2009. "Practical Applications of an Indigenous Research Framework and Two Qualitative Sharing Circles and Anishnaabe Symbol-Based Reflection." *International Journal of Qualitative Methods 8*(1):21–40.

Litosseliti, L. 2003. *Using Focus Groups in Research.* London: Continuum.

Martinez-Serrano, P., A.M. Palmar-Santos, M. Solis-Muñoz, C. Álverez-Plaza, and A. Pedraz-Marcio. 2018. "Midwives' Experience of Delivery Care in Late Foetal Death: A Qualitative Study. *Midwifery 66*:127–33.

Morgan, D.L. 1997. *The Focus Group Guidebook.* Thousand Oaks, CA: Sage.

Morgan, D.L. 2008. "Focus Groups." Pp. 352–4 in *The Sage Encyclopedia of Qualitative Research Methods,* edited by Lisa Given. Los Angeles: Sage.

Morgan, D.L. 2012. "Focus Group Interviewing." Pp. 141–59 in *Handbook of Interview Research: Context and Method,* edited by J.F. Gubrium and J.A. Holstein. Thousand Oaks, CA: Sage.

Morgan. D.L. and M.T. Spanish. 1984. "Focus Groups: A New Tool for Qualitative Research." *Qualitative Sociology 7*(3):253–70.

Running Wolf, P. and J.A. Richard. 2003. "Talking Circles: A Native American Approach to Experiential Learning." *Journal of Multicultural Counseling and Development 31*(1):39–43.

van den Hoonaard, D.K. 2001. *Student Culture at St Thomas University: A Report to the Committee on Academic Quality and Curriculum.* Fredericton, NB: St Thomas University.

van den Hoonaard, D.K. and W.C. van den Hoonaard. 2006. *The Equality of Women and Men: The Experience of the Bahá'í Community of Canada.* Douglas, NB: Deborah K. and Will C. van den Hoonaard.

Chapter 8

Altheide, D.L. 2008. "Ethnographic Content Analysis." Pp. 287–8 in *The Sage Encyclopedia of Qualitative Research Methods,* edited by L. Given. Thousand Oaks, CA: Sage.

Altheide, D.L. and R.S. Michalowski. 1999. "Fear in the News: A Discourse of Control." *The Sociological Quarterly 40*(3):475–503.

Atkinson, P. and A. Coffey. 1997. "Analyzing Documentary Realities." Pp. 45–62 in *Qualitative Research: Theory, Method, and Practice,* edited by D. Silverman. Thousand Oaks, CA: Sage.

Becker, H.S. 1986. *Doing Things Together: Selected Papers.* Evanston, IL: Northwestern University Press.

Best, J. 2020. "COVID-19 and Numeracy: How About Them Numbers?" *Numeracy 13*(2): Article 4.

Caissie, L. and D.K. van den Hoonaard. 2009. "Invented Identity and New Social Meanings of Aging: The Zoomers Are Coming! The Zoomers Are Coming!" Paper presented to Symbolic Interaction and Ethnographic Research, University of Waterloo, Waterloo, ON, 30 April–3 May.

Calasanti, T. and N. King. 2007. "'Beware of the Estrogen Assault': Ideals of Old Manhood in Anti-aging Advertisements." *Journal of Aging Studies 21*:357–68.

Clarke, J.N. and J. Binns. 2006. "The Portrayal of Heart Disease in Mass Print Magazines, 1991–2001." *Health Communication 19*(1):39–48.

Clarke, J.N. and G. van Amerom. 2007. "'Surplus Suffering': Differences between Organizational Understandings of Asperger's Syndrome and Those People Who Claim the 'Disorder.'" *Disability & Society 22*(7):761–76.

Curry, T. 1986. "A Brief History of the IVSA." *Visual Sociology Review 1*(1):3–5.

Diamond, T. 1992. *Making Gray Gold: Narratives of Nursing Home Care.* Chicago: University of Chicago Press.

Duneier, M. 1999. *Sidewalk.* New York: Farrar, Strauss, and Giroux.

Durkheim, E. 1897/1951. *Suicide.* Glencoe, IL: Free Press.

Ferrell, J. 2006. *Empire of Scrounge: Inside the Urban Underground of Dumpster Diving, Trash Picking, and Street Scavenging.* New York: New York University Press.

Funk, L.M., R.V. Herron, D. Spencer, and S.L. Thomas. 2020. "Aggression and Older Adults: News Media Coverage across Care Settings and Relationships." *Canadian Journal on Aging* doi:10.1017 .S07149808200000.

Gilchrist, K. 2010. "'Newsworthy' Victims? Exploring Differences in Canadian Local Press Coverage of Missing/Murdered Aboriginal and White Women." *Feminist Media Studies 10*(4):373–90.

Hammersley, M. and P. Atkinson. 1983. *Ethnography: Principles in Practice.* London: Tavistock Publications.

Holder, T.J.M. 2010. "Gender Ads: The Goffman Take." (www.intcul.tohoku.ac.jp/~holden/ Presentations/IAMCR-genderPres/Goffman .html).

Hookway, N. 2008. "Entering the Blogosphere: Some Strategies for Using Blogs in Social Research." *Qualitative Research 8*(1):91–113.

IVSA (International Visual Sociology Association). 2010. "About IVSA." (www .visualsociology.org/about.html).

Johnston, M.S., G. Johnston, M.D. Sanscartier, and M. Ramsay. 2018. "'Get Paid, Get Out': Online Resistance to Call Centre Labour in Canada." *New Technology, Work, and Employment 34*:1–17.

Kaminer, W. 1992. *I'm Dysfunctional, You're Dysfunctional: The Recovery Movement and Other Self-Help Fashions.* Reading, MA: Addison-Wesley.

Leggatt-Cook, C. and K. Chamberlain. 2012. "Blogging for Weight Loss: Personal Accountability, Writing Selves, and the Weight-Loss Blogosphere." *Sociology of Health and Illness 34*(7):963–77.

Leuenberger, C. and I. Schnell. 2010. "The Politics of Maps: Constructing National Territories in Israel." *Social Studies of Science 20*(10):1–40.

Manning, P.K. and B. Cullum-Swan. 1994. "Narrative, Content, and Semiotic Analysis." Pp. 463–77 in *Handbook of Qualitative Research,* edited by N.K. Denzin and Y.S. Lincoln. Thousand Oaks, CA: Sage.

McCloskey, R. 2008. "An Institutional Ethnographic Exploration of the Transitional Experience of Nursing Home Residents to and from a Hospital Emergency Room." PhD dissertation, Interdisciplinary Studies, University of New Brunswick, Fredericton, NB.

Mills, C.W. 1959/1976. *The Sociological Imagination.* New York: Oxford University Press.

Norman, M. 2012. "Saturday Night's Alright for Tweeting: Cultural Citizenship, Collective Discussion, and the New Media Consumption/Production of Hockey Day in Canada." *Sociology of Sport Journal 29*:306–24.

Pawluch, D. 1996. *The New Pediatrics: A Profession in Transition.* New York: Aldine de Gruyter.

Pawluch, D. 2009. "Conceptualizing a Profession in Process: The New Pediatrics Revisited." Pp. 318–30 in *Ethnographies Revisited: Constructing Theory in the Field,* edited by A.J. Puddephatt, W. Shaffir, and S.W. Kleinknecht. New York: Routledge.

Preston, K. 2020. "Tradition and Authoritarianism as a Solution to Social Decay—An Analysis of Canadian Right-Wing Extremism Online." MA thesis. Dalhousie University, Halifax.

Raby, R., C. Caron, S. Théwissen-LeBlanc, J. Prioletta, and C. Mitchell. 2018. "Vlogging on YouTube: The Online, Political Engagement of Young Canadians Advocating for Social Change." *Journal of Youth Studies* 21(4):497–514.

Reinharz, S. 1992. *Feminist Methods in Social Research*. New York: Oxford University Press.

Rose, D. 1998. "Television, Madness and Community Care." *Journal of Community & Applied Social Psychology* 8:213–28.

Rose, D. 2004. "Analysis of Moving Images." Pp. 350–66 in *Approaches to Qualitative Research: A Reader in Theory and Practice*, edited by S.N. Hess-Biber and P. Leavy. New York: Oxford University Press.

Schneider, C.J. 2016. *Policing and Social Media: Social Control in an Era of New Media*. Maryland: Lexington Books.

Statistics Canada. 2017. "Guide to the Census of Population, 2016." (www12.statcan.gc.ca/census-recensement/2016/ref/98-304/index-eng.cfm).

Stelzl, M., B. Stairs, and H. Anstey. 2018. "A Narrow View: The Conceptualization of Sexual Problems in Human Sexuality Textbooks." *Journal of Health Psychology* 23(2):148–60.

Thomas, W.I. and F. Znaniecki. 1918. *The Polish Peasant in Europe and America*. Boston: Gorham Press.

Thompson, B.Y. 2010a. "Director's Statement." (http://coveredthemovie.com).

Thompson, B.Y. 2010b. *Covered: Women and Tattoos*. Documentary. United States.

US Census Bureau. 2010. "United States Census 2010." (http://2010.census.gov/2010census/pdf/2010_Questionnaire_Info.pdf).

van den Hoonaard, D.K. 1997. "Identity Foreclosure: Women's Experiences of Widowhood as Expressed in Autobiographical Accounts." *Ageing & Society* 17:533–51.

van den Hoonaard, D.K. 2013. "Telling the Collective Story: Symbolic Interactionism in Narrative Research." *Qualitative Sociology Review* ix(3):32–45.

van den Hoonaard, W.C. and D.K. van den Hoonaard. 1991. "Airports as Caricature: Exploring Film and Children's Books." Paper presented at the Fifth Annual Qualitative Research Conference, Ottawa, ON, 14–17 May.

van den Scott, L.-J.K. 2016. "Mundane Technology in Non-Western Contexts: Wall-as-Tool." Pp. 33–53 in *Sociology of Home: Belonging, Community, and Place in the Canadian Context*, edited by G. Anderson, J.G. Moore, and L Suski. Toronto: Canadian Scholars Press.

van den Scott, L.-K. J., C. Forstie, and S. Balasubramanian. 2015. "Shining Stars, Blind Sides, and 'Real' Realties: Exit Rituals, Eulogy Work, and Allegories in Reality Television." *Journal of Contemporary Ethnography* 44(4):417–49.

van Gennep, A. 1909/1960. *The Rites of Passage*. London: Routledge.

Warren, C.A.B. and T.X. Karner. 2010. *Discovering Qualitative Methods: Field Research, Interviews, and Analysis*. 2nd ed. New York: Oxford University Press.

Webb, E.J., D.T. Campbell, R.D. Schwart, and L Sechrest. 1966. *Unobtrusive Measures: Nonreactive Research in the Social Sciences*, Chicago: Rand McNally.

Williams, T. 2017. *Teenage Suicide Notes: An Ethnography of Self-Harm*. New York: Columbia University Press.

Chapter 9

Albas, D. and C. Albas. 2009. "Behind the Conceptual Scene of Student Life and Exams." Pp. 105–20 in *Ethnographies Revisited: Constructing Theory in the Field*, edited by A.J. Puddephatt, W. Shaffir, and S.W. Kleinknecht. New York: Routledge.

Bagele, C. 2012. *Indigenous Research Methodologies*. Los Angeles: Sage.

Becker, G. 1997. *Disrupted Lives: How People Create Meaning in a Chaotic World*. Berkeley: University of California Press.

Becker, H.S. 1998. *Tricks of the Trade: How to Think about Your Research While You're Doing It*. Chicago: University of Chicago Press.

Bull, J. 2016. "A Two-Eyed Seeing Approach to Research Ethics Review: An Indigenous Perspective." Pp. 167–86 in *The Ethics Rupture: Exploring Alternatives to Formal Research Ethics Review*, edited by W.C. van den Hoonaard and A. Hamilton. Toronto: University of Toronto Press.

Çalişkan, G. and K. Preston. 2017. "Tropes of Fear and the Crisis of the West: Trumpism as a Discourse of Post-Territorial Coloniality." *Postcolonial Studies*. doi:10.1080/13688790.2017.1376367.

Charmaz, K. 2001. "Qualitative Interviewing and Grounded Theory Analysis." Pp. 671–94 in *Handbook of Interview Research: Context and Method*, edited by J.F. Gubrium and J.A. Holstein. Thousand Oaks, CA: Sage.

Charmaz, K. 2006. *Constructing Grounded Theory: A Practical Guide through Qualitative Analysis.* Thousand Oaks, CA: Sage.

Clarke, J.N. 2014. "Tracking Governance: Advice to Mothers about Managing the Behaviour of Their Children in a Leading Canadian Women's Magazine during Two Disease Regimes." *Critical Public Health* 24(3):253–65.

Denzin, N.K. 1987. *The Alcoholic Self.* Newbury Park, CA: Sage Publications.

Doucet, A. 2007. *Do Men Mother? Fathering, Care, and Domestic Responsibility.* Toronto: University of Toronto Press.

Dowling, M. 2008. "Reflexivity." Pp. 747–8 in *The Sage Encyclopedia of Qualitative Research Methods,* edited by L. Given. Los Angeles: Sage.

Duneier, M. 1999. *Sidewalk.* New York: Farrar, Strauss, and Giroux.

Ehrenreich, B. and D. English. 1989. *For Her Own Good: 150 Years of Experts' Advice to Women.* Garden City, NY: Anchor Books.

Esterberg, K. 2002. *Qualitative Methods in Social Research.* Boston: McGraw-Hill.

Garcia, A.C. 2019. "Bordering Work in Contemporary Political Discourse: The Case of the US/Mexico Border Wall Proposal." *Discourse and Society* 30 (6):573–99.

Ginter, A.C. and Radina, M.E. 2019. "'I Was There With Her': Experiences of Mothers of Women with Breast Cancer." *Journal of Family Nursing* 25(1):54–80.

Glaser, B. and A. Strauss. 1965. *Awareness of Dying.* Chicago: Aldine.

Glaser, B. and A. Strauss. 1967. *The Discovery of Grounded Theory.* Chicago: Aldine.

Goffman, E. 1959. *The Presentation of Self in Everyday Life.* New York: Anchor Books.

Goffman, E. 1963. *Behavior in Public Places.* Glencoe, IL: Free Press.

Grills, S. 2017. "Considering Essays: The Social Construction of Subcultural Value." *Qualitative Sociology Review* xiii(4):70–82.

Gubrium, J.F. 1986. *Oldtimers and Alzheimer's: The Descriptive Organization of Senility.* Greenwich, CT: JAI Press.

Gubrium, J.F. and J.A. Holstein. 2009. *Analyzing Narrative Reality.* Los Angeles: Sage.

Hochschild, A.R. 1979. "Emotion Work, Feeling Rules, and Social Structure." *American Journal of Sociology* 85(3):551–75.

Hochschild, A.R. 2011. "Emotional Life on the Market Frontier." *Annual Review of Sociology* 37:21–33.

Johnston, M.S. and J. Kilty. 2016. "'It's for Their Own Good': Techniques of Neutralization and Security Guard Violence against Psychiatric Patients." *Punishment & Society* 18(2):177–97.

Kaufman, S. 1986. *The Ageless Self: Sources of Meaning in Late Life.* Madison: University of Wisconsin Press.

Kenyon, G.M. and W.L. Randall. 1997. *Restorying Our Lives: Personal Growth through Autobiographical Reflection.* Westport, CN: Praeger.

Kenyon, G.M. and W.L. Randall. 1999. "Introduction: Narrative Gerontology." *Journal of Aging Studies* 13(1):1–5.

Lafrance, M.N. 2009. *Women and Depression: Recovery and Resistance.* London: Routledge.

Lafrance, M.N. 2011. "Reproducing, Resisting and Transcending Discourses of Femininity: A Discourse Analysis of Women's Accounts of Leisure." *Qualitative Research in Sport, Exercise, and Health* 3(1):80–98.

Lofland, J. and L.H. Lofland. 1995. *Analyzing Social Settings: A Guide to Qualitative Observation and Analysis.* Belmont, CA: Wadsworth Publishing.

Low, J. 2004. *Using Alternative Therapies: A Qualitative Analysis.* Toronto: Canadian Scholars Press.

Maines, D.R. 1993. "Narrative's Moment and Sociology's Phenomena: Toward a Narrative Sociology." *The Sociological Quarterly* 34(1):17–38.

Maines, D.R. 2001. *The Faultlines of Consciousness: A View of Interactionism in Sociology.* New York: Aldine de Gruyter.

March, K. 1995. *The Stranger Who Bore Me: Adoptee–Birth Mother Relationships.* Toronto: University of Toronto Press.

Mayan, M. 2009. *Essentials of Qualitative Inquiry.* Walnut Creek, CA: Left Coast Press.

McLuhan, A. 2020. "Adopting a Cloak of Incompetence: Impression Management Techniques for Feigning Lesser Selves." *Sociology Theory* 38(2):122–41.

McLuhan, A., D. Pawluch, W. Shaffir, and J. Haas. 2014. "The Cloak of Incompetence: A Neglected Concept in the Sociology of Everyday Life." *The American Sociologist* 45(4):361–87.

Mills, C.W. 1959/1976. *The Sociological Imagination.* New York: Oxford University Press.

Puddephatt, A.J. 2003. "Chess Playing as Strategic Activity." *Symbolic Interaction* 26(2):263–84.

Rabinow, P., ed. 1984. *The Foucault Reader.* New York: Pantheon Books.

Richardson, L. 1990. *Writing Strategies: Reaching Diverse Audiences.* Newbury Park, CA: Sage.

Riessman, C.K. 2001. "Analysis of Personal Narratives." Pp. 695–710 in *Handbook of Interview Research: Context and Method,* edited by J.F. Gubrium and J.A. Holstein. Thousand Oaks, CA: Sage.

Sanders, C.B. and S. Hannem. 2012. "Policing 'the Risky': Technology and Surveillance in Everyday Patrol Work." *Canadian Review of Sociology* 49(4):389–410.

Santin, M. and B. Kelly 2017. "The Managed Heart Revisited: Exploring the Effect of Institutional Norms on the Emotional Labor of Flight Attendants Post 9/11." *Contemporary Journal of Ethnography* 46(5):519–43.

Smith, L.T. 2012. *Decolonizing Methodologies: Research and Indigenous Peoples.* London: Zed Books.

Stelzl, M., B. Stairs, and H. Anstey. 2018. "A Narrow View: The Conceptualization of Sexual Problems in Human Sexuality Textbooks." *Journal of Health Psychology* 23(2):148–60.

Sunseri, L. 2011. *Being Again of One Mind: Oneida Women and the Struggle for Decolonization.* Vancouver: University of British Columbia Press.

van den Hoonaard, D.K. 1999. "No Regrets: Widows' Stories about the Last Days of Their Husbands' Lives." *Journal of Aging Studies* 13(1):59–72.

van den Hoonaard, D.K. 2010. *By Himself: The Older Man's Experience of Widowhood.* Toronto: University of Toronto Press.

van den Hoonaard, W.C. 1997. *Working with Sensitizing Concepts: Analytical Field Research.* Thousand Oaks, CA: Sage.

van den Hoonaard, Will C. 2011. *The Seduction of Ethics: The Transformation of the Social Sciences.* Toronto: University of Toronto Press.

van den Scott, L.-J. K. 2009. "Cancelled, Aborted, Late, Mechanical: The Vagaries of Air Travel in Arviat, Nunavut, Canada." Pp. 211–26 in *The Cultures of Alternative Mobilities: Routes Less Travelled,* edited by P. Vannini. Surrey, UK: Ashgate.

van den Scott, L.-J. K. 2018. "Role Transitions in the Field and Reflexivity: From Friend to Researcher." *Studies in Qualitative Methodology* (Special Issue: Emotion and the Researcher: Sites, Subjectivities and Relationships) 16:19–32.

van den Scott, L.-J.K., C. Forstie, and S. Balasubramanian. 2015. "Shining Stars, Blind Sides, and 'Real' Realties: Exit Rituals, Eulogy Work, and Allegories in Reality Television."

Wilson, R.A. 1966. *Feminine Forever.* New York: Evans.

Wisniewski, A. 2013. "'Are You a South Beach or an Atkins Girl?' A Qualitative Inquiry into Middle-Aged Women's Experiences as Consumers of Weight-Loss Media." PhD dissertation, University of New Brunswick, Fredericton, NB.

Wood, L.A. and R.O. Kroger. 2000. *Doing Discourse Analysis: Methods for Studying Action in Talk and Text.* Thousand Oaks, CA: Sage.

Chapter 10

Adams, T.E., S.H. Jones, and C. Ellis. 2015. *Autoethnography.* New York: Oxford University Press.

Albas, D. and C. Albas. 2009. "Behind the Conceptual Scene of Student Life and Exams." Pp. 105–20 in *Ethnographies Revisited: Constructing Theory in the Field,* edited by A.J. Puddephatt, W. Shaffir, and S.W. Kleinknecht. New York: Routledge.

Anderson, L. 2006. "Analytic Autoethnography." *Journal of Contemporary Ethnography* 35(4):373–95.

Becker, H.S. 1986. *Writing for Social Scientists.* Chicago: University of Chicago Press.

Bull, J. 2019. "Relational and Reflexive Research: Peoples, Policies, and Priorities at Play in Ethically Approving Research with Indigenous Peoples." PhD dissertation, University of New Brunswick, Fredericton, NB.

Castleden, H.E. 2007. "As Sacred as Cedar and Salmon: A Collaborative Study with Huu-ay-aht First Nation, British Columbia in Understanding the Meaning of 'Resources' from an Indigenous World View." PhD dissertation, Department of Earth and Atmospheric Sciences, University of Alberta, Edmonton, AB.

Castleden, H., T. Garvin, and Huu-ay-aht First Nation. 2008. "Modifying Photovoice for Community-Based Participatory Indigenous Research." *Social Science & Medicine* 66:1393–405.

Charmaz, K. 1991. *Good Days, Bad Days: The Self in Chronic Illness and Time*. New Brunswick, NJ: Rutgers University Press.

Charmaz, K. 2006. *Constructing Grounded Theory: A Practical Guide through Qualitative Analysis*. Thousand Oaks, CA: Sage.

Chazan, M. 2015. *The Grandmothers' Movement: Solidarity and Survival in the Time of AIDS*. Montreal: McGill-Queen's University Press.

Clarke, D. 2010. *A Sociological Study of Scholarly Writing and Publishing: How Academics Produce and Share Their Research*. Lewiston, NY: Edwin Mellen Press.

Creme, P. and M.R. Lea. 2008. *Writing at University: A Guide for Students*. 3rd ed. Berkshire, UK: Open University Press.

DeVault, M. 1999. *Liberating Method: Feminism and Social Research*. Philadelphia: Temple University Press.

Ellis, C.S. 1993. "'There Are Survivors': Telling a Story of Sudden Death." *The Sociological Quarterly* 34(4):711–30. (www.jstor.org/stable/4121376).

Ellis, C.S. 2008. "Autoethnography." Pp. 48–51 in *The Sage Encyclopedia of Qualitative Research Methods*, edited by L. Given. Los Angeles: Sage.

Emerson, R.M., R.I. Fretz, and L.L. Shaw. 1995. *Writing Ethnographic Fieldnotes*. Chicago: University of Chicago Press.

Esterberg, K. 2002. *Qualitative Methods in Social Research*. Boston: McGraw-Hill.

Gaudry, A. 2015. "Researching the Resurgence: Insurgent Research and Community-Engaged Methodologies in 21st-Century Academic Inquiry." Pp. 243–65 in *Research as Resistance: Revisiting Critical Indigenous and Anti-Oppressive Approaches*, 2nd ed., edited by S. Strega and L. Brown. Toronto: Canadian Scholars Press.

Gouliquer, L. 2000. "Negotiating Sexuality: Lesbians in the Canadian Military." Pp. 254–77 in *Women's Bodies, Women's Lives: Health, Well-Being and Body Image*, edited by B. Miedema, J.M. Stoppard, and V. Anderson. Toronto: Sumach Press.

Gouliquer, L., C. Poulin, and J. Moore. 2018. "A Threat to Canadian National Security: A Lesbian Soldier's Story." *Qualitative Research in Psychology* 15(2–3):323–35.

Hamadan, A. 2012. "Autoethnography as a Genre of Qualitative Research: A Journey Inside Out." *International Journal of Qualitative Methods* 11 (5):585–606.

Hine, C. 2020. "Strategies for Reflexive Ethnography in the Smart Home: Autoethnography of Silence and Emotion." *Sociology* 54(1):22–36.

Hochschild, A.R. 1979. "Emotion Work, Feeling Rules, and Social Structure." *American Journal of Sociology* 85(3):551–75.

Holt, N.L. 2003. "Representation, Legitimation, and Autoethnography: An Autoethnographic Writing Story." *International Journal of Qualitative Methods* 2(1):18–28.

Kamali, A. 1991. "Writing a Sociological Student Term Paper: Steps and Scheduling." *Teaching Sociology* 19(4):506–9.

Khyatt, M.D. 1992. *Lesbian Teachers: An Invisible Presence*. New York: State University of New York Press.

Kirby, S.L., L. Greaves, and C. Reid. 2006. *Experience Research Social Change: Methods beyond the Mainstream*. 2nd ed. Peterborough, ON: Broadview Press.

Klinker, J.F. and R.H. Todd. 2007. "Two Autoethnographies: A Search for Understanding of Gender and Age." *The Qualitative Report* 12(2):166–8.

Kontos, P.C. and G. Naglie. 2006. "Expressions of Personhood in Alzheimer's: Moving from Ethnographic Text to Performing Ethnography." *Qualitative Research* 6(3):301–17.

Lofland, J. and L.H. Lofland. 1995. *Analyzing Social Settings: A Guide to Qualitative Observation and Analysis*. Belmont, CA: Wadsworth Publishing Company.

Martin-Matthews, A. 1991. *Widowhood in Later Life*. Toronto: Butterworths.

Mitchell, R.G. and K. Charmaz. 1996. "Telling Tales, Writing Stories: Postmodernist Visions and Realist Images in Ethnographic Writing." *Journal of Contemporary Ethnography* 25(1):144–66.

Newmahr, S. 2011. *Playing on the Edge: Sadomasochism, Risk, and Intimacy*. Bloomington, IN: Indiana University Press.

Pascoe, C.J. 2012. *Dude, You're a Fag: Masculinity and Sexuality in High School*. Berkeley: University of California Press.

Poulin, C. 2001. "The Military Is the Wife and I Am the Mistress: Partners of Lesbians in the Canadian Military." *Atlantis* 26(1):65–76.

Randall, W.L. 2015. *The Narrative Complexity of Ordinary Life: Tales from the Coffee Shop*. Toronto: Oxford University Press.

Richardson, L. 1990. *Writing Strategies: Reaching Diverse Audiences*. Newbury Park, CA: Sage.

Richardson, L. 1994. "Writing: A Method of Inquiry." Pp. 516–29 in *Handbook of Qualitative Research*, edited by N.K. Denzin and Y.S. Lincoln. Thousand Oaks, CA: Sage.

Richardson, L. 2007. *Last Writes: A Daybook for a Dying Friend*. Walnut Creek, CA: Left Coast Press.

Saldaña, J. 2008. "Ethnodrama." Pp. 283–5 in *The Sage Encyclopedia of Qualitative Research Methods*, edited by L. Given. Los Angeles: Sage.

Stoddart, K. 1991. "Writing Sociologically: A Note on Teaching the Construction of a Qualitative Report." *Teaching Sociology* 19(2):243–8. (www.jstor.org/stable/1317857).

Sunseri, L. 2011. *Being Again of One Mind: Oneida Women and the Struggle for Decolonization*. Vancouver: University of British Columbia Press.

Thorne, S. 2008. *Interpretive Description*. Walnut Creek, CA: Left Coast Press.

van den Hoonaard, D.K. 2001. *The Widowed Self: The Older Woman's Journey through Widowhood*. Waterloo, ON: Wilfrid Laurier University Press.

van den Hoonaard, D.K. 2010. *By Himself: The Older Man's Experience of Widowhood*. Toronto: University of Toronto Press.

van den Scott, L.-J.K., C. Forstie, and S. Balasubramanian. 2015. "Shining Stars, Blind Sides, and 'Real' Realties: Exit Rituals, Eulogy Work, and Allegories in Reality Television." *Journal of Contemporary Ethnography* 44(4):417–49.

Van Manaan, J. 1988. *Tales of the Field: On Writing Ethnography*. Chicago: University of Chicago Press.

Wall, S. 2008. "Easier Said Than Done: Writing an Autoethnography." *International Journal of Qualitative Methods* 7(1):38–53.

Wall, S.S. 2016. "Toward a Moderate Autoethnography." *International Journal of Qualitative Methods* 15(1):1–9.

Williams, C.L. 2006. *Inside Toyland: Working, Shopping, and Social Inequality*. Berkeley: University of California Press.

Wolcott, H.F. 1995. *The Art of Fieldwork*. Walnut Creek, CA: AltaMira Press.

Wolf, D.R. 1991. *The Rebels: A Brotherhood of Outlaw Bikers*. Toronto: University of Toronto Press.

Glossary

Alfred, T. 2015. "A Talk by Taiaiake Alfred: Research as Indigenous Resurgence." Carlton, SPPA. (https://www.youtube.com/watch?v=myIUkzbiG_o).

Fine, G.A. 2012. *Tiny Publics: A Theory of Group Action and Culture*. New York: Russell Sage Foundation.

Goffman, E. 1959. *The Presentation of Self in Everyday Life*. New York: Anchor Books.

Hochschild, A.R. 1979. "Emotion Work, Feeling Rules, and Social Structure." *American Journal of Sociology* 85(3):551–75.

Kovach, M. 2015. "Emerging from the Margins: Indigenous Methodologies." Pp. 43–64 in *Research as Resistance: Revisiting Critical Indigenous and Anti-Oppressive Approaches*, 2nd ed., edited by S. Strega and L. Brown. Toronto: Canadian Scholars Press.

Lavallé, L.F. 2009. "Practical Applications of an Indigenous Research Framework and Two Qualitative Sharing Circles and Anishnaabe Symbol-Based Reflection." *International Journal of Qualitative Methods* 8(1):21–40.

Mills, C.W. 1959/1976. *The Sociological Imagination*. New York: Oxford University Press.

Smith, D. 1987. *The Everyday World as Problematic: A Feminist Sociology*. Toronto: University of Toronto Press.

Thomas, W.I. and F. Znaniecki. 1918. *The Polish Peasant in Europe and America*. Boston: Gorham Press.

van den Hoonaard, D.K. 1997. "Identity Foreclosure: Women's Experiences of Widowhood as Expressed in Autobiographical Accounts." *Ageing and Society* 17:533–51.

Weber, M. 1949. *The Methodology of the Social Sciences*. Translated by E.A. Shils and H.A. Finch. Glencoe, IL: Free Press.

Index

active interviews, 112–13
active voice, in report, 211
Adler, Patti and Peter, 36, 44–5
Adorjan, Michale, 131
advertisements, analysis of, 158–60
Agocs, Tricia, 107
Albas, Daniel and Cheryl, 28–30, 41–2, 187–8
Alfred, Taiaiake, 24
Altheide, D.L., 157–8
Ames, Herbert Brown, 81
Anderson, Nels, 80
anthropology, ethics in, 59
assumptions: and ethics, 61, 63; and questions,
    12–13, 25, 30–1; for researcher, 24–5, 27;
    in research process, 13–19; in standardized
    interview, 106–8; in symbolic interactionism,
    25–7
Atkinson, Michael, 51, 90, 91, 93–4
Atkinson, P., 160
Austin, Ashley, 28
autobiographies, analysis, 154
autoethnography, 215–16
autonomy, and ethics, 57

back-ups of data, 122
Bagele, Chilisa, 181–2
Bahá'í community, and equality, 132, 138
balanced views and writing, 72–3
Balasubramanian, Savina, 6, 162
bargain making, 90
Baym, Nancy K., 100
Becker, Gay, 192
Becker, Howard S.: on assumptions, 13; data and
    question, 177; influence of stories, 193; maps
    and reality, 153; and methods, 31; on report
    writing, 197, 198, 199, 210, 211, 213; on rep-
    resentation, 151; and sensitizing concepts, 26;
    and social meaning, 17, 26
"Becker principle," 193
Bella, Leslie, 45
Best, Joel, 152
bias and preconceptions, 25
Binns, J., 158
biomedical discourse, 189–90, 191
blogosphere research, 167–9
Blumer, Herbert, 13, 17, 183
Booth, Charles, 78–9
Bottorff, Joan L., 125
brainstorming, 49
breaching experiments, 18–19
Briggs, Jean, 31
Bull, Julie, 216

Buluing, Ronald, 114
bureaucratic documents analysis, 156–7

Caissie, Linda, 107
Calasanti, Toni, 160
Çalişkan, Gül, 190
Canadian Anthropology Society (CASCA), and
    ethics, 58, 59
Canadian identity, discourse analysis, 189
Canadian Qualitative Analysis Conference (the
    "Qualitatives"), 1–2, 3
Canadian Sociological Association (CSA), state-
    ment of ethics, 58–9
Castleden, Heather, and colleagues, 125–6, 214
causal knowledge, 15
celebrity culture, 35–6
census data, analysis, 152
Chamberlain, Kerry, 168
Chambers, Lori A., 38
Charmaz, Kathy, 42–3, 201, 209
Chazan, May, 200
Chicago School of Sociology, 31, 79–81, 82–3
children's books, analysis, 160–1
cities, and sociology, 79–81
civil inattention, 184
Clarke, Dawne A., 199
Clarke, J.N., 158
Clarke, Juanne, 168, 190–1
cloak of competence, 27–8
cloak of incompetence, 185
closed-ended (forced-choice) questions, 106,
    118–19
codes and coding, for data, 177, 178–80
collective outlook, 23, 181
collective stories, 192
colonial discourse, 190
complete observer, 86, 100–1
complete participant, 85
Comte, Auguste, 14–15
concern for human welfare, 57–8
conclusion, in writing up research, 208
confidentiality, 66, 141
conflict of interest, 62
consent and consent forms, 69, 71
content analysis: ethics in, 69–70; of television,
    162; in unobtrusive research, 150, 158, 159
convenience, and research topic, 44–5
Cooley, Charles Horton, 17
corporations, access to, 65
covert field research, 67–8
Crossley, Michele, 136
Cullum-Swan, B., 150

cultural studies, 166–7
cyber-ethnography, 101

daily life research, 4–6
data: back-ups, 122; codes and coding, 177,
    178–80
data analysis: ethics in, 70–1; in focus groups,
    145; and generic social processes, 186–8; and
    memos, 175–6; in qualitative research, 173–4,
    175, 176–7; and questions, 177; and reflexiv-
    ity, 174; and sensitizing concepts, 183–5; soft-
    ware for, 174; transcripts or field notes, 177–9;
    "trust the process" in, 8, 173, 178
data collection, 20
Davidman, Lynn, 49
Dawson, Carl, 82
Dawson, George, 79
deception, 67
deductive approach, in quantitative research, 20
deductive reasoning, 15
definition of the situation, 16
Denzin, Norman K., 40–1
DeVault, Marjorie, 107, 209
Diamond, Timothy, 43, 61, 63, 156
Dickson, Geraldine, 39
digital age. see Internet and digital age
discontinuous identities, 204
discourse analysis, 188–91
dissemination of findings, and ethics, 58, 59
documents analysis, in unobtrusive research,
    151–7
dog walking, and daily life research, 5
double-barrelled questions, 118
Doucet, Andrea, 45, 177
Duneier, Mitchell, 165, 193
Durkheim, Émile, 151

Ellis, Carolyn S., 215
email interviews, 123–4
Emerson, R.M., and colleagues, 98
emotion work, 184–5
Ermine, Willie, 59
Esterberg, Kristen, 201, 207
ethics: and assumptions, 61, 63; in data analysis,
    70–1; and discourse analysis, 191;
    in fieldwork, 64–7; and Indigenous peoples in
    Canada, 59–60; permission for research,
    65–6; principles of research in Canada, 56–9,
    73; in qualitative research, 56, 57, 60–2,
    64–71, 73; and research methods, 52;
    in writing up research, 71–3
ethnic groups, 17–18
ethnicity and identity, 152–3
ethnodrama, 216–17
ethnographic content analysis, 162
ethnographic fieldwork. see fieldwork

ethnography: autoethnography, 215–16; in
    Canada, 79, 81–3; Chicago School, 82–3; do-
    mestic ethnographies, 78–9; historical over-
    view, 78–9; virtual ethnography, 99–101
ethnomethodology, 18
"eulogy work," 6
everyday life research, 4–6
excerpts, in writing up research, 202–5

feeling rules, 184
feminism, and interviews, 107
feminist discourse, 191
Ferrell, Jeff, 163–4
Festinger, Leon, and colleagues, 68
fiction, analysis, 160–1
field notes: and data analysis, 177–9; example,
    224–5; importance, 84, 94–5; and inter-
    views, 121–2; jottings, 95–6; note-taking,
    94–5; and questions, 31; time for writing, 96,
    98; writing up, 97–9
field researcher: dress and punctuality, 92, 120;
    immersion in setting, 77–8, 87; participation
    levels and types, 85–7; storylines, 87, 89; see
    also researchers
field study and research: access to, 65–6, 87–8, 91;
    entering the field, 85–7, 91–2; historical over-
    view, 78–83; leaving the field, 67, 99; permis-
    sion for research, 65–6; place in group, 93–4;
    practice of, 84–99; purpose, 77–8; relation-
    ships with participants, 66–7; setting and site
    selection, 84; sponsors, 90–1; time spent in,
    64, 66–7, 76n3; trust from group, 87, 92–3
fieldwork: domestic ethnographies, 78–9; ethics
    in, 64–7; and gatekeepers, 65, 88–90, 93; his-
    torical antecedents, 78–83; length of research,
    64; questions in, 95; in sociology, 79–81
findings section, in writing up research,
    200–5
Fine, Gary Alan, 86–7, 93
first-person perspective, in report, 211–12
flash mobs, reactions to, 19
focused coding, 179–80
focus groups and focus-group research: career of
    group, 146–7; data and interactions analysis,
    144–7; description and use, 52, 129, 131–3,
    137; history of, 129–31; interactions in, 129,
    130–1; moderator and moderating, 138–40,
    141–2, 143–4; participant selection, 135–6;
    planning, 132–41; practice of, 140–4; ques-
    tions in, 137–8, 143, 144; recordings and
    equipment, 140–1; recruitment, 135, 136–7;
    start and discussion, 141–4; and talking
    circles, 133–4, 139; topic guide, 137–8, 140
"focussed interviews," 130
follow-up questions (or probes),
    116, 121

forced-choice (closed-ended) questions, 106, 118–19

Forstie, Clare, 6, 162

Foucault, Michel, 188

frames, in analysis, 157, 158

French Canada, ethnographies, 81, 83

Funk, Laura, and colleagues, 158

Furman, Frida, 44, 89–90

garbage, analysis, 163–4

Garfinkel, Harold, 18

gatekeepers, in fieldwork, 65, 88–90, 93

Gaudry, Adam, 214

gender: in advertisements, 158–60; in focus groups, 135, 140, 146; and researchers, 94; use of space, 4–5

generic social processes: in data analysis, 186–8; description, 27–30; and questions for research, 49–50

Gettys, Warner E., 82

Giddings, Lynne S., 23

Gilchrist, Kristen, 158, 159

Glaser, B., 185

Glassner, B., 4

glossary, 227–33

Goffman, Erving, 94–5, 159, 184

Gouliquer, Lynne, and colleagues, 217

government, access to, 65–6

Greaves, L., 206

Grills, Scott, 186–7

Gubrium, Jaber F., 44, 112, 192

Haas, Jack, 27–8

Haenfler, Ross, 94

Hall, Rebecca, 133–4

Hammersley, M., 160

"hanging around," and research topic, 44

Hannem, Stacey, 190

Harman, Lesley D., 42

Heilman, Samuel, 88

Henderson, Samantha, 77–8

Herodotus, 78

Hertz, R., 4

hierarchy of credibility, 36–9, 114

Hobo, The (Anderson), 80

Hochschild, Arlie R., 184

Holbrook, Beverly, 136

Hollander, J.A., 144, 145–6

Holstein, James A., 112, 192

homelessness, 80

Howard, John, 78

"how" vs. "why" questions, 60, 117

Hughes, Everett C., 17, 82–3

Humphreys, Laud, 68

Husting, Ginna, 42

Huu-ay-aht First Nation, 125–6

identity: and census, 152–3; in discourse analysis, 189; formation, 27–9; self-identity, 26–7

identity achievement, 50

identity foreclosure, 28, 154

images, in visual sociology, 164–7

impression management, 27–8

incorporation, 93

in-depth interviews: description and purpose, 8, 109–10, 111–12, 119; doing the interview, 119–21; guide, 110, 116–19; participants identification, 113–16; post-interview tasks, 121–3; practice of, 113–21; questions in, 116–19; types and approaches, 110–13

Indigenous methodologies, 23–4, 48

Indigenous peoples and groups: and discourse analysis, 189; and ethics in research, 59–60; fieldwork practices, 79; gatekeepers and permissions, 88; hierarchy of credibility, 38; and interviews, 108–9; missing/murdered women, 159; as PAR, 39; photovoice research, 125–6; presentation of research, 214; research by outsiders, 48, 59, 174; research "with" (not "on"), 24, 48, 79, 84, 86, 214; resurgence, 24; stories analysis, 181–2; and talking circles, 133–4, 139; see also Inuit

inductive approach, in qualitative research, 20

information technology (IT), and discourse, 190

informed consent, 69, 71

institutional ethnography (IE), 156

Internet and digital age: and ethics, 71; interviews, 123–4; recruitment of participants, 115; unobtrusive research, 160, 167–9; virtual ethnography, 99–101

interpretive content analysis, 159

interviews: ethics in, 69; field notes, 121–2; guide, 110, 116–19; and Indigenous peoples, 108–9; online or by email, 123–4; pauses and silences, 121; photo elicitation, 124–6; pitfalls and errors, 117–19; spontaneous interviews, 110–13; as standard protocol, 106; time for, 120; transcription, 122–3; see also in-depth interviews; standardized interview

intimate relations, 67

introduction, in writing up research, 209–10

Inuit: assumptions on, 20; gatekeepers, 88; and hierarchy of credibility, 38; housing, 97, 109, 165–6; identity foreclosure, 28; interviews, 109, 113; research by outsiders, 48; and sensitizing concepts, 183–4; and stories, 182; visual sociology, 165–6; see also Indigenous peoples and groups

Ispa-Landa, Simone, 114

Jackson, Peter, 136

Jamal, Aamir, 48

jargon, in report, 210–11

Johnston, Matthew S., and colleagues, 168–9
Jones, T.L., and colleagues, 22–3
jottings, 95–6
justice, and ethics, 57, 58

Kilbourne, Jean, 160
"killing time," 80
Kim, Wooksoo, 135, 145
King, Neal, 160
Kirby, S.L., 206
Kitzenger, Jenny, 135–6, 144–5
Klinker, JoAnn Franklin, 215–16
Kontos, Pia C., 217
Kuhn, Thomas, 16
Kyriakides, C., and colleagues, 3–4

Lafrance, Michelle N., 191
Landry, Deborah, 19
Langan, Debra, 107
language and words, 25–6
latent content, 150
Lazarsfeld, Paul, 129–30
Least Heat-Moon, William, 70
Leggatt-Cook, Chez, 168
letters and autobiographies, analysis, 154
Leuenberger, Christian, 153
Leuenberger, Christine, 90–1
Leyton, Elliott, 65–6
Li, J., 95
Liebow, Elliot, 90
literature, analysis, 160–1
literature reviews, 53, 205–7
Litosseliti, Lia, 139, 143
loaded questions, 117–18
"looking-glass self," 17
Loseke, Donileen R., 41
Low, Jacqueline, 45–6, 186
Luxton, Meg, 51

McCloskey, Rose, 156–7
McGill University, and ethnography, 82–3
McIntosh, Peggy, 18
McLuhan, A., and colleagues, 185
magic, as social process, 187–8
Malacrida, Claudia, 38, 41, 85
Mamali, Elizabeth, 125
manifest content, 150
Manning, P.K., 150
maps, analysis, 153
March, Karen, 88
Marshall, Albert and Murdena, 24
Martinez-Serrano, P., and colleagues, 133
meaning: in cultural artifacts, 150; social mean-
    ing, 17–18, 26
media content, and unobtrusive research, 157–62
memos, for research, 47, 175–6, 179

Merton, Robert C., 129–30
"me-search," 49
methods in research. see research methods
methods section, in writing up research, 207–8
Michalowski, R.S., 157–8
Mills, C. Wright, 35–6, 154
missing/murdered Indigenous and white
    women, 159
Mitchell, R.G., 209
mixed-methods research, 21–3
Moore, D., 95
Morgan, David L., 130–2, 141
motherhood, and risk discourse, 190–1
mundane technology, 165

Naglie, Gary, 217
narrative analysis, 191–3
Native Women's Association of the NWT, 134
Newfoundland and Labrador, ethnographies,
    82–3
Newmahr, Staci, 92
news media, analysis, 157–8, 159
Norman, Mark, 169
note-taking and notebooks, 84, 94–9, 139–40;
    see also field notes

Oakley, Ann, 107
objects, 17, 162–4
observational research, 51, 52
observer as participant, 85–6
OCAP principles (Ownership, Control, Access,
    and Possession), 60
Oliffe, John L., 125
online environment. see Internet and digital age
open coding, 177
open-ended questions, 116
opening sentences, in report, 209
operationalism, 15

"parachute research," 48
Parmelee, J.H., 22
participant as observer, 85, 86
participant observation, description, 78; see also
    field study and research
participants: assumptions about, 13–14; confi-
    dentiality, 66, 141; consent, 69, 71; ethics for,
    57–8, 60–1; in focus groups, 135–6; in in-
    depth interviews, 113–16; and photo elicita-
    tion, 124–5; pseudonyms, 204; relationships
    with, 66–7; and trust, 87, 92–4; in virtual
    ethnography, 100–1
participatory action research (PAR), 39–40
Pascoe, C.J., 94
passive voice, in report, 211
Pawluch, Dorothy, 155
performance ethnography, 216–17

Perkins, S.P., 22
permission for research, 65–6
personal experience, and research topic, 4–5, 34, 40–3
photo elicitation (photovoice research), 124–6
physical objects, analysis, 162–4
plagiarism, 213–14
positivism, 15
Potter, Beatrice, 78
PowerPoint, for presentations, 222
preconceived ideas. *see* assumptions
preconceptions and bias, 25
presentation of research, 214–17
presentations, guide for, 220–3
presentism, 69–70
Preston, Kayla, 150, 190
prewriting, 198
private problems *vs.* public issues, 36, 37, 154
probes (or follow-up questions), 116, 121
process of research. *see* research process
Prus, Robert, 27
pseudonyms, in report, 204
publications (professional), analysis, 154–5
public issues *vs.* private problems, 36, 37, 154
Puddephatt, Antony J., 186

qualitative data analysis. *see* data analysis
qualitative interviews: description, 51; types and approaches, 110–13; *see also* in-depth interviews
qualitative research: assumptions in, 15–19, 25; beginning of, 46–53; benefits, 20; conference in Canada, 1–2, 3; and daily life, 4–6; description and goal, 2–4, 15–19, 180; and hierarchy of credibility, 36–9; origins, 35–40; presentations guide, 220–3; *vs.* quantitative, 2, 14; topic ideas, 4–5, 34–5, 40–6; variety of approaches, 2, 50–1; *see also* specific topics
qualitative research methods: description, 2; mixed with quantitative, 21–3; *vs.* quantitative, 2–4, 20–1, 53
quantitative research: assumptions in, 14–15, 25; description, 14–15; literature reviews, 53; *vs.* qualitative, 2, 14
quantitative research methods: *vs.* qualitative, 2–4, 20–1, 53; sampling, 113
questions: and assumptions, 12–13, 25, 30–1; and data analysis, 177; development, 35, 49–50, 62, 64; and ethics, 60, 62, 64; in fieldwork, 95; in focus groups, 137–8, 143, 144; follow-up questions, 116, 121; importance, 12; in-depth interviews, 116–19; in interviews, 106; overview, 12–13; in qualitative research, 21, 49, 50, 60; standardized interview, 106; "why" *vs.* "how," 60, 117; *see also* specific types of questions

Raby, Rebecca, and colleagues, 168
race and racialization, 18, 152–3
random samples, 113–14
realist perspective, 15
reality shows, 6, 162
reflexivity, in data analysis, 174
Reid, C., 206
Reinharz, Shulamit, 5–6, 158–9
report writing: beginning of, 197–200; checklist, 226; cleaning up for submission, 212–14; drafts, 200; excerpts in, 202–5; findings section, 200–5; focus of and format, 199–200; introduction and conclusion, 208–10; literature review, 205–7; methods section, 207–8; plagiarism, 213–14; purpose, 197; style matters, 210–12; themes in, 200–1, 207; *see also* writing up research
research: bias and preconceptions, 25; ethics in (*see* ethics); "parachute research," ; 48 permission for, 65–6; and social processes, 27–30; topic ideas, 4–5, 34–5, 40–6; *see also* field study and research; qualitative research; quantitative research
research design. *see* research process
researchers: assumptions and questions, 24–5, 27, 30–1; identity in research, 94; influence, 193; participation levels and types, 85–7; and personal limitations, 46–9; presentations guide, 220–3; reflexivity, 174; and sensitizing concepts, 183; theoretical interests and stance, 45–6, 50–1; writing habits, 199; *see also* field researcher
research ethics boards (REBs), 57
research methods: and ethics, 52; Indigenous methods, 24, 48; mixed methods, 21–3; qualitative *vs.* quantitative, 2–4, 20–1, 53; selection and combination, 51–2, 84; *see also* qualitative research methods
research participants. *see* participants
research process: and assumptions, 13–19; beginning of, 46–53; literature search, 53; method selection, 51–2; qualitative *vs.* quantitative methods, 20–1; questions development, 35, 49–50; theoretical stance, 50–1
research questions. *see* questions
research reports. *see* report writing
research topic. *see* topic of research
respect for persons, 57
retirement communities research, 21, 45, 97
Ricciardelli, Rosemary, 131
Richardson, Laurel, 216
risk, and discourse, 190–1
Rose, Diana, 162
Ross, Timothy, 114

samples and sampling, 113–15
Sanders, Carrie B., 77–8, 107, 190
Sanders, Clinton, 43, 51
Sayre, J.J., 22
Scheibling, Casey, 101
Schneider, Christopher J., 169
Schnell, Izhak, 153
self-identity, 26–7
sensitizing concepts, 26, 183–5
serendipity, and research topic, 43–4
Shaffir, William (Billy), 27–8, 81–2, 88
signature stories, 180
skeptical ethnography, 86–7
Ślezak, Izabella, 93
Smith, Linda Tuhiwai, 24, 182
Smythe, S., 95
snowball sampling, 114
social disorganization, 154
social hierarchy or status, 36
social institutions, documents from, 156–7
social meaning, 17–18, 26
social processes. *see* generic social processes
social reality and context, 25–6, 35–6, 37
sociological imagination, 35–6, 37
sociology, fieldwork and ethnography, 79–81, 82
Spanish, Margaret T., 130–1
sponsors, 90–1
standardized interview (or surveys), 106–9
Statement of Professional Ethics (CSA), 58–9
statistical records, analysis, 151–3
Stelzl, Monica, and colleagues, 155
Stephens, Lorna, 125
stories, analysis, 180–2, 192
storylines, 87, 89
Strauss, A., 185
students: aces, bombers, and moderates, 28–30;
    presentations guide, 220–3
style matters, in writing up research, 210–12
Sunseri, Lina, 182, 214
symbolic interactionism, 17, 25–7
sympathetic understanding, 16
Syrian Refugee Resettlement, 4

tacit understandings, 18–19
talking circles, 133–4, 139
Tang, S.Y., and colleagues, 84
television, analysis, 161–2
theoretical saturation, 21
Thomas, Sara, 114
Thomas, W.I., 16, 154
Thompson, Beverly Yuen, 164–5
Thorne, Sally, 202
Thurairajah, Kalyani, 47
Todd, Reese H., 215–16
topic of research: finding topics, 4–5, 34–5, 40–6;
    and literature, 53; and personal limitations,

46–9; and questions, 35, 49–50; and theor-
    etical interests, 45–6; theoretical stance, 50–1
transcription and transcripts: and data analysis,
    177–9; in discourse analysis, 189; ethics in,
    69; of interviews, 122–3
trash, analysis, 163–4
*Tri-Council Policy Statement: Ethical Conduct for
    Research Involving Humans (TCPS),* 56–8, 60, 61
Trump, Donald, and Trumpism, 190
trust, from group, 87, 92–3
"trust the process," 8, 173, 178
truth, in research, 15, 87
Twitter, 169
"two-eyed seeing," 24

United States, 80–1, 152–3
unobtrusive research: description, 52, 149–50;
    documents of social institutions, 156–7;
    Internet research, 160, 167–9; media content
    and reflections of reality, 157–62; physical ob-
    jects analysis, 162–4; pre-existing documents
    analysis, 151–5; types of materials, 150, 151,
    156; visual sociology, 164–7
unwritten rules, 18–19

van Amerom, Gudrun, 168
van den Hoonaard, Deborah K.: daily life re-
    search, 6; as participant and observer, 86;
    retirement communities research, 21, 45, 97;
    see also widows and widowhood study
van den Hoonaard, Will C.: and discourse analy-
    sis, 191; fiction research, 160, 161; and focus
    groups, 132, 135, 136, 138–9, 143, 146; spon-
    taneous interviews, 111
van den Scott, Lisa-Jo K., research, 6, 162;
    see also Inuit
virtual ethnography, 99–101
visual sociology, 164–7
vlogs research, 168
voice, active and passive, 211

Weber, Max, 16
West, Candace, 5
Western cultures, stories analysis, 180–1
Whitehead, Krista, 100–1
whiteness, and ethnicity, 18
"why" *vs.* "how" questions, 60, 117
widows and widowhood study: gatekeepers,
    89; and in-depth interviews, 109–10, 113,
    118–19; media depiction, 160; memos and
    data, 175–6, 179; and narrative analysis, 192,
    193; notes in, 202; qualitative *vs.* quantitative
    methods, 2; recruitment of participants, 114,
    115; sample questions, 118–19; and serendip-
    ity, 43–4; stories in, 180–1; writing up process
    and examples, 201–2, 203–4, 205

Williams, Terry, 154
Wilson-Forsberg, Stacey, 41
Wisniewski, Angela, 174
Wolcott, Harry F., 198
Wolf, Daniel R., 47, 85, 86
women, 159–60, 190–1; *see also* gender
words and language, 25–6
Wright, Guy, 72–3
writing habits, 199
writing up research: active voice and first-person
    perspective, 211–12; beginning of, 197–200;
clarity and conciseness, 72; cleaning up for
submission, 212–14; conclusion, 208; and
ethics, 71–3; excerpts in, 202–5; findings section, 200–5; focus of, 199–200; introduction,
209–10; literature review, 205–7; methods
section, 207–8; plagiarism, 213–14; presentation of research, 214–17; report writing,
200–10; style matters, 210–12; *see also* report
writing

Znaniecki, Florian, 154